Voluntary Programs

Voluntary Programs

A Club Theory Perspective

edited by Matthew Potoski and Aseem Prakash

The MIT Press
Cambridge, Massachusetts
London, England

For information about special quantity discounts, please e-mail special_sales@mitpress.mit.edu.

This book was set in Sabon on 3B2 by Asco Typesetters, Hong Kong.
Printed and bound in the United States of America.

Library of Congress Cataloging-in-Publication Data

Voluntary programs : a club theory perspective / edited by Matthew Potoski and Aseem Prakash.
   p.   cm.
Includes bibliographical references and index.
ISBN 978-0-262-16250-0 (hardcover : alk. paper) — ISBN 978-0-262-66204-8 (pbk. : alk. paper)
1. Voluntarism. 2. Clubs. I. Potoski, Matthew, 1969– II. Prakash, Aseem.
HN49.V64V6384   2010
306.3'401—dc22   2009008122

10 9 8 7 6 5 4 3 2 1

To my family
—Matt

To Charu and Anshu
—Aseem

Contents

Preface

There is a strong and growing interest in voluntary programs among scholars, nongovernmental organizations (NGOs), and governments. With so many programs, in so many industries, with so many sponsors, there is a wealth of interesting cases, quirks, and questions that cry out for careful analytic scrutiny. An important task is to structure the voluntary program research agenda around critical issues and offer practitioners practical guidance for establishing effective programs. The analytic challenge we and our chapter contributors take up in this volume is to pull this research together using the club theory perspective in order to clearly communicate to scholars and practitioners crucial lessons about designing effective voluntary programs. While the chapters cover many important topics, we focus on the institutional design of voluntary programs, and assess the impact of program design on program membership and program efficacy.

Our theoretical endeavor is to link voluntary program scholarship to the more established literature on institutions and governance. Voluntary programs are rule structures ("institutions" in the scholarly vernacular) that seek to persuade firms to incur nontrivial costs of producing positive externalities beyond what the law requires of them. In this way, voluntary programs provide an institutional signal and assurance to firms' external stakeholders about the observed and unobserved activities that member firms are pursuing. Because programs vary in their abilities to attract participants and change participants' behaviors once they have joined the program, voluntary programs are likely to exhibit varying efficacy as policy tools. It is therefore important to not hastily reject or uncritically accept voluntary programs as policy tools. Rather, the theoretical and policy challenge is to identify the program characteristics that can ex ante predict program efficacy.

The chapters in this volume explore linkages between program design and efficacy across a range of policy areas using a variety of analytic techniques. In addition to examining programs developed by industry associations, they also investigate programs sponsored by governments and NGOs. In our recent book, *The Voluntary Environmentalists*, we conceptualize voluntary programs as clubs, in a political economy sense of the term. A club provides members with shared, group benefits from which nonmembers are excluded. Voluntary programs are like clubs in that they offer an excludable benefit that firms receive from their stakeholders (such as regulators, customers, and suppliers) because participation in the program signals that the firm is taking progressive environmental action. Because club membership benefits firms by enhancing their standing with stakeholders, clubs can require firms to incur the costs of taking progressive environmental action. While command and control regulations seek to persuade firms to adopt such policies via the stick of mandatory enforcement, green clubs seek to do so via the carrot of enhancing firms' reputations through their membership in the club. Once they have joined the club, participating firms have incentives to free ride and enjoy the goodwill benefits of affiliating with the club's brand without paying the costs of adhering to its rules. Just as firms need to be compelled to follow mandatory command and control regulations, effective clubs therefore need mechanisms to monitor and enforce club rules.

Club theory identifies to central collective action dilemmas that voluntary programs need to revolve in order to be effective. The first dilemma, the Olsonian dilemma, requires examining the following questions: Why do some firms join clubs and not others? What enhances a club's brand reputation among different stakeholders, and how do potential reputational benefits induce firms to join the club? The second dilemma, the shirking dilemma, stems from the fact that members may not live up to their program obligations once they have joined the club. Solving the shirking dilemma requires understanding how the club design ensures that members adhere to program requirements and do not free ride on the club's reputation. In sum, the book makes two key contributions:

• Theoretically, it outlines an accessible and yet robust framework for studying voluntary programs. The book expands on club theory to account for the different research findings on the efficacy of voluntary programs.
• Empirically, this book provides an empirical examination of the club theory across a range of programs and issue areas. These programs vary in terms of industry type, sponsor type, and target participant type.

Acknowledgments

Our previous book, *The Voluntary Environmentalists*, outlined the club framework for the study of voluntary programs and applied it in the context of a single program, ISO 14001. At conferences and other occasions where we shared our work, it became clear that our framework is useful for the study for a wide range of voluntary programs. This motivated us to think in terms of coediting a book that uses the club framework to examine voluntary programs across a range of issue and policy areas. We began working on this project in summer 2006. We wrote out an introductory chapter and contacted leading scholars writing on voluntary programs. Thanks to generous financial support from the Center for International Business Education Research (CIBER) and the Lindenberg Center both at the University of Washington, we held a workshop for the authors at the University of Washington in June 2007. At this workshop, the contributors presented the first drafts of their chapters to each other as well as an audience of both University of Washington and non–University of Washington faculty who were invited to serve as discussants. After the workshop, we provided additional detailed feedback on every chapter. The chapters went through two additional rounds of revisions in response to the suggestions and comments that the reviewers offered. The result is a series of strong chapters that cohere and make the volume greater than the sum of its individual contributions.

This project has received valuable support, input, and feedback from several individuals, including Laura Callen, Nives Dolsak, Steve Hanson, Sanjeev Khagram, Tom Koontz, David Layton, Margaret Levi, George Lovell, Peter May, Errol Meidinger, Stephen Page, Margaret Shannon, Rebecca Szper, and Mark Smith. We would like to extend our sincere gratitude to Clay Morgan, the commissioning editor, for his support and encouragement. Finally, we would like to acknowledge the support and encouragement from our families. We dedicate this book to them.

1

Voluntary Clubs: An Introduction

Matthew Potoski and Aseem Prakash

In recent years, voluntary programs have captured policy and scholarly attention. Firms participating in these programs promise to create positive social externalities beyond what government regulations require. Thousands of firms around the world have joined a voluntary program of one sort or another. This is an enticing phenomenon because it suggests a way to persuade firms to do socially desirable things at lower costs and with fewer conflicts than sometimes accompany government regulation. Voluntary programs are also perplexing, and perhaps even counterintuitive, precisely because governments regulate firms on the assumption that firms' pursuit of profit hinders them from doing socially desirable things in the first place. In exploring this puzzle, scholars have found that sometimes voluntary programs are successful in the sense that participation induces firms to increase their production of social externalities, but at other times programs fail to induce any positive change among the participating firms. It is time to move beyond examining whether these programs work and focus instead on identifying the conditions under which they work. Systematic inquiry along these lines requires a theoretical framework that helps identify ex ante the necessary conditions and institutional features of credible and effective voluntary programs.

This volume proposes an analytic framework for studying voluntary programs based on the economic theory of clubs, and rooted in social science theories of collective action and institutional design (Prakash and Potoski 2006b). Three features of our conception of voluntary programs are noteworthy: government regulations do not mandate that firms join voluntary programs; these regulations require members to adopt specific policies that are either not required by law (that is, the law is silent) or are beyond the legal requirements; and the objective behind the adoption of such policies is the production of positive social externalities. Through extensive theoretical and empirical analyses drawn from a variety of industries and regions of the world, the empirical chapters in this book show how the club approach can shed light on why firms join voluntary programs, why only some programs are successful, and what policy designers can do to harness voluntary programs' policy potential.

Building a social science–based analytic framework is important because voluntary programs are a fast-growing and crucial policy tool, and because the programs raise fundamental public policy questions. Firms, governments, businesses, and NGOs have all created and participated in a large variety of programs (Webb 2004; Vogel 2008). In the environmental field alone, Richard Morgenstern and William Pizer (2007) report that about three hundred voluntary programs have been negotiated between firms and national governments in Europe, and more than eighty-seven voluntary agreements have been sponsored by the U.S. Environmental Protection Agency (EPA).

The club approach to voluntary programs presented in this volume builds on the economic theory of clubs (Buchanan 1965; Cornes and Sandler [1986] 1996) in a novel way. Instead of treating clubs as organizations, we view clubs as institutions or rule systems (North 1990). We propose that voluntary programs can be viewed as rule systems that generate benefits having the characteristics of club goods. Firms that join a program enjoy the value of affiliating with the program's brand name. Brand affiliation is an excludable benefit because nonmembers are unable to receive these benefits. For members, the brand benefits are nonrival because their association with the club does not necessarily diminish the value others receive from the brand. Indeed, as we discuss subsequently, one firm's membership can often enhance the value that other members receive.

Membership in a well-regarded voluntary program allows firms' stakeholders to identify firms that are producing social externalities beyond the legal requirements by virtue of their club membership and differentiate them from nonmembers that are less likely to produce such social externalities. Effective voluntary programs that induce members to produce positive social externalities produce win-all-around outcomes: stakeholders win because firms produce the social externalities they desire, firms win because membership produces goodwill and other rewards from stakeholders, and club sponsors can share some credit for inducing firms to produce positive social externalities.

Of course, and importantly so, voluntary programs are not always successful. They can fail if their "brands" are not strong enough to attract firms to join or if they lack institutional mechanisms to ensure that firms live up to their obligations as program participants. In fact, the variability in program design and performance suggests the need for a framework that can help both scholars and practitioners make ex ante assessments of programs' potential strengths and weaknesses. Studies of voluntary program efficacy typically focus on describing the characteristics of program members or industries in order to identify causal lessons about program efficacy; rarely do these studies look at voluntary program attributes as exogenous drivers of program efficacy. Our club framework seeks to bring attention to this important but neglected issue of scholarly inquiry. The empirical chapters presented in this volume examine voluntary programs in specific industries and issue areas using the club framework. In doing so, they examine the value of the club framework in explaining the efficacy of the voluntary program in a range of contexts and with different types of membership.

The Rationale for Voluntary Programs

Voluntary programs' policy potential is to stimulate the creation of positive externalities and mitigate the production of negative ones. Externalities are negative or positive consequences of transactions experienced by those not involved in a transaction. Externalities imply that the social costs and benefits of a transaction differ from the private costs and benefits that the actors receive. Actors tend to underproduce goods with positive externalities because they cannot capture (all or most of) the benefits that society enjoys, yet they bear all the costs. For example, if I pay all the costs of a streetlight that I install at the end of my sidewalk, my neighbors enjoy the positive externalities of a safer neighborhood and an easier nighttime path to their homes. Actors likewise tend to overproduce goods with negative externalities because while they enjoy the benefits, they only partially bear the costs that society incurs, such as when factories pollute the air and water. Voluntary programs seek to alter firms' cost-benefit calculus to channel their private self-interests in ways that lead to the reduction of negative externalities and/or production of positive externalities.

Externalities imply a market failure because the socially optimal quantity of the good has not been produced. The traditional response to market failure has been government intervention in market transactions (Pigou [1920] 1960), though markets can solve some externality problems without governmental intervention. If the producers and receivers of externalities could bargain easily—that is, if there are few information asymmetries, and low transaction costs for negotiating and writing contracts—externality receivers could compensate externality producers, leading to socially optimal production levels (Coase 1960). But such bargains are difficult and perhaps impossible to strike where there are many actors with large information asymmetries among them. A consumer might be willing to pay extra for goods produced in environmentally friendly ways, but only if he or she can identify the goods and firms making them. For example, a prospective groom might pay extra for an engagement diamond if he is confident that proceeds from the sale would not be supporting military conflicts in Africa (see chapter 5). Consumers sometimes need assurance that the money they spend is indeed supporting firms that produce goods in ways that cohere with their preferences.

Firms can unilaterally declare that their goods have been produced in socially responsible ways. While consumers might trust some firms, for most people such self-declarations might not be persuasive on their own simply because consumers are unable to verify which firms are telling the truth. More broadly, information asymmetries coupled with the lack of assurance mechanisms prevent actors from transacting business. In such situations the market has "failed," and the gains from win-win exchanges have not been realized.

The term "market failure" is somewhat unfortunate because it seems to imply that all markets have failed. A market is a specific rule configuration: market failure suggests that a specific rule system is not working in a specific context. In the same setting, a different market with a different rule system might successfully facilitate transactions.

This is where voluntary programs add value. They seek to reconfigure the institutional space between the potential exchange participants by providing new rules and a new mechanism to facilitate exchange. In effect, they create a new market for corporate reputation—one could perhaps call it a "market for virtue" (Vogel 2005). To consumers and other firm stakeholders, voluntary programs signal that the participating firm has agreed to adopt polices that lead to the production of social externalities beyond legal mandates. Program membership may also provide assurance that the firm is abiding by its commitment to produce positive externalities. If firms' consumers and stakeholders favor the production of such externalities, they can reward the firms that become members. Voluntary program membership allows participating firms to appropriate benefits from appreciative consumers and stakeholders that they would not be able to enjoy without joining the program. In other words, joining a voluntary program confers a branding benefit on firms, allowing their stakeholders and consumers to reward them for producing the social externality program that membership requires.

As institutional responses to market failures, voluntary programs facilitate a bargain among three categories of actors: firms that produce social externalities beyond legal requirements and receive the excludable branding benefits that the program offers; program sponsors that establish the program and create mechanisms to ensure participants follow the program rules; and firms' stakeholders who value the externalities that the participating firms generate and reward them for doing so. To illustrate with examples presented in this volume, Tim Bartley (chapter 6) shows that apparel companies joined a fair labor practices program to protect their brand image and escape criticism from social activists. The voluntary programs were expressly created to show that participating firms were using fair labor practices, and stakeholders who wanted labor conditions improved in overseas facilities received a signal about firms' labor practices. The chapters by Virginia Haufler on the diamond industry (chapter 5), Elizabeth DeSombre on the shipping industry (chapter 7), Tim Büthe on the accounting industry (chapter 8), and Mary Kay Gugerty (chapter 12) all show how voluntary programs were created in response to pressures from stakeholders who wanted firms to produce more positive social externalities. The analytic approach to the study of voluntary programs proposed in this volume takes into account the institutional and stakeholder context in which programs function.

While governmental interventions play a valuable role in correcting market failures (Pigou [1920] 1960), governments themselves can also fail (Wolf 1979). In this light, voluntary programs can be viewed as correctives to both market and government failures (although these programs are also vulnerable to their types of institutional failures, as we will discuss), and can be seen as creating a new public policy domain (Falkner 2003). We do not mean to suggest that a proliferation of voluntary programs will or should lead to the "retreat of the state" (Strange 1996), or "governance without government" (Rosenau and Czempiel

1992). Carefully designed voluntary programs can actually support public regulation given that governments seldom have the resources to legislate and monitor every detail of human activity (Ruggie 2004). Regulatory gaps exist in all governance systems. Perceptions of governmental failures (or successes) in one area tend to spill over to other issue areas. By filling in regulatory or governance gaps, voluntary programs can improve the broader regulatory and governance climate. While the extant research has not yet quantified the value or welfare gains via such "soft effects," this is an interesting research area for scholars who study spillovers facilitated by institutional linkages.

It is fair to say that some voluntary programs have the potential to help governments and public authorities to focus resources on areas where public regulations are most effective (Gunningham and Sinclair 2002; Wilson 2002). Dan Fiorino (chapter 10) and Cary Coglianese and Jennifer Nash (chapter 11) show how the EPA has been in the forefront of establishing voluntary programs in the United States. For one, these programs can aid government regulation by requiring firms to go beyond the government's regulations—an important contribution especially in jurisdictions where governmental enforcement capacities are limited or where international agreements such as the World Trade Organization constrain governmental action (Bartley's chapter 3 on labor codes in the apparel industry, and Daniel Drezner and Mimi Lu's chapter 9 on ISO 14001). Nevertheless, despite potential complementarities with public regulations, there are theoretical reasons to believe that some voluntary programs might be designed to preempt and shape governmental regulation in ways that reduce social welfare (Segerson and Miceli 1998; Maxwell, Lyon, and Hackett 2000; Heritier and Eckert 2008). This is an important area that merits careful empirical investigation.

Some critics charge that voluntary programs create "democracy deficits" on the grounds that governments can be "democratic" in ways that voluntary programs cannot (Porter 2001). For example, a voluntary program's rule-making procedures might not be open to public input, or interested stakeholders might not be allowed to review the program's rules. Voluntary programs might not reflect the "public will" to the same extent as government regulation. While some voluntary programs are amenable to "capture," and may not afford adequate opportunity to all stakeholders to participate in rule making and enforcement, such sweeping generalizations are difficult to support. For one, democracy is a recent invention. Even in 2006, most countries could not be termed as fully functioning democracies; the *Economist* (Economist Intelligence Unit 2007) labels only 28 of the 167 countries it examined as full democracies. And even in established democracies, there is debate regarding the degree to which governments respond to public concerns. Indeed, the significant literature on capture was first developed in the context of the United States (Stigler 1971), often touted as a well-functioning democracy. Instead of praising or criticizing any ideal governance type, the analytic challenge is to explore conditions under which any institution can function democratically and effectively.

While some voluntary programs might substitute for governmental regulation, as the chapters by Haufler (chapter 5), DeSombre (chapter 7), Bartley (chapter 6), and Büthe (chapter 8) demonstrate, the two can coexist and even complement one another, as illustrated in the chapters by Fiorino (chapter 10), Coglianese and Nash (chapter 11), and Drezner and Lu (chapter 9). Public laws and regulations influence voluntary programs as well as vice versa. Voluntary programs operate not just in the shadow of government regulations but also in coordination with them. Some voluntary programs may induce participants to comply better with public regulations (Börkey, Glachant, and Lévêque 1998; Dasgupta, Hettige, and Wheeler 2000; Potoski and Prakash 2005)—an important issue in countries where the laws are weakly enforced. As we discuss below, from the stance of potential program participants, the value of joining a program is often contingent on its fit with public institutions and regulatory culture. While some voluntary programs are certainly shams, it is critical to assess voluntary programs on their analytic and policy merit and deficiencies—a task admirably accomplished by the empirical chapters in this volume.

Book Outline

This book seeks to contribute to the growing literature on voluntary programs, also termed as private authority regimes, private law, and private regulation (Cutler, Haufler, and Porter 1998; Coglianese and Nash 2001, Mattli and Büthe 2003; Cashore, Auld, and Newsom 2004; Prakash and Potoski 2006b). The book has three theoretical chapters and nine empirical ones. Building on Prakash and Potoski (2006b), the book outlines a deductive, theoretical approach rooted in club theory to examine voluntary programs and then submits this approach to empirical examination. The three theoretical chapters (2–4) explore the club approach to the study of voluntary programs. Chapter 2 presents the core ideas in a broad and general form. Chapters 3 and 4 select portions of the club approach for rigorous, formal analysis. These two chapters look at the trade-offs between the stringency of the obligations that a voluntary program imposes on its members (a proxy for the levels of social externalities that the members produce) and programs' ability to attract participants. The nine empirical chapters examine the usefulness of the club framework for the study of voluntary programs that vary across issue areas, sponsorship, and the object of governance. These chapters scrutinize programs in diverse policy areas, including shipping, labor, accounting, diamonds, human rights, and the environment. The chapters include programs that have been sponsored by industry, NGOs, and governments. While clubs are predominantly targeted to shape the behaviors of firms, Gugerty's chapter (12) explores how clublike programs are proliferating to regulate the practices of nonprofits. Thus, the wide diversity of empirical studies across sectors, sponsoring organizations, and objectives of governance provides a broad assessment of the robustness of the club framework, and generates new insights for the future research on voluntary programs.

To preview the empirical chapters to come, Haufler (chapter 5) focuses on the diamond industry, Bartley (chapter 6) on the labor sector, DeSombre (chapter 7) on the shipping industry, Büthe (chapter 8) on the accounting industry, and Drezner and Lu (chapter 9) compare an environmental club (ISO 14001), a social responsibility club (United Nations Global Compact), and a human rights club (the Free Burma campaign). The chapters by Fiorino (chapter 10) and Cogalianese and Nash (chapter 11) study programs in the environmental arena, where voluntary programs have proliferated in recent years in the United States. Given the important role of the EPA in sponsoring voluntary programs, these chapters present comparative case studies of different programs sponsored by this agency as well as state governments, with the recently discontinued National Environmental Performance Track program being the common case discussed by the two chapters. The EPA has launched over sixty voluntary programs. As the central actor in U.S. environmental policy, the EPA has the potential to shape voluntary programs' future in significant ways. Indeed, its experience with voluntary programs has much to inform other actors that have sponsored voluntary programs in other policy areas. What emerges overall from the empirical research in this volume are lessons about when programs are more likely to fail—weak monitoring and enforcement programs are the most frequent culprits—and how political, economic, and policy conditions shape voluntary programs' performance.

Chapter Outline

The book has twelve chapters divided into three parts. Part 1 presents three theoretical perspectives on voluntary programs. Chapter 2, "A Club Theory Approach to Voluntary Programs," by Potoski and Prakash, introduces the club theory of voluntary programs that is at the heart of this book. It describes voluntary programs' two central institutional features: club standards that specify how members are to produce social externalities, and monitoring and enforcement rules to ensure that the members live up to their program obligations. The chapter then investigates the analytic features of different types of programs and program brands. It ends with a discussion of how the club approach fits with other voluntary program research.

Chapter 3, "Clubs, Credence Standards, and Social Pressure," by Baron, presents a theory of industry collective action in the face of social pressure arising from "private politics" led by an activist NGO seeking to change the practices and policies of the firms in the industry. An example would be environmental NGOs campaigning to change the practices of timber companies to conform to the NGO-sponsored forestry club, the Forest Stewardship Council. The response of the U.S. industry (under the aegis of the American Forestry and Paper Association) was to counter by developing its own forestry club, the Sustainable Forest Initiative. This chapter seeks to explain which firms would join an industry-sponsored club and which would not, the governance rules for such a club, what standard the club would choose, and how the firms would perform. In addition, the theory attempts to explain whether social pressure would be directed to the firms in the club or those not in the club.

Chapter 4, "An Economics Perspective on Treating Voluntary Programs as Clubs," by Kotchen and van 't Veld, outlines a research agenda for nesting club theory within a model of more general public goods provision. Specifically, it highlights the strengths and weaknesses of existing club theory for understanding voluntary programs and takes initial steps to show how club theory can be expanded to account for the provision of more general public goods. Finally, it discusses how the broader conceptualization of club theory draws our attention to new questions and answers about the increasingly important role of voluntary programs for solving collective action problems. Using a formal model, the chapter demonstrates how standard club theory illuminates several important features of voluntary programs, including but not limited to the following: a membership condition that clarifies the trade-offs associated with the decision to join a club, a level of provision condition that shows how club standards emerge, and a congestion mechanism that shows how club benefits are increasing in the number of members, but only to a point, after which rivalry begins to take effect. In addition, the chapter shows how heterogeneity among potential members can result in the formation of clubs with differing standards. The analysis underscores the conceptual distinction between clubs and standards that emerge endogenously, and those that can be established exogenously by a third party.

Part 2 addresses industry and international clubs, and has five chapters. Chapter 5, "The Kimberley Process, Club Goods, and Public Enforcement of a Private Regime," is contributed by Haufler. The Kimberley Process is an example of an effective voluntary program and shows the value of the club perspective for analyzing how voluntary programs work. The Kimberley Process's club standards are rules for verifying diamonds' chain of production and custody so that certified diamonds are "clean," as distinct from the "blood diamonds" whose proceeds are used to fund violent civil wars and rebellions. The program thus provides a positive social externality—a more peaceful world—through the production of a club good—a "brand" signal that identifies clean diamonds and thereby boosts the collective reputation of the legitimate diamond industry. The history of the Kimberley Process's struggle against blood diamonds is itself fascinating and suggests some reason for optimism: many people point to the way that funds dried up after the Kimberley club was put in place as a factor that brought combatants to the negotiating table in Sierra Leone. Yet the case also shows the importance of designing and maintaining effective institutions to solve collective action problems. The program relies on public sector monitoring and enforcement, which on paper appears to be a strong sword, although it may have weaknesses in practice. And the program has struggled to build the strength of its brand signal, although the success of the movie *Blood Diamond* may have helped the Kimberley Process brand penetrate public consciousness.

Chapter 6, "Standards for Sweatshops: The Power and Limits of the Club Approach to Voluntary Labor Standards," by Bartley, examines the apparel industry's struggles to establish and maintain voluntary programs. The apparel industry's collective reputation suffered greatly in the early 1990s when activists accused Nike, Wal-Mart, the Gap, and others of profiting from exploitation, brutality, and child labor in their supply chains. Early voluntary programs to rebuild the industry's reputation were largely failures, with weak club standards and weaker monitoring and enforcement. Even the subsequent later voluntary programs, created through multistakeholder processes, have had little positive consequence, perhaps due to weak club standards that require participants only to "pay attention" to labor problems, or perhaps due to monitoring and enforcement regimes that while moderately strong on paper, are weak in practice. Club theory reveals its analytic power in this case by showing that effective institutions must be as strong in practice as in theory. Yet as Bartley points out, the club theory of voluntary programs laid out in the first chapter of this volume has a blind spot to the crucial questions about the often political process of establishing and governing voluntary programs—a limitation we take up as well in chapter 13.

Chapter 7, "Voluntary Agreements and the Shipping Industry," by DeSombre, examines several voluntary programs in this industry where the absence of a global sovereign government makes externality problems particularly difficult to solve. DeSombre's analysis shows that while voluntary programs can address different types of problems—lax labor standards, inadequate safety, overfishing, and environmental protection—and provide different types of private and public benefits, effective programs have in common strong club standards as well as effective monitoring and enforcement regimes. In a sector otherwise characterized by the kind of "race to the bottom" that others hypothesize but rarely find in practice, these clubs, largely voluntary, have been the only successful mechanisms for raising environmental, safety, and labor standards in international shipping. DeSombre's careful account of these programs reveals the importance of aligning voluntary programs' standards and enforcement with existing governance structures.

Chapter 8, "Technical Standards as Public and Club Goods: Who Is Funding the International Accounting Standards Board and Why?" by Büthe, examines the International Accounting Standards Board (IASB), and how it provides rule systems for the international finance and accounting industry. Büthe's analysis shows the value of the club approach to voluntary programs: firms join the program and thereby finance the public goods it produces, in exchange for the excludable club goods that membership provides. Sovereign governments ceded authority to the IASB to induce industry acceptance of regulations by granting them standing in the rule-making process. The IASB, in turn, exploited governmental institutions to strengthen the monitoring and enforcement of its club standards. The IASB's success in providing public benefits stems largely from how well its institutional design matched both the policy problem and its political and policy context.

Chapter 9, "How Universal Are Club Standards? Emerging Markets and Volunteerism," by Drezner and Lu, begins by noting that the focus on voluntary standards has rested on an implicit assumption: most multinational corporations (MNCs) joining voluntary clubs are headquartered in advanced, industrialized democracies. The chapter then asks, if this assumption is correct, are voluntary clubs truly a global phenomenon, or has the predominance of Organization for Economic Cooperation and Development (OECD) multinational firms created a misperception among scholars of the global political economy? Variation in national preferences and institutions could have a profound impact on the club perspective on voluntary programs. Firms based in emerging markets might not value the club benefits of certification as much as Western-based MNCs because citizens in emerging markets might place a lower value on the positive social externalities created by such clubs. Both of these factors might undercut the incentive-based logic of voluntary standards. This chapter engages in a "tough test" of the power of voluntary clubs by examining the participation and compliance of firms headquartered in Pacific Rim developing countries to three different sets of voluntary clubs: the United Nations Global Compact, the Free Burma campaign, and the ISO 14001 regime. Firms demonstrate greater adherence to "strong sword" programs than "weak sword" ones, suggesting the value of the club model for voluntary programs.

Part 3 examines clubs sponsored by governmental and nonprofit actors. It has three chapters. Chapter 10, "Green Clubs: A New Tool for Government?" by Fiorino, analyzes how the EPA and U.S. state governments design voluntary environmental programs, or "green clubs," to recruit firms to participate and then prevent them from shirking once they have become members. The chapter shows the value of club theory's analytic lens for comparing across government programs, and between government and nongovernmental-sponsored programs. Government programs have an important advantage in that they can reward participating firms with not just "soft" club benefits such as greater recognition but also "harder" club benefits such as regulatory flexibility and lower fines for environmental accidents. Green clubs can also reshape conflictual relations between firms and regulators into more cooperative, even relational interactions. Realizing the full potential of government-sponsored green clubs is hampered by laws and regulations that restrict governments' ability to reward cooperative firms that join green clubs with anything more than soft club benefits. The political free pass that government-sponsored green clubs have enjoyed in the United States has expired; Fiorino suggests ways that governments can adapt their clubs' standards and enforcement regimes, and perhaps even amend their laws and regulations, to better harness their potential as a policy tool.

Chapter 11, "Government Clubs: Theory and Evidence from Voluntary Environmental Programs," by Coglianese and Nash, extends Fiorino's analysis in chapter 10 by first digging more deeply into the EPA's experience with its recently discontinued Performance Track voluntary program and then examining twenty-eight other EPA voluntary programs through the club theory analytic lens. Where the Performance Track has stringent club standards and strong enforcement swords, the standards of other EPA voluntary programs tend to be more variable, with strong club standards generally coupled with strong enforcement regimes. Like Fiorino, Coglianese and Nash suggest that while governments can offer substantial club benefits in the form of regulatory benefits, political and legal constraints prevent them from doing so, resulting in the limited membership rosters of so many government-sponsored voluntary environmental programs.

Chapter 12, "Self-Regulation and Voluntary Programs among Nonprofit Organizations," is contributed by Gugerty. Where we traditionally view NGOs as voluntary program sponsors, Gugerty turns the question around, and sees NGOs as actors that demand the type of public and club benefits that voluntary programs can provide; NGOs, for example, use voluntary program membership to signal their quality to donors. Drawing global data from fifteen nonprofit voluntary programs, Gugerty finds that most NGO voluntary programs appear to be at least somewhat effective, which may not be surprising given the premium NGOs place in building and maintaining a credible reputation. Moreover, programs with stronger institutional design—stronger club standards as well as more effective monitoring and enforcement mechanisms—generate more club benefits for their members and more positive externalities for the public at large. Gugerty's prescriptions for improving NGO voluntary programs suggest both the analytic similarities among NGO, industry, and government-sponsored programs—the importance of strong institutional design, and matching rules to policy and political contexts—and how these issues are manifested differently across settings.

Finally, chapter 13 by Prakash and Potoski outlines the book's conclusions. First, it examines the terrain covered in the previous chapters, showing how club theory adds value to the study of voluntary programs. Second, while these chapters demonstrate the strengths of applying the club lens to voluntary programs, they also identify some areas where the theory is weak and underdeveloped. For example, they highlight the various types of voluntary programs where the insights from the club perspective are most useful. The concluding chapter summarizes these issues and suggests how future research might address them.

I

Theories of Voluntary Clubs

2

A Club Theory Approach to Voluntary Programs

Matthew Potoski and Aseem Prakash

The club theory approach to voluntary programs builds on long-standing political economy traditions that address the theoretical bases of collective action. Collective action research poses fundamental questions about social organization. Why do or don't individuals work together to pursue common objectives, and with what consequences? If collective action is desirable, then how can it be fortified, what are its impediments, and how can these impediments be removed? While much of the political economy literature tends to assume that collective action or inaction is voluntary—such as Mancur Olson's work examining interest group dynamics in a well-functioning democracy—collective action can be coerced in the sense that actors can be made to work in groups against their will, such as through public law. Indeed, in such situations, actors may even be forced to bear the costs of collective action while being denied its benefits.

We are interested in studying collective action through voluntary programs. This behavior is voluntary in the sense that it is not coerced by the state via regulation or statute. Of course, states (and other stakeholders) can create different types of incentives for actors to embrace or shun collective endeavors. The key point is that the voluntary collective action we study is not mandated by legal or regulatory requirements.

To produce effective voluntary collective action, the participating actors need to share the costs *and* benefits of their actions. By and large, collective action is likely to fail if some actors want to reap the benefits but not share the costs. Indeed, Olson's (1965) insight was that collective action is undermined by free-riding actors who seek to enjoy the benefits of collective action without paying for them. Thus, for successful voluntary collective action, rule systems need to curb free riding.

This volume examines collective action by firms in the form of participation in voluntary programs. Firms seek to signal to their stakeholders that they are socially responsible. But adopting socially responsible policies is often costly, especially ones that are beyond legal requirements. Arguably, a typical firm would want to enjoy a reputation for social responsibility without having to actually pay the costs of being socially responsible. It might believe that if other firms are willing to bear the cost of being socially responsible, it would be able to enjoy some of the "warm glow" (chapter 4) that emanates from their actions.

Why might firms not want to take socially responsible action? First, the goodwill created by socially responsible firms might spill over to all firms. Citizens might begin to believe that most firms are socially responsible and consequently take benign attitudes toward all businesses. As a result, citizens might ease their political pressure for new regulations or restrictions on businesses, benefiting all firms. In political economy terms, a firm might hope that the benefits of socially responsible action are nonexcludable and it can avail of them without bearing the costs of being socially responsible itself.

A second reason a firm might not take socially responsible action is that its stakeholders may not be able to identify that it is doing such good deeds. Stakeholders may not have a low-cost way of differentiating the virtuous firms from other ones. Baron (chapter 3) terms the unobservable traits of firms as "credence attributes" to emphasize that stakeholders have difficulty verifying firms' behavior. Hence, stakeholders may have to spread their goodwill across all firms—an option that would reward the free-riding firms as well as those doing the socially desirable things. Or stakeholders may also decide to withhold rewards from all firms—an option that would punish the virtuous firms. Recognizing the information problems faced by the stakeholders, a firm considering socially responsible action might wonder why it should bear the costs of such action if no matter what it did, the firm would still receive the same level of benefits from its stakeholders. The implication is that if stakeholders want to encourage firms to produce social externalities beyond legal requirements, they need low-cost mechanisms to identify virtuous firms and focus their rewards only on them.

The policy challenge is to find ways to curb free riding among firms through a mechanism that creates excludable benefits that can be appropriated only by those firms that bear the costs of producing positive social externalities. This mechanism would serve as a low-cost vehicle for stakeholders to differentiate the virtuous firms from the other ones. Below we explain how voluntary programs accomplish these tasks. There is an additional collective action to be resolved for voluntary programs to be effective, however. Suppose a group of firms joins a voluntary program that requires it to produce some social externality. Some firms in this group might fail to live up to their obligations, either by intention or ignorance, yet these firms would continue to receive the benefits of program membership simply because outside stakeholders could not differentiate the shirking firms from the nonshirkers. This problem has serious implications for voluntary programs. Nonshirker members would be less inclined to continue with the program. Eventually, shirking by some program members can threaten the reputation of the program as a whole, making it less attractive for all, and perhaps leading the remaining nonshirkers to select themselves out of the program. (Effective voluntary programs must have monitoring and enforcement mechanisms to curb shirking.)

Inducing firms to promise to be socially responsible and then live up to their promises are the two central collective action problems confronting voluntary programs. This book investigates how voluntary programs' rule structures might mitigate these two problems, which we call the Olsonian problem and the shirking problem. We first extend the traditional economic theory of clubs in an innovative way and apply it to the study of voluntary programs. Next, we present voluntary programs' core institutional features, discuss how they look to solve collective action problems, and present a typology of voluntary programs. Finally, the chapter relates the club approach to voluntary programs to other voluntary program research as well as the theoretical and empirical analyses that follow in the remainder of this volume.

Toward a Club Theory of Voluntary Programs

In traditional economic theory, clubs are institutions that supply impure public goods. While the literature on "impure public goods" has an impressive lineage (Pigou [1920] 1960; Tiebout 1956; Wiseman 1957), James Buchanan (1965) is generally credited with introducing the theoretical concept of clubs in an economic sense. Paul Samuelson (1954) classified goods as either public or private, and Buchanan (1965) identified clubs as institutions for producing and allocating goods that are neither fully private (rivalrous and excludable) nor fully public (nonrivalrous and nonexcludable). In recent years, Richard Cornes and Todd Sandler ([1986] 1996) have been responsible for important theoretical advances in and empirical applications of these club concepts.

Unlike pure public goods, where the benefits one recipient receives are made available to all, club goods are excludable so that their benefits can be appropriated only by those who pay for them. To defray the costs of creating such goods, club sponsors are able to charge fees to club good recipients because they can deny the goods to those who do not pay up. Club goods are nonrivalrous in that what one individual consumes is still available for others to consume, at least until the good becomes congested or overcrowded. An illustrative example of a club in this traditional sense is a golf club: the excludable benefit club members receive is use of the club's golf course and facilities, for which they pay yearly dues. From a broader social welfare perspective, markets can allocate club goods efficiently. The market for golf club memberships can be efficient because once tee times become too scarce, the club can hike its fees to bring membership to optimal levels, and an entrepreneurial dairy farmer can turn his cow pasture into golf courses to meet the demand for golf club memberships. Another instance of a Buchanan club is a movie theater. The product it provides is nonrival (several patrons can watch the movie at the same time) and yet excludable (unless you buy the ticket, you cannot gain entry into the theater). The central purpose of a movie theater is to supply a club good for the benefit of its patrons. If there is excess demand, entrepreneurs will consider establishing new theaters—or in some cases, raising the price of a movie ticket. Thus, the price mechanism can be expected to efficiently balance demand and supply for movie entertainment.

We use the club approach in a way that is somewhat different from the original economic sense of the term, although our framework is grounded in the familiar economic assumptions (Prakash 2000b; Kollman and Prakash 2002; Prakash and Potoski 2006b). Voluntary programs (or voluntary clubs) differ from traditional "Buchanan" clubs because their central purpose is not to produce club benefits for their members. Instead, their intention is to induce members to produce positive social externalities beyond what government regulations require them to produce. In exchange, members receive the program's "club good," a benefit that only those participating in the program can enjoy.

In traditional economic clubs, members pay fees directly to the club sponsors, such as monthly dues to use the golf facilities, special tolls for driving on a particular road, or tickets for a movie. In voluntary programs, "membership fees" are not direct payments to club sponsors. Membership fees instead can be viewed as the monetary and nonmonetary costs of producing the positive social externalities that club membership requires of them. Clubs may require members to reduce pollution (see chapters 7, 9, 10, and 11), pay higher than market wages (chapter 6), provide the financing for more comprehensive accounting standards (chapter 8), have lower administrative overheads (chapter 12), or eschew diamonds from conflict zones (chapter 5). We identify three types of benefits that clubs create:

• *Social externalities* that constitute the policy payoff of clubs and provide their public policy rationale
• *Private* benefits that accrue to individual club members only
• *Branding* benefits (having the characteristics of club goods) that accrue to all club members but not to nonmembers[1]

The production of positive social externalities is the important welfare gain to society and *the* central justification for voluntary clubs. Externalities can have the attributes of private goods (a club obligating participating firms to pay higher wages), public goods (a club obligating participating firms to reduce greenhouse gas emissions), or even club goods (a club prescribing participating forestry firms from harvesting a forest revered by an aboriginal group). This distinction in the nature of externality benefits is critical because it sheds light on the external actors (and their motivations) that are likely to pressure firms to join a club. The externality beneficiaries may use public or private politics to induce or perhaps compel firms to join a club, as chapter 3 shows. Externalities create asymmetrical benefits for different stakeholders, and therefore different stakeholders might want firms to join different types of voluntary programs. Thus, to understand how branding benefits get created and perceived by firms, it is important to investigate the attributes of the externalities that the club is expected to generate, and how firms' stakeholders respond to them. As chapter 7 demonstrates, labor unions pressured shipping firms to join a labor club that requires them to pay higher wages for their crews. And it is also essential to examine how stakeholder input affects the program design (see chapter 3) or who might be eligible to become members (see chapters 10 and 11).

Private benefits accrue only to individual club members, not to other club members and certainly not to nonmembers. Private benefits are not central to the analysis of voluntary programs from a collective action standpoint. For example, a club designed to protect the environment might require policies that help firms uncover waste, and therefore reduce costs and increase profits. This is similar to the "win-win" scenario that Michael Porter and Claas van der Linde (1995) describe in the context of public regulation. Such private benefits, however, have limited utility for evaluating voluntary clubs because an instrumental actor (such as a profit-oriented firm) is likely to take these actions unilaterally, without joining the club. If private gains from unilaterally taking such actions were sufficient to induce the firm to produce positive social externalities, then voluntary clubs (or governmental regulations for that matter) would not be necessary.

Branding benefits are the compensation that club sponsors bestow on members and withhold from nonmembers, allowing members to advertise that they are different from nonmembers by virtue of their club participation. Affiliating with a club's positive brand reputation can benefit club members in several ways. In its broadest sense, membership reduces information asymmetries between firms and stakeholders. By providing information and assurance about members' unobservable activities, clubs reduce stakeholders' transaction costs for identifying which firms are producing positive externalities. Hence, clubs facilitate "Coasian exchanges" between firms and their stakeholders: the club is the intermediary that allows stakeholders to receive the positive externalities they value, and club members to receive the branding benefits that are valuable to them. To employ Neil Gunnigham, Robert Kagan, and Dorothy Thornton's (2003: 35–38) terminology, these clubs can supply members with the "social license to operate." Affiliation with a club and its reputation is thus akin to building organizational reputations that shape how stakeholders interact with the organization (Carpenter 2001).

Mitigating Collective Action Dilemmas through Voluntary Programs

The club approach is an analytic tool to bring together many concepts previously discussed in the voluntary programs literature, such as problems associated with free riding and shirking (Arora and Casson 1995, 1996; King and Lenox 2000; Rivera and deLeon 2004; Delmas and Keller 2005), program membership as a signaling mechanism (Darnall and Carmin 2005; Terlaak and King 2006), the collective nature of reputations (Hoffman 1997; Cashore, Auld, and Newsom 2004; Barnett and King 2006), and the importance of monitoring and enforcement to prevent shirking (Börkey, Glachant, and Lévêque 1998; Kolk and Tulder 2002). In addition to linking these insights and generating new ones, the club approach focuses inquiry on two salient collective action dilemmas that bear on recruitment and efficacy questions, and links these dilemmas to club design.

Like any other institution, voluntary programs are susceptible to institutional failures if they do not solve their collective action dilemmas. Two collective action dilemmas are analytically most salient for voluntary programs. First, what we call the Olsonian dilemma centers on firms' incentives to free ride on the effort of others: to take advantage of a reputation for being socially responsible without incurring the costs of producing positive social externalities. Why might this happen? Suppose some firms decide to reduce pollution. As the word spreads, this generates a warm glow (see chapter 4) about the environmental consciousness of firms in general (or perhaps in an industry, if these firms were in a single industry). Firms have the incentive to free ride because all firms would bask in the warmth of this glow. The subset of firms that incurred costs to create the warm glow in the first place is essentially subsidizing the goodwill that all firms receive. A firm might be willing to produce more social externalities if the benefits of its actions were not shared among all firms but instead went only to the one firm.

The free rider problem stems from the fact that stakeholders cannot tell how much social externalities firms are producing, and consequently, they withhold their rewards lest they be caught in the sucker's trap of rewarding firms whose claims of social responsibility were empty—a dynamic akin to a lemons market (Akerlof 1973). Even if a firm tries to mitigate the information asymmetries by informing stakeholders that it produced a social externality, without verification, such claims might be viewed as self-serving and therefore not credible. As a result, while some firms might want to produce the externalities because their stakeholders would reward them for doing so, the externality does not get produced. Clubs mitigate this information problem by providing a credible signal about which firms deserve stakeholder rewards because they are producing social externalities. In doing so, they solve the free rider problem because the benefits of club membership can then be appropriated only by firms that have joined the club.

The second dilemma, what we call the shirking dilemma, pertains to the incentives for firms to join a voluntary club and enjoy the benefits of membership without adhering to a club's obligations. Widespread shirking undermines the production of social externalities and dilutes a club's credibility. If the club strictly monitors adherence to its rules and sanctions noncompliance, shirking can be mitigated. A club with a reputation for effectively policing its participants is likely to have a stronger standing among firms' stakeholders and therefore eventually be more attractive to potential participants.[2]

Club Standards

Clubs seek to attract members by providing affiliation with a program brand that signals to firms' stakeholders that they are producing social externalities. The extent of such branding benefits is contingent on the stakeholders' perceptions of what types and levels of externalities firms are producing through their program membership. The compliance requirements that the clubs impose on their participants, which we call club standards, serve as a proxy to assess the levels of externality production.

Club standards specify what firms need to do to join the club and remain members in good standing. Club standards can come in different types, depending on what they require of members. Club standards might specify performance requirements (sometimes called outcome standards). Other standards are more process oriented, such as requirements that members adopt a management system or that members regularly consult with community groups. Finally, some club standards limit membership eligibility by descriptive preconditions, such as whether firms operate in a specific industry or have already established high levels of social performance.

Club standards specify requirements beyond the mandates of government law (or where the law is silent); it is through reference to mandatory government regulations that we can gauge the "voluntary" dimension of the club. This means that the same action that is voluntary in a jurisdiction with less stringent regulations could be mandatory in a jurisdiction with more stringent regulations. Government regulation also is the analytic referent for measuring the social value that a voluntary program creates: How much more positive social externality does a voluntary program compel its members to produce than they would produce in the absence of the program?

While the obligations that the club imposes on its members can be viewed as a continuum, for analytic purposes, we will examine two ideal types: lenient and stringent club standards. Lenient club standards require little of their members beyond what government regulations require. These are low-cost clubs that lead to the production of small amounts of social externalities. Of course, even lenient club standards must mandate that members produce some positive social externality (or mitigate a negative one), or else the club would be a mere empty gesture. While it might be easy for a firm to join such a lenient voluntary club, the club is likely to have a weak reputation—after all, why would stakeholders favor clubs that lead to only trivial amounts of externalities? Clubs with such lenient standards are likely to face adverse selection problems because firms with superior social performance (which might be well beyond the legal minimum) would not want to subsidize or identify with laggards (that barely meet the regulatory requirements), and therefore would not join the club. Thus, the club is likely to be saddled with firms that neither have stellar social performance nor are likely to acquire one because the club's standards impose marginal requirements on them.

Yet there might be some advantages to relatively lenient standards. First, lower membership costs may encourage a large number of firms to become members. High membership might produce more "network effects" that enhance the value of the club brand. Second, many of the firms that join may be making true improvements to their performance to become members (rather than simply seeking certification for the social externalities they are already producing)—a dynamic akin to a production possibility frontier. From a public policy perspective, then, the "value added" by a club with more lenient standards might still be substantial if enough firms join it.

Stringent club standards impose obligations on firms that are well beyond the requirements of public law and regulations. As a consequence, firms that become club members are each likely to produce large amounts of positive social externalities. To ensure that only "serious" firms join the club, a club with stringent standards may admit only firms that have already achieved superior social performance. In this way, entry-level requirements could signal to the various stakeholders the stringency of obligations that the club imposes on its members. The advantage of stringent standards is that the club's brand would be more credible and serve as a low-cost tool for signaling club members' commitment to producing social externalities. Stakeholders would more readily differentiate leaders (members) from laggards (nonmembers) among firms. Armed with this information, these stakeholders could reward and punish firms accordingly. Chapters 10 and 11 discuss clubs sponsored by the EPA with stringent club standards.

Stringent standards, however, have two potential downsides. First, the high cost of meeting the standard may dissuade firms from joining. As we discuss subsequently, low membership might not allow the generation of sufficient levels of "network effects" to enhance the overall value of the club brand. The second disadvantage might be that because these clubs are likely to attract "leaders," club membership might not be able to induce additional production of social externalities because such firms are already operating on the outer boundaries of the externality production frontier. From a public policy perspective, the "value added" by the club might be marginal.

Monitoring and Enforcement Rules

Shirking is a second major source of institutional failure. Shirkers formally adopt the club's standards without implementing and practicing them, but still claim to be socially progressive by virtue of their club membership. While nonmembers are excluded from enjoying the benefits of club membership, shirkers continue to enjoy club benefits unless they are discovered and sanctioned. As word spreads about large-scale shirking, the club's reputation is likely to be diminished and the brand reputation undermined.

Clubs' sponsors and stakeholders have incomplete and imprecise information about how an individual club member is adhering to club obligations. Such information asymmetries might encourage some members to believe that they can get away with shirking because their behaviors will not be detected. The incentives to shirk are further accentuated if members believe that even if detected, shirking will go unsanctioned. It is therefore important for voluntary clubs to establish monitoring and enforcement mechanisms that reduce information asymmetries, and signal to club members that their adherence to club obligations is under scrutiny and their shirking will be sanctioned.

Creating monitoring mechanisms increases the costs of governing a voluntary program. Club sponsors need to make careful assessment of the marginal benefits of increasing monitoring stringency. We identify three components to effective and credible monitoring and enforcement systems: third-party monitoring, public disclosure of audit information, and sanctioning by program sponsors. Third-party monitoring means that participating firms are required by the club sponsor to have their club-related actions or policies audited by accredited, external auditors to verify that they are adhering to the obligations that the club membership requires. The idea is that because firms and their managers recognize that accredited, external actors have the abilities and incentives to identify and report shirking, they are less likely to shirk. In some cases, program sponsors may require the public disclosure of audit information. The logic is that public disclosures empower external actors to scrutinize participating firms' club obligations and then expose the shirkers. Sanctioning by external stakeholders might follow, thereby mitigating club participants' incentives to shirk in the first place. Finally, the sponsoring organization may itself act on the audit information and sanction the members that have been found to be shirking on their obligations. The threat of such sanctioning is most credible because club sponsors have a vested interest in ensuring the club's credibility. By sanctioning shirkers, club sponsors send out a message to club participants as well as external stakeholders that they will hold participants accountable regarding their club obligations.

We call clubs' monitoring and enforcement programs swords. Strong sword programs have all three components: audits, disclosure, and sanctioning mechanisms. They are most likely to curb shirking because they mitigate information asymmetries between participants and program sponsors/stakeholders, and allow sponsors to sanction shirkers. In extreme cases, sponsors may expel participants from the program. As discussed in chapters 10 and 11, the EPA's Performance Track is an example of a strong sword program. In addition to third-party audits of participants' environmental management systems, the EPA required Performance Track members to submit an annual report demonstrating their environmental accomplishments and that they are adhering to Performance Track's membership requirements. This helped to mitigate the information asymmetries between the EPA and the Performance Track club members. Importantly, because program membership had to be renewed every three years, the EPA could sanction shirkers simply by not renewing their club membership. It is fair to say that Performance Track's institutional design reduces information asymmetries and creates credible threats that shirkers will get sanctioned once their nonadherence to club obligations is brought to notice. Thus, we expect low levels of shirking in strong swords program. These clubs also have high governance costs, though eventually the cost of monitoring and sanctioning mechanisms is borne by the participating firms.

Medium sword programs require third-party audits and public disclosure. Although their institutional design does not provide for sanctioning of the shirkers by the sponsoring organization, they are likely to curb shirking because with public disclosure of audit information, firms' stakeholders can punish the shirkers. In this way, sanctioning is outsourced by the sponsoring organization to external stakeholders. The EPA's 33/50 program and the European Union's Environmental Management and Audit System are examples of medium sword programs. In both programs, firms are required to undergo third-party audits, and the information about their adherence to club obligations is available to the public. Because it is not clear how the sponsoring organization sanctions shirkers, we place them in the medium sword category.

Weak swords programs require only third-party audits. In such clubs, information asymmetries between the sponsoring actor and club members are sought to be mitigated by audits. External stakeholders, however, do not have access to information regarding adherence to club obligations by individual participants. As a consequence, they cannot reward or sanction firms. ISO 14001 is an example of a weak sword program. The International Organization for Standardization, the sponsoring organization, is not known to aggressively sanction shirkers, and the absence of public disclosure of audit information weakens stakeholders' ability to sanction shirking. Weak sword clubs also impose minimum governance costs of installing monitoring mechanisms. On this count, they could be attractive to a large number of firms that are wary of overinvesting in the production of social externalities.

Based on the above discussion, we can identify six club types whose appeal is likely to vary across actors and contexts. *Shams* pertain to clubs that have weak monitoring and enforcement mechanisms, and that impose modest obligations on participating firms. These clubs have little policy merit in terms of the production of social externalities; however, they can be employed to create an erroneous impression about firms' commitment to socially desirable policies. In effect, these clubs pay only lip service to social goals. At the opposite spectrum, *mandarin* clubs impose significant obligations on their participants, and have strong mechanisms to monitor and enforce adherence to club obligations. They are likely to produce sizable levels of social externalities on a per member basis, but might have limited membership due to stringent club standards. While *country clubs* are likely to have a small roster due to their stringent club standards, members are less likely to comply with their high club standards. Their overall impact on social goals is likely to be modest. *Boot camps*, in contrast, expect less from their members in terms of the production of social externalities (lenient standards), but their strong swords might significantly reduce shirking. Depending on the roster size and the level of shirking, they could have a sizable aggregate impact. *Boy Scouts* and *prep schools* are in the middle of the spectrum in terms of the obligations that they impose on members and the strength of their swords. They are likely to create moderate levels of desirable social externalities.

Table 2.1
Toward an analytic typology of clubs

Enforcement and monitoring rules Club standards	Weak sword	Medium sword	Strong sword
Lenient standards	Participation cost: low Shirking: high Branding benefits: marginal Policy implication: low levels of social externalities **Shams**	Participation cost: low to moderate Shirking: moderate Branding benefits: low to moderate Policy implication: low to moderate levels of social externalities **Boy Scouts**	Participation cost: low to moderate Shirking: low Branding benefits: low to moderate Policy implication: moderate levels of social externalities **Boot Camps**
Stringent standards	Participation cost: moderate to high Shirking: high Branding benefits: marginal Policy implication: low levels of social externalities **Country Club**	Participation cost: moderate Shirking: moderate Branding benefits: moderate Policy implication: moderate levels of social externalities **Prep Schools**	Participation cost: high Shirking: low Branding benefits: high Policy implication: high levels of social externalities **Mandarins**

The production of social externalities (per club member) is likely to be minimal in clubs with lenient standards and weak swords. In contrast, we expect the production of social externalities to be the highest per member in clubs with stringent club standards and strong swords. This, of course, raises the question, Are the Mandarin clubs always the best and Shams always the worst? The answer depends on the context in which the club operates. Mandarin clubs are the high-cost clubs in terms of both the costs of complying with club standards and the governance costs associated with monitoring and enforcement. While some stakeholders might favor such clubs because they maximize the production (per firm) of the desired externality, potential participants might not perceive an adequate payoff of joining such costly clubs. As a result, such clubs might have low levels of membership, leading to modest production of externalities in the aggregate. Sham clubs, on the other hand, might attract a larger roster of firms, and although participants would produce only modest levels of externalities per capita, they could produce a substantial level in the aggregate. Hence, the analyst has to pay close attention to the nature of club standards, what types of externalities are generated, at what levels, how clubs' reputations are established and communicated, and so on. This typology should help the analyst in structuring their analysis and then posing the appropriate questions in the context of the fit of the club within the policy environment. After all, given the political implications of voluntary clubs, different club types are likely to serve as the most appropriate fits for varying policy contexts.

The chapters in this volume suggest the value of this typology. On the theoretical front, chapters 3 and 4 formally explicate the dynamics among clubs' reputations, institutional design, and firms and their stakeholders. Many interesting insights emerge. For example, there is some evidence that no good deed goes unpunished: the models predict that members of mandarin clubs are sometimes more attractive targets for "private politics"—protests from activist groups—than are members of weaker shams (chapter 3). Also surprising is that from a social welfare perspective, mandarins are not always the most desirable club (see chapter 4).

The typology also has value for the empirical chapters in this volume. Chapter 5 suggests that the Kimberley Process for diamond certification may eventually fail because of potential weaknesses in its monitoring and enforcement program. While the program has stringent club standards, weak enforcement could shift it from an effective mandarin to an empty country club. Likewise, chapter 6 shows that the apparel industry's early voluntary programs were certainly country clubs—there was little monitoring and enforcement of the standards—and in some cases were outright shams with minimal enforcement of weak standards. No wonder they lacked legitimacy among labor rights activist groups. The shipping industry (chapter 7) is a fascinating case where there are several voluntary programs having both strong and weak enforcement and club standards. This chapter finds some correlation among the strength in standards, the strength in benefits from accepting those standards, and the strength or reliability of enforcement mechanisms. In a sector often noted for the race to the bottom, shipping clubs are probably the only effective mechanisms at raising environmental, safety, and labor standards on ships globally. The analysis in chapter 8 suggests the accounting industry created mandarin clubs with effective club standards as well as effective monitoring and enforcement. Chapter 9 shows that firms in the Pacific Rim countries see greater value in joining strong sword clubs than those with weak swords. Chapters 10 and 11 illustrate the variability in how government-sponsored clubs have performed. The EPA's Performance Track, discussed in chapters 10 and 11, is certainly a mandarin club, but its membership roster fell well short of expectations, and it's not clear how well the EPA was able to reward firms that joined the program. Chapter 12 points out that nonprofit clubs are likely to have substantially weaker standards and enforcement than their commercial counterparts. This is due both to the difficulty of measuring nonprofit output and the relatively lower institutionalization of reporting standards in the nonprofit sector. Thus, this chapter shows a range of clubs including shams that operate in the area of NGO voluntary regulation.

Institutions, Program Brands, and Collective Action

Voluntary clubs must cultivate a reputation for requiring their members to produce social externalities. A program's brand reputation is influenced by its club standards because these rules critically shape the levels and types of externalities that members produce beyond the regulatory requirements. The brand reputation is also influenced by the size of a program's membership roster (and associated network affects), how stakeholders view a club's monitoring and enforcement rules, and the credibility of the program's sponsors.

The value that members receive from the brand is also influenced by each firm's own characteristics and the extent to which their stakeholders—consumers, regulators, investors, suppliers, and so forth—can identify club members and reward them. How these stakeholders reward club members is contingent partly on stakeholders' desire to encourage the production of specific externalities, and partly on whether stakeholders have the information and resources to act on their desires. As chapter 3 illustrates, activists such as those in environmental groups can signal their preferences by pressuring firms to join a voluntary club (Sasser et al. 2006). Large or more profitable firms might benefit more from the club because they have capabilities to capitalize on stakeholders' goodwill. As chapter 8 suggests, actors in a "privileged group" (Olson 1965) who are disproportionately affected by an industry's collective reputation are likely to take the lead in establishing an industry club and ensuring that other industry firms join it. Indeed, this is the story of Responsible Care in the chemical industry (Gunningham and Rees 1997; Prakash 2000a; King and Lenox 2000) and the Sustainable Forestry Initiative in the forestry industry (Cashore, Auld, and Newsom 2004). As chapters 10 and 11 suggest, in the context of clubs sponsored by the EPA, firms that are often out of compliance with the law might perceive different types and levels of benefits flowing from club membership in relation to firms that are always in compliance. Thus, in addition to club design and the credibility of the club sponsor, the attractiveness of a given club is likely to vary with the institutional and stakeholder context as well as firm-level characteristics (see chapter 4).

Some firms unilaterally take actions to boost their reputation with stakeholders. Indeed, it is not hard to think of companies with well-earned reputations for social leadership. If firms can take unilateral action to boost their standing among stakeholders, what is the advantage of joining voluntary clubs, which in all likelihood is a costlier route to achieve this objective? Club membership can offer important advantages over unilateral action. First, positive action by one member of a club can boost other club members' reputations as stakeholders paint the entire club roster with the same brush (a bad apple can tarnish the bushel as well). Because clubs can capture these scale economies and create network externalities through their brand, progressive social action taken as part of a club can do more to boost a firm's reputation than the same action taken unilaterally. Second, firms' unilateral commitments to socially desirable action may be less credible because they are less institutionalized. When individual firms make their own rules, they can also easily change them. As the "credible commitment" literature suggests (North and Weingast 1989), of course, actors can devise mechanisms for tying their hands—that is, credibly committing to upholding the rule system and not opportunistically changing it. Nevertheless, it is fair to say that as an institutionalized governance system, clubs enjoy a degree of legitimacy that an average firm alone may find difficult to acquire. By joining a club whose rules they cannot change easily in the short run, firms credibly signal their commitment to producing positive externalities.

Size, Scope, and Voluntary Clubs

The size of a club's membership roster influences the value of club benefits in significant ways. On the one hand, members create more opportunities to capture economies of scale in building reputations (McGuire 1972), a dynamic akin to network effects (Bessen and Saloner 1988). Network effects pertain to the changes in the benefit that an actor derives from a good (joining a club in our case) when the number of other actors consuming the same good (participating in the club) changes. Positive network effects create increasing returns to scale to club membership: with every additional member, the marginal benefits of being associated with club membership increase (or the marginal costs of creating benefits decrease). Language groups can be thought of as clubs amenable to network effects: the more people who speak a given language, the higher are the benefits from learning it. Having more members helps advertise a policy club broadly among stakeholders as one member's socially desirable activities creates positive externalities for other members, so that the value a member derives increases as others join.

While the benefits of club membership are nonrival because the positive reputational benefits one member enjoys can be simultaneously enjoyed by other members, crowding may set in as the club roster grows—a question that has not been sufficiently examined in the voluntary program literature. The issue of optimal club size has been discussed in the traditional Buchanan club literature (Cornes and Sandler [1986] 1996). Chapter 4 applies a similar approach by examining optimal size in the context of voluntary clubs: the point at which crowding sets in influences the amount of social externality and overall social welfare gain that the club produces.

The issue of optimal club size can be examined from the perspective of different actors. We previously suggested that for most clubs, the participants are likely to prefer a higher membership roster simply because it increases the benefits they receive from affiliating with the club brand. Now imagine a club with universal membership. Arguably, from the perspective of a firm that has joined a club in order to distinguish itself from its peers, this might not be the optimal club size. In contrast, for stakeholders interested in the maximizing the production of the desired social externality, the optimal club size might be universal membership. Chapter 4 formally demonstrates that from a social welfare perspective, clubs with unrestricted access lead to the dissipation of the overall surplus and are therefore not socially optimal.

Industry-sponsored programs, such as the American Chemistry Council's Responsible Care program and the American Forestry and Paper Association's Sustainable Forestry Initiative, clearly illustrate club size issues. Club sponsors and most participating firms might desire universal membership because the "bad behavior" of one member (say, an industrial accident) carries negative consequences for the rest. This is because the stakeholders might not be able to differentiate members (with desired policies) from nonmembers (without desired policies). If club membership imposes substantial obligations and thereby reduces the chances of "bad behavior," universal membership serves as a sort of collective insurance for firms operating in that industry. The efficacy of such insurance falls with the increasing number of "leaks" (firms that do not join the club), and in response, industry associations might then require their members to join an industry-wide voluntary program—as they do in the chemical (Prakash 2000b) and forestry industries (Cashore, Auld, and Newsom 2004).

Just as a farmer can establish a new golf course to solve crowding in neighboring clubs, congestion in voluntary clubs might be solved through additional clubs that emphasize different types or amounts of externality production. A new program, for example, may require that its members produce even more social externalities to distinguish its brand (and members) from members of a more populous but less stringent program.

Voluntary Programs in Research and Practice

Readers familiar with the literature on voluntary programs will see echoes of familiar themes in the club approach. The preceding sections traced the social science roots of the club theory approach; the section below shows how the approach fits with and draws from the voluntary program research tradition. This research is richly multidisciplinary, with many theoretical and methodological approaches, and as we will see in this volume, the voluntary programs themselves vary in many ways, such as the type of sponsor, the nature of the industry—or industries— in which they operate, the types of firms that join them, and so on. An important merit of the club approach is its ability to facilitate the cross-fertilization of research findings and theoretical insights from this diverse research agenda.

Categorizing Voluntary Programs

Voluntary program classification schemes have mostly been developed in the environmental arena. Peter Börkey, Michael Glachant, and François Lévêque (1998) of the Centre d'economies industrielle (CERNA) classify programs in four categories based on the characteristics of actors involved in the voluntary institution: public voluntary programs sponsored by public authorities, negotiated agreements between public authorities and an industrial sector or individual firms, unilateral commitments by an industrial sector that do not involve public authorities, and private agreements between firms and their stakeholders.[3] This is a useful way to think about how voluntary approaches to regulation relate to public law, given that the involvement of public authorities is a critical characteristic of this typology. For example, this typology can be useful for predicting how business-government relations, political institutions, and culture more broadly might influence the emergence of a given category of voluntary program. The CERNA (Börkey, Glachant, and Lévêque, 1998, 5) framework notes the "distinct national patterns" in the use of voluntary approaches. In Japan, negotiated agreements at the local level are popular, while in the European Union, which consists of countries with corporatist structures, negotiated agreements at the country level are well established. In the United States, both public voluntary programs motivated by public relations reasons and unilateral commitments seem to be in vogue.

The club approach coheres with the CERNA framework in that the four program types can be viewed as different types of clubs. As we discuss in the conclusion, our approach is most useful when there are significant information asymmetries between firms and their stakeholders, and when public image is a key payoff for firms to join these programs. Yet our approach differs from the CERNA approach on two counts. First, the club approach applies more generally, extending, for example, to programs that are sponsored by NGOs. As chapter 6 on the apparel industry and chapter 7 on the shipping industry suggest, NGOs are emerging as crucial players in sponsoring voluntary programs. Second, analytically, the club framework emphasizes *program attributes* instead of *actor attributes* as drivers of program efficacy. This is because to study program efficacy, one needs to focus on factors that are reasonably exogenous to program performance. At least in the short run, program design is exogenous to program performance.

Nicole Darnall and JoAnn Carmin (2005) classify voluntary environmental programs by their requirements, such as establishing environmental improvement targets, and conformance requirements, such as monitoring and sanctions. The club approach mirror's this typology in that environmental requirements are similar to club standards, and conformance standards are similar to monitoring and enforcement procedures, but the club framework goes further by allowing the development of a more general vocabulary for classifying club standards that can apply across different programs, in different industries, and in different policy settings.

We should note that the club approach does not address all cases where firms take progressive action to produce positive externalities. A firm might unilaterally decide to take such action because its owners and managers simply want to, in response to stakeholder pressure, or because it found new ways to produce profits through its good deeds (Porter and van der Linde 1995). Likewise, the club approach does not address cases where there is no club, such as individual bilateral agreements negotiated among a single firm along with its government and perhaps nongovernmental stakeholders (Delmas and Marcus 2004; Börkey, Glachant, and Lévêque 1998). Finally, Thomas Lyon and John Maxwell (2003) suggest that sponsors establish voluntary programs to provide information about how they can produce positive externalities more efficiently, such as by introducing novel clean production technology. Such programs may create positive externalities by overcoming firms' ignorance about how to cheaply produce externalities and may be an important policy tool. In the Lyon and Maxwell approach, however, firms do not join voluntary programs for reputational gain. The club framework focuses on designing institutions that can solve the collective action problems that prevent the production of desirable externalities. We return to the limitations of the club framework in the concluding chapter.

Research Voluntary Program Efficacy

Program by program, scholars have studied conditions under which firms join voluntary programs and under which programs are effective. Firms' stakeholders are not always able to perceive salient firm characteristics. Several innovative studies suggest that firms join voluntary programs as a mechanism to signal difficult-to-observe features about themselves (Darnall and Carmin 2005; Terlaak and King 2006). A firm might join a voluntary program to boost its reputation (Terlaak and King 2006), and an industry association might sponsor a program of its own to boost the collective reputation of its members (King and Lenox 2000). This signaling function makes membership in voluntary programs an important stakeholder management tool (Delmas 2001), and indicates that sponsors build program brands that transmit strong and clear signals (Harbaugh, Maxwell, and Roussillon 2006).

There is a strong theoretical argument that firms take beyond compliance action to forestall more stringent government regulations (Pfaff and Sanchirico 2000; Maxwell, Lyon, and Hackett 2000). Indeed, governments themselves may have reason to create a voluntary program rather than wait for government regulation in response to political and market pressures (Lyon and Maxwell 2003). Empirical verification of these arguments has been elusive—a firm is unlikely to admit to such motives when it is trying to "voluntarily" do good things—although forestalling regulations appears to have been a motive for the apparel industry's voluntary labor programs in the early 1990s, as shown in chapter 6. This motivation is not inconsistent with the club approach: firms and industries are targeted for regulation when there is a perception that they are producing negative externalities, and firms have a free rider problem in terms of who pays the cost of reducing their own negative externalities for benefits that would be shared by all firms facing the threat of regulations.

Research on the efficacy of voluntary programs—whether they induce members to improve their performance—has produced mixed results (Ramus and Monteil 2005). Jorge Rivers and Peter deLeon (2004) report that ski resorts that participated in the Sustainable Slopes Program were not any more green than their nonparticipating counterparts. Similarly,

Andrew King and Michael Lenox (2000) found that chemical firms participating in the Responsible Care program did not reduce the emission of toxic chemicals any faster than nonparticipants, and Magali Delmas and Arturo Keller (2005) present a similar weak affect of the EPA's WasteWise Program. Madhu Khanna and Lisa Damon (1999), however, report that firms that joined the EPA's 35/50 voluntary program reduced their emissions of toxic pollutants more than the nonparticipants. Our own work suggests that ISO 14001 improved participating firms' environmental performance (Potoski and Prakash 2005a) and compliance with government regulations (Potoski and Prakash 2005b). An explanation for these disparate findings is that successful voluntary programs have effective monitoring and enforcement mechanisms that prevent shirking among participants—a conclusion echoed in several of the chapters in this volume.

An important advantage of the club approach to voluntary programs is that its focus on institutional design and collective action helps scholars and analysts to make *ex ante* predictions and proposals about how rule structures will affect program efficacy. Inquiry grounded in these core theoretical actors can then focus on how the program sponsorship, market context, and political environment affect how programs function. What features do voluntary programs need to be effective where firms' brands are weak? How does sponsorship affect programs' reputations? Chapter 12 is instructive on this count. As this chapter points out, NGOs are increasingly creating voluntary programs to signal to their funders their commitment to utilize funds as per the guidelines laid out by donors.

The club framework should also facilitate the comparative study of voluntary programs established by one sponsor or across multiple sponsors. Indeed, scholars have recognized the significance of this issue when conducting comparative analyses of voluntary programs (Cashore, Auld, and Newsom 2004; Lenox and Nash 2003; Darnall and Carmin 2005). While such cross-program studies can shed light on why some programs are successful and others are not, advancing research and practice requires an encompassing theoretical and analytic framework that identifies voluntary clubs' important features, and ties them to program efficacy, thereby leading to a better understanding of what types of voluntary clubs work, where, and why. Such a theoretical framework should facilitate comparisons not only among voluntary programs but also with other policy instruments. We believe the club theory framework for voluntary clubs makes a contribution in this direction.

Conclusion

All in all, we believe the club approach has much to offer not only for improving the study of these policy mechanisms but also for suggesting ways that these programs can be better designed. The approach targets key institutional features that affect the extent to which voluntary programs can overcome the critical collective action problems that most directly threaten their efficacy. It also lays out a common vocabulary and analytic lens that can guide comparative research across multiple programs in diverse political and policy arenas. And because it is firmly grounded in well-established social science traditions—with roots in club theory, institutional analysis, and collective action—the club approach helps scholars to both draw guidance from a broad social science foundation and speak back to these important research traditions.

All of this is not to say that the club approach is not without its blind spots. Indeed, the chapters that follow highlight the approach's strengths as well as crucial areas in which it is underdeveloped. After the club approach has been vetted through ten chapters of rigorous theoretical and empirical scrutiny, we will be in a better position to discuss its strengths and weaknesses, and how the approach might be improved—tasks that we take up in the volume's concluding chapter.

3

Clubs, Credence Standards, and Social Pressure

David P. Baron

In addition to their physical and performance characteristics, products have unobservable credence attributes that consumers cannot learn through search, experience, or consumption. Such attributes could include the conditions under which the product is produced, including any unregulated externalities associated with production, how workers are treated and how well they are paid, how and where the product is marketed, hidden hazards associated with the consumption of the product, associated environmental externalities, and whether the product is made from sustainable inputs. Some consumers value the credence attributes of products and are willing to pay a premium for their supply. Firms then have an incentive to add those attributes to their products as a form of product differentiation. Even if they do not consume the products, citizens who value credence attributes that correspond to positive social externalities or redistribution to preferred recipients can generate social pressure to induce firms to supply more of those attributes. When a demand pull from consumers' willingness to pay is present, the push from social pressure can increase the supply of credence attributes. This chapter provides a theory of the supply of credence attributes in the presence of both consumers' willingness to pay and social pressure.[1]

Social pressure can be directed at firms through public or private politics. Public politics in the arenas of government institutions can result in legislation mandating the supply of credence attributes, the promulgation of regulations by agencies, and decisions by courts about any rights and entitlements pertaining to those attributes. In addition to pursuing their objectives through public politics, citizens can use private politics to pressure firms to supply credence attributes. Private politics is the direct application of social pressure in an attempt to change the behavior of economic agents.[2] NGOs and social activists are frequently the agents of social pressure. That is, they are funded by citizens and draw their influence from the support of citizens for their causes. Empirical studies have documented the impact of NGOs on environmental performance (see Lyon and Maxwell 2004), although the studies typically do not distinguish between the underlying public and private politics (see, for example, Binder and Newmayer 2005).

The targets of private politics and social pressure can respond by forming a private organization to promulgate voluntary standards and then certify that their products meet those standards. In the footwear and apparel industries, a group of firms and NGOs formed the Fair Labor Association (FLA) that promulgates standards for working conditions in overseas factories and sponsors independent inspections of those factories to verify compliance. In response to demands that timber companies comply with the standards of the NGO-sponsored Forest Stewardship Council (FSC), U.S. timber companies formed the Sustainable Forest Initiative (SFI) that establishes standards and provides for independent inspections.[3] In the aftermath of the Bhopal tragedy, a group of chemical companies formed Responsible Care to promote safety and environmental protection in their firms (King and Lenox 2000, 2002). Many chemical companies, however, chose not to participate. Under pressure from NGOs, project finance banks formed the Equator Principles governing the environmental and worker standards for the projects, such as dams, pipelines, roads, and telecommunications systems, that they finance in developing countries.

These organizations typically adopt less stringent standards than demanded by the NGOs. For example, when the FLA was formed, some NGOs and labor unions refused to participate and instead formed the Workers Rights Consortium to campaign for stronger worker rights in the footwear and apparel industries. Similarly, the NGOs backing the FSC criticized the SFI for its standards and the absence of mandatory independent inspections. Environmental NGOs have also criticized the Equator Principles because they do not go far enough to protect the environment.[4]

This chapter focuses on the formation of such voluntary organizations (referred to here as clubs), their choice of a standard for the credence attributes of the products of their members, and how that choice and participation in the organization are affected by social pressure. The SFI is an example of a club, and the standard pertains to timber sustainability practices, certification, and verification by the club and its member firms. The club is assumed credibly to assure compliance with the standard, although as Prakash and Potoski discuss in chapter 2, shirking by club members can be a concern.[5] Assurance could be provided by government, an independent third party, or the club if it can credibly give a seal to products meeting an agreed-to standard. NGOs can also supply credible certification through independent monitoring and inspection. The information provided ensures that the standard is met or that any unintended shortcomings will be quickly corrected. The seal or certification that the product receives provides an excludable benefit to the club members.

In the model, the only reward for supplying a product with credence attributes comes from the price premium that consumers pay, although the rewards could take other forms such as regulatory relief, as considered in chapters 10 and 11. The club is assumed to be formed by the firms in the industry, but a club could also be formed by activists and NGOs, as in the case of the FSC. A club could also form at the initiative of the government, as in the case of the voluntary programs sponsored by the EPA, as discussed in chapter 10. Government-sponsored programs are often intended to attract good performers to set an example in the hope that others will follow. The club itself serves as an intermediary between citizens who are willing to reward firms for the credence attributes of their products and the firms that through the club can credibly supply those attributes.

With regard to social pressure, the objective is to answer three questions about its effect on club formation and conduct. The first is whether a club would be formed in the absence of social pressure, and if so, what credence standard would the firms choose? Second, if a club would form in the absence of social pressure, how is its conduct affected by the presence of social pressure? For instance, does the club choose to supply more credence attributes when it is under social pressure than when social pressure is absent, and does social pressure affect how many and which firms join the club? The third pertains to the locus of social pressure. That is, under which conditions is social pressure directed at the club firms or those firms that do not join the club? For example, an NGO could act opportunistically and target the club firms because they have demonstrated a willingness to supply credence attributes. They are viewed as soft, in other words. Paul Argenti (2004), for one, concluded that the selection of Starbucks as a target by the NGO Global Exchange was because Starbucks was viewed as soft and responsive.

Prakash and Potoski (2006b) consider voluntary environmental agreements from the perspective of club theory. Chapter 4 presents a theory of clubs in which a social planner or administrator forms a club that maximizes social welfare. It then contrasts the chosen standard and the club size with those resulting when an environmentalist organizes a club to maximize environmental benefits. In the model considered here, firms form a club to maximize their expected profits taking into account the strategic interactions among the firms that join the club and those that do not. The firms may establish a club voluntarily in the absence of social pressure, and social pressure led by an activist can result in a higher or lower standard. The firms can fight the social pressure, but if the activist campaign is successful, a higher standard results.

The response of firms to the threat or actuality of private or public politics pressure has been studied in the self-regulation literature. Thomas Lyon and John Maxwell (2004) as well as Maxwell, Lyon, and Steven Hackett (2000) provide theory and empirical evidence on self-regulation by firms. Andrew King and Michael Lenox (2000, 2002) and Lenox and Jennifer Nash (2003) provide empirical studies of industry self-regulation programs. Seema Arora and Timothy Casson (1996) and Magali Delmas (2006) studied the performance of firms participating in voluntary programs sponsored by the EPA. I (Baron 2007, 2008, 2009a) present theories of self-regulation in the form of corporate social responsibility. Kotchen (2006b) and Aleix Calveras, Jaun-Jose Ganuza, and Gerald Llobet (2007) provide theories of self-regulation by consumers.

Relationship to the Framework

The theory presented here can be related to the framework in chapter 2, but differs from that framework on several dimensions. On the demand side of the product market, the credence attributes are supplied only to the extent that consumers value those attributes—that is, are willing to pay for them. The credence attributes could, but need not, correspond to social externalities or represent public goods. That is, the credence attributes could reflect private redistribution to particular recipients, such as workers in overseas factories. Consumers' valuation could reflect altruism for those who benefit from the credence attributes or could reflect warm glow preferences for the act of purchasing a product with credence attributes. Consumers also will pay for credence attributes only if those attributes are credibly assured.

On the supply side, the credence attributes are supplied privately by firms that are assumed to be able to assure credibly that the attributes are actually supplied. Credibility is assumed to be provided collectively by firms, and the organization that assures credibility will be referred to as a club. The firms in the club do not act cooperatively but instead compete directly in the product market. Credible credence attributes represent a form of product differentiation, since consumers are willing to pay for those attributes. Consequently, the club firms compete with each other in the product market. In contrast to the economic theory of clubs (Cornes and Sandler [1986] 1996), there is no exogenously assumed congestion cost. Competition among the firms limits club size.

The club that arises in equilibrium is self-sponsored, and it is based solely on self-interest. That is, the objective of the club is to maximize the profits of its members, and the credible supply of credence attributes is the instrument to accomplish this objective. The amount of credence attributes supplied, which is referred to as the standard, is assumed to be determined collectively by the members of the club, and although there are many governance structures that the club could use to make the collective choice, the club is simply assumed to maximize the aggregate profit of its members.

The focus of this model is not on the internal organization of the club nor on how it prevents shirking. The organization is assumed to prevent shirking, and in order to focus on the size of the club and the standard chosen, the costs of the organization are assumed to be zero.[6] The club does not face a free rider problem, since only the members of the club can have the provision of their credence attributes assured. Participation in the club is, however, endogenous and voluntary. In the model, participation is limited by the private cost that a firm incurs in meeting the standard. Conversely, the private costs of meeting the standard affect the choice of the standard.

The model has complete information, so there is no adverse selection in the participation decisions of firms. Nevertheless, due to the discrete number of firms, a club may not be composed of the firms with the lowest costs of meeting the credence standard. There are thus multiple equilibriums with clubs of different sizes and standards as well as equilibrium clubs of the same size but with different memberships and standards. The focus in the chapter, is on efficient clubs—clubs that include the firms that are the most efficient in meeting the credence standard. In the theory there is no notion of an optimal club size. Instead, club size is determined in equilibrium by the participation decisions of the individual firms. That is, there is an equilibrium club size and standard.

The opportunity for the private provision of credence attributes need not be due to a government failure. That is, a majority of citizens may not support the provision of the credence attributes. The private provision can result instead from the preferences of a minority. Private provision thus can serve the interests of minorities.

In addition to the valuation of credence attributes by some consumers, citizens who are not consumers can have preferences for the credence attributes. These citizens do not participate in the product market but they can participate in the political market. Government is not present in the model, so the political market involves only private politics. Citizens are assumed to fund activists and NGOs that put private politics pressure on the firms to supply more credence attributes. Like the consumers who are willing to pay a premium for the credence attributes, the citizens who fund social pressure through private politics may have minority preferences.

The club firms anticipate the social pressure, so their choice of a standard is affected, as is the size of the club. The activists and NGOs that engage the firms in private politics have a choice between targeting the club firms and targeting the firms that do not provide credence attributes. Their campaign, if successful, is assumed to force the targeted firms to increase their supply of credence goods.[7] The target of social pressure can fight back, and the incentive to fight depends on the demand of the activist, the public support for the campaign, and the number of firms targeted and any standard they may have adopted. Credence attributes therefore are supplied voluntarily by the club firms at the level of the standard they choose, and in addition credence attributes may be forced on the club or nonclub firms by social pressure.

The club firms can affect the targeting choice of the activists through both the standard chosen and the club size. Conversely, the anticipation of social pressure affects the participation decisions of firms and the standard chosen by those firms that participate. The higher the standard chosen, the less likely is it that the club firms will be targeted. If targeted, the club firms can have incentives to fight, but they may prefer to concede to the activist's demand. Moreover, they may prefer to be targeted so as to avoid a reduction in their product differentiation advantage that would result if the nonclub firms were targeted, the campaign succeeds, and the nonclub firms then provide credence attributes. The club firms can assure that they will be targeted by setting a low standard. Social pressure thus can result in low standards if the club firms sacrifice themselves or high standards if they prefer that the nonclub firms be targeted.

This chapter uses two standard models to study the formation and operation of a club in the presence of social pressure. One is a vertical differentiation model from industrial organization where the differentiation is analogous to quality differences among products. The other is a contest model used in political economy in which the probability of the activist or the club winning the social pressure conflict is determined by the resources each commits to the contest as well as other factors such as reputation and trust. The combination of these two models results in complexity, so a numerical example is used to illustrate the properties of equilibriums.

This chapter develops a number of potentially testable results. When consumers value the credence attributes of products, firms can have an incentive to form a club to assure the supply of those attributes. The credence attributes provide product differentiation and yield a price premium. Consequently, firms can voluntarily adopt standards in the absence of social pressure, and their motivation is profit maximization. Although consumers value a higher standard, the quantity sold by the club firms is decreasing in the standard, since the effect of the price premium outweighs the credence effect of a standard. Hence, the market share of the club firms is decreasing in the standard for a club of a given size.

The firms in an efficient club are those with the lowest fixed costs, and some firms do not join because their costs of meeting the standard are too high. Clubs with higher standards are thus smaller than clubs with lower standards. The lower standard need not, however, be the lowest common denominator, since the club maximizes the aggregate profit of its member firms and the standard provides product differentiation. Higher fixed costs result in smaller clubs.

The market share of the club is decreasing in the standard for two reasons. First, the price is higher, and this price effect outweighs the credence effect resulting from consumers' higher willingness to pay. Second, a higher standard can reduce the number of firms in the club, which reduces the intensity of competition, increases the price premium, and decreases the market share.

In the presence of social pressure, the probability that an activist campaign targeting the club firms succeeds is decreasing when those functions are strictly convex. The firms in the club, in this case, can have an incentive to choose a higher standard in anticipation of being targeted, so as to reduce social pressure. If the fixed cost functions are sufficiently convex, the club chooses a higher standard in the presence of social pressure than in its absence. If the nonclub firms will be targeted by the activist, the club firms may choose a lower standard unless doing so would shift social pressure to them.

The activist does not necessarily target the worst offender. Instead, it takes into account both the performance of its potential targets and the number of firms it can target. For example, targeting the nonclub firms can be attractive because a successful campaign yields a greater change in credence attributes. Targeting the club would result in a smaller change in credence attributes, but if the club is large more firms would change their conduct in the event of a successful campaign. The activist's choice of a target thus depends on both the standard and the size of the club. When activists follow a practice of targeting "soft" firms—that is, the club firms that supply credence attributes—fewer firms join the club. The example shows that the activist can prefer to target the nonclub firms.

The chapter is organized as follows. The next section introduces the model, and the following section summarizes the analysis and results for the case of a voluntary club. Social pressure is then considered, the activist's choice of a target is explored, and then an example is presented. Conclusions are offered in the final section. The details of the analysis and proofs of results are available in Baron (2009b).

The Model

The model includes a set of firms in an industry, a continuum of consumers, and one activist that is the agent of social pressure. The industry produces a product that has credence dimensions. A firm can produce the product with accompanying credence attributes, but consumers must be confident of the firm's claims about those attributes before they will pay a premium for the product. A firm's claims, as in its advertisements, are assumed to lack credibility unless they are verified or confirmed. The firms can establish a club with a standard for the credence attributes, ensure compliance, and credibly make compliance with the standard public information, using a seal, for instance. Credibility could be assured through monitoring and on-site inspections by independent third parties and public disclosure of the results. The FLA uses independent third-party organizations to conduct inspections, and members of the SFI can elect to use independent third-party monitors. NGOs could also certify the credence attributes of a product and make that information public.

Meeting a standard for credence attributes is costly in terms of both the marginal cost of production and the fixed costs of meeting the standard, and those costs are increasing in the stringency of the standard. The firms participating in the club are assumed to act jointly in choosing the standard and monitoring compliance with it, but they compete in the product market. Those firms that do not participate in the club are assumed not to have access to a mechanism that would verify any claims they might make about the credence attributes of their products. Those firms then produce the basic product. The club thereby provides product differentiation that segments the market into products that meet the standard and products that do not.

The higher willingness to pay of consumers for a product that meets a credence standard offers an incentive to join the club, but entry into the club has a competitive effect on the price. The focus here is on a market in which the equilibrium price for the club product is greater than the price of the basic product and some firms—those with high fixed costs, for example, choose to produce the basic product with no credence attributes.

Consumers   Consumers are represented as a continuum of mass N. A consumer has a type $w \in [0, \overline{w}]$, which is assumed to be uniformly distributed, reflecting their warm glow preferences for the credence attributes of the good. Each consumer is assumed to have a demand for one unit of the good and a willingness to pay u given by

$$u = \overline{w}_o + ws,$$

where $\overline{w}_o$ is the willingness to pay for a unit of the basic product, which meets a standard normalized to 0, $s \in [0, \bar{s}]$ is the credence attributes standard, and $\bar{s}$ is an upper bound on the standard. The basic product is assumed to be produced in a globally competitive industry with a world price w_o, which is less than $\overline{w}_o$. The price p_c of a product with standard s is established in the market for the product with credence attributes.

Firms   The industry is composed of n identical firms that produce a homogeneous physical product, and entry is assumed to be prohibited by sunk costs. A group of m firms can form a club C and choose a standard s_c for the product produced by its members. The choice criterion used by the club firms is assumed to be the maximization of the aggregate profit of the members. Once the standard has been chosen, the club firms engage in Cournot competition. The firms in the club produce a homogeneous product, and meeting the standard entails a common marginal cost $c_c(s_c)$ that is increasing in the standard with $c_c(0) = c_o$, which is the marginal cost of the basic product. The common marginal cost is assumed to result from the requirements of meeting the standard. To allow for more specific results, let $c_c(s_c) = c_o + \gamma s_c$, where $\gamma \leq \bar{w}$.

The standard once chosen is assumed to be fixed and not easily changed, since the product must be branded and differentiated, and production facilities and practices must be altered. Once established, the standard is changed only when the firms are forced to do so by a successful activist campaign.

A club firm $i \in C$ also incurs a fixed cost of developing the capability to meet the standard, monitoring compliance, and enforcing the standard. The fixed costs can differ among the firms, as Erica Sasser and her colleagues (2006) discuss in the context of the timber industry. For example, International Paper purchases timber from a large number of small, independent timber producers and would incur high costs of implementing a stringent chain of custody tracking system, whereas Domtar owns or has long-term leases covering most of its timber sourcing, so its chain of custody costs would be low. The fixed cost function $K_i(s)$ is assumed to be strictly increasing and differentiable with $K_i(0) = 0$. The fixed costs are assumed to be orderable in s, so identify the firms by their fixed costs so that

$$K_1(s) < K_2(s) < \cdots < K_n(s), \quad \forall s \in (0, \bar{s}).$$

The firms producing the basic product incur no fixed costs.

The profit $\Pi_{ci}(s_c)$ of a club firm is

$$\Pi_{ci}(s_c) = \pi_{ci}(s_c) - K_i(s_c), \tag{3.1}$$

where $\pi_{ci}(s_c) = (p_c - c_c(s_c))q_{ci}$ is the operating profit, and q_{ci} is the quantity produced by firm $i \in C$. The operating profit $\pi_{nj}(s_c, 0)$ of a firm $j \in \mathcal{N}$, the set of firms producing the basic product with standard 0, is

$$\pi_{nj}(s_c, 0) = (w_o - c_o)q_{nj}, \tag{3.2}$$

where q_{nj} is the quantity. So that the firms producing the basic product can earn rents, let $w_o \geq c_o$. The firms producing the basic product are assumed to split equally the residual demand.

The Activist The activist could be an individual NGO or a coalition.[8] The activist makes a demand s_A on the industry prior to a club being formed, where s_A is assumed to be a principled demand rather than a bargaining position. The activist subsequently chooses a target and conducts a private politics campaign against the target. The campaign represents a threat to the target as in the case of a boycott (Innes 2006) or other harmful activities. The activist chooses between targeting the club firms and targeting the firms producing the basic product, depending on which yields the higher expected utility. The demand is that all targeted firms meet the standard s_A. The theory does not provide an explanation for the activist's choice of a campaign demand, and the activist is assumed to demand the same standard s_A from either target. In the timber industry, for example, environmental NGOs demand that U.S. timber producers meet the standards of the FSC.

The target counters the private politics campaign, and a contest ensues. If the campaign fails, the targeted firms maintain their precontest standard. If the campaign succeeds and the activist wins the contest, the targeted firms implement the standard s_A, which is monitored by the activist for compliance. For instance, the Rainforest Action Network trains volunteers who walk the aisles of Home Depot stores looking for lumber made from old-growth timber. As in the case of the FSC, the activist certifies the standard s_A to consumers as with a seal.

The Nonmarket Contest The outcome of the private politics campaign is assumed to be determined by a contest function that depends on the expenditures A by the activist and the expenditures of the firms. The expenditures A may be thought of as reflecting social pressure that could harm the targeted firms. The harm could correspond to damage to the reputations or brands of the firms. In the data collected by Lenox and Charles Eesley (2006), compliance with the activist's demand had a correlation of 0.59 with the harm delivered by an activist. This is consistent with the contest specification below in equation (3.3) that the probability of a successful campaign is increasing in A. This component of the campaign has a public goods property in the sense that criticism, allegations, and demands can be directed at all firms in the group. For example, information about the practices of a firm can pose a threat to the reputation of all firms in the group.

If it is targeted, the club counters the activist by expending an amount r per member, and the probability p_c that the campaign succeeds is specified as

$$p_c = \frac{\beta A}{\beta A + mr},$$
(3.3)

where $m = |C|$ is the size of the club and $\beta > 0$ is a parameter that reflects the public sentiment favoring the activist's cause relative to the interests of the target. The parameter β also could reflect the quality of the activist, where higher-quality activists have at their disposal more effective tactics. Eesley and Lenox (2006) found that the probability that the target complied with a demand was greater the more harmful the tactics used by the activist. For example, boycotts and protests were more effective than proxy measures and letter writing but less effective than civil lawsuits. The parameter β also reflects characteristics of the target, such as a brand or public reputation that can be damaged by a campaign. A more vulnerable target corresponds to a higher β, and a less vulnerable target corresponds to a lower β. Higher values of β thus reflect an advantage for the activist. Forty-four percent of the firms targeted in Eesley and Lenox's database acquiesced to the activist's demand.

The activist is assumed to maximize the expected aggregate supply of credence attributes. The expected utility EU_A^C of the activist when the club is the target is thus

$$EU_A^C = \frac{\beta A}{\beta A + rm} ms_A + \frac{rm}{\beta A + rm} ms_c - A + (n - m)0,$$
(3.4)

where s_A is implemented by the club firms if the campaign succeeds and s_c is implemented if it fails, and $s_n = 0$ is the standard of the basic product produced by the firms not in the club.[9]

The club firms choose their expenditures r to maximize their expected profits less their expenditures on the contest. The (aggregate) expected profit $E\Pi_C$ of the club firms is

$$E\Pi_C = \frac{\beta A}{\beta A + rm} \sum_{i \in C} \Pi_{ci}(s_A) + \frac{rm}{\beta A + rm} \sum_{i \in C} \Pi_{ci}(s_c) - rm.$$
(3.5)

The preferences of the firms producing the basic product when they are the target are similar and are specified in the "Private Politics and Social Pressure" section below along with the expected utility of the activist when those firms are targeted.

Timing   The model consists of five stages. In the first stage social pressure is initiated by an activist that makes a demand that the industry meet a particular standard s_A. In the second stage a collection of firms forms a club that chooses under a specified governance rule—for example, aggregate profit maximization—a credence standard for its members. In the third stage the activist chooses to launch a private politics campaign targeting the club firms or the firms producing the basic product. Fourth, the activist and the target contest the campaign, and the success or failure of the campaign is realized. Fifth, firms compete in the product market with the standard resulting from their choices and the outcome of the campaign. The equilibrium concept is subgame perfect Nash.

A Voluntary Club

The Product Market Equilibrium
In the final stage after the club has formed and chosen a standard and the campaign has been conducted, the club firms and the firms producing the basic product compete. The competition among the firms depends on which firms the activist targets and whether the campaign succeeds or fails. If the activist campaign fails, the club firms with standard s_c compete among themselves as well as against the firms producing the basic product with standard 0. If the activist targets the club and the campaign succeeds, the club standard is s_A, and the product market equilibrium is the same with s_A replacing s_c. If the activist targets the firms producing the basic product and the campaign succeeds, the competition is between the club firms with standard s_c and the other firms with standard s_A.

This section considers the case in which there is no social pressure. So that the activist has a choice among potential targets, the focus is on parameter values such that both the basic product and the product meeting the club standard are produced in equilibrium. This requires that the standard be at least a minimum level s_c^-.

Consumers self-select with those with a high willingness to pay for the credence attributes buying the product of a club firm and those with a low willingness to pay buying the basic product. In the product market equilibrium, a higher standard increases consumers' willingness to pay, and the equilibrium price is higher. The former is a *credence effect*, and the latter is a *price effect*. The price effect always outweighs the credence effect, so the quantity produced by the club firms, and hence their market share, is decreasing in the club standard.

The operating profit $\pi_{ci}(s_c)$ of a club firm is a strictly convex function of the club standard. As in the standard Cournot model, the operating profit is a decreasing function of the size of the club and an increasing function of the size N of the market. A shift in consumer preferences as indexed by $\bar{w}$ has two effects analogous to those for a change in the standard. First, the price increases, and second, the preference for credence attributes is stronger. A shift in consumers' willingness to pay for the standard thus increases operating profit. If some proportion η of consumers receive no warm glow from a product with credence attributes, the size of the market is $(1 - \eta)N$. The equilibrium price is unaffected, but the quantity produced and the operating profit of a club firm are lower by a factor of $1 - \eta$.

The operating profit of the firms producing the basic product is increasing in the club standard, since the market share of the club firms decreases. That is, the price effect for the club product exceeds the credence effect, so more consumers purchase the basic product.

These results are summarized in the following proposition.

Proposition 1   (A) A credence standard provides product differentiation, and consumers with a high willingness to pay for credence attributes purchase from the club firms and those with a low willingness to pay purchase the basic product. (B) The price of the club product is increasing and the quantity produced by a club firm is decreasing in the standard, so a higher standard causes some consumers to shift from the club product to the basic product. The market share of the club is thus decreasing in the standard. (C) The profit of the firms producing the basic product is strictly increasing in the club standard.

The Club Standard
No theory is provided to explain the process by which the club is formed. One view is that a firm initiates the formation of an open club and announces a choice rule. Firms then choose whether to participate, and those participating choose a standard according to the choice rule.

As in the case of the SFI, an industry association could initiate the formation. Here, the club is assumed to choose a standard, and if targeted, contests the campaign to maximize the expected aggregate club profits. In the absence of social pressure the club chooses a standard s_c^* that maximizes the sum of the profits in equation (3.1).

Taking the fixed costs into account, a club firm could prefer the minimum standard s_c^- if its fixed costs are sufficiently high. Alternatively, if fixed costs are low, a firm could prefer the maximum standard. The choice of a standard depends importantly on the form of the fixed cost functions. Consider first the case in which the fixed cost function is concave. Since operating profit is strictly convex in the standard, the profit $\Pi_{ci}(s_c)$ in equation (3.1) is strictly convex, so all firms prefer either the minimum or maximum standard. The club then is unanimous in choosing either the minimum or maximum standard.

If, as seems reasonable, it is relatively more costly to meet higher standards than lower ones, the fixed cost functions would be strictly convex. If $K_i(s)$ is strictly convex for all s, a club firm i can have an interior ideal standard $\hat{s}_{ci}$ that satisfies the first-order condition equating the derivative of equation (3.1) to 0 and the corresponding second-order condition. The results are summarized in the following proposition.

Proposition 2   If the fixed cost functions are concave, the club chooses either the minimum or maximum standard. If the fixed cost functions are strictly convex, the club standard can be strictly between the minimum and the maximum.

Participation in the Club

Firms would voluntarily participate in a club in the absence of social pressure provided that consumers reward them sufficiently for the credence attributes of their product. Competition, however, drives down operating profits, so the reward depends on the size of the club as well as the club standard. A club must be an equilibrium club with respect to the choice of a standard, the participation of the firms in the club, and the nonparticipation of firms not in the club. Thus, an equilibrium requires that the standard be an equilibrium choice given the firms participating in the club, and given an equilibrium standard, the set of firms that join the club must be identical to those that chose the equilibrium standard. That is, given the equilibrium standard, the profit of a club firm must be at least the profit it could earn if it quit the club and produced the basic product, and the remaining members of the club chose a new standard. In addition, given an equilibrium standard and a set of club firms, no firm not in the club can prefer to join the club taking into account the new standard that would be chosen by the larger club. In addition to these stability requirements, the equilibrium must be subgame perfect. This is illustrated in the example presented in the "Numerical Example" section below.

Since the operating profit of all club firms is the same, the firms with the strongest incentives to join the club are those with the lowest fixed costs. Firms with high fixed costs of meeting the standard can avoid those costs by producing the basic product. Firms thus can be viewed as self-selecting into the club based on the fixed cost of meeting the standard as well as the operating profit. Because the number of firms is discrete, there are multiple equilibriums. The focus here is on an efficient equilibrium in which firms with lowest fixed cost functions are in the club. Since fixed costs are strictly increasing in the standard, the higher the standard, the (weakly) smaller will be the (efficient) club. Cleaner clubs are therefore smaller than dirtier clubs.

The characterization of the participation in the club is summarized in the following proposition, and the equilibrium size of the club is illustrated in the "Numerical Example" section below.

Proposition 3   For a given standard s_c, the efficient club is composed of firms with the lowest fixed costs. Suppose that the fixed cost functions are strictly convex so that the optimal standard $s_c^*(m)$ is not at a boundary. Then, $s_c^*(m)$ is strictly decreasing in m, so larger (efficient) clubs have lower standards. Higher fixed cost functions $K_i(s)$, $i = 1, \ldots, n$, result in a (weakly) smaller efficient club.

To provide a more specific analysis, let the fixed cost functions be specified as $K_i(s) = \frac{1}{2} b_i s_c^2$, where $b_1 < b_2 < \cdots < b_n$. Let $\bar{b} \equiv \frac{1}{|C|} \sum_{i \in C} b_i$. The standard chosen by the club is a normal good in the sense that it is increasing in consumers' willingness to pay and decreasing in the cost. The effect of club size on the standard chosen can be identified by noting that $\bar{b}$ is increasing in m, since the lowest-cost firms join the club. The standard s_c^* thus is strictly decreasing in the size m of the club, so if m were exogenous, larger clubs would have lower standards. This results because the marginal operating profit is decreasing in m due to more intense competition, so the reward to an individual firm from a higher standard is lower. Aggregate club profit is strictly decreasing in club size, since competition is more intense the larger the club. A limit on club size, then, can come from more intense (Cournot) competition.

The following proposition summarizes the results of this section.

Proposition 4   For $K_i(s) = \frac{1}{2} b_i s^2$, $i = 1, \ldots, n$: If $s_c^* \in (s_c^-, \bar{s})$, the operating profit is strictly increasing in the standard when evaluated at the optimal standard s_c^*. The club standard is increasing in N and $\bar{w}$, and decreasing in $(w_o - c_o)$, γ, η, and $\bar{b}$. Also, larger clubs choose lower standards.

Private Politics and Social Pressure

Social Pressure and the Activist

The activist can direct social pressure to either the club firms or the firms producing the basic product. The choice depends on how likely a campaign is to be successful and what the gain in credence attributes would be in targeting each group. Campaign success depends in principle on many factors, but in the model considered here it depends on the resources available to the activist and the expenditures of its target. The resources available to the activist could come from donations made by citizens (as in Baron 2009a), but here the activist is assumed to be able to call on citizens for whatever resources it chooses to spend on the campaign. (For a richer model and analysis of activist campaigns, see Baron and Diermeier [2007].)

The activist is assumed to maximize the expected aggregate credence attributes of products, which is equivalent to the aggregate compliance with standards, less the campaign expenditures, as specified in (3.4). The instrument of the activist is a private politics campaign that consists of a demand, a target, and the conduct of the campaign. As indicated earlier, the demand is viewed as absolute, such as meeting the FSC standards. The model is specified as s_A being the result of a successful campaign.

In implementing its campaign, the activist could target one firm at a time. The firms, however, understand that they are in line to be targeted and have an incentive to act together in opposition to the activist. The firms in the club are organized and hence can act collectively by jointly contesting the campaign. Although the firms producing the basic product are not organized, they are assumed to form an ad hoc coalition to contest the campaign.

This section first considers the case in which only the club firms can be targeted and then the one in which only the nonclub firms can be targeted. The following section then examines the activist's choice of a target.

Targeting the Club Firms

The club must be worse off as a result of a successful campaign, since the standard s_A could have been chosen rather than s_c^* and the cost of the contest avoided. The standard s_A resulting from a successful campaign has two effects on the club firms. First, the operating profit is affected. For example, if the fixed cost functions are sufficiently convex, the operating profit is increasing at the optimal club standard, so the operating profit is higher at s_A. Second, fixed costs are higher, and the fixed costs are what limited the club standard in the first place. Not all firms in the club, though, need be worse off if the campaign succeeds, since some, those with low fixed costs, preferred a higher standard than chosen by the club. Also, the club that would form in the absence of social pressure may differ from the one that forms in the presence of social pressure.

Directing social pressure to the club firms could represent environmental NGOs demanding that the club firms adopt the more stringent standard (s_A) of the FSC rather than the standard (s_c) of the SFI. Alternatively, it could represent an activist targeting firms that take half measures instead of full ones. It also could represent an activist that chooses the softer target. The club firms are softer in the sense that their incremental fixed costs $K_i(s_A) - K_i(s_c)$, $i \in C$ are smaller than the fixed cost $K_j(s_A)$ from targeting the firms $j \in \mathcal{N}$ producing the basic product.[10]

The equilibrium probability ρ_c^* that a campaign against the club firms succeeds is determined by the choices of A and r by the activist and the club firms, respectively. The following proposition characterizes the effect of the club standard on that probability.

Proposition 5   If $K_i(s)$ is concave for all $i \in C$ and $s \in [0, \bar{s}]$, an increase in the club standard increases the probability of a successful campaign against the club—that is, $\frac{d\rho_c^*}{ds_c} > 0$. If $K_i(s)$ is strictly convex for all $i \in C$ and $s \in (0, \bar{s})$, an increase in the club standard strictly decreases (increases) the probability of a successful campaign as

$$\frac{(s_A - s_c)^2 (w_o - c_o)^2 N}{(m+1)^2 \bar{w} s_A s_c^2} <(>) \frac{1}{m} \sum_{i \in C} (K_i(s_A) - K_i(s_c) - (s_A - s_c) K_i'(s_c)).$$

$$(3.6)$$

That is, the fixed costs must be sufficiently convex and the margin on the basic product sufficiently small for an increase in the club standard to decrease the probability of a successful campaign. Conversely, when the b_i are high, the stakes of the firms are high, and their incentive to contest the campaign is strong. The probability of a successful campaign is then decreasing in the standard. This provides an incentive for the club firms to choose a higher standard to reduce the likelihood of a successful campaign.

A higher demand s_A by the activist increases the stake, $\sum_{i \in C}(\Pi_{ci}(s_c) - \Pi_{ci}(s_A))$, of the club firms and strengthens the contest incentives of the activist. The former effect increases the incentive of the club firms to contest the campaign, whereas the latter effect increases the incentive of the activist to contest the campaign. Analogous to proposition 5 if the fixed cost functions are concave, an increase in the demand by the activist increases the probability of a successful campaign. The same is true if the fixed cost functions are not "too convex," but if those functions are sufficiently convex, the probability of success is decreasing in s_A. This results because the incentives of the club firms to contest the campaign are stronger when the fixed cost functions are strongly convex.

The comparative statics of the probability of a successful campaign are complicated by competing effects. Higher fixed costs (b_i higher) increase the stake of the club firms, which act to reduce ρ_c^*. Higher fixed costs also (weakly) reduce the standard $s_c^*(m)$ of a club of size m, and a lower standard can increase ρ_c^* by strengthening the contest incentives of the activist. Insight into one of the incentives can be obtained by holding the club standard fixed.

The probability of a successful campaign is strictly increasing in β in equation (3.3), holding s_c fixed, so higher-quality activists are more successful than lower-quality ones. Similarly, if the product is branded so it is easier (higher β) for the activist to harm the firm, a successful campaign is more likely. If a higher β corresponds to a greater trust gap between the activist and the firms, the greater the public's trust in the activist relative to that in the firms, the more likely is the campaign to succeed. For example, a 2005 survey based on interviews with over twenty thousand people in twenty countries found that for fourteen tracking countries, the average level of trust in NGOs was twenty-nine, compared to two for large domestic companies and minus fifteen for global companies, whereas trust in national governments was minus nine.[11] The meaning of trust was left to the interviewee, but in the context of the model it might be interpreted as the extent to which the public finds credible the advocacy of the activist and its targets during the campaign.

When only the club firms can be the target of social pressure, their choice of a standard is affected. The expected profit $E\Pi_c^C$ of the club firms, where the superscript C denotes that the club is targeted, can be expressed as

$$E\Pi_c^C = \sum_{i \in C} \Pi_{ci}(s_A) + (1 - p_c^*)^2 \sum_{i \in C} \Delta\Pi_{ci}. \tag{3.7}$$

It is immediate from equation (3.7) that the club firms always contest the campaign rather than concede. That is, $E\Pi_c^C > \sum_{i \in C} \Pi_{ci}(s_A)$ for $p_c^* < 1$, and $p_c^* < 1$, provided the stake of the club firms is positive.

To identify the incentive effects of social pressure, consider the club's choice of a standard to maximize equation (3.7) when the fixed cost function is sufficiently convex—that is, when it satisfies the condition in equation (3.6). Evaluating the first-order condition for the maximization of equation (3.7) with respect to s_c at the standard $s_c^*(m)$ chosen by a voluntary club of size m indicates that the club facing social pressure chooses a standard $s_c^{c*}(m)$ higher than s_c^*. The club firms then prefer a higher standard than in the absence of social pressure. Conversely, when the optimal standard $s_c^{c*}(m)$ satisfies the first-order condition, the probability of a successful campaign is decreasing in the standard, which is the case when the fixed cost functions are sufficiently convex.

In this case a higher standard is chosen because of social pressure. The higher standard decreases the probability of a successful campaign and does so because it weakens the incentive of the activist to expend resources on the campaign. This is due to the smaller gain $s_A - s_c$ for the activist in the event that the campaign succeeds. The following proposition states this result.

Proposition 6 If only the club firms can be targeted, EU_c^C is strictly concave, and $K_i(s)$, $i \in C$ is sufficiently convex as specified in equation (3.6), a club of size $m = |C|$ chooses a higher standard in the presence of social pressure than in the absence of social pressure. The number of firms in the club could also change because of social pressure, as considered in the "Numerical Example" section below.

The equilibrium expected utility EU_A^c of the activist, where the superscript c denotes that the club is the target, is

$$EU_A^c = ms_c^{c*}(m) + mp_c^*(s_A - s_c^{c*}(m)) - A^*$$

$$= ms_c^{c*}(m) + mp_c^{*2}(s_A - s_c^{c*}(m)), \tag{3.8}$$

so the activist gains from a campaign. The expected utility depends on the size of the club. A larger club means that more firms have adopted the club standard, and hence more will meet a higher standard if the campaign succeeds. The club size also affects the probability of a successful campaign and the choice of a standard. The net effect of an increase in club size is indeterminate in general. The example is informative.

Targeting the Nonclub Firms
Some activists target the "worst offenders," which here are the firms producing the basic product. Compared to targeting the club firms, targeting the firms producing the basic product is attractive to the activist because the gain s_A from a successful campaign is greater than the gain $s_A - s_c$ from targeting the club firms. Targeting the firms producing the basic product would also be attractive if the firms did not act collectively in contesting the campaign, since then given the contest function analogous to equation (3.3), the firm with the highest fixed cost would contest the campaign and all the others would free ride on its efforts. The campaign expenditures A would still constitute a public bad for the nonclub firms, however, which provides an incentive for the firms producing the basic product to act collectively in contesting the private politics campaign, and they will be assumed to do so.

If the campaign succeeds so that the nonclub firms produce a product with standard s_A, the club firms have the product with the lower standard and thus have the lower price. In the equilibrium, some consumers with a low willingness to pay are priced out of the market. The equilibrium is presented in Baron (2009b) along with the equilibrium profits. Some firms with high fixed costs can be forced out of the industry by a successful campaign, in which case the remaining firms split the demand.

The club's choice of a standard is affected when the firms producing the basic product will be targeted, since the probability p_n^* of a successful campaign determines how likely the club firms are to face the basic product with a standard 0 or a product with standard s_A. For example, an increase in β increases p_n^*, so it is more likely that the club firms will compete against a product with standard s_A. This provides an incentive to choose a lower standard, since the club firms prefer greater product differentiation if the campaign is expected to succeed. In addition to the effect on the standard, the equilibrium size of the club can be affected.

The expected utility of the activist is

$$EU_A^n = ms_c^{n*}(m) + (n - m)s_A\rho_n^* - A_n^*$$

$$= ms_c^{n*}(m) + (n - m)s_A\rho_n^{*2}. \qquad (3.9)$$

The activist gains from conducting a campaign against the firms producing the basic product.

Choosing a Target

The activist chooses its target based on which yields the higher expected credence standards from an equilibrium campaign, and this choice must be consistent with the expectations of the club firms about which target will be chosen.[12]

The activist bases its choice on three factors in comparing the expected utilities in equations (3.8) and (3.9). The first is the relative gain, s_A versus $(s_A - s_c)$, from targeting the nonclub firms rather than the club firms. The second is the probabilities of a successful campaign against the two potential targets, where those probabilities depend on the gains as well as the stakes of the firms. The third is the size of the club, where ceteris paribus targeting more firms is attractive, since the campaign has the characteristic of a public bad for the targets. The choice of a target is considered in more detail in the example.

The club influences the activist's choice of a target through the standard it sets. Suppose that for a club of size m with standard s_c the expected utility of the activist in equation (3.8) is greater than that in equation (3.9), so the club firms anticipate being targeted. If the fixed cost functions are sufficiently convex so that $\frac{d\rho_c^*}{ds_c} < 0$, to avoid being targeted the club can choose a standard higher than $s_c^{c*}(m)$ so as to shift social pressure to the nonclub firms.

The club firms, however, may prefer to be targeted. That is, if the club firms choose a high standard, and the activist targets the nonclub firms and the campaign succeeds, the club firms would have the lower standard. This means that they sell to consumers with a lower willingness to pay for credence attributes, and their profits could be lower. Moreover, the product differentiation $(s_A - s_c^*)$ could be lower, resulting in more intense competition and lower profits. These effects could be sufficiently strong that the club firms prefer to be targeted, and to assure that they will be targeted, they choose a low standard.

Lenox and Eesley (2009) found that the probability that a firm was targeted by an activist was increasing in the level of its emissions of toxic pollutants as well as its emissions relative to those of other firms in the same four digit Standard Industry Classification code. This is consistent with firms having an incentive to choose a higher standard to shift the activist to a different target.

A Numerical Example

This section presents a numerical example to illustrate the analysis and results in the previous sections. The fixed costs are assumed throughout to be strictly convex with the specification $K_i(s) = \frac{1}{2}b_i s^2$, $i = 1, \ldots, n$.

A Voluntary Club   Consider the model with parameter values: $n = 5$, $w_o = 1$, $c_o = 0$, $\bar{w} = 7$, $N = 10$, $\gamma = 3$, $s_A = 5$, $\beta = 2$, and $b_i = 0.5 + 0.1(i - 1)$, $i = 1, \ldots, 5$. For a club $C = \{1, 2, 3\}$ the minimum standard is $s_c^- = \frac{3}{16}$, and the fixed cost parameters and ideal standards $\hat{s}_{ci}$ of the individual firms satisfying the first- and second-order conditions for equation (3.1) are given in the following table, along with the profits evaluated at the standard $\hat{s}_{c2}$.

Firm	b_i	$\hat{s}_{ci}$	$\Pi_{ci}(\hat{s}_{c2})$
1	0.5	2.83	2.729
2	0.6	2.35	2.453
3	0.7	2.01	2.177

The club maximizes the aggregate profit of its members, and the mean parameter $\bar{b}$ of the fixed cost functions is 0.6, so it chooses the standard $s_c^*(3) = 2.35$. The profits given in the table indicate that all club members have positive profits. Since the market share of the two firms not in the club increases, they are also better off than in the absence of a club and have profits $\pi_n = 2.63$.

Next, the equilibrium club size is determined. For a club of size 3 to be an equilibrium, firm 4 must prefer not to enter the club, and with $b_4 = 0.8$, it prefers not to enter, since in addition to the fixed costs the more intense competition drives club profits down. In addition, firm 3 must prefer not to quit the club. If it quit, the club $C' = \{1, 2\}$ composed of the remaining firms 1 and 2 would choose $s_c^*(2) = 4.605$, and the profit of the 3 firms producing the basic product would be $\pi_{nj} = 1.994$, so firm 3 will not quit the club C. The (efficient) equilibrium thus is $(m^*, s_c^*(m^*)) = (3, 2.35)$. Moreover, this equilibrium is unique. That is, there is no efficient equilibrium club with 4 members, since firm 4 would quit, and there is no efficient club with 2 members, since firm 3 would join the club.

Social Pressure and the Choice of a Target   When social pressure is directed at the club firms, participation in the club poses the risk that the campaign will succeed, which would impose the fixed cost $K_i(s_A)$. Particularly when the cost function is strictly convex, this risk can discourage participation in the club. Participation, however, can be encouraged if the club standard diverts the social pressure to the firms producing the basic product. Targeting those firms then provides incentives to participate in the club.

As indicated in the previous section, the club firms may have an incentive to choose a high standard to divert social pressure to the nonclub firms, or may have an incentive to set a low standard to attract social pressure and avoid the risk of reduced product differentiation. For a club of size 3, the aggregate expected profit of the club firms is maximized at a standard $s_c^o(3) = 1.39$, the club firms are targeted by the activist, and the probability is 0.80 that the campaign succeeds. The average expected profit of the club firms is 0.448, whereas the expected profit of each nonclub firm is 0.551. The expected profit of firm 3 is -0.571. To check whether firm 3 will quit the club, a club of size 2 concedes to the activist's campaign for all $s_c < 4.21$. At $s_c^o(2) = 1.89$, the activist is indifferent between targeting the club firms and targeting the nonclub firms. The maximal aggregate expected profit of the club firms is when they are targeted. Their average expected profit is 7.125. The expected profit of firm 3, though, is 2.000, so firm 3 quits a club of size 3. The equilibrium is then $(m^*, s_c^*(m^*)) = (2, s_c^*(2) \in [0.154, 1.89])$. The activist targets the club firms, and they concede without contesting the campaign—that is, $p_c^* = 1.$[13]

For this example, the presence of social pressure results in a smaller club than in the absence of social pressure, and the club firms choose a low standard that makes them the target. The club does so to make certain that it will be targeted by the activist, since it wants to avoid the risk that product differentiation will be worsened in the event of a successful campaign against the nonclub firms. With $s_A = 5$, the activist's demand is sufficiently low that the club firms do not contest the campaign. If $s_A = 8$, the club $((m^*, s_c^*(m^*)) = (2, s_c^*(2) \in [0.154, 3.42])$ contests the campaign and $\rho_c^* = 0.767$.

If the demand of the activist is more extreme, both club size and its strategy are governed by additional strategic considerations. Because of the extreme demand firms want to avoid being targeted, particularly when they will have direct competitors that will drive the price down. In contrast, if a firm will have no direct competition, it may benefit from being targeted. It may also want to concede to the activist's demand so that it will have the higher level of credence attributes and benefit from the differentiation. For example, if the activist demand is $s_A = 10$, the equilibrium efficient club is $m^* = 4$ with a standard $s_c^* \in [0.154, 0.210]$. The nonclub firm is then targeted and concedes with probability one. The activist does not target the club firms because they would fight hard against the campaign, since if they were to lose they would have an extreme standard and would have strong competition among the four firms. In essence, the club firms put themselves in a position in which they have to fight hard if targeted. With the club firms locked in to fight hard, the activist is better off targeting the nonclub firm.

Conclusions

The objectives of this chapter were to explain the formation of industry programs pertaining to credence attributes of products, the choice of a credence standard by the firms participating in a program, and how social pressure and private politics affect both which firms participate and the standard they choose, and to also identify the locus of social pressure. This required a model of industry behavior and a model of social pressure. The chapter combined a standard model of vertical product differentiation with a contest function representing the outcome of the private politics campaign. The resulting model is complex, and results can depend on the functional forms and the parameter values. For example, the product market has a credence effect as consumers reward the firms for the credence attributes of their products, but the credence standard also affects costs, and hence competition and prices. In the presence of social pressure, the credence standard also affects the incentives of both the activist and its target. If the costs of meeting the credence standard are sufficiently convex, social pressure induces the club firms to choose a higher standard when they anticipate being targeted. The club firms do so because a higher standard decreases social pressure by reducing the incentive of the activist to contest the campaign. In addition, the club firms could choose a higher standard to divert social pressure to the firms producing the basic product.

A number of aspects of the collective choice of credence standards warrant additional research, and three are mentioned here. The first is to explain in which industries and in which circumstances firms would be expected to form a club to assure credence attributes. In some industries rewards may not be present, since consumers may not reward the firm nor support social pressure. In other industries firms may face high costs of collective action that prevent forming a club. In such industries the supply of credence attributes might be assured through government regulation and enforcement, obviating the need for private action. The second is the choice rule used by the club firms. The model assumed that the firms maximize aggregate club profits, but the preferences of the member firms differ for both the credence standard and the intensity with which the activist campaign is contested. A variety of choice rules could be used, and the rule chosen can affect both the standard and the participation in the club. In the model a high cost firm has only one alternative to a high standard, and that is to quit the club. A choice rule that gave each firm an opportunity to influence the choice could better serve the firms. The third is the interplay with public politics. NGOs and firms may be able to turn to government for regulation or protection against regulation. Even if the NGOs and firms do not formally engage in public politics, private politics is conducted in the shadow of laws and regulations as well as the possibility of government action. Allowing NGOs and firms to engage in both private and public politics would enrich the theory of the provision of credence attributes.

4

An Economics Perspective on Treating Voluntary Programs as Clubs

Matthew J. Kotchen and Klaas van 't Veld

The overall theme of this book is to examine how club theory can advance our understanding of voluntary programs, defined as regulatory institutions under which businesses voluntarily agree to comply with environmental or other standards. Drawing on insights from the economics literature on club theory, Potoski and Prakash (2005b; Prakash and Potoski 2006b) develop a political science perspective on how voluntary programs can be interpreted as clubs.[1] Their analyses, along with the contributed chapters in this volume, open a new area of inquiry into the conceptual underpinnings of voluntary programs and the potential for voluntary programs to function as decentralized mechanisms for mitigating collective action problems.

According to one definition, "a club is a voluntary group of individuals who derive mutual benefit from sharing one or more of the following: production costs, the members' characteristics, or a good characterized by excludable benefits" (Cornes and Sandler [1986] 1996, 347). To see the parallel with voluntary programs, interpret "individuals" to mean firms, and consider the example of forest certification programs that seek to promote sustainable forest practices. The certification program establishes a benchmark of best practices, and firms that satisfy the benchmark, which is assumed to be costly, may seek voluntary certification. The benefits to the firm are reputational, in that consumers trust the certification and may be willing to pay a premium for sustainably harvested forest products. In this instance, the forest certification program is effectively a club that is based on member characteristics (sustainable practices) and offers excludable benefits (reputation). When described in this way, voluntary programs appear to be compatible with much of the existing economic theory on clubs.

Many voluntary programs, however, have an additional feature that as far as we know has not been accounted for in the existing theory. These voluntary programs are designed to promote the spillover of positive externalities outside the club. The intent of forest certification programs, for example, is to promote habitat conservation for external benefits such as the protection of biodiversity and recreational opportunities. Note that these positive externalities—which flow outside the club—are public goods. Hence, in order to fully understand the institutional arrangements of voluntary programs, we need to expand the conceptualization of clubs to account for the broader context of public goods provision. Among the cases discussed in this volume that are consistent with this conceptualization are the Kimberley Process for diamond certification (chapter 5), voluntary labor standards (chapter 6), and government-sponsored environmental programs (chapters 10 and 11). Other examples can be found in Morgenstern and Pizer's (2007) collection of papers on voluntary environmental programs in the United States, Europe, and Japan.

The aim of our chapter is to develop a formal economic model that nests elements of club theory within a model of the private provision of a public good. The model is intentionally simple, yet it provides a useful starting point for addressing a number of fundamental questions raised in chapter 2. Are voluntary clubs an effective mechanism for mitigating collective action problems? How do club standards emerge? How are club standards related to club size? And under what circumstances, if any, will club standards and/or membership be socially optimal?

We motivate the model with a consumption good that can be produced with different levels of a "green characteristic"—namely, the environmental friendliness of practices used in its production. Producers choose the level of this characteristic, whereby greener production is assumed to be more costly. Consumers care about the characteristic, but cannot directly observe it (because, say, they cannot observe production practices). As a result, green production is only credible if it is certified by a "green club" that producers can voluntarily join.

Establishing and managing such a club is itself costly, however, and it is reasonable to assume that the average club costs—the total costs divided by the number of member firms—eventually increase with the club size (for example, due to additional layers of bureaucracy, or greater complexity of monitoring and enforcing the club's green production standard). This eventual increase in the average club costs plays a key role in our model, because it in effect gives rise to a negative congestion externality. As Sandler and Tschirhart (1997) note, the presence of some form of crowding is a defining premise of club theory, and it has the effect of making the level of whatever benefit the club provides interdependent with the club's membership size. In our model, the congestion externality creates an interdependence between the club standard and the number of firms in the club.

In the next section we present the model, beginning with the special case in which consumers have purely "warm glow" preferences; that is, consumers care only about the private provision of the green characteristic through their own purchase of the green good.[2] We show that in this case, the socially optimal club standard balances the benefit that consumers of the green good derive against the higher cost of green production, while the socially optimal club size balances the benefit from expanding the club's overall provision of the green good against the higher cost of managing the club. We demonstrate also that in a market setting with no restrictions on club membership, the equilibrium club size will be inefficiently large, to the point where the club makes no net contribution to social welfare. The reason is that when firms decide whether or not to join the club, they consider only their private benefit and cost of doing so, but ignore the congestion externality they impose on existing members.

We then extend the model to account for more general preferences over the green characteristic as a public good, and again compare the socially optimal club with the club that arises in open-access market equilibrium. We show that the positive public good externality of providing the green good increases both the socially optimal club standard and club size. Because firms ignore the positive externality, though, while continuing to ignore the negative congestion externality, the market equilibrium club size may now be either too small, too large, or socially optimal. Nevertheless, the club always contributes to social welfare, because the public good benefit is not dissipated in equilibrium.

Following that, we analyze policies that can improve the equilibrium club's efficiency, but also discuss realistic constraints on such policies. We switch gears to consider an "environmentalist club" that simply seeks to maximize the provision of the public good. Here we show that a government concerned with the different objective of maximizing social welfare may in some cases find it optimal to simply encourage an environmentalist group to sponsor the club, and then we offer some concluding thoughts.

Warm-up with Warm Glow

Consider an economy of identical producers, each of which is able to produce one unit of a particular consumption good using either conventional production or a green production process with different levels of environmental friendliness. Let $\theta \geq 0$ denote a producer's chosen level of green production, where $\theta = 0$ corresponds to conventional production. Green production is assumed to be more costly, such that the total cost of producing a unit of output is $c + \alpha\theta$, where c is the cost of conventional production and $\alpha\theta$ is the additional cost of green production.

The economy includes N identical consumers. Each consumer is assumed to purchase one unit of output and have preferences of the form

$$U(\theta) = b + f(\theta),$$

where b is the benefit from consuming the conventionally produced good, and $f(\theta)$ is the additional benefit from consuming a good produced at green production level θ. This additional benefit is assumed to be strictly increasing in θ, but at a decreasing rate.[3] This form of the utility function is considered a warm-glow specification, because each individual cares only about the green production associated with their own consumption. In the next section, we generalize consumer preferences to account for the public good aspect of green production.

To keep things simple, we assume that green production is not observable to consumers, and that it is not credible for producers to claim green production at any level unless they are certified by a green club. It follows that without a club, no producer would engage in green production (i.e., $\theta = 0$), as they would have no incentive to incur the additional cost. We assume that b exceeds c, so that producing a unit of the conventional good improves social welfare with positive surplus $b - c$. How this surplus is split between consumers and producers depends on the price for the good, which in turn depends on market conditions.[4] Regardless of the price, however, the level of social welfare—equal to the sum of consumer and producer surplus—would be $N(b - c)$ without a club.

We consider the case of a single green club that requires its members to meet a benchmark standard of θ. Moreover, we assume that the club can perfectly monitor and enforce this standard, so that there is no issue of shirking by the member firms. The club thus provides a mechanism that makes its members' green production at the benchmark θ fully credible to consumers. But there are costs associated with establishing and managing the club. These include both "fixed" overhead costs, which are incurred regardless of the club size n, and "variable" administration costs, which increase with n. Overall club costs are shared equally among members, so that each must pay the average cost $A(n) = C(n)/n$. Provided, then, that variable costs do not increase too rapidly with n, the fact that fixed costs can be spread over more members will cause the average costs to initially decrease with n. Yet we assume that as n increases further, the increased complexity of administering a large club will cause the average costs to eventually increase with n. As noted in the introduction, this assumption plays a key role in our model. Formally, we assume that there exists a critical $\check{n}$ such that $A'(n) < (>)0$ for $n < (>)\check{n}$.

The Socially Optimal Club

A green club is fully characterized by the combination of its standard θ and membership n. We first consider the $\{\theta, n\}$ combination of the socially optimal club—that is, the combination that would be chosen by a hypothetical social planner concerned with maximizing social welfare. Formally, if we let W denote welfare, the planner's optimization problem would be

$$\max_{\theta,n} W = n[b + f(\theta) - (c + \alpha\theta) - A(n)] + (N - n)(b - c).$$

The first term on the right-hand side represents the overall surplus generated by the n firms in the club that each produce a single unit of the green good. This is equal to the aggregate benefit enjoyed by n consumers, $n[b + f(\theta)]$, less the aggregate cost of production, $n(c + \alpha\theta)$, and the cost of managing the club, $C(n) = nA(n)$. The second term represents the surplus welfare generated by the $N - n$ firms outside the club that each produce a single unit of the conventional good. Rearranging terms, we can rewrite the problem more simply as

$$\max_{\theta,n} W = n[f(\theta) - \alpha\theta - A(n)] + N(b - c), \tag{4.1}$$

where the first term is now the *additional* surplus generated by the club, over and above the surplus $N(b - c)$ that is generated even without the club.

The socially optimal $\{\theta^*, n^*\}$ combination that solves this problem is implicitly defined by the first-order conditions

$$f'(\theta) = \alpha \qquad\qquad (4.2)$$

and

$$f(\theta) = \alpha\theta + A(n) + nA'(n). \qquad\qquad (4.3)$$

Equation (4.2) shows that at the optimal combination, the marginal benefit of increasing the standard should equal the marginal cost. Equation (4.3) equates the marginal benefit and marginal cost of increasing the club size. Adding a firm to the club yields a marginal benefit $f(\theta)$, because one additional consumer will consume the green good. At the same time, adding a firm implies a marginal cost $\alpha\theta + A(n) + nA'(n)$, because producing the additional unit of the green good costs $\alpha\theta$, and because the overall club costs increase by $C'(n) = A(n) + n'A(n)$.

Note that as long as the average surplus generated by the club, as given by the term in brackets in expression (4.1), is positive, condition (4.3) will hold only if $nA'(n) > 0$. That is, average club costs must be increasing, implying that the socially optimal club size n^* must be strictly larger than the club size $\check{n}$ at which the average costs are minimized. At any such n, a firm's joining the club increases the overall club costs by *more* than the average club cost $A(n)$ before it joined. The difference, equal to n times the increase $A'(n)$ in all member firms' average costs, is essentially an external cost that the new firm imposes on existing members.

Figure 4.1 illustrates the solution graphically. The figure shows how, at the socially optimal standard θ^* defined by equation (4.2), the average club cost AC varies with club size n, and how this cost compares with the social marginal cost SMC as well as the marginal benefit $f(\theta^*)$ of adding a firm to the club. Beyond club size $\check{n}$, the average cost increases with the club size, which implies that each additional firm must contribute above-average additional costs—that is, the marginal club cost exceeds the average club cost. The socially optimal club size n^* occurs where the SMC is just offset by the marginal benefit. At that size, the average surplus from the club, $f(\theta^*) - \alpha\theta^* - A(n^*)$, is strictly positive and equal to the external cost $n^*A'(n^*)$ imposed by the last firm that joined.

Equations (4.2) and (4.3) capture how the surplus is optimally created through the exchange of club-certified goods. When green production is

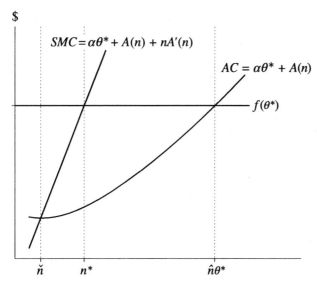

Figure 4.1
Socially optimal and equilibrium club size

credible, consumers are willing to pay a premium up to $f(\theta)$ for each additional unit produced by the club, and this more than covers the increased production costs $\alpha\theta$. Because of this, the optimal standard should maximize the difference between the two, as captured in equation (4.2). Equation (4.3) shows, though, that from the perspective of maximizing social welfare, club membership and thereby the output of the green good should be limited. This is because of two additional costs of expanding club membership and output: the average cost $A(n)$ of club administration and the external cost $nA'(n)$ that each additional member imposes on all other members.

The Equilibrium Club
We now examine the characteristics of the club that will emerge in market equilibrium if the club is open access, allowing any firm that meets its standard to join. In order to analyze this equilibrium, we must consider the price that will emerge for the club-certified good. It turns out that we can focus exclusively on the price premium that will emerge—that is, the difference between the price for the green good and that for the conventionally produced good.

Denoting the premium p, let us take a given club standard θ as a starting point for considering the equilibrium size of the club. Firms have an incentive to join the club as long as the premium they receive exceeds their increase in costs from joining (i.e., $p - \alpha\theta - A(n) \geq 0$). Moreover, consumers have an incentive to purchase the additional firm's output as long as their utility gain from doing so exceeds the price premium (i.e., $f(\theta) - p \geq 0$). It follows that as long as the *overall* surplus from additional green production is positive (i.e., $f(\theta) - \alpha\theta - A(n) \geq 0$), some price premium exists that meets both conditions, allowing a further expansion of the club. Once club membership grows beyond the critical size $\check{n}$, however, the component $A(n)$ of firm costs will start to increase, until eventually the overall surplus is exhausted and it must hold that

$$f(\theta) = \alpha\theta + A(n). \tag{4.4}$$

No further expansion is then feasible, because it would raise firm costs $\alpha\theta + A(n)$ above the consumer willingness to pay $f(\theta)$, leaving no price premium that can satisfy both sides of the market.

It is important to recognize that equilibrium condition (4.4) does not define a unique set of club characteristics $\{\theta, n\}$. In fact, there are an infinite number of combinations that will satisfy the equation. Nevertheless, if we start with a given club standard θ, then the mapping to an equilibrium club size n is unique. We can write this mapping as a function $\hat{n}(\theta)$, which is illustrated in figure 4.2. Notice that no equilibrium club exists if the standard is set lower than $\underline{\theta}$ or higher than $\bar{\theta}$. This follows because at both low and high standards, the difference between consumers' willingness to pay and green production costs is too small to cover the average club costs, even at the club size $\check{n}$ where the average club costs are minimized.

Figure 4.2 also shows how $\hat{n}(\theta)$ is inversely U shaped. The intuition for this result is straightforward. For low-standard clubs, raising the standard raises consumers' willingness to pay for green production at a faster rate than the cost of green production. It follows that more firms have an incentive to join, even though the average club costs are increasing. In contrast, for high-standard clubs, consumers' willingness to pay increases at a slower rate than the cost of green production, so firms must drop out in order to reduce the average club costs.

Formally, it can be shown that the slope of $\hat{n}(\theta)$, or the change in the equilibrium club size for any change in the club standard, is

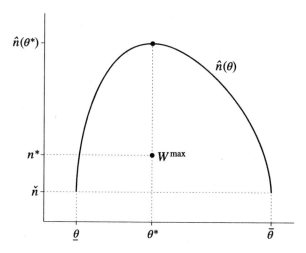

Figure 4.2
Equilibrium club size as a function of the club standard

$$\hat{n}'(\theta) = \frac{f'(\theta) - \alpha}{A'(\hat{n}).} \tag{4.5}$$

Comparing the numerator of this expression with equation (4.2) implies that the slope of the function equals zero at θ^*. Hence, equilibrium club membership is maximized at the socially optimal club standard. Note that the equilibrium size $\hat{n}(\theta^*)$ at this standard is strictly greater than the socially optimal club size n^* indicated by the point W^{max}. It follows that the socially optimal club cannot arise in open-access market equilibrium.

Recall from figure 4.1 that at the efficient club size n^*, the consumers' benefit from an additional unit of the green good equals the social marginal cost of having a new club member. In the open-access equilibrium, however, potential club members consider only their *private* marginal cost (equal to the average cost AC), which excludes the external cost that their joining imposes on other members. They thus continue to join as long as the consumers' benefit, or willingness to pay, exceeds the average cost, which is true up to club size $\hat{n}(\theta^*)$.

At this higher, equilibrium club size, the surplus generated by the club is completely dissipated. That is, the equilibrium club makes no contribution to social welfare. Moreover, this is true not just at the socially optimal standard but also at any standard that the club might set. This constitutes a market failure in economic terms. Rather than maximizing overall surplus, leaving the market to determine the club size ends up driving the surplus to zero. The underlying mechanism is essentially that of the well-known "tragedy of the commons." Just as herders ignore the external costs that their grazing imposes on fellow herders, resulting in overgrazing, firms ignore the external costs that their joining the club imposes on other members, resulting in excess entry.

Generalization to Public Good Preferences

We discussed previously how many voluntary programs seek to promote the provision of public goods. Thus far we have assumed only warm-glow benefits from voluntary provision. This section expands the model to account for public good benefits that might arise from green production.

The model setup remains unchanged, except for the specification of consumer preferences. To account for both warm-glow and public good benefits, we now assume that consumers have preferences of the form

$$U(\theta) = b + f(\theta) + g(n\theta),$$

where the term $g(\cdot)$ increases at a decreasing rate in the overall production of the green good $n\theta$. This term captures public good benefits that result from overall green production, in the form of nonrival and non-excludable improvements to environmental quality that all N consumers enjoy equally, regardless of whether they contribute to such production by purchasing the good.[5] We assume additive separability between warm glow and the public good for analytic simplicity.

The Socially Optimal Club

We analyze the public good version of the model following the same steps as those above. The social planner's objective is to solve the following maximization problem:

$$\max_{\theta,n} W = n[f(\theta) - \alpha\theta - A(n)] + N[g(n\theta) + b - c]. \tag{4.6}$$

The first-order conditions, which again uniquely define the socially optimal club characteristics $\{\theta^*, n^*\}$, are now

$$f'(\theta) + Ng'(n\theta) = \alpha \tag{4.7}$$

and

$$f(\theta) + Ng'(n\theta)\theta = \alpha\theta + A(n) + nA'(n). \tag{4.8}$$

Comparing equations (4.2) and (4.7) shows that the social marginal benefit from increasing the club standard now includes an additional term, $Ng'(n\theta)$, which captures the social marginal benefit to all N consumers of increasing the public good. Similarly, comparing equations (4.3) and (4.8) reveals that the marginal benefit of increasing the club size now includes an additional term, $\theta Ng'(n\theta)$, which captures the social marginal benefit to all N consumers from having one additional firm produce the green good.

Using equations (4.7) and (4.8), it is straightforward to verify that both θ^* and n^* are strictly greater than in the pure warm-glow case of the previous section. Driving this result are the public good benefits that all consumers now enjoy from the club, regardless of whether they purchase the club-certified good. In effect, the club is now more socially beneficial because it generates public good spillovers to all individuals in the economy.

The Equilibrium Club
We can show that the change in consumer preferences to account for public good benefits has no effect on the forces that drive the equilibrium club size. Firms still have an incentive to join the club as long as the price premium p exceeds their private costs $\alpha\theta + A(n)$. Moreover, consumers still have an incentive to purchase the green good as long as their private warm-glow benefit from the purchase, $f(\theta)$, exceeds the price premium p. The reason why the public good benefit plays no role in this decision is that for any reasonable club size n, consumers receive the same level of the public good $n\theta$ regardless of whether they themselves contribute. This is captured implicitly with our assumption that n is continuous. It follows that the equilibrium club size continues to be determined by equilibrium condition (4.4).

Comparing the equilibrium condition (4.4) with the social planner's first-order condition (4.8), we now see two sources of market failure. The first, which we described as a tragedy of the commons, is unchanged from the warm-glow version of the model. When firms decide whether to join the club, they still ignore the negative externality that they impose on other club members. The new source of market failure arises because of free riding with respect to the private provision of the public good. Because consumers enjoy the public good regardless of whether they themselves purchase the club-certified good, they have no additional willingness to pay for the good beyond that derived from warm glow. Accordingly, when firms continue to join the club, they ignore the positive externality, $Ng'(n\theta)\theta$, that they impose on all consumers.

In the special case where the two externalities are exactly equal at $\{\theta^*, n^*\}$, the two market failures will offset each other, and the equilibrium club size for standard θ^* will equal n^*. More generally, however, the two externalities will differ in size, resulting in an equilibrium club that is suboptimally large or small.

Finally, it is important to recognize that the public good case differs from the pure warm-glow case because the equilibrium club does in fact contribute to social welfare. The reason is that even though the warm-glow surplus $n[f(\theta) - \alpha\theta - A(n)]$ is still driven to zero through excess firm entry, all consumers still enjoy positive public good benefits $Ng(n\theta)$. In effect, the warm-glow benefit to the n consumers that purchase the club-certified good "pays" for the public good benefit to all N consumers. Consumer purchases of warm glow, in other words, produce a positive externality.

Club Policies

Up to this point, we have considered how a hypothetical social planner would optimally choose both the club standard and size, and how given any club standard, market forces will determine the equilibrium club size. We have not yet considered how a real-world administrator—possibly a government agency, an NGO, or some other third party—would choose the club standard in anticipation of the equilibrium response. Nor have we considered how the administrator might take advantage of various policy instruments. In order to analyze the latter questions, we must specify the administrator's objective function. In this section we assume that the administrator aims to maximize social welfare, just like the social planner. In the next section we consider an alternative.

We have already shown that in order to implement the welfare-maximizing club combination $\{\theta^*, n^*\}$, it is not in general sufficient to simply set the standard at θ^*. Without any restrictions on club entry, a tragedy of the commons will tend to increase the club size above n^*, while free riding by consumers will tend to reduce the club size below

n^*. That being said, in many circumstances it may be difficult legally or politically to impose restrictions on a club's size.

A more practical alternative may be to charge a uniform admission fee τ, over and above the average club administration costs $A(n)$. Since this fee just acts as an additional cost for firms, which all else equal reduces their incentive to join, the equilibrium condition (4.4) becomes

$$f(\theta) = \alpha\theta + A(n) + \tau. \tag{4.9}$$

Comparing this condition with the social planner's first-order condition (4.8) shows that setting the fee at level

$$\tau^* = n^* A'(n^*) - N g'(n^*\theta^*)\theta^* \tag{4.10}$$

will implement the socially optimal club. In effect, the admission fee forces entering firms to internalize the two externalities associated with membership. The first term on the right-hand side of equation (4.10) captures the negative externality of increasing average club costs for all other club members. The second term captures the positive externality of increasing the level of the public good for all consumers. Depending on which of these terms is larger, τ^* may be either positive or negative. In the latter case, the optimal policy would be to subsidize club membership, thereby raising it to n^* from what would otherwise be suboptimally low.

An equivalent mechanism to the admission fee is a tax τ on the green good. Such a tax drives a wedge between the premium p_c paid by consumers and the premium p_f received by firms, such that $p_c = p_f + \tau$. Nevertheless, club entry will as always continue until both $f(\theta) - p_c = 0$ and $p_f - \alpha\theta - A(n) = 0$. Combining these three conditions and substituting away p_c and p_f leaves exactly the same equilibrium condition (4.9). Hence, setting tax τ as in equation (4.10) would also implement the socially optimal club, and again τ^* can be negative, implying a subsidy on the green good.

An important concern relating to the different policy instruments has to do with revenue. Specifically, if $\tau^* > 0$, the aggregate revenue raised from the club through either an admissions fee increase or a tax on the club good cannot be returned to either the n member firms or the n consumers buying from the club without canceling the policies' incentive effects. The revenue must instead be used in a manner that benefits *all* consumers or firms equally, regardless of whether they respectively buy or produce the green good. Similarly, if $\tau^* < 0$, the aggregate revenue $n\tau^*$ required to finance the admissions fee reduction or subsidy on the club good must be raised from all consumers or firms equally. Alternatively, revenue could be raised in some other sector of the economy, but then one would need to consider potential inefficiencies there.

These constraints may in practice make club policies less attractive or even infeasible. If the whole rationale for establishing a "voluntary" club is that it provides an alternative to government regulation, whether through command-and-control mandates, taxes, fees, or subsidies, then the program may have to operate under what amounts to a budget-balancing constraint: any fees associated with club membership must be set at levels that neither exceed nor fall short of covering club administration costs. In such contexts, if the club administrator *can* choose the club size directly, it will be constrained from choosing any size greater than that consistent with the equilibrium condition (4.4). In other words, given whatever standard θ the administrator chooses, it will be constrained to set n less than or equal to the club size $\hat{n}(\theta)$ implicitly defined by condition (4.4).

If the club administrator *cannot* choose the club size directly at all, then a budget-balancing constraint will reduce its role to simply choosing the club standard θ, knowing that the resulting club will be of the equilibrium size $\hat{n}(\theta)$. This implies that in the pure warm-glow case discussed earlier in this chapter, a welfare-maximizing club administrator will be indifferent between all standards within the interval $[\underline{\theta}, \bar{\theta}]$, and what is more, between establishing a club and not establishing one. This is because, as shown previously, the equilibrium club for any θ will make no contribution to social welfare. In contrast, in the public good case examined earlier, we found that the equilibrium club does contribute to social welfare. Even though club-related benefits are driven to zero, the club generates public good spillovers $Ng(n\theta)$ to all individuals in the economy. The implication is that the welfare-maximizing club administrator will choose θ to maximize the public good spillovers.

Environmentalist Clubs

Having considered a club whose administrator aims to maximize social welfare, we now explore the alternative of a club whose administrator aims to simply maximize the provision of the public good. Analyzing this objective seems appropriate for a variety of scenarios, including ones in which the public good is an environmental amenity and the administrator is not a government agency but an environmental group.

In terms of the model presented here, an environmental group may establish a club that certifies a particular good as green, with the explicit objective of maximizing $n\theta$. In principle, the group may be able to choose not just the club characteristics $\{\theta, n\}$ but also the premium p charged for the club-certified good. Following the same reasoning used above, we find that the familiar equilibrium condition must continue to hold. We can thus write the environmentalist club's problem as follows:

$$\max_{\theta,n} n\theta \quad \text{subject to} \quad f(\theta) = \alpha\theta + A(n)$$

In other words, the club seeks to maximize the provision of the public good subject to the constraint of the familiar equilibrium condition.

Figure 4.3 illustrates the problem graphically. The downward-sloping curves labeled G_0, G_1, and so on, represent the club's indifference curves—that is, combinations of n and θ that yield a particular value $G_i = n\theta$ of its objective function, with higher curves yielding higher values ($G_0 < G_1 < G_2 < G_3$). As in figure 4.2, the bold, inverse U-shaped curve represents the function $\hat{n}(\theta)$ implicitly defined by the equilibrium

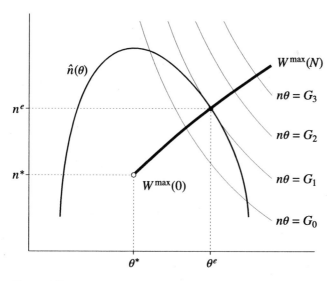

Figure 4.3
The environmentalist club's optimization problem and socially optimal combinations with public good preferences

condition. Graphically, the club's problem involves choosing a standard θ such that the associated point on the constraint $\hat{n}(\theta)$ reaches its highest indifference curve, thereby maximizing $n\theta$ subject to the equilibrium condition. This is achieved at the point $\{\theta^e, n^e\}$, where the constraint is tangent to indifference curve G_1.

Although figure 4.3 is drawn for a particular parameterization of the model, we can describe some general results comparing the environmentalist club with the socially optimal club. We know that because the club's indifference curves are downward sloping, the tangency point that defines $\{\theta^e, n^e\}$ must lie on the downward-sloping segment of the $\hat{n}(\theta)$ curve. This implies that the tangency must lie to the right of the socially optimal standard when preferences are purely warm glow, because we saw earlier (recall figure 4.2) that the latter standard is where the $\hat{n}(\theta)$ curve is maximized. In the purely warm-glow case, in other words, the environmentalist club will choose a standard θ^e higher than the welfare-maximizing standard θ^*. It can also be shown that the environmentalist club size n^e will be greater than the welfare-maximizing size n^*.

When preferences include a public good component, these results continue to hold, but only if N is not too large. Recall from the analysis above that both θ^* and n^* increase from their values in the pure warm-glow case. This increase can be shown to be larger the greater that N is. It can also be shown that at a critical value of N, which we denote N^e, the socially optimal $\{\theta^*, n^*\}$ coincides with the environmentalist club's optimal $\{\theta^e, n^e\}$. For values of N greater than N^e, the relationship between the two optima becomes reversed—that is, the environmentalist club standard and size both become smaller than would be welfare maximizing. The reason for the difference is that the environmentalist club is constrained by the equilibrium condition, while the social planner is not.

The upward-sloping curve in figure 4.3 from $W^{\max}(0)$ to $W^{\max}(N)$ illustrates these results graphically. The curve is the locus of socially optimal combinations of $\theta^*(N)$ and $n^*(N)$ when these are treated as functions of N. The lowest point on the curve, labeled $W^{\max}(0)$, corresponds to the socially optimal club in the warm-glow case, when the public good benefits $Ng(n\theta)$ are zero. When the public good benefits are positive, the social optimum will lie further up the curve, and more so the larger N is. Clearly, then, there exists a critical N^e such that the social optimum will coincide with point $\{\theta^e, n^e\}$, and at higher N it will lie above and to the right of that point.

An important observation about the environmentalist club relates back to the discussion in the previous section about a real-world club administrator whose aim is to maximize welfare. It was noted there that if such an administrator faces a budget-balancing constraint, and in particular cannot subsidize the club with outside funds, it will not be able to choose a club size that exceeds the equilibrium size $\hat{n}(\theta)$ conditional on whatever standard it sets. In terms of figure 4.3, the administrator's choices would be limited to the segment of the $W^{\max}$ locus below the $\hat{n}(\theta)$ curve. It follows that for N greater than N^e, when the administrator's unconstrained optimum would lie above the $\hat{n}(\theta)$ curve, its constrained optimum will coincide with the environmentalist club outcome. Interestingly, this provides the administrator with an alternative policy option: rather than creating and administering the club itself, it can simply encourage an environmental group to create the club, and achieve the same constrained-optimal outcome.

The same implication follows when the welfare-maximizing administrator cannot choose the club size directly, in addition to facing a budget-balancing constraint. As also discussed in the previous section, the administrator's effective optimization problem then reduces to maximizing public good spillovers alone, subject to the equilibrium condition. But since those public good spillovers $Ng(n\theta)$ increase monotonically in $n\theta$, that optimization problem is effectively identical to that of the environmentalist club, with the same solution.

Conclusion

The economic model developed in this chapter offers a starting point for thinking formally about voluntary programs as clubs, nested within the context of public goods provision. Voluntary programs are treated as clubs because they provide nonrival but excludable benefits to members, yet these benefits are subject to negative congestion externalities when the club membership expands. Because the club monitors and certifies certain production practices that consumers value but cannot themselves verify, they allow member firms to earn a premium for their goods. But these profits are reduced by shared club administration costs, which eventually increase as the club membership expands. The model is distinct from other applications of club theory in that the club promotes the spillover of positive externalities. In the context of clubs that promote green production practices, this positive externality consists of an environmental public good.

In the special case where consumers derive only private, warm-glow utility from the club good, there are no public good spillovers. If club membership is open to all firms that agree to meet its certified production standard, the congestion externality internal to the club gives rise to a tragedy of the commons: new firms will continue to join the club as long as there are profits to be made. The result is a market failure due to the complete dissipation of the potential benefits of the club.

In the more general case where consumers derive both private and public good utility from the club good, the same tragedy of the commons can arise. But in this case, there is a further source of market failure because of free riding among consumers. Consumers have no incentive to consider the public good benefits to others of their own purchases of the club good. We find that the first market failure still results in an equilibrium where direct club benefits are completely dissipated. The second market failure, however, still leaves an indirect benefit of the club: consumers' purchases of the club good for warm-glow reasons end up "paying" for a public good benefit to all consumers—even those who do not purchase the club good. Moreover, because the second market failure tends to discourage firm entry relative to what is socially optimal, the equilibrium club size with both market failures combined may be either greater than, less than, or equal to the welfare-maximizing size.

We also considered several policies that welfare-maximizing club administrators might employ in order to address the two market failures. Most obviously, these include direct limits on club size, or if such limits are infeasible, taxes or subsidies that discourage or encourage firm entry. If the latter policies are infeasible as well, perhaps because they are viewed as inconsistent with the "voluntary" nature of the club, we find that the club administrator's constrained optimal policy reduces to simply maximizing the overall provision of the public good. Interestingly, then, its optimal policy may be to leave club administration to an outside group whose objective is to maximize such provision to begin with, rather than to maximize welfare. Third-party certification and ecolabeling programs are examples.

In conclusion, we hope that the model presented here provides a useful start for developing formal models that capture the institutional arrangements of voluntary programs. Although the setup of our model is intentionally simple, the treatment of club formation within the context of the private provision of a public good generates several new insights. Further extensions not considered here, but left for future work, include the consideration of imperfect monitoring and the enforcement of club standards, heterogeneity among consumers and firms, rival clubs that may arise, cases in which firms can credibly signal their own standards, and game-theoretic strategies.

II

Industry and International Clubs

5

The Kimberley Process, Club Goods, and Public Enforcement of a Private Regime

Virginia Haufler

One of the most innovative institutions designed to address the problem of illicit financing of violent conflict is the establishment of the Kimberley Process Certification Scheme (KPCS) to control the trade in diamonds from regions of conflict.[1] During the protracted civil wars and rebellions that devastated parts of Africa in recent years, many people sought innovative means to end these long-running conflicts. Leading activist organizations pointed to the financing of conflict as a key point of leverage, particularly through the sale of natural resource commodities to pay for soldiers and weapons. The most prominent of these commodities is diamonds—or blood diamonds, as the activists labeled them. Other commodities also were singled out for attention—timber, coltan, gold, and oil. But it was only in the diamond sector that the industry voluntarily instituted a certification system to keep diamonds from conflict-affected regions out of world markets.

This chapter examines the Kimberley Process through the lens of the club approach to voluntary programs, as laid out in the first chapter of this volume. The KPCS is a system in which a set of diverse actors overcame the dilemmas of collective action to establish a voluntary program that can be characterized as a voluntary club. At its core is a system that establishes strict standards for club members to identify, certify, and audit rough diamonds to assure that they do not come from conflict-ridden regions. The Kimberley Process establishes a chain of custody within the industry to ensure the integrity of the certification process as the stones go from source to export. Enforcement at this stage is through the World Diamond Council, and is voluntary.

Yet there is a wider and more effective monitoring and enforcement mechanism within which the industry voluntary program is embedded —a strong swords mechanism, to use Prakash and Potoski's terms.

States that participate in the Kimberley Process commit to upholding strict standards that no diamonds will be exported or imported without certification. States are sanctioned by being excluded from the diamond trade if they are not members of the Kimberley Process, or if they violate its standards—an excludable benefit of participation. The KPCS is structured as a club within a club, as the industry voluntarily establishes the standards and mechanisms of certification and chain-of-custody systems, with weak monitoring and enforcement; and governments voluntarily enforce those standards through trade controls, with strong sanctions.

The social externality provided by the KPCS is the reduction or cessation of the use of diamonds to finance violence and war. The KPCS raises the cost of trading diamonds from war zones, making it difficult for combatants to raise the money they need for weapons and soldiers. This is a positive externality of the voluntary program, which provides reputational benefits for both industry and state participants. The material benefits are clear for the members of the club, because they have essentially established (or reestablished) a diamond cartel. But the voluntary nature and weak enforcement of the actual certification process at the industry level, along with loopholes in the state border control system, have allowed a certain amount of shirking, as conflict diamonds enter legitimate markets. Shirking in this case includes the falsification of certification documents by industry and government officials; a lack of controls as the rough diamonds change hands and are transferred among brokers, distributors, polishers, and retailers; and an unwillingness by some states to enforce export and import controls. This threatens to undermine the reputational benefits on which the system ultimately depends.

The diamond sector has institutionalized a complicated voluntary program that provides private and public benefits. It contrasts with the lack of similar institutions for other commodities also implicated in the financing of violence. The explanation of these differences may lie in a number of unique features of this sector—for example, high industry concentration, limited sources of the product, and extreme sensitivity to reputation. This system also contrasts with many other voluntary programs because the industry voluntary program is overlaid with a public system of monitoring and enforcement. The analysis of this case provides important insights into the creation of new and innovative international institutions for the development of global rules and the provision of public goods.

Civil Conflict and Diamonds

In the decade immediately following the end of the cold war, civil conflicts in the developing world, especially Africa, came to the attention of the international community. There is no international regulatory system for internal conflicts, and until recently, internal conflicts were in principle "off-limits" to the international community. Despite numerous examples of intervention in local disputes, there has been up to now a general commitment to sovereignty and nonintervention. (Krasner 1999, Finnemore 2003) This norm was challenged, however, by an increase in international concern about the rising death toll and increasing horror of war in some of the poorest countries in the world.

Civil wars in Angola, Sierra Leone, Rwanda, the Democratic Republic of the Congo, and Côte d'Ivoire spilled across borders and garnered worldwide attention. The brutality of genocide in Rwanda and the cruelty of rebel practices in Sierra Leone generated media attention and galvanized activism on behalf of the victims. Early in the decade, advocacy groups that were determined to bring an end to the long-running bloodshed in places like Angola and Sierra Leone publicized the link between natural resources and the financing of war. A series of reports by Global Witness in 1998 and 1999 put companies on a par with governments as at fault in facilitating the ongoing conflict in Angola, focusing especially on oil companies and banks (Global Witness 1998; 1999). Ian Smillie, of Partnership Africa Canada, released a report in 2000 highlighting the way in which diamonds financed violence in Sierra Leone (Smillie, Gberie, and Hazleton 2000). The idea of conflict diamonds entered political debates, propelled in part by highly effective campaigns by advocacy organizations targeting consumer sentiment by relabeling them blood diamonds.

By 2000, a series of significant political actions were taken by the international community regarding diamonds and conflict. The UN General Assembly passed unanimously a resolution condemning the role of diamonds in financing conflict. The United Nations defines conflict diamonds as "diamonds that originate from areas controlled by forces or factions opposed to legitimate and internationally recognized governments, and are used to fund military action in opposition to those governments, or in contravention of the decisions of the Security Council." (http://www.un.org/peace/africa/Diamond.html) The United Nations focused its attention initially on Sierra Leone, Angola, and Liberia. The UN Security Council had already applied sanctions against the UNITA rebels in Angola, including an embargo on trade in diamonds in 1998. It followed up with a High Level Expert Panel to investigate sanctions busting, and the resulting report for the first time "named names" of individuals and companies involved in illegal trade (the "Fowler Report"). (Fowler 2000) The Security Council also applied sanctions to the trade in diamonds from Sierra Leone in 2000, following the signing of the Lomé Peace Agreement. An expert panel was established in this case as well, which reported on the links between the trade in Sierra Leone and the role played by Liberia, against which further sanctions were sought.

The diamond industry initially tried to ignore the campaign against conflict diamonds, with De Beers in particular reluctant to discuss any change in industry behavior. The diamond sector has been operated for over a century on the basis of an international cartel, one of the most successful in history. By the early 1990s, Debora Spar (1994) described it as

an intricate network of production quotas, quality controls, and stockpiles. It is a formidable system of fixed prices and controlled distribution. It is an incredible array of rules and regulations, rarely violated and meticulously enforced. Most of all, however, the diamond cartel is a staggering edifice of cooperation.

This cooperation within the industry was based on a common interest among all players in maintaining tight control of diamond supplies in order to ensure the illusion of scarcity that contributed to the myth that diamonds are valuable. The cartel was established by Cecil Rhodes and, later, Ernest Oppenheimer and his successors as managers of De Beers. De Beers controlled the supply and distribution of diamonds by its ownership of South African mines and diamond stockpiles, and through the Central Selling Organization based in London, which handled distribution. The cartel was supported by long-term contracts between De Beers and most diamond producers.

This began to break down in the 1990s, partly as a result of the conflicts in Africa that pushed large amounts of rough diamonds into world markets. The challenge to De Beers was exacerbated by the collapse of the Soviet Union, which was the other major source of diamonds; as a result of domestic changes there, more diamonds "leaked" into markets through channels outside De Beers' control (www.debeersgroup.com).

The negotiations between De Beers and Russia over the amount the Russians would sell to De Beers became increasingly tense, and threatened to break down. In addition, new smaller players entered the market and began challenging De Beers for its market share. Africa is no longer the main source of diamond production in the world; Canada, Australia, Brazil, China, and Russia together account for more than half of the world's diamond mining. According to *The Economist*, in the early 1990s De Beers produced about 45 percent of the world's rough diamonds, but sold about 80 percent of the total world supply through its Central Trading Organization (*The Economist* 2007). If other producers were no longer willing to sell the majority of their stocks to the Central Trading Organization, then the cartel would be weakened significantly.

By 2000, the management of De Beers decided to end its "custodial" role in controlling the diamond supply, and shifted from being, as its Web site states, "buyer of last resort to supplier of first resort" (www.debeersgroup.com). It did this under competitive pressure, as the diamond market changed and its control weakened. De Beers also wanted to end its antitrust problems in the United States so that it could develop a consumer market there. To demonstrate its changed policy, De Beers committed to selling much more of its stock. The trading arm of De Beers stopped buying diamonds on the open market, which was one of the primary means to build up its stockpiles and control supply. It was simply becoming too expensive to support diamond prices by restricting supply, as new suppliers entered the market and undermined the cartel. De Beers also began investing significant funds in new diamond fields outside South Africa, primarily in the Northwest Territories of Canada. It still controls over half of the diamond market, but De Beers is no longer enforcing the old cartel.

Creating the KPCS

By 2000, leaders within the diamond industry realized the threat posed by the increasingly heated campaigns over conflict diamonds as well as the sanctions imposed on the diamond trade by the United Nations. The value of diamonds, at least those used for jewelry, is essentially a myth maintained by a clever marketing campaign. The major use of gemstone diamonds is in jewelry, a luxury consumer good with no intrinsic value. The diamond cartel reinforced the perception that the diamond was a special gem by controlling supply and ensuring that diamonds remained scarce, obtainable only by those with wealth. Diamonds were "branded" not with a trademarked name such as De Beers but instead established as a class of status goods. The idea that an engagement ring must be a diamond was one promoted by the diamond sector, and is of fairly recent origin.

An equally clever advocacy campaign was now calling them blood diamonds, linking them with horrific practices such as the mutilation of children by rebels in Sierra Leone. This campaign could potentially lead to a significant collapse in the market for diamonds, with the worst-case scenario one in which consumers stop buying diamonds and no longer consider them appropriate symbols of love and marriage. It was a direct attack on the reputation of both the industry and the product it produced—a reputation carefully nurtured by the diamond sector for almost a century. The industry initially had been dismissive of efforts to campaign against other ethical issues in the mining industry, such as labor conditions and smuggling, but a few perceptive industry insiders realized that this campaign could be different. The stakes were significantly higher. Transnational campaigns were becoming increasingly influential, and it would be essential for the industry to prevent this campaign from succeeding.

The debate among industry participants revealed the dilemmas of collective action, even within a tight-knit community and an industry that was highly concentrated. Not everyone took seriously the potential threat, and those who did see the danger to the diamond market— both from continuing international sanctions and the blood diamond campaign—feared the only solution would be to turn to government regulation, which they wanted to avoid. Instead, the participants proposed a voluntary program within the industry in order to shore up reputations, preserve markets, and elude regulations. The World Federation of Diamond Bourses and the International Diamond Manufacturers Association passed a resolution creating the World Diamond Council (WDC) in 2000. The mandate of the WDC was to develop a tracking system for the export and import of rough diamonds to prevent their illicit use (www.worlddiamondcouncil.org). The WDC established a set of committees to explore options, producing proposals that would become the basis for a new international regime. We can view the WDC as a large club, in which members to some degree stood in a hierarchical relationship to the central sellers—De Beers and its Central Trading Organization (although this hierarchy had been diminished by changes in the industry, as described above).

The WDC proposed strict standards for a system of warranties and chain-of-custody practices within the industry, certifying that rough diamonds did not come from an area of conflict and traders in polished diamonds knew the origins of their stones. Industry participants committed not to trade in uncertified stones. They also proposed that other sectors—banks, insurers, shippers, and others—commit to cease doing business with anyone dealing in conflict diamonds (Rapaport 2000). The industry went forward with implementation, establishing internal controls to prevent the purchase and distribution of conflict diamonds among the members of the WDC.

Such a voluntary program, however, could not be implemented effectively by the industry alone. The WDC explicitly called for the implementation by governments of a system of export and import control. The global trade in diamonds could only be regulated through border controls, which meant that governments had to cooperate in establishing a parallel system of standards, monitoring, and enforcement. Although it is conceivable that the industry itself could establish limits on its own exports and perhaps even on imports, this is one area where the private sector is clearly at a disadvantage. A more effective trade regime would have to rely on the border controls instituted by governments. This would not be a typical sanctions regime, based on a trade ban with a country; instead, it would be a sectoral regime based on a trade ban on particular products—in this case, noncertified diamonds.

A number of producing states were particularly concerned about the campaign against diamonds. Botswana, Namibia, and South Africa all were major producers of diamonds—indeed, diamonds were Botswana's main export. Even the antidiamond campaigners were sensitive to the fact that a collapse in the diamond market would severely injure a developing country (Botswana) that was widely recognized to be managing its resource wealth responsibly. Legitimate producing states recognized that a certification system and export-import controls would be in their best interest to support. The UN General Assembly in 2000 called for the development of a mechanism to end the diamond-conflict link, and it too suggested a certification system. Later that year, the United Nations sponsored initial negotiations among industry representatives from the WDC, African diamond-producing states, and civil society organizations

(Global Witness and Partnership Africa Canada) in Kimberley, South Africa. By the end of the year, the UN General Assembly adopted a resolution supporting the establishment of a diamond certification system. Negotiations over the next two years produced in 2002 the KPCS, which was implemented in 2003.

Country Clubs and Mandarins: Private and Public Clubs

The KPCS is, as noted above, a club within a club. It is designed specifically to generate a social good: the reduction of diamond financing for violent conflict. The central problem is one of government failure, not market failure; almost by definition, the areas where conflict diamonds are a problem are failed states. The scheme is designed to provide both the diamond industry and diamond exporting states with the reputation that they need to maintain and even strengthen their markets. Their reputation is solidified by providing branding benefits through the certification system.

All participant states must ban exports and imports of noncertified diamonds. They must ensure that diamonds are in sealed containers and properly certified, and they cannot trade diamonds with nonparticipants. States must also institute a system of internal controls to ensure that conflict diamonds are eliminated from internal markets and prevented from ever reaching export markets. Member states are required to be transparent in the exchange of information about production levels, trade data, and any implementation problems that arise, to facilitate monitoring and enforcement. Annual plenary meetings decide which members to review, what issues exist, and to propose reforms. In 2003, members agreed to establish a system of peer review, and there have been ongoing initiatives to strengthen this aspect of the system. There is a Working Group on Monitoring to undertake regular review of member country implementation (www.kimberleyprocess.com). States that violate the terms of the KPCS or are unable to control corruption and other forms of shirking are kicked out of the Kimberley regime and excluded from its benefits. The states are supposed to ensure that the industry participants also live up to their commitments under the regime.

The member states constitute a club with stringent standards and fairly strong enforcement. The member states are subject to monitoring and auditing by other states as well as the two NGOs that are official observers of the Kimberley Process; there is also informal monitoring by nonparticipant activists and observers. The enforcement mechanisms include oversight, technical assistance, and the costly sanction of losing membership status—which means losing access to legitimate diamond markets. The state-based club in Kimberley is close to what Prakash and Potoski label mandarins.

The Kimberley Process entwines a voluntary industry program within this state-based trade control regime. Industry representatives are considered to be official observers within the KPCS. The Kimberley Process documents state that it "will provide for a system of warranties underpinned through verification by independent auditors of individual companies and supported by internal penalties set by industry, which will help to facilitate the full traceability of rough diamond transactions by government authorities" (KPCS section 4). The WDC has established guidelines on how to implement a certification system, offering technical expertise in this area, but there is variation in the degree to which these guidelines have been adopted across countries. To date, the KPCS has not established clear oversight and sanctioning of industries in response to some problems revealed by audits, and the audit system itself is not clearly established. This has been one of the primary complaints of the two civil society participants in the KPCS—Global Witness and Partnership Africa Canada. The private sector has formed a new cartel to ensure the branding benefits of this voluntary program and protect the market for gem diamonds. The standards under KPCS are stringent although the enforcement is weak; this is a country club that primarily provides benefits to members, but through the larger trade control regime also has significant social benefits.

By 2008, the KPCS had forty-nine member states including the European Community as one member, constituting all major producers, traders, and polishing centers along with the majority of diamond consumer markets. The industry has implemented its certification system and chain-of-custody standards within each member state, and the major industry associations and firms have joined. Diamond shipments that have occurred outside the KPCS have been seized. Most member state participants have been reviewed, and a few have been barred from the KPCS for noncompliance, such as the Democratic Republic of the Congo and Liberia. The latter was permitted to rejoin in 2007, after the lifting of UN sanctions in response to a change in government and significant reforms there. Venezuela, however, withdrew in 2008 after years of noncompliance, while Panama is applying to join. There have been expressions of concern about specific firms, particularly the Russian firm Alrosa, which has opposed action on conflict diamonds and is suspected of violating the terms of the Kimberley Process.

The creation of these intertwined clubs, with a private sector voluntary program embedded within a state-based system, was driven in large part by the pressing desire on the part of industry, states, and even their critics to maintain the value of diamond markets. All the participants in the diamond sector had a powerful common interest in the reputation of the product, allowing them to overcome barriers to collective action. The "club good" that the KPCS supplies is the system's promise to identify "clean" diamonds, holding the industry accountable through establishing and implementing standards for certification. Participating states would enforce the system internationally by only permitting the export and import of certified diamonds. This system was critical to maintaining the value of the diamond in the minds of consumers, by rehabilitating the reputation of the product in the face of the blood diamonds campaign. The branding of clean diamonds through the certification process is a key element of the club goods that the system provides. In order to obtain those reputational benefits, members joined the club with a commitment to the peaceful resolution of conflicts. For industry and exporting nations, the social externalities were the only way to obtain the club goods they desired, although of course the social externalities were the main demand of stakeholder NGOs involved in the blood diamonds campaign.

Certification systems are designed to assign liability and monitor ownership of valuable resources. They establish a club whose members partake of the benefits of an assured market, free of sanctions or legal repercussions for market transactions. They are essentially the opposite of a traditional sanctions regime, which typically applies negative punishments and not positive enticements. The certification is a clear and public symbol of membership in the club, which conveys reputational information to consumers, activists, and public officials. International certification systems have been established in recent years in a number of different sectors, including most prominently the certification for labor standards and environmental sustainability (chapter 6, this volume).

The KPCS, as a club, deliberately excludes from valuable international trade all nonparticipating states. The costs to Kimberley Process members of excluding others are relatively low, while the costs of being one of the excluded are extremely high. The club good provided by the KPCS is one of reputation, based on a set of standards and enforcement mechanisms that ensure the accountability of members. The system itself is clearly nonrivalrous, although the underlying good being exchanged—diamonds—is a purely private good. As more participants join, they offer a higher level of social externalities in the form of a more highly regulated market that excludes conflict diamonds. Network benefits may increase as more members join, providing positive returns to scale. As the number rises, though, we may reach a "tipping point," where the norms underlying the system become ingrained within society and the value of the club may decline (Finnemore and Sikkink 1998).

Many of the features that should enhance cooperation and facilitate the creation of a club are present in this sector: small numbers, long shadow of the future, and extensive sharing of information. The private club is made up primarily of diamond producers and distributors, dominated by De Beers. It is clear that the structure of the industry, which is still influenced significantly by this one company, facilitated agreement among the players. Without the support of the De Beers group of companies, it is doubtful that the industry would have supported the creation of the KPCS. Even as De Beers has changed direction and brought in new managers, it still retains its influence on its business partners. Indeed, we may look on De Beers as constituting its own "k-group," in game theory terms, since it gains so much from maintaining first the original cartel and later the new cartel that underlies the KPCS. Although the cartel has been weakened, the economic and personal relationships among industry insiders remain strong. The industry is well organized through the World Federation of Diamond Bourses and the International Diamond Manufacturers Association, which meet annually. All of this facilitates cooperation among the industry players, and motivated them to overcome their divergent interests and support the Kimberley Process.

At the same time, the industry itself is divided between the big, hierarchical mining of South Africa and Russia, and the alluvial or artisanal mining that is found in many other countries. Most conflict diamonds come from the latter sources, which are much more difficult to monitor and control. Establishing a chain-of-custody system is difficult in even the most advanced states, and can be an impossible task in lawless and corrupt environments. Small-scale players are less likely to be fully committed to the certification scheme, and can act as spoilers within the regime. To some degree, they are disciplined by the larger players, the industry buyers such as De Beers, but there is much room for shirking at this level.

The voluntary program by industry would mean nothing if there were no action by governments. Once the industry leaders realized the need to act, they supported from the start a global system of export and import control by governments, under which only conflict-free zones would be able to trade in rough diamonds. The interstate part of the KPCS was driven largely by the interests of diamond-producing states, led by regional hegemon South Africa, a major force behind the KPCS. States sought to protect an important source of revenue, and had a strong common interest in maintaining the value of the diamond. They feared the rising political backlash against the use of diamonds to finance bloodshed, particularly through the successful link made to the plight of child soldiers in Sierra Leone. The pressure for action was intensified by political activism in the United States, a major market for gemstones. NGOs were active in lobbying legislators on the conflict diamond issue. Within the United States, diamond companies and trade groups launched a lobbying and public relations campaign in support of the Conflict Diamonds Act of 2001 (although critics accused it of being too weak and favorable to industry) (Silverstein 2001). U.S. industry leader Lazare Kaplan International had earlier worked closely with De Beers to negotiate the creation of the WDC in 2000.

While initially the KPCS did not include a monitoring system, the participants quickly agreed to establish one within a year of implementation, and almost all members have requested that they be reviewed (www.kimberleyprocess.com). This would reinforce the reputational benefits of belonging to the Kimberley Process. State participants in the KPCS would also receive private benefits that would come from continued access to legitimate diamond markets. Industry participants based within these states would obviously also benefit from access to world markets. They both would receive the secondary benefit of facilitating the peaceful resolution of regional conflict, which can reduce the threat for those countries that are in "bad" neighborhoods. By eliminating markets for rough diamonds sourced from conflict-affected regions, the funds for rebels and secessionists would dry up, at least in theory. The countries actually experiencing conflict but nevertheless capable of meeting KPCS standards expected that rebels would be forced to the negotiating table by the sanctions on diamond sales from conflict-affected regions.

Since the KPCS's establishment, the level of legitimate diamonds traded in international markets has risen dramatically. More government and industry players are taking advantage of the opportunity to market themselves as responsible diamond sellers, with De Beers, for instance, now marketing a "Forever" diamond that is certified as conflict free. The social externalities of the voluntary program may be seen in the fact that some of the conflicts that first generated headlines about diamonds have been settled, although we cannot say that the new restrictions on the diamond trade truly caused peace to break out. There is continuing concern about shirking by weak governments, and the problem of "spoilers"—that is, smugglers and criminals who evade the Kimberley Process controls. Attention has shifted recently to the Côte d'Ivoire as the main source of illicit diamonds in the world today, but even Canada—which has the strictest oversight of its diamond industry—is concerned about smuggling and criminal activity. Still, most observers (and certainly the WDC) affirm that this constitutes only a tiny fraction of the broader market. While it is difficult to draw a direct line between the restrictions on trade in conflict diamonds and the end of civil conflicts, there is the perception that the Kimberley Process has had significant positive social externalities.

Weaknesses in the KPCS Voluntary Program

Representatives of consumers, citizens, and peace interests all supported the KPCS system largely due to the social externalities they expected to gain from the end of trade in diamonds as a source of conflict finance. A recent outside evaluation of the KPCS praised the system overall for the success it has had in only a few years of operation. "Three years into operation, the scheme has been credited with exponential growth in legitimate diamond exports." (Global Witness and Wexler 2006, 5). But there are a number of weaknesses in the system.

One source of weakness, also identified by Spar in her study of cartels, and prominently mentioned in the preamble to the KPCS itself, is the need for effective internal controls. Some member countries are weak governments, with high levels of corruption and an erratic commitment to the process. The certificates of origin from these states may be suspect, as officials can be richly rewarded for certifying diamonds from suspicious sources. The problem of shirking poses a challenge to the KPCS, due to deliberate or accidental noncompliance by such governments.

There is evidence that diamonds are financing the conflict in Côte d'Ivoire, and the Kimberley Process has not acted quickly to address it. The system of peer review that is the central means of monitoring implementation is still evolving, and needs to be strengthened. As noted above, however, countries can and have been removed from the list of KPCS participants, which is a strong enforcement mechanism.

Another source of weakness is the determination of nonparticipants to circumvent the rules. For instance, diamonds from rebels operating in excluded states can be smuggled into participating states, given a certificate, and exported as certified diamonds. Some argue that the system is undermined or has the potential to be undermined by the large number of stones from conflict regions that were bought and stockpiled by De Beers prior to the negotiation of the KPCS, and that may be circulated today as certified diamonds. There is too little government oversight of the industry within each country, throughout the supply chain from diamond miners to brokers, which means that diamond certificates may be awarded to some conflict diamonds. The corrupt practices of many of the unsavory characters acting as buyers and brokers create incentives to circumvent the system.

One of the key weaknesses in the system, and one that has been identified in studies of other types of certification systems, is the degree to which the value of certification is driven by consumer choices. The campaign against conflict diamonds sought to influence the buying habits of consumers by painting them as blood diamonds and shaming the industry into ending the trade in conflict diamonds. The negotiators of the KPCS genuinely feared the collapse of the value of the diamond if the campaign succeeded. Creating a label that would signal clean diamonds appeared to be the most effective way to address the problem. But the reality is that few consumers or even retailers know about conflict diamonds, even fewer are aware of the certification system, and only a handful actually insist on buying only conflict-free certified diamonds (although this may have changed a little following the release of the movie *Blood Diamond*). This is despite the fact that retailers are members of the KPCS, and the prominent retail jeweler Tiffany's has been publicly active in supporting the system. It is difficult to ensure that consumers are well informed, and labels signifying certification may mean little to the average buyer.

One potential future problem is that of free riding once the number of participants rises high enough. There is a possibility that the certification label will become even less noticeable to the public as it becomes more ubiquitous, allowing nonparticipants to free ride on the positive reputation built up by others. There may be a sort of reputational spillover effect, in which once the KPCS is well established, everyone simply assumes that all diamonds being sold are certified, whether or not the salesperson can produce an actual certificate. This may be the equivalent to crowding effects seen in other types of clubs. Yet given the difficulty of establishing the certification system in the minds of consumers and retailers, this is unlikely to happen any time soon.

The Kimberley Process as a Club Good

The Kimberley Process is a fairly unique institution. It combines private and public sector groups into a larger system which is greater than the sum of its parts. It privileges neither state nor market, and thus does not fit easily into contemporary debates about the decline of the state and the rise of the market. The distribution of power among the states that created the system was less important in the creation of the system than the distribution of power among industry players. State power did come into play in terms of market power, though—regional powerhouse and major diamond producer South Africa promoted the Kimberley Process, and the U.S. position mattered as it was the major consumer market for diamond gemstones.

As described above, the Kimberley Process is a club of state and nonstate actors—a "double club"—providing the club good of reputational benefits. It does this by establishing a set of standards for the certification of diamonds that are conflict free. This system is backed by both internal industry controls, and a state-based monitoring and enforcement system applied to international trade. The system excludes from diamond markets those states and industry players that are not participants in the system. By establishing the KPCS, the diamond industry and diamond exporting states prevented a potential decline in the market for their product as a result of global activism against conflict diamonds. This reputational benefit accrued only to KPCS members. But the system also provided an important social externality by severely restricting the ability of rebels to finance violence through the sale of diamonds. While the system is clearly not airtight, it has influenced the shape of both markets and politics in conflict-affected regions.

The club approach to analyzing this case allows us to better understand some of the dynamics of the interaction between state and market. The distribution of power among exporting states and within the industry facilitated the creation of a club. The system required voluntary action by both states and firms, with the goal of preserving the reputation of the product by providing a social externality. The high value placed on the reputation of the product further facilitated cooperative action to sustain that reputation and overcome dilemmas of collective action. Diamonds are interesting because it is the reputation of the entire class of goods, as noted earlier, and not the branding of particular company products that was at stake. The creation of the Kimberley Process was in response to the danger that diamond markets would weaken significantly if consumers associated diamonds with war instead of weddings, and if activists continued to shame the industry publicly.

The Kimberley Process reestablishes a diamond cartel, but in a new and "improved" version. It is not a cartel in the traditional sense in which industry players collude formally or informally to restrict supply with the primary goal of increasing prices or dividing up market shares. In this case, the participants engaged in public negotiations, and included an unusually wide range of actors—firms from every stage of the production process, both producing and consuming states, intergovernmental organizations, and NGOs. The goal was not explicitly about the levels of supply, prices, profits, or market shares. Instead, the goal was to deliver a social externality that would enhance the market for diamonds. But the end result of establishing limits on trade in a particular type of diamond—conflict diamonds—is to reaffirm the market power of legitimate diamond players. This system reduces competitive pressures on market players to some degree, since non-KPCS states and firms cannot sell into KPCS member state markets. On the other hand, these same states had in most cases been subject to UN sanctions prior to the implementation of the Kimberley Process, so they already had limited access. Many of the formerly sanctioned states have implemented reforms and seek to become Kimberley Process members themselves. While we might label this club a cartel, it is perhaps more accurate to describe it as an international sanctions regime with public and private elements.

While there are many unique aspects to the KPCS, the way in which public authority overlays and supports the industry voluntary program through monitoring and oversight can be seen in other issue areas too, such as the accounting standards discussed in this volume's chapter 8. Many of the authors in this book ask under what conditions states are most likely to take on this role. The Kimberley Process case illustrates a situation in which sovereignty is still central to cooperation, but not unchallenged—where border control is essential to the success of the private voluntary program. Monitoring and restricting transactions across borders is still a major function of the modern state, despite the ways in which globalization may undermine the effectiveness of such control. And in fact, the portability of diamonds and their susceptibility to smuggling demonstrate the real limits to government oversight.

One question that must be asked, though, concerns the notion of accountability itself. Voluntary programs often obscure the lines of accountability. To whom are participants accountable, and for what? To consumers? To innocent civilians caught up in war? Or to a vague notion of the international community? In a legalistic sense, we do not have an international system in which there are official lines of delegation established by democratic governments, which is the gold standard for accountable systems (Grant and Keohane 2005). There is little participation by those most affected by the system—consumers, miners, and laborers in the mining sector, and more important, those who suffer the consequences of continued violent conflict. Willie Nagel, an international diamond trader who contributed to the creation of the Kimberley Process, commented that the system was designed to stem the flow of conflict diamonds, but "conflict-free diamonds should not be confused with ethical diamonds" (*The Economist* 2007). Philippe Le Billon (2006), a scholar who has been following the conflict diamond issue from the beginning, makes an interesting argument about the nature of the diamond campaign in the modern era. It was successful at linking spaces of violent conflict (African civil wars) with spaces of peaceful consumption (U.S. jewelry stores). But it leaves us with extremely negative images of Africans as brutal and Africa as lawless, and with positive images of major multinational corporations such as De Beers.

Nevertheless, the Kimberley Process is an innovative means of resolving social problems through voluntary action by a mix of public and private actors. These mixed public-private voluntary programs are an advance in the development of global governance in areas where public action alone has been difficult to achieve, and where the failure of governments is a barrier to the achievement of things we value such as peace (Benner, Reinicke, and Witte 2004). While the Kimberley Process cannot claim that it was the main mechanism for bringing peace to many African states, it is an institution that provides significant incentives for peaceful commerce and represents a positive development in global governance.

6

Standards for Sweatshops: The Power and Limits of the Club Approach to Voluntary Labor Standards

Tim Bartley

In the early 1990s, when activists first accused apparel and footwear companies like Nike, Wal-Mart, and the Gap of profiting from exploitation, child labor, and the suppression of labor rights in their supply chains, most companies responded by denying responsibility. Confronted in 1992 with images of child labor in a Bangladeshi factory, Wal-Mart's CEO famously dismissed them, telling *Dateline NBC*, "The pictures you showed me mean nothing to me" (quoted in Ramey and Barrett 1996, 10).

Less than two decades later, major consumer products firms are much more likely to portray themselves as upholders of labor rights around the world, and point to an array of codes of conduct, social audits, factory certifications, and corporate social responsibility professionals to back up their claims (Bartley 2005; Esbenshade 2004; Haufler 2001; O'Rourke 2003; Rodríguez-Garavito 2005; Schrage 2004). The 1990s witnessed the formation of voluntary programs like the Fair Labor Association, Social Accountability International, and Ethical Trading Initiative, which set collective standards for participating companies and purport to verify compliance in factories around the world. These programs were designed for (and partially by) apparel, footwear, toy, and other consumer products firms producing through global supply chains, and selling in North American and European markets. Participating firms incur private costs to fund external auditing and/or the certification of factories, and potentially to rectify problems that are identified (though both sets of costs are often partially left to the supplying firms). For the participants, the programs promised branding benefits in the form of an improved reputation with consumers, investors, business partners, and government officials, while also generating positive externalities in the form of improved working conditions, more adequate wages, and reductions in worker abuse and harassment.

Although these programs have not always delivered on these promises, their formation and operation deserve close attention. How did these voluntary programs emerge? Why would firms in labor-intensive industries sign up for potentially costly voluntary standards? How should we understand their impacts and significance? In this chapter, I explore the potential and limits of the club approach in answering these questions.

First, I examine how voluntary programs were formed in response to antisweatshop pressures. The power of the club approach lies in explaining how responses to stakeholder pressure might shift from unilateral actions (like individual company codes of conduct) and those open to blatant shirking, to programs with shared standards and some degree of monitoring and enforcement. I look at firms' initial attempts to organize such systems, which largely failed, as well as the eventual role of companies in creating and designing the Fair Labor Association (FLA) and Social Accountability International (SAI). Yet the mobilization of firms, as described by this approach, cannot fully account for the rise and contours of voluntary programs for labor. To do so, the club approach's emphasis on solutions to firms' Olsonion dilemmas and pursuit of club goods must be embedded in an analysis of political conflicts over regulation and standard setting at the national and international levels. Voluntary labor standards programs represented not merely a solution for companies but also an outcome of political battles over the legitimate means of regulating capitalism in a context of globalization and neoliberalism. Paying heed to the broader political conditions that have made voluntary programs so prominent can strengthen the account of how programs form and provide insight into the relationship between voluntary programs and public policy.

This chapter also looks at factors that led firms to participate in these voluntary programs and their impacts to date. Although the leading initiatives have—on paper, at least—reasonably strong club standards and medium-to-strong swords, the participation rates have been low, and their impact has been limited due to weaknesses in both design and implementation. The rise of voluntary programs in this sector has for the most part not disrupted the durable inequalities and price/speed pressures that lead to "sweating" the workforce. Serious questions remain about the effects of voluntary programs for labor standards in the apparel and footwear industries.

Good organization

Overall, this chapter makes three main contributions to the analysis of voluntary programs. First, it examines the *formation* of voluntary programs, considering the impact of both collective action dilemmas among firms and broader political processes. It then demonstrates the importance of social movement pressure—not only in the formation of voluntary programs, but also in spurring firms' participation. Third, it highlights a case in which the effectiveness of voluntary programs (as currently configured) is very much in doubt (see also Locke, Qin, and Brause 2007; Seidman 2007).

Before proceeding, it is crucial to put the case of voluntary labor standards in context. The distinction between standards on the books and standards in practice is central to understanding both labor law and voluntary programs. Some advocates have argued that voluntary programs are necessary precisely because governments are unwilling or incapable of enforcing labor laws—even though these laws are quite strong in principle in some developing countries. Likewise, the standards used by groups like the FLA and SAI resemble not merely "Western" labor standards but also *internationally negotiated* conventions of the International Labor Organization on forced labor, child labor, discrimination, health and safety, and freedom of association (though sometimes with loopholes added). They do not stipulate specific wage rates but call for conformance with minimum wage laws, prevailing local industry wages, and in the case of SAI also for a wage "sufficient to meet basic needs" and "provide some discretionary income" as well. Although there are some shortcomings and contradictions to these voluntary standards, if vigorously implemented they would nevertheless represent a step up from labor practices and conditions in many apparel and footwear factories in developing countries (although not always a step up from the law on the books). But implementing them is not a simple task, and the rise of a "market for virtue" in this arena has not erased fundamental conflicts between brand-name firms, suppliers, and workers, making this a difficult case for voluntary programs.

Labor Standards from the Perspective of the Club Approach

Why have some of the same firms that initially sought out cheap sources of labor in repressive political environments now adopted voluntary standards for labor conditions and worker rights in their supply chains? The answer lies largely in the pressures that have been brought to bear on companies by antisweatshop activists, labor unions, shareholder activists, and consumer groups. While firms like Nike, the Gap, and Polo Ralph Lauren have invested heavily in "branding" and "reputational capital" (Fombrun 1996; Klein 1999), they have also found that high-profile scandals and political pressures can tarnish that reputation. In the face of such pressure, it is not surprising that firms would adopt voluntary standards to try to deflect criticism, preempt regulation, and signal their social responsibility to consumers and investors. But one would expect firms to pursue low-cost, unilateral solutions that do not require any substantial loss of autonomy in production decisions—solutions like public relations campaigns and codes of conduct designed for and by the company. This has, in fact, been the most common response to antisweatshop pressure, and most consumer products firms now have a code of conduct for their suppliers. It is in explaining why firms might go beyond individual responses to create and join collective programs with at least some enforcement capacity, however, that the club approach to voluntary programs becomes useful.

The keys to applying the club approach to the case of labor standards are to consider the limited credibility of unilateral strategies and conceptualize reputation as a "good held in common." First, corporations' claims about their social responsibility are subject to credibility problems. Reasonably savvy consumers and investors may discount companies' own self-serving claims, especially if activists are able to expose "sham" elements in them. In response, firms may search for ways of lending credibility to their claims, such as employing auditors to assess them. Still, even if a watchdog is employed, the question of "who watches the watchdog" remains, and the "spiral of distrust" continues (Djelic and Sahlin-Andersson 2006; Shapiro 1987). Given substantial uncertainty about the credibility of firms' claims, the market for information about production practices will fail (Akerlof 1970). In this situation, firms may develop an interest in external and at least partially independent systems for monitoring, verifying, or certifying claims as well as upholding corporate reputations (Milgrom, North, and Weingast 1990; Viscusi 1978). Spiraling debates about the credibility of "no sweat" claims, in sum, may create the conditions for independent voluntary programs to emerge.

Second, conceptualizing reputation as a "good held in common" (see concluding chapter) further illustrates why individual firm-level strategies for protecting or improving reputations may be insufficient. If activists target specific firms, others in the industry may find themselves tarred by the same brush, such that one firm's reputation is partially dependent on the actions of its competitors (King, Lenox, and Barnett 2002). Firms thus face a collective action problem:unilateral action may not be enough to improve their reputation, and firms that do take steps toward improving production practices are likely to be undercut by competitors (Spar 1998). Yet cooperative responses will probably be hampered by free riding. For instance, industry-wide codes of ethics that lack sanctions may be undermined by some firms free riding on the efforts of others (King and Lenox 2000). There may even be a problem of adverse selection, wherein the *worst* firms (in terms of their labor practices) are the *most attracted* to voluntary programs.

Certification and monitoring associations represent a potential solution to this problem (Garcia-Johnson 2001; Spar and Yoffie 2000). By certifying or otherwise branding firms that are found to be in compliance, such systems seek to distinguish the good apples from the bad. In this way, reputation becomes an excludable club good rather than a nonexcludable public good (see chapter 2). The benefits of an improved reputation can be limited to those firms that contribute to this effort, while free riders can be excluded. On the other hand, as Prakash and Potoski (2007a) point out, industry reputation need not be thought of as rivalrous, since many firms can conceivably join the club and enjoy reputational benefits without subtracting from the benefits accruing to other club members.

If the club approach is to be broadly applicable, then it ought to not only provide an interpretation of outcomes but also describe the *process* of innovation and institution building. As one looks at the historical record, one should find evidence of firms coping with the sort of collective action dilemmas described above and developing innovative systems for certifying credible claims. Such evidence may be found through a process-tracing analysis that uncovers both how actors talk about their dilemmas and the strategies used to solve them. Relevant data might be collected from interviews, trade journals, and/or archival sources. Regardless of the source, the evidence should speak to at least three types of questions: How were problems diagnosed in industry circles, and did firms recognize a collective action dilemma? What sets of actors attempted to solve these problems, and were they the sorts of actors emphasized by the club approach? What sorts of voluntary programs were proposed, and how robust were they? By moving in this direction, analysts can better use the club approach to explain the *formation* of voluntary programs in addition to their structure and impact.

In the next section, I apply the theory in this way, examining how apparel and footwear firms responded to external pressures and reputational threats. The analysis draws on interviews ($N = 28$) with a variety of individuals involved in the formation or development of voluntary programs in this sector, articles from the leading trade journals (*Bobbin* and *Women's Wear Daily*), and various secondary sources.

Reputation Threats and Firm Responses

Concerns in the early 1990s over child labor, physical and verbal abuse, and violations of core labor rights in the production of toys, soccer balls, rugs, and garments marked the beginning of a wave of antisweatshop protests and media campaigns (Cavanagh 1997; Spielberg 1997; Varley 1998).[1] Some of the earliest campaigns focused on production in China—for companies like Levi Strauss, Toys"R"Us, and others—where the Tiananmen Square massacre in 1989 and U.S.-China trade negotiations drew special attention to human rights abuses. Other early sweatshop exposés highlighted child labor in the production of soccer balls in Pakistan, rugs in India, and garments in Bangladesh and Honduras; the suppression of labor rights in Indonesia, El Salvador, and elsewhere; and several shocking instances of physical abuse. Wal-Mart, Nike, the Gap, and Liz Claiborne were among the first major companies to be implicated in these international sweatshop scandals.

Yet one of the most dramatic early sweatshop scandals occurred in the United States, in the Los Angeles, California, suburb of El Monte. It was there, in 1995, that government inspectors discovered Thai immigrants working as indentured servants in an apartment complex, sewing garments to be sold by major retailers, including Montgomery Ward, Target, and Sears (Bonacich and Appelbaum 2000; Su 1997). The next year, labor rights activists brought sweatshops further into the U.S. media spotlight by exposing child labor in a Honduran factory producing Kathie Lee Gifford's line of clothing for Wal-Mart as well as a New York City sweatshop also producing Kathie Lee Gifford's brand (Bonacich and Appelbaum 2000; Krupat 1997). As *Women's Wear Daily* noted, "Allegations about the production of the Kathie Lee line follow other very public black eyes for the garment industry" (Reich Says 1996, 1).

These black eyes were compounded by a growing antisweatshop movement, which was adding firms like Phillips-Van Heusen, Guess, JCPenney, Eddie Bauer, and many others to the list of companies hit with the sweatshop stigma. Government pressure had also mounted by the mid-1990s. The U.S. Department of Labor had begun stepping up its enforcement of wage and hour law in domestic garment factories in the early 1990s, and had experimented with holding manufacturers and retailers responsible for the back wages owed by their contractors and subcontractors (Bonacich and Appelbaum 2000; Esbenshade 2004; interviews with Department of Labor officials June 27, 2002, July 19, 2002, August 23, 2002). Congressional representatives were introducing a number of bills designed to restrict the import of products linked to child labor and human rights abuses (Barrett 1994; Ramey and Barrett 1996).

In this context, companies displayed increasing concern about what a trade journal called the attempt to "publicly tarnish the reputation of the industry as a whole" (Nett 1997, 38). Faced with threats to their images and autonomy, some companies began looking for ways to, as one industry adviser phrased it, "put a muzzle on these watchdog groups" (Rolnick 1997, 72).

El Monte and the Initial Attempts at Voluntary Labor Standards Programs

The El Monte incident spurred one set of firms to begin to develop voluntary labor standards programs to certify compliance. El Monte made the collective character of the industry reputation clear, especially for firms in California. It was explicitly described as such by a *Bobbin* editor in an article called "Bad Apples Need Not Apply":

Unfortunately, the old saying about a bad apple spoiling the whole bunch can be true—at least on the surface. Perhaps no one knows this better than reputable contractors, who must bend over backwards to distance themselves from illegitimate businesses that tend to give the whole apparel industry a bad rap.... How do the "good" contractors, manufacturers and retailers convince John Q. Public that the El Monte situation is not the norm? (Black 1995, 2)

As California industry leader Ilse Metchek put it, "The Labor Department considered [El Monte] as the norm—that we're a sweatshop industry. That isn't the norm. It's an aberration. Our job now is to show that [the El Monte sweatshop incident] isn't the way things are. It's the way *some* things are" (quoted in Abend 1996, 28).

Faced with direct threats to a reputation held in common, domestic manufacturers and contractors began to develop certification and labeling systems, since as Metchek observed, "certification is the answer" (ibid., 29). One set of firms developed the Compliance Alliance in 1995 to coordinate factory monitoring and develop a no-sweat labeling program (Bonacich and Appelbaum 2000; Marlow 1995; interview with Department of Labor official August 23, 2002). Meanwhile, the Coalition of Apparel Industries in California developed a plan to certify contractors and manufacturers at this time. In early 1997, it created a separate NGO to administer it, called the California Apparel Industry Certification Board. This was designed as a "voluntary certification program [that] will allow manufacturers and contractors to be recognized for their efforts to curb labor law violations" (Bobbin 1997, 44). In industry circles, the Coalition of Apparel Industries in California program was touted as an attractive initiative, through which "companies meeting the standards would be 'certified' and retailers and manufacturers would be encouraged to use only those firms that are certified, driving out the sweatshop operations" (Black 1997, 1).

Yet the outcome of this moment of forward-looking collective action among firms was not the emergence of robust certification initiatives, but instead several *failed* voluntary programs. Industry actors in California were somewhat divided over the two plans, which differed in the formalization of the certification procedure as well as the responsibilities assigned to brands and contractors (Bonacich and Appelbaum 2000; Marlow 1995). Neither initiative managed to take hold. The Compliance Alliance never introduced a labeling program, and the Coalition of Apparel Industries in California initiative was pronounced definitively dead in 1998 (Black 1998). Although the precise reasons for these failures are not entirely clear, it appears that these attempts suffered from divisions within the industry and a lack of endorsement from other stakeholders.

Reconstructing this case of a "failed club" holds several broader lessons for scholars of voluntary programs. First, while analysts typically focus only on clubs that have successfully emerged, digging through the historical record can reveal alternative paths that would otherwise be forgotten. In addition, this instance serves as a further reminder that cooperation is hard to secure, and even initial agreements can falter under the weight of setting up a new organization and promoting a novel set of practices. Such organizations did emerge—in the form of the FLA and SAI—but it took a different set of actors to accomplish this.

From Individual Codes of Conduct to Monitoring Associations

Large, image-conscious firms also developed an interest in voluntary labor standards. Levi Strauss had designed the first code of conduct pertaining to labor conditions in its suppliers' factories in 1991, and by the mid-1990s these sorts of voluntary commitments were nearly ubiquitous in the apparel and footwear industries. A 1996 study by the U.S. Department of Labor identified thirty-six apparel manufacturers and retailers with labor codes of conduct for their supply chains. This included firms that had been at the center of highly visible sweatshop scandals, like Wal-Mart, Nike, the Gap, and Kellwood (the manufacturer of Kathie Lee Gifford's line), as well as firms that had largely escaped activist attention, such as Fruit of the Loom, Jones Apparel, Talbots, and VF (maker of Lee, Wrangler, and many other brands) (U.S. Department of Labor 1996).

The rapid diffusion of codes of conduct stems from the low cost of this response to external pressures (actual or threatened) from activists, government, and consumers. Yet the mere existence of codes of conduct, absent evidence that they were actually affecting labor practices, was a weak riposte to sweatshop allegations. Activists quickly challenged them as purely symbolic responses that were radically decoupled from conditions in factories (Campaign for Labor Rights 1997; Shaw 1999). Some companies attempted to verify compliance by sending internal auditors or hiring accounting firms, NGOs, or firms from the growing industry of specialized labor standards auditors to inspect factories around the world. Activists quickly challenged the adequacy of this response as well. Ernst and Young's factory monitoring for Nike became the focus of one exposé, which showed that auditors overlooked a variety of occupational health and safety hazards, and failed to gather accurate information from workers (O'Rourke 1997). One specialized auditor, Cal Safety Compliance Corporation, turned out to have monitored the California manufacturer that was funneling some of its production to the El Monte slave shop, raising questions about the quality and integrity of this auditor (Esbenshade 2004). Overall, even as companies adopted codes of conduct and employed external auditors, activists kept the pressure up, and companies continued to struggle to make their no sweat claims credible.

As with the El Monte case, one might expect these large, high-profile firms to cooperate to build collective programs with stronger standards and verification procedures, in order to fend off social movement pressure, preempt government intervention, and distinguish themselves from sweatshop operators. Although the major trade associations—the American Apparel Manufacturers Association and the National Retail Federation—did little at this point aside from developing fairly weak codes of conduct, several large brands did come together to support and help design groundbreaking programs like the FLA and SAI.

Initially, even large brand-name corporations seem to have found direct cooperation on factory monitoring difficult. As one executive explained, "There was one effort in '95 or '96 where we attempted to reach out to our primary competitor and share, and we were rebuffed. And you know, there was a lot of sort of backroom competition between the companies in those days, so sharing was not easily possible" (interview with apparel executive September 30, 2005). Yet these companies had begun to coordinate their actions in forums like Business for Social Responsibility, an NGO formed in 1992 with leadership from companies like Levi Strauss and Stride Rite. By 1996, this group also had representatives of Reebok and Phillips-Van Heusen on its board of directors, and was serving as a "chamber of commerce" of sorts for companies interested in corporate social responsibility (Ramey and Barrett 1996; Internet archive at ⟨http://www.bsr.org/bodlist.html⟩ (accessed October 30, 1996); interview with CSR professional March 16, 2004). The Council on Economic Priorities had also organized an informal study group of firms with codes of conduct, the Partnership for Responsible Global Sourcing, in which companies like Levi Strauss, Liz Claiborne, L. L. Bean, and Eileen Fisher participated (Council on Economic Priorities 1994; Ramey and Barrett 1996; interview with SAI organizer July 18, 2002).

These companies became some of the key players in the construction of labor standards monitoring and certification associations. In summer 1996, the Clinton administration brought together a group of companies, NGOs, and labor unions in what would soon become known as the Apparel Industry Partnership (AIP). The companies included Liz Claiborne, L. L. Bean, Nike, and Phillips-Van Heusen as well as Business for Social Responsibility itself. This group soon began developing plans for the FLA, with representatives from Liz Claiborne, Reebok, and Business for Social Responsibility playing especially prominent roles (Arnold and Porter 1996; interview with NGO-based FLA organizers August 22, 2002, February 19, 2004, August 8, 2002; interview with apparel executive/FLA organizer March 9, 2004; interview with independent monitor

July 18, 2002). The value of the nascent FLA was, according to one corporate participant, that "companies will be better able to protect their reputations" (quoted in Ramey 1997, 14). While many of the largest apparel firms were working within the AIP, Toys"R"Us, Eileen Fisher, and several other companies had teamed up with the Council on Economic Priorities, which founded SAI (originally called the Council on Economic Priorities Accreditation Agency) in 1997.

In sum, a handful of large branded companies played an important role in organizing labor standards certification systems, much as the club approach to voluntary programs would expect. This was not their first strategy for responding to sweatshop criticism but rather one that evolved out of their earlier attempts to maintain their reputations and garner credibility for their claims of being the responsible good apples in the industry.

Politics, Neoliberalism, and the Limits of the Club Approach

The story about firms organizing to solve reputation and credibility problems, significant as it is, captures only part of the impetus for the formation of the AIP/FLA and SAI. The AIP was, after all, a *government-led* initiative, while the SAI was a project of the Council on Economic Priorities, an NGO promoting socially responsible consumer and investor choices. When one looks more closely at how these initiatives were formed, their *political* roots become clearer.

The Clinton administration brought companies, NGOs, and labor unions together to convene the AIP after a long string of attempts by Secretary of Labor Robert Reich to use publicity to spur improvements in labor conditions both internationally and domestically. In many ways, the AIP/FLA was simply a more systematized version of Reich's "Trendsetter List," which named companies that were engaged in the monitoring of their contract factories, but came under fire from both companies and labor unions for its ambiguous standards for inclusion (Bonacich and Appelbaum 2000; Levy 1998; interview with Department of Labor officials June 27, 2002, July 19, 2002; interview with NGO-based FLA organizer August 22, 2002). In addition, promoting voluntary labor standards was a way for the Clinton administration to appease its Left/labor constituency while still forging ahead with a free trade agenda. Clinton had reneged on earlier promises not to sign the North American Free Trade Agreement without strong labor and environmental standards and had delinked trade with China from human rights considerations (Tsogas 2001; Varley 1998). When the El Monte and Kathie Lee scandals hit, the Clinton administration stopped short of endorsing binding intergovernmental regulation (which unions and many labor rights advocates would have preferred) and instead convened the AIP. Although it was a nominally private sector program, several Department of Labor and administration officials shepherded the project in its early stages (interview with FLA representative June 27, 2002; interview with NGO and FLA organizer July 18, 2002).

In the ensuing years, Clinton initiated a $4 million per year grant program, administered through the U.S. Department of State, to fund voluntary labor standards programs. This provided nearly half of the funding for the FLA and SAI as these programs grew in 2000 and 2001. In those years, government funding accounted for 48 percent of the FLA's $2.46 million in revenues and 46 percent of SAI's $3.92 million in revenues (analysis of IRS forms 990 accessed via Guidestar.org). So even though the Clinton administration did not directly create SAI, as it created AIP/ FLA, government funding was an important source of early support.[2]

In addition to companies and the U.S. government, a few NGOs played crucial roles in crafting the procedures and governance structure of the FLA—especially the Lawyers Committee for Human Rights and the International Labor Rights Fund. The latter group had previously called for labor standards in the form of a "social clause" to be added to the General Agreement on Tariffs and Trade (Collingsworth, Goold, and Harvey 1994). But the campaign for the social clause fell to defeat in 1994 and again in 1996–1997, in part due to charges that it amounted to protectionism and conflicted with the General Agreement on Tariffs and Trade rules about nontariff barriers to trade. It was in this context that the International Labor Rights Forum turned to the market and the potential for consumer pressure to serve as "an additional weapon in the arsenal for human rights" (interview with NGO-based FLA organizer August 22, 2002). Initially, organized labor and several other NGOs saw some promise in the AIP as well, but they eventually dropped out in protest over weaknesses in the workplace standards and monitoring provisions, generating a firestorm of controversy that continues to surround the FLA.

These observations cast labor standards systems in a different light. Whereas the club approach puts the analytic focus squarely on the ways in which voluntary programs solve collective action dilemmas, the case of labor standards reveals several other factors that have facilitated the rise of voluntary programs. Governments have actively supported voluntary systems and stimulated cooperation among private sector actors (potentially helping them overcome collective action problems). Governments have done this, in part, because voluntary programs are less likely than binding law and regulation to conflict with free trade agendas or World Trade Organization rules against imposing nontariff barriers to international trade (Bernstein and Cashore 2004; Ward 1996). The neoliberal project of encouraging free flows of capital and limiting government intervention must to some degree be credited with facilitating the ascendance of voluntary clubs. In addition to setting limits on how governments can regulate trade (through World Trade Organization rules), the rise of neoliberalism has legitimated arguments against "hard" government intervention and has widely diffused scripts about the power of markets to solve a variety of social problems. Taking this broader political environment into account helps to explain the recent wave of club formation, and may also open up new lines of argument how voluntary programs, governments, and NGOs intersect (see Bartley 2007). Comparing the failed institution-building projects led by firms in the wake of El Monte with the more successful projects that led to the FLA and SAI suggests that the involvement of government and NGOs may in fact be decisive for the formation of some types of clubs, although the contingencies of history get in the way of being able to make a firm conclusion on this point (since not all else was equal in these two moments). Paying close attention to the intersections of private programs and public policy should improve our understanding of the origins of voluntary regulation as well as the stakes that different players have in it.

Why Do Companies Participate in Voluntary Programs?

Both the FLA and SAI have the formal properties of strong sword programs, in that they include third-party auditing along with limited forms of disclosure and sanctioning. In practice, though, they are better characterized as carrying blunted medium swords, since they have largely refrained from sanctioning participating companies. Their standards are stronger than those of the industry association's Worldwide Responsible Apparel Production program (O'Rourke 2003), but weaker than the International Labor Organization conventions and provisions typically backed by labor unions. Despite the well-documented shortcomings of these programs (Esbenshade 2004; Rodríguez-Garavito 2005), they do represent external bodies with some degree of monitoring and enforcement capacity, however imperfect. The FLA, SAI, and UK-based Ethical Trading Initiative include representation by NGOs and other nonindustry actors, making them multistakeholder initiatives (MSIs) of a sort, though not all have the support of organized labor. With a weak sword, more lenient standards, and no involvement of credible labor rights or human rights NGOs, the Worldwide Responsible Apparel Production program—created in response to the FLA and SAI—can be considered a sham club. On the other side of the aisle, activists and labor unions developed a more stringent alternative for collegiate apparel, the Worker Rights Consortium, which rejects the standard model of voluntary programs altogether in favor of a "fire alarm" approach to intervening in labor conflicts.

Given the existence of an industry-based sham program and corporations' general reluctance to relinquish their autonomy, why have some companies signed on to MSIs like the FLA and SAI? Surprisingly, for all the debate about these programs, no research has tried to answer this question systematically. In this section, I present the results of some analyses of participation in MSIs (the FLA, SAI, and Ethical Trading Initiative) among the fifty largest U.S.-based corporations (measured by total sales in 2000) that make or sell apparel, footwear, or textiles.[3] I examine the impact of reputational capital, social movement pressure, and firm size on the likelihood of participating in an MSI.

Data on Companies, Reputational Capital, and Social Movement Pressure

I utilize data on firm size and sector from the Compustat Industrial Annual database, and draw on several other sources to measure reputational capital and social movement pressure. To generate a rough measure of whether firms have made major investments in consumer-oriented reputational capital, I utilize external evaluations of companies' advertising and branding efforts during the 1990s—namely, the "100 Leading National Advertisers" and "Marketing 100" lists, each published yearly by *Advertising Age* magazine. The former simply ranks the top companies by advertising expenditures, while the latter results from the magazine's attempt to find "current brand success stories" each year and profile their creators (Edwards 2005). Together, they capture both traditional marketing efforts and the innovative branding strategies that came into fashion in the 1990s. Twenty-four of the fifty large firms in my sample were included on at least one of these lists sometime between 1991 and 2000, and are therefore considered to have significant investments in consumer-oriented reputational capital.

Since corporate reputations may be rooted in perceptions of investors and the rest of the business community, not just end consumers (Fombrun and Shanley 1990; Podolny 2005), I also measure whether companies were recognized for a positive reputation in the business community, using the *Fortune* magazine's lists of "Top 100 Most Admired Companies" from 1991 to 2000. This measure captures a type of reputational capital valuable in (and recognized by) the business community.

To measure social movement pressure, I draw on an intensive coding of a rich source of data on the politics of the apparel industry—the two major trade journals, *Bobbin* and *Women's Wear Daily*. The latter source, a daily newspaper of the industry, provided especially detailed coverage of labor rights and antisweatshop campaigns targeting U.S. firms. All relevant articles in these journals from 1993 to 2000 were collected and coded for details about which companies were targeted. (For more details on the data collection procedure, see Bartley and Child [2007].) The trade journal data were supplemented with data on corporate targets gleaned from the leading secondary sources on the antisweatshop movement (Armbruster-Sandoval 2005; Bonacich and Appelbaum 2000; Louie 2001; Manheim 2001; Ross 1997). I use these data to discover whether a particular company was "named and shamed" by antisweatshop activists in a given year, and look at how commonly they were targeted—thus capturing the differences between firms that were never targeted, those that were targeted briefly or occasionally, and those (like Nike) that were the focus of sustained social movement pressure.

Results

Overall, the rate of participation in MSIs among the fifty largest U.S. corporations (that make or sell apparel or footwear) was fairly low. Only nine of these firms (18 percent) participated in the FLA, SAI, or Ethical Trading Initiative at any point between 2001 and 2004.[4] Many of the largest firms in the industry stayed away from MSIs. None of the "big four" discount retailers (Wal-Mart, Sears, Kmart, and Target) participated. Nor did major apparel manufacturers like VF, Sara Lee, or Jones Apparel, nor department store chains like Federated, May, or Dillards.

Table 6.1 shows that retailers were significantly less likely than others to participate in MSIs. Nordstrom and the Gap were the only two large

Table 6.1
Retailers and participation in MSIs

Participation in MSI?	Nonretail firms	Retailers	Total
No	13 (65%)	28 (93%)	41 (82%)
Yes	7 (35%)	2 (7%)	9 (18%)
Total	20	30	50

Chi-squared = 6.53, p < .011
Cramer's V = −.36

Table 6.2
Corporate reputation and participation in MSIs

	Major brand investment?		
Participation in MSI?	No	Yes	Total
No	24 (92%)	17 (71%)	41 (82%)
Yes	2 (8%)	7 (29%)	9 (18%)
Total	26	24	50

Chi-squared = 3.90, p < .048
Cramer's V = −.28

U.S. retailers that did participate, while the other 93 percent refrained. The limited participation by retailers is somewhat surprising, given their direct interface with consumers. If direct consumer demand for non-sweatshop clothes were driving the rise of voluntary labor standards systems—as analysts like Elliott and Freeman (2003) suggest—then one would expect retailers to be more heavily involved.

If direct contact with consumers is not a key factor, then what else might be driving participation? Given the importance of reputational benefits to the club approach to voluntary programs, it is possible that firms with major investments in reputation have more to gain from participating (or more to lose from not participating) than other firms do. Table 6.2 provides initial support for this idea, showing that firms with especially salient brand reputations are more likely than others to participate in MSIs. This resonates with findings from other sectors, such as King and Lenox's (2000) result that chemical companies with well-known reputations had a higher likelihood of participating in the Responsible Care program. While only 8 percent of apparel and footwear firms *without* a major brand reputation participated in MSIs, the rate of

Table 6.3
Social movement pressure and participation in MSIs

	Targeted by activists in 1990s		
Participation in MSI?	No	Yes	Total
No	22 (100%)	19 (68%)	41 (82%)
Yes	0 (0%)	9 (32%)	9 (18%)
Total	22	28	50

participation was significantly higher—around 29 percent—for those firms with major investments in this type of reputational capital.

Yet the effect of reputation may not be as direct as this makes it seem. In fact, it may be the social movement pressure that reputation-intensive firms attract—rather than the reputational capital itself—that determines participation in MSIs. An initial look at the data suggests that social movement pressure is indeed an important piece of the picture. As shown in table 6.3, every one of the nine companies that participated in MSIs had been targeted over sweatshops or labor rights at some point between 1993 and 2000. This means that social movement pressure was a *necessary condition* for participation by large U.S. corporations. It was not sufficient, however, since some companies (nineteen, to be specific) were targeted at least once, but still did not participate in MSIs. In the analyses below, I show that the *intensity* of social movement pressure (measured as the number of years that a company was targeted by activists) can help to explain participation in MSIs.

In order to better understand the various determinants of participating in MSIs, I use a logistic regression analysis that examines how participation is shaped by firm size, retail status, reputational capital, and the intensity of social movement pressure.[5] Because these last two factors are analytically intertwined, I assess their effects using a two-stage model designed to adjust for the possibility of endogeneity. The goal of this procedure is to develop measures of reputational capital and social movement pressure that are independent of the tendency for activists to direct their energies at reputation-intensive firms. To do this, I first analyze the intensity with which companies were targeted by social movements, using reputational capital and several other control variables as predictors.[6] I then take the residuals from this model—which represent the difference between the observed amount of social movement pressure and the amount predicted by these factors—and use them as the measure of social movement pressure in a model explaining participation in MSIs. This

Table 6.4
Logistic regression of the likelihood of participating in MSIs (2001–2004), fifty largest U.S. apparel, textile, and footwear firms

Major brand investment (1 = yes, 0 = no)	4.6968*
	(2.1591)
Recognition for business reputation (1 = yes, 0 = no)	4.3676*
	(2.2015)
Intensity of social movement pressure (resid. from stage1)	1.4296*
	(.6849)
Retailer (1 = retailer, 0 = other)	−3.1602[+]
	(2.0055)
Size (assets in 2000)	−2.0383*
	(1.1378)
Constant	9.90688
	(7.2944)
N	50
Likelihood ratio Chi-squared test	27.33***
Pseudo-R^2	.5798

Note: Estimated SEs in parentheses.
[+] $p < .10$ * $p < .05$ ** $p < .01$ *** $p < .001$ (one-tailed tests)

allows me to assess whether reputation has direct effects on participation, or whether its effect is fully reducible to the social movement pressure it attracts. The model of participation in MSIs (the main concern in this chapter) in shown in table 6.4, while the first stage is included for interested readers in appendix 6.1.

I find that both social movement pressure and reputational capital shape companies' participation in multistakeholder labor standards initiatives. Table 6.4 shows that reputational capital increases the likelihood of firms participating, controlling for social movement pressure, size, and retail sector. Firms with consumer-oriented reputational capital (major brand investments) were significantly more likely than others to participate in MSIs. Business-based reputational capital (positive recognition in the business community) also significantly raises the likelihood of participating in MSIs.

Social movement pressure has a statistically significant effect on participation in MSIs as well. The more intensely companies were targeted by activists during the 1990s, the greater their likelihood of participating in MSIs, controlling for reputation, size, and retail status.

The negative effect of size indicates that among the firms in this analysis (the fifty largest in the industry), being bigger is associated with a lower likelihood of participating in an MSI, which is consistent with the earlier observation that many of the largest firms have shied away from multistakeholder engagement. Retailers are also less likely than other firms to participate (although this effect does not reach the conventional .05 level of statistical significance).

The stage one model (reported in the appendix 6.1) found that reputational capital increases the intensity with which firms are targeted. We can therefore conclude that reputational capital has both direct effects on participation and indirect effects that go through social movement targeting. Reputation-intensive firms do indeed attract more social movement pressure, which is a major determinant of participating in MSIs. But they also face a higher likelihood of participating for reasons that are not fully reducible to social movement pressure.

Overall, these results underscore the contentious character of this case of voluntary clubs. Absent some degree of activist pressure, *no* major U.S. corporations have chosen to participate in MSIs, and the intensity with which firms were confronted by activists shapes their likelihood of participating. In addition, the idea that firms join voluntary labor standards programs in order to protect valued reputations from threats (actual or potential) or otherwise maintain their reputational investments is supported by the finding that major investments in reputational capital increase the likelihood of participation.

Of course, there are several caveats to these results. First, a few *smaller* companies, like Patagonia and Eileen Fisher, have joined MSIs without experiencing intense social movement pressure. Among smaller firms, there may be some that pursue corporate social responsibility initiatives purely as a signal of their corporate culture or the market niche they occupy. But this has not generally occurred among the largest firms. Second, somewhat different findings about retailers and firm size might be obtained if one looked at companies in Europe, where some of the big retail chains have been more interested than their U.S. counterparts in engaging with MSIs, perhaps due to a more developed "market for virtue" there. Finally, over time, we might expect the importance of social movement pressure as an impetus for joining MSIs to decrease. If multistakeholder versions of certification and monitoring get institutionalized and become more routine features of industries—as ISO 9000 and 14001 standards have become—one would expect the importance of intense social movement pressure to decline. Whether this sort of institutionalization could occur without a significant weakening of standards and blunting of swords is, of course, a crucial question.

The Limited Impact of Voluntary Labor Standards Programs

It is tempting to assume that the rise of voluntary programs constitutes a win-win outcome, in which firms' pursuit of private and branding benefits generates broader social externalities. In fact, there is no evidence that voluntary labor standards have dramatically transformed working conditions or power asymmetries at the point of production. Nor have the potential benefits fully materialized for companies—with the possible exception of private benefits accruing to those in the burgeoning social auditing industry. Corporate participation in MSIs has remained low, and no market for independently verified "sweat-free" apparel or footwear has emerged. Unfortunately, it is not possible to measure the value that certification programs have had for companies in terms of protecting their brand reputation or preempting more stringent regulation; surely membership has had its privileges. But social movement pressures and reputational threats have not disappeared, and certification associations themselves have had to defend their credibility on many occasions.

The existing evidence, though highly fragmentary, suggests that the impact of voluntary codes of conduct, factory monitoring, and certification systems on wages, working conditions, and worker empowerment has been modest at best. No research has systematically demonstrated positive impacts, and certification and monitoring associations themselves have begun to express serious doubts about the efficacy of their work. A recent report from the Ethical Trading Initiative (2006) cited cases of "audit fraud" and declared a "growing crisis in ethical trade auditing." The FLA has even moved away from its original monitoring model—calling it an "inadequate tool to create sustainable change in working conditions"—to emphasize "capacity-building" at the factory level (Fair Labor Association 2007).

In general, the academic research paints a mixed picture of whether voluntary labor codes of conduct are actually being implemented or are merely facades decoupled from shop-floor practices. For instance, while Stephen Frenkel (2001) found that Chinese footwear firms producing for two major brands were largely in compliance with the basic workplace standards set by those companies, Niklas Egels-Zanden's (2007) study of Chinese toy factories found *no* factories (out of nine studied) in compliance with voluntary standards for working hours, and less than half in compliance with standards for labor contracts (namely, that contracts exist), minimum wage, and overtime. Neither is it clear that sustained monitoring significantly improves the rates of compliance. In one innovative study utilizing Nike's internal ratings of factories, Richard Locke, Fei Qin, and Alberto Brause (2007) found that even as Nike engaged in a great deal of monitoring, the vast majority of factories (around 80 percent) failed to improve over time, and some actually experienced a decline in their compliance rating. It is clear that monitoring has not brought about radical shifts in production practices, although it may be improving compliance with basic health and safety measures as well as preventing the most egregious forms of physical abuse.

When it comes to empowering workers and altering the power relationships in the workplace, researchers agree that voluntary standards have proven useful only in rare circumstances. Frenkel (2001) saw no evidence of collective worker empowerment, and Ngai-Ling Sum and Pun Ngai (2005) found evidence that voluntary codes of conduct are sometimes used *against* workers, as a tool of managerial discipline. In a few cases in Latin America, companies' engagement with voluntary standards and the work of the Worker Rights Consortium (a voluntary club with universities as members) facilitated the recognition of independent unions in factories in Mexico (Kukdong, producing for Nike and Reebok) and Guatemala (Choishin, producing for Liz Claiborne). But the success of these campaigns depended on a rare confluence of factors, including grassroots union movements, strong cross-border civil society linkages, and international trade pressures on domestic governments (Rodríguez-Garavito 2005; Seidman 2007; US/LEAP 2003). Without these sorts of other factors, it is doubtful that voluntary standards will have an empowering effect for workers. Like the rise of human resource management in the previous century, the recent rise of voluntary regulation of labor conditions is more likely to introduce technocratic solutions than to alter fundamental power differentials.

Why have the impacts of voluntary labor standards programs been so limited? The answer appears to be twofold. First, there are limits rooted in the fundamental design of standards in programs like the FLA, SAI, and Ethical Trading Initiative. The club standards appear to be too circumscribed to solve the deeply entrenched problems of sweatshops in this sector. In particular, voluntary programs failed to tackle the inequalities and price pressures that underlie many sweatshop practices and labor rights abuses. Participation in voluntary programs has not for the most part required companies to restructure their sourcing practices or explore alternatives to lean-and-mean production models. Instead, membership has only required a willingness to *pay attention* to the dark side of this model and occasionally try to persuade suppliers to rectify problems. Apparel production remains the terrain of cutthroat competition among contract factories, and major brands have continued to demand low prices and quick turnaround times on orders. These pressures facilitate sweating the workforce—by imposing long but unstable work hours (including forced overtime), intense discipline, downward pressure on piece rates, and cheating on wages (Bonacich and Appelbaum 2000; Piore 1997). Even where conditions have improved, these pressures have occasionally led to backsliding or high-standards suppliers losing business.

Second, although they are in theory strong-to-medium sword programs, some weaknesses in these programs' monitoring and enforcement *in practice* appear to have hampered their achievements. Part of the problem lies with the auditing process. Early critics of factory monitoring showed that some auditors lacked training in labor relations or occupational health and safety, and questioned their ability to collect accurate data from workers due to cultural differences and status inequalities (Esbenshade 2004; Labor Rights in China 1999; O'Rourke 2002). While some local nonprofits have entered the field in order to counteract these tendencies, and other auditors have upgraded their competencies, questions remain about whether auditors are missing (or turning a blind eye to) actual practices. Recent exposés in *Business Week* and the *Financial Times* have shown how factory managers—in China in particular—have become more sophisticated at falsifying records of wages and working hours, coaching workers to give the "correct" answers, and even bribing auditors directly (Secrets, Lies, and Sweatshops 2006; Foster and Harney 2005). Of course, even rudimentary and flawed monitoring turns up frequent violations of company and association codes of conduct. Yet many observed problems go unresolved. The FLA and SAI seem reluctant to brandish their swords in response to violations. The FLA has endorsed the compliance programs of companies even when independent monitors found numerous problems in their factories. SAI's certification of hundreds of factories in China, where wage and hour laws are routinely flouted and freedom of association is problematic, suggests that this program has set the bar fairly low, serving as less of a mandarin badge of honor and more of a signal that a factory is not among the worst in the industry.

Some have argued that voluntary labor standards could have consequences that are unintended and *harmful*, by disrupting markets, artificially inflating the price of labor, and reducing employment levels (Bhagwati 2004). Again, the evidence to evaluate these contentions broadly is not currently available, but proponents of this view have been unable to point to cases in which employment has declined as a result of voluntary labor standards. One of the only empirical studies to address this question examined wages and employment in Indonesian factories, and found that sectors subject to antisweatshop pressures did experience wage gains that outpaced those in other sectors (in part because they started at low levels), but these were *not* offset by declines in employment (Harrison and Scorse 2006). More broadly, it appears that voluntary standards have rarely had a big enough impact to generate either especially positive or negative effects.

Conclusion

This chapter has examined the formation and operation of voluntary labor standards systems for apparel, footwear, and similar consumer products. I have shown that the club approach usefully describes some of the processes through which firms develop an interest in associations for monitoring and certifying labor conditions. In some instances, however, this interest is not sufficient to generate robust voluntary programs—as demonstrated by the failed clubs in the wake of the El Monte incident. Attempts to protect their reputation and gain credibility for their claims did underlie the work of companies like Liz Claiborne, Reebok, Nike, and Toys"R"Us in developing the FLA and SAI. On the other hand, absent the work of the U.S. government and several NGOs, it is not clear that these programs would have come into existence. This serves as a reminder of the importance of embedding the club approach in a broader account of the political and institutional terrain.

It is also critical to take the politicized character of labor standards systems seriously for understanding their consequences. The analysis of firm participation showed that social movement pressure was a crucial determinant of participation in MSIs. Although it is not possible to make definitive conclusions about the impacts of these systems, it is clear that the mere existence of voluntary standards does not automatically translate into large-scale changes in working conditions or respect for labor rights.

Clearly, improving global labor conditions is a complex and power-laden problem. In this respect, the sweatshop case resembles the case of conflict diamonds analyzed in chapter 5. Both deal with problems that are intertwined with extreme inequality and domestic politics in developing countries. Similarly, the forestry case analyzed by Cashore and colleagues (2006) includes a recognition that even with the growth of a respected forest certification program, the problem of illegal logging remains severe. These and other lines of research remind us of the limits of voluntary programs.

Analytically, the sweatshop and conflict diamond cases also illustrate the importance of social movement pressure as an impetus for firms to begin to consider forming or joining a club. In fact, across a number of cases of clubs concerned with labor, human rights, or the environment (see chapters 7 and 9), the catalyzing force of social movements—in the form of protest, community organizing (e.g., over the "right to know" about toxins), and NGO-sponsored media campaigns—can hardly be understated. While firms may frame their decisions to participate in voluntary programs as a matter of ethical commitments, these cases (and the club approach developed in this book) serve as a reminder that such decisions are most commonly rooted in concrete threats to firms' reputation, revenue, and autonomy. In a slightly different fashion, chapter 8 on the IASB also lends weight to this point.

The role of government in forming voluntary clubs is apparent not only in the Clinton administrations' work in creating the FLA but also in the chapters 10 and 11 on the EPA. Clearly, the U.S. government in the 1990s was a major source of voluntary programs—sowing the seeds of voluntary regulation in a variety of industries and policy domains. On the other hand, in the case of labor standards, the government played more of a facilitating role—convening and supporting voluntary programs, but not operating them directly, as the EPA does.

Finally, the case of labor standards—like that of forestry (Cashore, Auld, and Newsom 2004)—features competition among multiple programs (the FLA, the SAI, Worldwide Responsible Apparel Production, and the Worker Rights Consortium). Theorizing this type of regulatory competition among private initiatives is a crucial task for the literature on voluntary programs. Does the sort of competition, conflict, and mutual adjustment observed in these cases water down or ratchet up compliance? To date, few have provided empirical purchase on this question, even though a variety of sectors (forestry, apparel, coffee, and organics) feature competing clubs.

Appendix 6.1

Stage 1 Model—Targeting Analysis: Negative Binomial Regression of the Intensity of Social Movement Pressure on the Fifty Largest U.S. Apparel, Textile, and Footwear Firms

DV: number of years firms were targeted by social movements (1993–2000)	
Constant	−2.5510*
	1.3896
Major brand investment (1 = yes, 0 = no)	1.1103**
	.4199
Recognition for business reputation (1 = yes, 0 = no)	.7284+
	.4956
Log assets (average 1993–2000)	.2604+
	.2025
Financial performance (ROA, average 1993–2000)	−1.9587
	2.9930
Retailer	−.2554
	.4014
Textile manufacturer	−1.1631
	1.1345
Headquarters in CA or NY (loci of movements)	.3731
	.4240
N	50
Likelihood ratio Chi-squared test	32.72***
Alpha	.3112*
	(.2155)
Pseudo-R^2	.1757

Notes:

1. Estimated SEs in parentheses.

$^+$p < .10   *p < .05   **p < .01   ***p < .001   (one-tailed tests)

2. The measure of social movement pressure analyzed in this chapter (see table 6.4) is based on the residuals from this model, which regresses the number of years that companies were targeted by social movements (between 1993 and 2000) on indicators of reputational capital and controls for firm size (log assets), financial performance (return on assets), sector (retail, textile, and others), and location in California or New York (loci of antisweatshop activism). The residuals (the difference between the observed amount of social movement targeting and the values predicted by this model) are then used as a predictor in table 6.4.

7

Voluntary Agreements and the Shipping Industry

Elizabeth R. DeSombre

There are numerous externalities from the global transport of goods on the oceans. Shipping uses fossil fuels that produce air pollution and contribute to climate change. Ship operations create solid waste that is most easily disposed of overboard if nothing prevents such dumping. Water taken on as ballast in one part of the world and deposited in another moves species from an ecosystem where they may be kept in check to one in which they may become invasive. Accidents from the transport of oil also deposit oil in the oceans annually, and shipping generally results in additional ocean pollution from operational discharges.

These potential problems are made worse by the globalization of international shipping and, especially, the open ship registration system. All ships have to have a nationality, and for most of history the nationality of the shipowner has determined the state of registry of the ship. A ship must follow the domestic and international rules adopted by the state in which it is registered. Beginning nearly a century ago, Panama, followed especially by other states in the post–World War II era, began to allow ship registration by nonnationals. Open registry states (also called flags of convenience) allow ship registration by nonnationals, and compete to keep environmental, safety, and labor standards low in order to promise low costs to shipowners who register in these locations. These states can earn significant portions of their national income through registration fees and taxes paid by ships registered by foreigners, and thus seek to lure ship registrations by promising shipowners that their costs will decrease if they register in open registries (DeSombre 2006).

This process has essentially caused a race to the bottom in international ship standards. Most ships engaged in international trade—two-thirds of container vessels, and an even greater number of those that transport passengers—are now registered in open registries (Institute of

Shipping Economics and Logistics 2004), with a consequent decrease in the standards that the ships are required to follow. More important, as new international rules are adopted, open registries may refuse to take them on (causing one scholar to characterize rules as "stuck in the mud" [Zarsky 2002]), ships may change registries from those that accept these rules to those that do not, and new registries open as the standards of older registries rise, creating a system where there is always an option to escape international rules.

States have been reluctant to mandate increased standards for ships. Although traditional maritime states decry the "unfair" competition from open registry ships that do not adopt high standards, they benefit from the cheap goods made possible by international trade conducted on low-cost, low-standard ships. The open registry states themselves receive all the positive utility of ship registrations that flow only to them, whereas any negative utility (say, from environmental disasters, globally decreased wages, or increased risk in working conditions) is shared internationally.

In the case of shipping, the most effective efforts to raise standards on ships have come through the benefits from which low-standard ships or ship registries are excluded. The creation of benefits to which shipowners desire access makes use of exclusion to keep those out that are not willing to accept higher standards voluntarily. The process by which these mechanisms of exclusion operate transform the locus of regulation to focus on a resource (such as a market or a set of services) that are not rival in the way that the resource itself might have been.

The shipping case has a number of voluntary clubs that differ across the dimensions examined on this project. Their standards are of varying strength between reasonably strong labor standards at one end of a spectrum to weaker codes of conduct for ships transmitting certain types of chemicals. Similarly, the enforcement mechanisms vary in strength as well, from document inspection as a part of every transaction for the selling of seafood to self-reported information on shipping practices.

Another important dimension on which these clubs vary is the strength of the benefit gained from membership (or conversely, lost by a lack of membership or noncompliance with membership requirements). In some cases, clubs may almost cease to seem voluntary if the benefit they provide is so central to the industry in which they operate—as can be the case with classification or access to markets for fishery products—that a lack of membership or compliance may undermine one's ability to operate successfully. Other benefits are clearly weaker, such as the reputational advantage that may—or may not—accrue to those listed on a Web site as having provided information about their safety practices.

The programs described in this chapter are voluntary to the extent that no ship registry need ever take on these standards, and ships need only to uphold the standards required of them by their registries. The challenge represented in this issue area is to persuade registry states to adopt these international standards or persuade ships whose registries have not done so to take them on voluntarily. The creation of clubs—of states or ships that have voluntarily accepted these standards—whose members receive benefits from belonging has been the key to increasing the number of actors bound by existing international rules.

The number and variation of clubs within the sector of ocean shipping offers the opportunity to evaluate how the voluntary nature of clubs intersects with the strength of both the standards themselves and their enforcement mechanisms. Perhaps not surprisingly, in the shipping case there seems to be some correlation among the strength in standards, the strength in the benefit from accepting those standards, and the strength or reliability of enforcement mechanisms. In a sector otherwise characterized by the kind of race to the bottom that others hypothesize but rarely find in practice, these clubs, largely voluntary, have been the only successful mechanisms at raising environmental, safety, and labor standards on ships globally.

Ships and the Variety of Voluntary Clubs

At the outset it is worth noting that the issue area of international shipping provides some complications for the voluntary clubs framework examined in this volume, and requires some choices about how to characterize activities and options for ships. To the extent that the voluntary clubs in this book are those in which members agree to go "beyond compliance," all the clubs discussed here are voluntary, but that distinction is less clear for international rules than domestic ones.

In the international arena, adopting standards collectively negotiated or put forth by international organizations is voluntary on the part of states (although once adopted these rules are legally binding). Since ships are only required to undertake the domestic and international obligations put forth by their flag states, and it is perfectly legal to choose flag states that specifically avoid taking on these international standards, the standards examined here *are* voluntary. But almost all the standards discussed in this chapter came about (regardless of how they are implemented) through a process of intergovernmental negotiation, which is not frequently the kind of standard considered to be voluntary.

A related issue is the role that domestic law plays. Ships are only bound by the laws of the state in which they register, but states that they visit or conduct business with can impose requirements that those ships have to meet—that they must follow international fishery rules in order to off-load their catches, say, or must have certain safety equipment to be allowed to enter (or leave) a port. Technically all these rules are voluntary since ships do not have to sell in those markets or visit those ports, but they come with the enforcement mechanisms of the state and an element of coercion, which is a far cry from what we see in many voluntary clubs.

Within the broader issue area of standards on ships, there are a large number of voluntary standards that are available within clublike organizations. Several categories of these clubs are examined here. The most significant are certification for labor standards offered by a global labor union and fishing restrictions under regional fishery management organizations. There are also a number of industry-led clubs, from classification societies and protection and indemnity insurance clubs (and clubs of clubs for both these organizations) whose members apply higher safety and environmental standards on ships than they might otherwise be required to, to organizations of industry groups that vow that their shipping of dangerous substances is subject to higher safety standards than otherwise required.

Discussion of each set of clubs begins with an overview of the actors that can be club members, the costs to those actors of joining the club, the benefits to them for joining, and the positive externalities that result from actors joining the club in question. Also considered are the strength of the club standards and the enforcement mechanisms to ensure that club members implement the requirement of the clubs.

The International Transport Workers Federation and Labor Standards

Among the most interesting sets of voluntary standards in the shipping case are those created by the International Transport Workers Federation (ITF), a global labor union that addresses shipping issues. The ITF has created a club of ships that have adopted high labor standards in return for unfettered access to ship services in port. Potential members of this club are individual ships (or more accurately, their owners, although a given owner can enroll one ship in the relevant club while leaving others outside—a strategy that is sometimes pursued). The costs to the ships are high: the increased labor standards, wages, and fees paid to the club can double the labor costs on ships. The social benefits of the ITF's club are greater labor rights and higher wages for ship workers, and an external organization that can intercede on behalf of seafarers.

The set of labor standards discussed here were created by the ITF for several reasons: to protect ship workers from exploitative labor practices, raise labor standards and wages worldwide, and increase the costs to ships of registering in flags of convenience in order to drive these ships back to registering in traditional maritime states, thereby increasing opportunities for ship workers (the ITF's membership) in these countries. This latter hope has not come to fruition, but the others have indeed been realized. Shipowners take on the set of standards offered by the ITF because the retaliation if they do not, or if they do not live up to the standards they have accepted, can be extremely costly, depending on the areas of the world in which they choose to do business.

The ITF flag of convenience campaign offers shipowners who agree to certain international standards a "collective agreement" between the shipowner and the ITF, which then gives the ship a blue (or green, depending on the process by which the agreement is negotiated) certificate, attesting to its acceptance of these standards. The collective agreement covers such things as duration of labor, hours of duty, wages (laying out a specific scale of acceptable minimum wages), medical attention, insurance and compensation, food and accommodation, safety, and the rights of seafarers to join unions (International Transport Workers Federation 2001). Most collective agreements are actually between the national union of the state where the shipowner is a citizen (rather than where the ship is registered) and the ship, though the ITF examines these agreements to make sure that they conform to ITF standards. In cases where there is no appropriate or available national union, the ITF can negotiate and sign agreements with the ship operators.

The standards contained in the collective agreement are predominantly derived from existing international agreements on labor and safety, under the International Maritime Organization and the International Labor Organization. The wage rates that must be paid on a ship in order to meet the ITF requirements of the collective agreement have traditionally been determined by the ITF alone, through a decision-making process within its Fair Practices Committee, although more recently the ITF has created a parallel process in which some shipowner organizations have collectively negotiated the benchmark wage that will be used for agreements with their ships.

A shipowner who signs an ITF-approved collective agreement indicates an intention to be bound by these obligations with respect to the specified ship, which includes allowing the organization to inspect its ships, and allowing the appointment of an onboard safety representative, who can inspect the ship and investigate accidents without fear of reprisal. In addition, the shipowner agrees to contribute an amount of money per seafarer annually to the Seafarers' International Assistance, Welfare, and Protection Fund (usually referred to simply as the "welfare fund"). Currently, the required contribution to the welfare fund is $230 per seafarer. The money in this fund is used to finance the flags of convenience campaign, including the inspection of ships, so the system pays for itself.

All seafarers on the ship must be enrolled in an ITF-affiliate union (and if a suitable union is not available, the shipowner must pay to enroll them in the Special Seafarer's Section of the ITF, which acts as a union for those for whom there are no ITF-affiliated national unions), and the shipowner agrees to pay the union or ITF contributions for the seafarer. Moreover, if the ship has not previously been operating under a collective agreement and has paid wages below the ITF minimum, the ship operator must agree to contribute "back pay." This pay is calculated as the differential between the rate of pay previously in effect and the higher ITF scale for the time from when the seafarer signed on board the ship. This money is collected by the ITF and given to the individual seafarers (DeSombre 2006).

As suggested already, the club standards are strong, and meeting them is costly and difficult for shipowners. It is interesting to note, however, that one potential side effect has been to raise labor standards and wages even on ships that are not a part of the club. Shipowners who prefer not to negotiate ITF collective agreements but want high-quality ship labor must pay the prevailing wage for skilled workers—a wage that has increased because of the number of ships that do have ITF collective agreements. The benefits to shipowners are nevertheless reasonably high, or more accurately, the costs of not joining the club are high for ships that travel to ports with a strong ITF presence.

The benefits to the shipowners who accept the club standards are high but variable; it is not that club membership entitles you to something but rather that the lack of club membership comes with the risk that your ships will be subject to a work boycott in port. Such a boycott is not certain (although there are some ports in which it is more likely than in others), so if a ship never happened on an ITF inspector who chose to call for a labor action, the shipowner would not have gained a material benefit from club membership.

Enforcement is undertaken by ITF inspectors. Ships that have collective agreements have been given a certificate, indicating that the workers on the ship will be afforded a specific set of international labor protections, regardless of those mandated by the vessel flag state. ITF inspectors seek to board a flag of convenience–registered ship when it is in port and ask to see its certificate. If there is any reason to question whether the ship is upholding the relevant standards, ITF inspectors can look at its books or question the crew. In addition, they may respond to complaints by workers on the ship who indicate that their rights under the collective agreements are not being upheld.

If a ship does not have a certificate, it is given the opportunity to agree at that point to uphold the required standards. If the ship does not have an ITF-approved collective agreement and refuses to agree to ITF demands, the organization attempts to convince crew members to leave, or dockworkers to refuse to unload or service the vessel (Northrup and Scrase 1993). (If the ship's officers refuse to let it be boarded, the ITF can similarly encourage a work boycott.) Because the type of agreement offered when a ship is boarded in port requires even higher wages and more stringent standards than those entered into when a ship is not a target of industrial action, shipowners have an incentive to negotiate agreements before they are targeted for action.

What effect has the ITF process had on the standards that ships take on and uphold? Northrup and Rowan (1983) suggest that the threat of ITF boycotts and the associated campaign to sway public opinion "have forced FOC countries to raise their standards, to devote more attention and legislation to safety practices, and have greater concern with the rights, training, and well-being of seafarers." They claim as well that the ITF's work has influenced open registries to move their standards towards International Labor Organization levels of labor protections.

These collective agreements have been influential. According to the ITF, approximately 30 percent of ships flagged in open registries currently have collective agreements with the ITF, covering more than ninety-five thousand seafarers. As of 2004, there were more than five thousand total collective agreements of this type, up from fifteen hundred in 1990 (DeSombre 2006). Although it is impossible to know for sure, it is likely that the ships that have negotiated collective agreements with the ITF are living up to much of what is required of them, since the ITF inspects frequently and provides avenues to hear complaints from ship workers.

Regional Fishery Management Organizations and Trading Clubs

Some regional fishery management organizations (RFMOs) have created trading clubs in which states (and ships) take on fishery management obligations in return for market access for their fish products. For the most part the club members are flag states: the standard way that the club is enforced is to permit only imports or transshipments of fish products from vessels flagged in registries that accept the relevant rules (and when individual vessels can document that their catches followed these rules). But these mechanisms also explicitly provide for ships whose registries have not joined the relevant agreements to do so on their own; as long as they can demonstrate that they are following the rules of the RFMO, they gain access to the markets of member states. The costs to a flag state of joining the club is that its vessels are legally obligated to follow the rules set by the fishery organization; because some ships seek registries specifically to avoid being bound by such rules, membership may cost flag states some registry revenue. The ships registered in that state are also limited in the amount of fish they can catch. The benefits to the flag states are that they might be able to attract registration from ships that want access to the major markets for fish products, and the benefits to the ships are that they can sell their fish in these markets at a higher price than the fish would fetch elsewhere. The beneficial social externality created by this club is the increased protection of the fishery that, if successful, eventually benefits those who own or operate fishing vessels, because they can continue to harvest the resource on which they depend.

One of the major reasons fishing vessels register in open registries is to seek out a registry that has not joined an RFMO for the region or species of fish that the vessel operator seeks to pursue. In reaction, a number of RFMOs focusing on high-value or highly migratory high seas fish species have created what amounts to a trading club in which only vessels that follow the rules of the fishing organization can sell or transship the fish they caught in states that are members of the RFMOs.

Although the clubs were instituted by the RFMOs themselves, and member states are legally bound (to slightly varying extents depending on the particular RFMO) to implement their policies, the incentive for creating such a program came from the fishers within registries that accept the relevant fishery regulations. These fishers suffered from the fishing done by vessels outside the regulations. The extent of fishing outside the agreements could increase the availability of a given fish product and thus drive down its price, meaning that those who observed the restrictions would catch a smaller amount of fish and earn less money for it. Most important, this unregulated fishing meant that the restrictions that fishers observed would not have the intended effect: fishing done outside the regulatory process would undermine the ability of those who did restrict their fishing activity to have a beneficial effect on the health of the fish stocks. Changing the point of regulation, to create a club good, was the solution that could provide a sufficient incentive for unregulated fishers to change their behavior (DeSombre 2005a).

The significance of the provision that allows individual fishing vessels to document that they meet RFMO rules if their flag state has not accepted these rules is not clear. There is no evidence yet of individual ships taking on the rules when their registry states have not, and it seems likely that the RFMOs have included this provision primarily to avoid running afoul of international trade rules. But at least technically, individual fishing vessels may choose to accept higher standards than they would otherwise be required to, in order to gain membership in the trading club, and flag states are encouraged to take on standards they previously had not, so that their fishing vessels can gain access to markets for fishery products.

While there are a number of RFMOs that are at different points in the process of creating trading clubs, two examples here will suffice. The first is the International Commission for the Conservation of Atlantic Tunas, which regulates tuna and tunalike fishes in the Atlantic Ocean. The second is the commission associated with the Convention for the Conservation of Antarctic Marine Living Resources (CCAMLR), which has focused, in its clublike regulatory process, on Patagonian toothfish.

The process works via catch documentation that accompanies traded fish from the regulatory area (or landed in or transshipped through member states) to allow member states to distinguish between fish caught legally and within the regulatory framework, and those caught by ships not bound by regulations. This documentation process is followed by a requirement by the relevant commission that members refuse to accept imports of fish from ships or states that have kept themselves outside the regulatory framework.

The recent trend has been to augment these measures by a vessel monitoring system that allows flag states (at a minimum) or fisheries commissions (more intrusively) to keep track of where ships are fishing. One of the immediate aftereffects of the catch documentation process was that a statistically unlikely number of catches were reported as taking place just outside the regulatory area, without good evidence of where they actually were caught. To address this potential problem, CCAMLR required that as of 2001, satellite tracking equipment be installed on ships fishing for toothfish to enable their flag states to track their location, to ensure that they are fishing legally. But since this mechanism depends on flag state oversight, it has been subject to abuse. Those member states with little regulatory oversight capacity lack either the will or ability to track their vessels. More controversial has been the question of whether this tracking would be augmented with a centralized electronic tracking mechanism that would allow the organization to track vessels. This process has now been implemented preliminarily within CCAMLR.

The standards under the RFMOs are reasonably strong; states must agree to collectively restrict their catches of fish (and follow other restrictions on such things as gear and seasons) and take responsibility for the actions of their fishing vessels. For individual fishing vessels the standards, especially in comparison to not joining the club, are quite high: instead of being allowed to catch as much fish as they can, in whatever manner they choose, they are severely restricted in their catches.

The benefits to the owners and operators of fishing vessels are quite high: they gain access to a much more lucrative market for their catches. Fish caught outside the documentation schemes do find a market, but fetch a price at a minimum 20 to 40 percent lower (and sometime even more so) than fish caught within the cooperative agreements (DeSombre 2005a). This latter process is what provides the incentives for ships or states to agree to take on the rules in question; fishers can choose to fish outside the international regulatory process (and registries can intentionally and legally avoid joining), but if they do so, they will have difficulty finding a market for their fish, and will earn less money for it. The benefits to the registry states are harder to quantify. In some cases, flag states that joined RFMOs and/or began to accept international fishing rules found that fishing vessels left their registry (DeSombre 2006). Whether that departure, and the accompanying loss of registry revenue, is balanced by increased registrations by those who desire access to the major fish markets is hard to tell. The enforcement of the mechanism relies on the power of the states in which it operates. Inspectors at ports check for documentation on each shipment of fish that is landed; the new requirement for satellite tracking increases the ability to check that fish were caught where fishers indicate. Moreover, this documentation is required for the sale of the fish in question, and is therefore inspected by those who buy and sell fish, and checked against RFMO records.

There have been several notable results from these programs as implemented by the International Commission for the Conservation of Atlantic Tunas and CCAMLR. First, in both cases, a number of flag of convenience states whose vessels have been excluded from markets under this system have either agreed to join the RFMOs or at least to cooperate with them. Second, there is some evidence that ships are changing registry either to a registry that has joined the RFMOs for the area/species they wish to fish or, in the case of those that do not want to be bound by the rules and whose flag states have newly joined RFMOs, to new registries that are not members. The ultimate effect—the increased protection of the fishery resource itself—is harder to measure, but there do appear to be fewer vessels fishing in the regulatory areas without having taken on the relevant rules.

Classification and Insurance Clubs

Technically, classification (the certification by an outside organization that ships are constructed to specific standards) and insurance are voluntary for ships. In practice, most states (even flags of convenience, although not all of them) require ships to be classed in order to register, and port states can require classification if a ship is to visit a port. Protection and indemnity (P&I) insurance is also technically voluntary, but becoming expected or required in certain circumstances. In addition, clubs to provide these services also organize themselves into voluntary, higher-standard clubs of clubs.

For classification and P&I insurance clubs, the potential members are ships that are classed or insured by a particular organization. The costs are moderate: they need to meet the basic safety and environmental standards mandated by the organization, which are standards most ships meet. On the other hand, it is not difficult to find some organization that will be willing to class or a group that will insure a ship. The benefits are significant but basic: having P&I insurance and classification may be required for entry into certain ports; at a minimum, not having them will make a ship an increased target for port state inspection. The positive social externalities are that ships with classification and P&I insurance are less likely than those without to experience a major disaster on the oceans, causing harm to seafarers and the environment; if these disasters do happen, P&I insurance will help pay for the costs and damages that arise. In addition, classification and insurance decrease the work for port inspectors, who do not have to ascertain for themselves that ships have the required equipment and processes.

For the clubs of higher-standard classification societies and P&I clubs, the targets are the initial clubs themselves; those with higher standards are brought into a group that is able to trumpet these higher standards and reap the reputational benefits. The costs to the first-order clubs of joining are fairly low; they include increased inspection and oversight, and the possible loss of income that comes from having a smaller pool of ships to draw their membership from. Conversely, however, the benefits include an increased attractiveness to ships that want the reputational benefits (and a decrease in the likelihood of inspection and detention) that comes from belonging to a high-quality club; they also include the ability to raise standards without having to fear the loss of ship registrations from doing so unilaterally. In the case of P&I insurance, to the extent that attracting high-quality ships decreases the likelihood of a shipping disaster, membership in a club of quality clubs can have a cost savings if there are fewer accidents that require payment from the P&I club. The positive social externalities from these second-order clubs are similar to those from the first-order clubs: less harm to seafarers and the environment.

Both classification and P&I insurance are (by the definition used here) voluntary standards in their own right. They have clublike characteristics: a given classification society may refuse to class a ship that does not meet its standards, and because port inspectors can single ships out for inspection based on the detention record of ships classed by a given society, ships want to choose reputable classification societies if they hope to avoid being targeted for inspection. (And on the other end of the spectrum, what the European Union has called the "classification societies of convenience" [Moloney 1997] are the classification societies known for refusing to apply high standards.)

P&I clubs, as their name suggests, explicitly operate as clubs; a group of shipowners self-insures. In other words, shipowners put money into a collective fund from which each draws in case of an accident. Because it is the group that is responsible, shipowners only know in advance what proportion of the overall year's costs they will have to pay, but the actual amount depends on the extent to which shipowners collect from the fund during the year (Braithwaite and Drahos 2000). For that reason, shipowners within a P&I club have the incentive to admit only those to the club who do not pose a particularly high risk of accident or other liability. In order to make this determination, most club managers interview representatives of the shipowner, find out the credit rating of the owner, and gather information from current club members. Most also hire inspectors to inspect ships that are more than ten years old, and refuse to insure passenger ships, oil tankers, and bulk carriers that are not certified as complying with the International Maritime Organization's International Safety Management code (Bennett 2001).[1]

The second layer of voluntary clubs that the classification and insurance organizations themselves (rather than the ships or shipowners) participate in is also notable for the purposes of this volume. Classification societies and P&I insurance providers themselves have an incentive to distinguish themselves as providers of a reputable service, but cannot afford to do so unilaterally because the costs of the higher standards would make them noncompetitive unless these standards can be more widely applied and an advantage can accrue to those that adopt them. These processes have been done through the creation of clubs of high-standard classification societies or P&I clubs.

Classification societies are in competition with each other, based on reputation and cost. Those societies vying for higher status will take on stricter requirements and refuse to class questionable ships. But classification societies that raise their standards unilaterally are likely to lose business if there are other reputable societies that are still accepted by those that discriminate based on the classification society. The American Bureau of Shipping learned this lesson when it introduced stricter standards for tankers and bulk carriers before other high-standard societies did, and twenty tanker owners left the American Bureau of Shipping for other societies (DeSombre 2006). To raise the standards, the most reputable classification societies have banded together in the International Association of Classification Societies (IACS), whose member societies collectively class half of the world's ships. The IACS sets minimum standards that all member societies are required to accept (Braithwaite and Drahos 2000). The IACS audits its member societies to ensure reliability, and has maintained its prominent reputation by excluding member societies with poor records. For example, the IACS expelled Polish classification society Polski Rejestr Statkow after a ship it classed sank in a way that showed "serious shortcomings" (PRS Must Shake 2000).

P&I insurance clubs have also self-organized into the International Group of P&I Clubs. This club of clubs plays several functions, one of which is to serve as a clearinghouse for information. If a shipowner from one P&I club in the International Group applies to join a different club, the club it previously belonged to is obligated to tell the new club what the rates and performance of the ship were. Since nearly 90 percent of the new members in a club come from another club within the International Group, this policy can make it difficult to hide bad performance records by moving to a new club. P&I groups seek to become members of the International Group because of the reputational advantages that will allow them to seek high-quality ships for their group, especially as industry groups (discussed further below) have begun to require that members maintain P&I coverage with a member of the International Group (DeSombre 2006).

The first-order clubs apply moderately strong standards to ships concerning safety and environmental practices and equipment. For the ships, meeting these standards is (at least in the short run) considerably more costly than not meeting them, although the minimum standards for classification and insurance have become the industry standards (and most ships are built to these standards), so it is hard to consider them exceptional. The benefits from classification and P&I insurance include access to ports along with a decreased likelihood of inspection and detention. Most of the standards in question decrease the likelihood of disaster in the longer run, providing a cost advantage to ships. To that extent they may help shipowners implement their own long-term self-interest, when short-run incentives might otherwise have prevented it. The standards are enforced by inspections conducted by the classification societies and the P&I clubs (along with documentation that the ships need to provide).

The second-order clubs require that their member clubs increase standards above the minimum required for classification and P&I insurance. The costs to the member clubs are fairly low assuming that the club of clubs works. It is hardly any more difficult or expensive to require a high standard for classification than a low one; the cost would come if raising standards drove away ships from the societies. Some ships certainly do leave when a society raises its standards and joins a high-standard club of clubs. But the benefits are the attraction of new ships that want the advantages that being in a higher-standard club confers. The enforcement by the second-order clubs appears to be minimal; these clubs take the word of the member societies that they are implementing the higher standards they claim to have taken on.

Industry Self-governance Clubs

Among the weakest voluntary standards, both in terms of the standards themselves and their enforcement, are clubs created within functional segments of the shipping industry. These clubs have shipowners within a particular sector as their potential members. The costs to joining generally involve the costs of undergoing increased inspection and meeting the standards of the most demanding classification societies (although these standards differ only somewhat from lower-standard classification societies). The benefits are nebulous: the hope is that ships with membership in these industry clubs will be seen as safer ships on which to transport hazardous materials and will therefore be more likely to be hired (or hired at higher rates) than other ships. It is difficult to measure the extent to which this reputational effect is borne out in practice.

Beginning in the mid-1990s, as inspections of ships in port increased and held ships to stricter standards (and detained them if they had any egregious environmental or safety shortcomings), industry organizations created their own inspection systems and clubs of ships that agreed to take on higher-than-required environmental and safety standards. These are primarily undertaken by groups of companies responsible for shipping hazardous substances—such as chemicals or oil—to indicate that their members accept and implement high standards, or by groups of shipowners.

The producer organizations are run by segments of the industry. One such organization, the Oil Companies International Maritime Forum, "a voluntary association of oil companies having an interest in the shipment and terminalling of crude oil and oil products," formed in 1970 in the wake of the Torrey Canyon oil spill in response to increasing public concern about oil pollution. In 1993, the organization created the Ship Inspection Report Program. This program mandates a uniform inspection process in which information is collected electronically and made available to member organizations (as well as governmental organizations such as port state inspectors and international agreements about inspectors) so they can ascertain how well maintained and managed a given tanker is. The organization's membership currently stands at fifty-nine (OICMF 2007).

Another similar organization, the Chemical Distribution Institute, created an audit process for ships. This program does not give ships a passing or failing grade but rather makes available to those considering using shipping services the information about what equipment and procedures the ship has in place; this information is loaded into a Chemical Distribution Institute database that can be accessed by member organizations. Sixty-seven companies participate in this organization and its inspection system (CDI 2007). While ships may decide to participate in this audit process or not (and the results are publicly available), no ship is removed if it is found to be lacking.

Other such industry clubs are run by shipowners themselves. The two most prominent are designated by the types of ships operated. The International Association of Independent Tanker Owners (known as INTER-TANKO) provides a variety of services to its members, but the relevant ones for these discussions include requiring certain evidence that the ships are both safe and environmentally sound. Beginning in 1994 and 1995, ships of member states were required to be classed by the highest-ranked classification societies (Porter 1994), and to carry protection and indemnity pollution insurance for at least $500 million per tanker (Abrams 1994). The organization also required that ships met the International Ship Management Code requirements by 1998, whether or not these standards were required by the flag states. Ships must also have a "satisfactory oil pollution response plan." Most important, INTER-TANKO began to remove members that did not comply with these new rules, beginning with the Adriatic Tankers Shipping Company, which refused to give evidence of the classification or insurance status of its twelve ships (Porter 1995b).

A similar organization, the International Organization of Dry Cargo Ship Owners (called INTERCARGO), has undertaken a similar process of raised standards for members, so that membership would be seen as "a seal of quality operation" (Porter 1995a). Membership guidelines specify that members must have "quality ships and operation." The organization explored setting up its own inspection system (Bray 1997), but appears not to have done so.

None of these clubs has especially strong standards, and the benefits to the club members, difficult to measure, are unlikely to be especially great. The clubs also have fairly weak enforcement, primarily relying on self-reporting from the ships. These reports are, however, backed in part by classification, and are examined by those running the club, so they are not entirely meaningless. The clubs do vary a bit in terms of the penalties for meeting the standards: INTERTANKO has been willing to remove ships from its organization, while the others have not as yet done so.

These types of inspections processes give those that use the services of ships the opportunity to choose ships to use that are likely to be in good condition and that are unlikely to be stopped by one of the other inspection processes like port state control, and gives shipowners the ability to advertise their ships as being of better quality and meeting higher standards than the competition.

The Shipping Clubs in the Model

Because there are many different programs under which ships or states can take on voluntary standards in the context of global shipping, they provide the opportunity to ascertain how these different programs fit within the framework this book puts forth, and analyze any patterns that emerge from the variety of different programs within this one issue area.

How do the various voluntary standards taken on within the context of ships fare in the model laid out in this project? A preliminary effort to characterize the strength of the different voluntary standards and their enforcement is represented in table 7.1. Some characterizations prove difficult: there is no absolute clear line between stringent and lenient

Table 7.1
Typology of shipping industry voluntary programs

	Enforcement standards		
Club standards	Weak sword	Medium sword	Strong sword
Lenient standards	SIRE, CDI Int'l Grp P&I clubs INTERCARGO	IACS INTERTANKO Classification → P&I clubs →	
Stringent standards			RFMOs ITF

standards. For the purposes of the categorization above, the cost and difficulty of meeting standards is used to classify them as weak or stringent. Although the categorization is not made in a relative manner, if the majority of ships follow a set of standards (although few are required to do so by law), it is considered as evidence that the standards are weak. Those that are characterized as stringent are those that most ships have not taken on and that require a substantial cost to implement. That line is not easy to draw, and many of the standards characterized here as lenient might better belong in a middle category were one to exist.

Similarly, this case problematizes the question of what constitutes enforcement, partly because the types of voluntary standard programs in the shipping industry differ from the examples that underlie the initial conceptualization of voluntary standards within the framework. It is useful to consider both the costs to not meeting the standards (or conversely, the advantage that accrues to club members and not to those outside the club) and the manner in which it is determined whether ships or states are meeting the standards.

Most of the programs here are considered to be relatively weak; in no cases are ships or states asked to go beyond internationally agreed-on rules. The industry-run groups (the Ship Inspection Report Program, the Chemical Distribution Institute, INTERCARGO, and INTERTANKO) as described above simply require that shipowners agree to undergo regular inspections and meet a set of standards that classification societies require; likewise, the classification societies and insurance organizations hold ships to standards that most shipping destinations require or request. More stringent are the Regional Fishery Management Organization standards that limit catches of fish in ways that would be unlimited to those that did not take on those standards, and the International Transport Workers Federation labor standards that many ships have not otherwise met, and that include paying union fees for ship workers.

The major difference across programs comes in terms of the strength of the enforcement mechanisms. Most of the industry-run clubs rely primarily on self-reporting and have little in the way of sanctions for members that are not fulfilling their obligations. The main consequence to those participating in the programs listed in the upper-left section of table 7.1 (which includes most of the corporate programs) if they do not fulfill their obligations is that they cannot list their names on the Web site of the organization. It is difficult to measure the reputational boost that might accrue from the Web site listing, and therefore also difficult to determine the impact of no longer being listed. It is not always even clear that the organization would do anything of consequence on determining that ships are not meeting the standards. In addition, the information about whether ships are living up to the obligations or not is entirely self-reported.

The medium sword programs add some level of external inspection to the process; there are inspectors for both P&I clubs and classification societies. Classification societies and P&I insurance clubs on their own (the first-order clubs discussed above) can also be considered medium (or possibly even strong) enforcement on the same basis: they do inspections and can remove members that do not meet their standards. More important, the consequences of not upholding the standards accepted are more meaningful. If a ship does not receive classification or insurance many ports will not allow it to visit, and ship-run inspection systems single out ships without high-quality classification or insurance for additional scrutiny. The enforcement mechanisms for the IACS and INTERTANKO are not strong, but they do have strong sanctioning mechanisms that have actually been used to remove members that could not demonstrate that they were meeting club standards.

The only two strong sword programs are international fishery rules and those put forth by the ITF. Not only do both organizations have intrusive ways of making ships document that they are meeting the standards in question but the consequences of doing so are high: fish products will be refused access to markets, and port workers may refuse to unload or service ships in port.

It may not be surprising that the difficulty of required behavior change and strength of enforcement are strongly correlated. When ships gain a large benefit from being in the club, there is a strong incentive to have external validation that they are indeed meeting the membership criteria. The strongest are the labor standards overseen by the ITF; there is a clear external evaluation of the labor standards, and ships that do not live up to their agreements can suffer a strong penalty. Close in stringency to the ITF (such that it is unclear whether it belongs in the strong or medium category) is the documentation process for RFMOs. The sanctioning mechanisms are clear and severe (seafood not allowed to be landed or traded), and the inspection process happens by external actors at several stages of the transaction. The one factor that makes it weaker than ITF enforcement is the possibility that ships could falsify documentation at sea (though that becomes less likely as satellite tracking becomes more common) without being caught.

A critical aspect that arises in the shipping standards is the strength of the incentives to take on the standards in the first place. In the case of the ITF, for instance, the sanctioning mechanism for not living up to the relevant standards (the strong likelihood of a labor boycott in port) is also applied to those that do not agree to take on the standards in the first place, and is likely to be the primary reason that shipowners agree to adopt the standards. This observation is truer of fishing standards; those that do not agree to adopt them (even though international law does not require that they do) are the ones that experience the major sanctioning.

In addition, the shipping case shows the spectrum of strength of enforcement is not a clear continuum. INTERTANKO's willingness to expel members that would not provide information about whether they met the classification and insurance standards required should count as a strong sanctioning mechanism, but it is not clear that the organization meets the weaker requirements of "third party audits and public disclosure," since information about insurance and classification is not publicly available. In fact, in this example the tankers were not expelled for failing to live up to the standard but rather for not providing information to prove that they were.

What does the above categorization process suggest more broadly about voluntary standards and enforcement? Most significant, there appears to be a relationship between the strength of the standard and the strength of the enforcement process. That relationship makes intuitive sense: if actors are going to bear the cost of having to live up to difficult standards, they want to ensure that others that gain the advantages of being in the club are actually also living up to its obligations. Likewise, if they are going to take on strong standards, the payoff needs to be bigger than the simple reputation advantages from some of the weaker clubs.

Why Are Clubs Created?

The first part of the answer to the question, why clubs at all, has to do with the ability of club goods to avoid the participation problems that collective action poses. For those that want to manage a collective effort, such as one dealing with oil pollution in the ocean or the depletion of a fishery, the anarchic international system makes addressing these problems especially difficult. When states do not have to take on international rules and ships can choose to register in states that avoid these rules, those states that do choose high standards can have their effectiveness undermined by states that can't be excluded from the resource and whose use of it can diminish its use for others.

The same issue structure that makes these resource problems difficult to manage rules out the likely effectiveness of efforts to regulate what states or ships are allowed to do. For decades, scholars, politicians, and activists attempted to address international ship regulation by mandating the conditions under which states could run registries, the ships they could register, or the international rules they would have to follow, such as mandating a "genuine link" between ship and registry state (Dempsey and Helling 1980). But the international rules mandating a genuine link or particular standards are created by international rules. And since those rules are only binding on states that choose to take them on, the states running open registries did not. Because of that, international rules pertaining to ships are doomed to have free riders, and in a common pool resource structure, those free riders can undermine the effectiveness of the cooperation that takes place. From that perspective, an approach that transforms the regulated issue from a common pool resource to a club good provides a way around the problems that faced international cooperation.

For individual industry-based actors (shipowners, transport companies, etc.) that choose to implement high standards—either because they are forced by their flag state to do so or because they care about protecting the resource (such as a fishery) on which they depend—the club approach allows them to avoid the competitive disadvantage of competing with less-well-regulated actors in their industry. Fishers pushed the trading clubs, for example, because the fish they catch under restrictions will not have to compete in the market with those caught without restrictions. The system has even greater advantages if the process brings more ships under regulatory control and thereby better protects the resource on which these fishers hope to rely over the long term. The actors within the club benefit from both the exclusion it makes possible and the increased standards others take on in order to become part of the club.

Conclusion

The shipping industry experience analyzed in this chapter showed the initial weakness of standards imposed by governments. In efforts to escape mandated regulations, shipowners began to register ships in locations that would not impose stringent rules, and eventually the vast majority of commercial shipping worldwide was registered in open registries with low standards. The ability of shipowners to change their registration in order to evade international rules emphasizes the voluntary nature of these rules, and the extent to which international regulation is voluntarily adopted. It is the club aspect of efforts to persuade ships to adopt international standards that made the difference: shipowners or registry states could gain an advantage from meeting high standards, and those that did not could be kept from the benefits given to those that took on those standards. In the absence of high-standard clubs, shipowners were afraid that they would be disadvantaged by taking on high standards—and the high costs these standards entail—when other continued to avoid the rules. The creation of clubs made it possible for ships inside the high-standard clubs to gain benefits denied to those outside the clubs, thereby increasing the advantages to ships that took on the voluntary standards.

Voluntary clubs have had a major effect in raising standards on ships; indeed, they are just about the only thing that has succeeded in doing so. The standards vary in what they demand of members, what benefits members receive in return for joining, and how club standards are enforced, in ways that are roughly correlated with each other. These voluntary clubs have provided benefits for their members; ships that belong are less likely to be inspected or detained, less likely to suffer from a labor boycott, can gain access to markets for fish products, and may be more likely to be hired to transport goods. The positive social externalities that result include better-managed fisheries, less risk of environmental disaster at sea, and better labor protection and wages for seafarers worldwide.

This issue area provides support for the general proposition that voluntary regulations can make a crucial difference to individual behavior and a broader collective social good, and that a club framework can be a beneficial way to operate voluntary rules. In this issue the stringency of rules varies across a number of initiatives, as does the extent to which clubs are willing to self-police. Interestingly, the stricter the voluntary rules that clubs take on, the more strenuous the enforcement mechanisms as well. There is a clear logic for that relationship, and it will be interesting to determine the extent to which it holds across issue areas. Finally, an examination of voluntary clubs in the context of international shipping suggests that the distinction between what is voluntary and what is not is less clear on the international level than it might be in a domestic context. All international rules have some voluntary component, in that states choose whether to take them on. A club approach can persuade states to do so when they might not have initially intended to, or can persuade their substate actors to adopt rules beyond what the state might require, which provides fruitful avenues for increasing international standards.

8

Technical Standards as Public and Club Goods? Financing the International Accounting Standards Board

Tim Büthe

This chapter seeks to push the boundaries of the club approach by examining its analytic usefulness in a substantive realm to which it might not appear easily amenable: corporate financial reporting.[1] Most countries today recognize the legal construct known as a corporation and allow the shares in such "joint stock companies" to be publicly traded. To protect investors against (some of) the risks that arise from the information asymmetries between owners (shareholders) and the company's managers, most countries also require publicly traded companies to disclose at regular intervals certain information about the company's financial performance and health, using a specified set of accounting or financial reporting standards. These financial reporting standards specify, for instance, how research and development expenses, performance incentives for managers such as stock options, assets in an employee pension fund, and other particular types of transactions and events should be reflected in the accounts that firms make public in their financial statements. The consistent application of those standards is supposed to result in aggregate measures of the firm's value and financial position, which are accurate and easily comparable across firms (see Mattli and Büthe 2005a, 401; see also Solomons 1983). Since their use is mandated by laws or regulations, their "adoption among the targeted population" (Prakash and Potoski 2006b, 43–44) is not voluntary. Similarly, monitoring (most importantly the external audit of corporate accounts, in which the auditor certifies *inter alia* the proper use and compliance with the specified standard) is usually required by governments or financial market regulators. And enforcement is either conducted by public authorities or enabled by legal provisions (e.g., provisions for shareholder lawsuits).

Yet, while governments or public agencies require, monitor, and enforce compliance with financial reporting standards, they have in many countries delegated the rule making (i.e., the task of actually setting those standards) to private bodies. Most notable among those private bodies is the International Accounting Standards Board (IASB). Its standards are, as of March 2007, required for some or all corporate accounts by publicly traded companies in seventy-four countries, including all of the member states of the European Union. And after an increasingly public debate within their respective countries, the Securities and Exchange Commission of the United States (SEC) and the government of Japan in summer/fall 2008 announced plans for requiring the use of IASB standards by 2014. Numerous other countries allow the use of these standards in lieu of or in addition to national (domestic) standards and/ or have announced plans to switch to them.

The IASB is a private organization, based in London. Its fourteen board members and staff (most of them accounting experts from around the world, especially from the United States, the United Kingdom, and Commonwealth countries) develop International Financial Reporting Standards (IFRSs) and issue revisions of the International Accounting Standards developed by the IASB's predecessor.[2] The IASB's annual budget of £12–16 million ($20–30 million) has during its first seven years been financed overwhelmingly by voluntary contributions from the major international accounting firms and companies that are actual or potential users of IFRSs. The number of contributing companies has increased substantially since 2001, but remains small relative to the number of companies that use IFRSs (and includes some who do not [yet] use IFRS at all). Substantial funding from the private sector has thus enabled the IASB to produce financial reporting standards that appear to have first and foremost the characteristics of a public good: high-quality financial reporting standards boost public trust in financial markets in general, thereby increasing the amount of capital available for productive financial investments. They also foster the efficient operation of integrated financial markets by enhancing the international comparability of financial reports. These benefits are nonexcludable in that they accrue to all financial market participants and nonrival in consumption in that any one company's use of IFRSs does not diminish their beneficial usability for any other company.

While adoption and compliance with IFRSs is surely an interesting issue, it is the IASB's financing arrangement that raises the central analytic question that I seek to answer in this chapter: *Why would profit-maximizing corporations from around the world voluntarily finance a private international body that produces public goods?* I submit that club theory (Buchanan 1965; Casella 2001)—and specifically Potoski and Prakash's club approach—can help answer this question. As discussed in greater detail below, the club approach can help us understand the existence and financial viability of this global private standard setter by leading us to consider the possibility that public goods might merely be positive social externalities from the production of club goods.

This chapter consists of three sections after this introduction. In the first, I provide a brief overview of financial reporting standards, their political-economic importance, and the IASB as *the* source of international financial reporting standards. This empirical sketch motivates the central analytic question noted above. In the second section, I develop the analytical question in greater detail and put forth two possible explanations, building on the logic of hegemonic stability theory and the club approach, respectively. I derive from each of these theoretical perspectives a number of empirical implications. In the final section, I provide some tentative empirical tests of the hypotheses.

I seek to make three contributions to the current volume. First, I provide a case study of a private transnational "club" that exercises governance authority over an important aspect of global financial markets. Such a case study of global private politics is helpful to ground theorizing empirically. By exploring a case that goes beyond voluntary programs strictly speaking, it also allows us to explore the limits of the club approach. I discuss some of the implications of my case study for the club approach in the conclusion. Second, by focusing not just on the institutional structure of the IASB but also on some of the key actors that make this institution financially viable, the chapter addresses the common criticism that the "global governance" literature is often devoid of actors. Third and more broadly, the chapter seeks to contribute to the small but fast-growing literature on international financial reporting standards. While there is much research, especially from an economics and accounting perspective, on the consequences of certain accounting principles or particular provisions in financial reporting standards, there is still little research on where these standards come from. Such research is particularly sparse for IFRSs, which are becoming ever more important in the context of the international integration of financial markets, as ever more financial market regulators accept accounts based on these international standards in lieu of accounts based on national standards (e.g., Deloitte 2008). Even social science research that focuses on these international standards tends to provide little analysis of the standards development or the IASB (e.g., Nölke 2005; Porter 2005).[3] Such analyses are warranted since recent research suggests that the decision-making procedures and funding arrangements for institutionalized standard setting have a major impact on the content of the resulting standards (Mattli 2001; Mattli and Büthe 2003, 2005b; Büthe and Mattli 2010).

Accounting Standards and the IASB: An Empirical Introduction

Recent research has drawn attention to the important role of technical standards as instruments of governance in product markets and for trade in goods (e.g., Büthe and Witte 2004; Kollman and Prakash 2001; Mattli 2001; Prakash and Potoski 2006a; Salter 1999; WTO 2005). Standards also play important roles in domestic and international financial markets, but have until recently attracted little scholarly attention beyond capital adequacy standards for banks and other financial institutions (Oatley and Nabors 1998; Singer 2007). Financial reporting standards are a key example of such standards for financial markets, and a particularly interesting set of standards for social science analysis. As noted in the introduction, these standards regulate how assets and liabilities are reported in annual reports or other corporate financial statements. If followed in letter and spirit, accounting standards allow the control of management by the stockholder-owners of a corporation by decreasing information asymmetries, which is why Nicholas Véron (2007, 6) appropriately calls them the "operating system of capitalism." From a broader social science perspective, these standards create incentives for firms to engage in some activities and avoid others, as well as to choose particular means in pursuit of a given goal. In sum, financial reporting standards matter because they shape the behavior of firms and consequently important aspects of a country's political economy.

Moreover, as one might expect from the product of a political process, financial reporting standards have traditionally differed significantly across countries. While systems of *inventory* accounting—a hallmark of virtually all the leading premodern civilizations—have largely independent origins and histories, the early history of *financial* accounting is mostly the transnational history of double-entry bookkeeping (Braudel 1981). Nonetheless, financial accounting *standards* developed quite differently in the context of different local financial markets as well as different national legal and regulatory environments. Governments began to regulate accounting when perceptions of the role of government changed (and the potentially taxable assets and profits of corporations greatly increased) in the second half of the nineteenth and early twentieth century. But when governments did so, they had a variety of interests in mind, including those of tax authorities, financial market investors, creditors, and customers or suppliers of firms. Accounting standards therefore differed across countries on many dimensions, including the degree to which they promulgated highly specific rules or broad principles, or the extent to which private interests were involved in the standards-setting process (e.g., Banner 1998; Benston 1975; Carmona 2002; Hopwood 2002; Moonitz 1970; Nobes and Parker 2008; Roberts, Weetman, and Gordon 2008; Véron, Autret, and Galichon 2006, 7–20; Zeff 1972).

In the late twentieth century, however, the internationalization and arguably globalization of financial markets led to demands from multinational corporations (MNCs), investors, and sometimes government officials for the international harmonization of accounting standards, at least for the regular financial reports issued by publicly traded companies. The IASB then became the focal institution for developing such harmonized standards; it arose as the predominant source of "international" accounting/financial reporting standards in the late 1990s and early 2000s (see Jupille, Mattli, and Snidal 2008; see also Camfferman and Zeff 2007; Leblond 2006; Posner 2007; Steinberg, Arner, and Olive 2002; Véron 2007). While accounts based on IFRSs are not yet accepted everywhere, the IASB is on its way toward becoming *the* source of international and in many respects truly global financial reporting standards. A major turning point for IFRSs was the 2002 decision by the European Union to require consolidated financial statements, which have to be filed in EU countries under national law or regulations, to be based on the IASB's standards, starting in 2005. The EU Directive 1606/2002 "on the application of international accounting standards" from July 2002 (*OJ* L243/1) sparked a cascade of IFRS adoption by financial market regulators around the world. As of March 2007, IFRSs were required to be used by domestic listed companies in seventy-four countries.[4] Six further countries (Brazil, China, Kazakhstan, Morocco, Russia, and the United Arab Emirates) require their use by some domestic listed companies; and Brazil, South Korea, and the Russian Federation have passed laws or adopted regulations requiring their use starting within the next three years (see Deloitte 2007, 12–22). In addition, twenty-two countries (and seven other countries without a domestic stock exchange) allow—

but do not require—the use of IFRSs (Deloitte 2007); among them, Israel has announced plans to abandon national standards in favor of IFRSs (IASCF 2007b, 2). Finally, several countries that currently restrict or forbid the use of IFRSs have announced plans to switch to IFRSs in the coming years or are considering the option (IASCF 2007b, 2; SEC 2008). Canada, for instance, is switching from Canadian accounting standards to IFRSs in 2009; and the U.S. Securities and Exchange Commission as well as Japan's financial market regulators have announced plans in 2008 for adopting mandatory IFRS-based reporting by 2014.

Notwithstanding the important role that governments and public regulatory agencies have played in elevating IFRSs to their prominent position, the IASB—the standard setter—is a *private* organization. It is based in London, nominally as a subsidiary of the International Accounting Standards Committee Foundation (IASCF), a Delaware-incorporated not-for-profit corporation.[5] The IASCF pays the salaries and operating costs of the IASB. It has a modest endowment, but raises most of the funds that it needs to cover the costs of the IASB's operations from regular and irregular *voluntary* contributions, mostly from the private sector.

The Puzzle of IASB Financing: Two Explanations for Public Goods Provision

The IASB puts forth explicit behavioral norms for firms that publish financial statements. Developing these standards is expensive. The members of the board are recognized experts in accounting and financial reporting; for all or almost all of them, being a member of the board is a full-time position, and there are tight constraints on any other positions they might hold, in order to safeguard against conflicts of interest. The board members therefore command high salaries, and they are supported by a small but growing, highly qualified (and therefore expensive) staff. Consequently, the IASCF/IASB's annual budget has been growing, from about £12 million annually in 2001–2006 to about £16 million (about $30 million) annually in 2007–2008 (see IASCF 2007a, 7). In addition, the technical work of standard setting requires expert input from practitioners, which is often provided by large accounting firms and corporations.

The IASB asserts—and many financial market regulars agree—that the primary objective of these standards is to increase public trust in financial markets and make them operate more efficiently on an international or global scale. Indeed, good financial reporting standards should supply the kind of high-quality, easily comparable information that reduces information asymmetries between managers and owners as well as between buyers and sellers of financial securities. It should therefore also raise trust in the operation of financial markets, which in turn should increase the willingness to invest in financial securities and hence lower the cost of capital in financial markets. These benefits of having the IASB develop IFRSs are diffuse, nonrival, and nonexcludable, which suggests that financing the IASB may be seen as the provision of a public good (see Kindleberger 1983).

Despite these public goods characteristics of IFRSs, IASB standard setting is financed by voluntary contributions from a large number of profit-maximizing firms. This should not happen, due to what Potoski and Prakash call the "Olsonian" problem of free riding (see Olson 1965): If one can enjoy a good for free, why pay for its provision? The problem of free riding is of course the classic reason why Adam Smith and even most libertarians recognize that governments have a useful role in the provision of essential public goods such as national defense and public safety, and why groups who have sought to increase the provision of public goods have time and again turned to the state to demand such goods (e.g., de Swaan 1988): the superior coercive capacity of the modern state makes it uniquely capable of ensuring that (almost) all beneficiaries of a public good contribute toward its provision (Büthe 1998; Büthe 2004, 288). Yet governments are not necessary for the provision of public goods (Ostrom 1990). In fact, most corporate managers surely know that, if too many free ride, the public good will be underprovided and at the extreme no one may get to enjoy it. This recognition may under some conditions suffice to overcome the collective action problem of public goods provision. Such a high-spirited motivation, however, seems unlikely to explain why profit-maximizing corporations would voluntarily finance a private international body that produces public goods. If there are no material rewards (directly or indirectly) for contributing to the provision of a public good—or more precisely, if any such rewards (including reputational rewards) do not equal or exceed the costs—then firms that are in competition with other firms that might not incur such costs have strong material incentives not to contribute to the provision of a public good, even if doing so were considered "appropriate" in

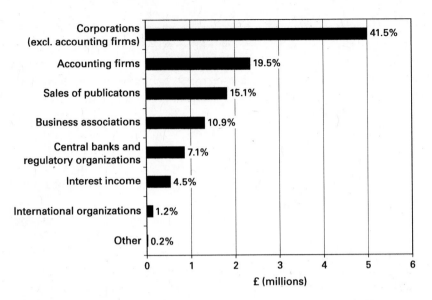

Figure 8.1
IASC foundation funding by source in 2005

a sociological institutionalist sense (see, e.g., March and Olsen 1998). What, then, has allowed the IASB to attract the financial support to prosper and grow?

I develop in this section two possible explanations for why private sector (for-profit) companies finance the IASB. These companies contribute the largest share of the IASB's budget, as shown for 2005 in figure 8.1 (IASCF 2006a).[6] The first explanation is based on hegemonic stability theory (HST), which has a long tradition in international relations theory as an explanation for the provision of goods with positive externalities (e.g., Kindleberger 1986; Krasner 1976; Gilpin 1981; Lake 1983; see also Keohane 1984; Mattli 1999). Here, I focus especially on the variant of HST developed by Duncan Snidal (1985). The second explanation draws on Potoski and Prakash's club approach.

Generalized HST Explanation
The core logic of hegemonic stability theory's explanation for the provision of public goods is simple: if there is an actor whose size allows it to capture such a large share of the benefits that they exceed the total costs that he or she has to bear, then the actor will provide the public good—

or ensure its provision.[7] Taking on such a leadership role is what makes the actor the "hegemon," from which the theory's name is derived (Keohane 1980). The literature then often distinguishes between two ideal types: the benign hegemon, which provides the public good without regard for the free riding of other beneficiaries (e.g., Kindleberger 1986; Keohane 1984), and the malign one, which forces others to pay for it (e.g., Krasner 1976; Gilpin 1981; see also Lake 1993). To be sure, forcing others to pay is costly, too, but in either case, the provision of the public good is—according to this theory—a rational decision based on a cost-benefit analysis, with the hegemon's share of the benefits exceeding the sum of the direct and indirect costs it incurs.

Much of the literature on HST assumes that the role of the hegemon must be played by a single actor. It therefore has focused on the question of how large/dominant such a hegemon would have to be for the hegemon to provide the public good. Size is here usually measured by the share of the global economy or global trade, the share of global (or subsystem) power resources, or sometimes by the absolute amount of resources—frequently leading to atheoretical claims about thresholds. But as Snidal (1985) shows, the assumption that there must be a single hegemon is logically unsustainable. Building on Russell Hardin's (1982) and Thomas Schelling's (1978) work on collective action, Snidal shows that a "k-group" of k actors (with $k > 1$) can equally provide and sustain public goods based on the HST logic, as long as the size of the group remains sufficiently small (and its coherence sufficiently high) that the k actors can overcome their own collective action problems—for instance, through the creation of appropriate institutions (Snidal 1985, esp. 597ff).

While developed primarily to explain cooperation among sovereign states, there is nothing in the theory to suggest that it cannot be applied to the realm of global private politics. Does HST, as modified by Snidal, allow us to explain the transnational cooperation of firms in providing for the public good of accounting standard setting through the IASB? Exclusive reliance on the benign hegemon variant seems problematic: the IASB has been financially viable thanks to annual contributions by corporations from many countries, as well as some national and international government entities. It is hard to see how so many actors would spontaneously overcome their collective action problems. A variant of the coercive hegemon argument, however, might be applicable, where the four (until 2002, five) major multinational accounting firms play the role of the k-group, paying for the IASB's operations partly themselves and partly by railroading others into contributing. We might expect the major accounting firms to be able to play this coercive hegemonic role vis-à-vis those firms that are for all practical purposes too large to use any auditors other than the "Big Four" (see Stevens 1981; 1985; Stevens with Stevens 1991). In fact, this argument has some prima facie plausibility. In interviews that I have conducted with current and former chief financial officers (CFOs), several noted that when their company's auditor suggests that the firm do something, a CFO will at a minimum listen carefully and often will do as requested. The HST-based explanation therefore is worth exploring empirically. What observable implications does it have?

One observable implication of the HST explanation is that contributions should come from large and/or multinational firms that must rely on one of the Big Four accounting firms for auditing services. And indeed, many of the private sector contributors to the IASB since 2001 have been large MNCs. This finding, however, offers only weak support for the HST explanation because firms that are financially capable of making commitments to give $100,000 or more for several years (the magnitude of contributions initially sought by the IASB) are bound to be quite large and likely multinational. Moreover, this observable implication of HST can also be derived from an alternative explanation (the club approach discussed below) and hence does not allow us to differentiate between the alternative explanations.

A second observable implication of the above variant of HST is that firms should be willing to be publicly identified as funders of the IASB, given that public identification provides a seemingly neutral, yet public way for the auditing firms to obtain confirmation that (or whether) a given firm has contributed to the IASB. But here, too, we face the problem of observational equivalence: such visibility might also be sought for other reasons (see below).

More decisive tests need to be tied more closely to the stipulated causal mechanism. Here, one might look for indications that the major accounting firms' own contributions (and possibly their actions to solicit contributions by others) are indeed motivated by the share they expect to gain from the public goods benefits of international standards harmonization, rather than being motivated by any private or club good benefits. Unfortunately, motivations and intentions are inherently difficult to observe. But if it were indeed the Big Four accounting firms that obliged their audit clients to make contributions to the IASCF/IASB budget, then the cross-national distribution of corporate contributors should correspond closely to the cross-national distribution of the four accounting firms' audit clients. Moreover, it should be the case that financial executives of the contributing firms have indeed been approached by their auditors about funding the IASB. And we should expect those who have been cajoled into contributing to seek to broaden the group of contributors in order to share the costs—possibly by asking governments to make contributions mandatory (DeSombre 2000; Vogel 1995).

A Club-Theoretic Explanation

An alternative explanation can be derived from the club-theoretic approach (Prakash and Potoski 2006b; Potoski and Prakash 2009 (chapter 2, this volume)). It leads us to consider the possibility that the public goods benefits of IASB standardization might only be positive externalities of a process through which nonrival, but excludable goods are produced—that is, club goods. To determine whether funding the IASB's standard setting can be characterized as yielding some benefits that can be treated analytically as club goods, and whether the public good benefits might be treated for analytic purposes as positive externalities of the provision of those club goods, a more general discussion of the benefits of (international) accounting standards is needed.

Based on the existing literature on accounting standards and preliminary interviews with corporate financial executives, financial analysts, lenders, investors, and regulators, Büthe and Mattli's International Accounting Standards Survey identifies seven objectives of (international) accounting standards (Büthe and Mattli 2008):

• Increasing the stability of capital markets
• Increasing the comparability of corporate information
• Providing a level playing field internationally for companies
• Enhancing market efficiency
• Improving the transparency and usefulness of accounts to shareholders, investors, and creditors
• Improving public confidence in the market
• Preventing legislation or government regulation

Not all stakeholders will consider every item on the above list a goal of financial reporting standards, and some items might therefore not qualify as positive externalities of IASB standard setting. Most of them, however, should bring nonexcludable, nonrival benefits to all market participants. And achieving objectives such as increased public confidence in the market brings benefits that, at a minimum, accrue to all publicly traded companies, regardless of whether they contribute to financing the IASB. Consequently, and even though the use of a particular set of accounting standards is mandatory for most publicly traded companies, we can characterize private sector contributions to the IASB's financial viability for analytical purposes as a voluntary program, with the features specified by Potoski and Prakash in chapter 1: there are no government regulations mandating that firms contribute to the IASB; such contributions thus go "beyond legal requirements" (p. 2), and the objective of the IASB (if not necessarily the objective of each financial contributor) may reasonably be assumed to be the production of standards that have positive social externalities.

The production of public goods, though, is surely not the whole story. Shifting from differing national standards to a single set of international standards entails adjustment costs, at least for some market participants. For any given firm, the net benefit of accounting standards harmonization at the international level therefore should depend upon how high these adjustment costs will be. This creates the opportunity for an explanation of IASB funding based on the club approach: if contributing to the IASB budget provides privileged access to members of the IASB or a more indirect means of influencing the content of IFRSs, firms may be able to use contributions to the IASB budget as a way to reduce their adjustment costs. This excludable benefit might then explain IASB funding and the public goods provision that comes with it.

Moreover, these benefits may be expected to differ across firms (as well as across countries), because the required and optional use of these standards differs across firms. European firms above certain thresholds have been obligated to file their consolidated accounts based on IFRSs since 2005; they may have a strong incentive to seek avenues for influencing the specific provisions of the international standards, all the more so the more that IASB proposals for bookkeeping, valuation, and so on tend to diverge from the firm's prior practice. That prior practice might differ considerably across firms, even within a given country, depending on the filing requirements of the various exchanges on which a firm is listed, the extent to which the firm has integrated the accounting of subsidiaries in various countries, and which standards it uses for this purpose. In sum, financing the IASB and thus enabling the production of high-quality internationally harmonized accounting standards with their public good characteristics may yield benefits that are excludable such that the financing of IASB accounting standardization may be suitably analyzed using the club approach.

What specifically might we expect to observe empirically—especially regarding contributions by nonaccounting private sector firms—if the logic of the club approach is driving funding for the IASB? First, we should expect European (EU) firms to be especially willing to provide funding for the IASB, given that they have to follow IFRSs (which was essentially known to happen almost from the moment when the IASB was established). We also should see changes over time, particularly an increase in corporate contributions from countries such as the United States and Japan in 2006–2007, when these countries started to consider allowing or adopting IFRSs.

Second, we should expect contributors to be disproportionately multinational, since having a single set of rules and procedures for record-keeping and accounting benefits such companies through economies of scale (relieving them of the obligation to issue different financial statements in each national jurisdiction). Moreover, the international harmonization of accounting standards facilitates the consistency of internal accounts, which increases the control of central management over subsidiaries in various jurisdictions and may even improve financial performance—benefits that also accrue primarily to large, multinational firms. These benefits should generally outweigh the lost opportunities for arbitrage that otherwise arise from differences in national accounting rules. Private sector contributions to the IASB from countries with no current or imminent obligation to use/implement IFRSs should be limited to companies with subsidiaries in countries where such filings are required or where such a requirement is imminent. Yet, unfortunately, a finding that contributors are mostly MNCs does not allow differentiating between the explanation based on the club approach and the HST-based account developed above, since both of them yield this prediction.

Third, and in contrast to the expectation derived from HST, we might expect that those who are already contributors are *not* keen to see the IASCF broaden the group of contributors, at least if such a change involves increasing the diversity of preferences, since such a broadening diminishes the potential influence derived from any given firm's financial contribution.[8] Such a preference may be impossible to ascertain directly, but a corollary might be easily observable: large contributors (underwriters) and contributors from countries that require the use of IFRSs (who therefore have a high stake in the content of these standards) should be the least likely to terminate their contributions, lest it create the need for the IASCF to seek out financial contributions from others, whose interests may differ.

Finally, direct evidence of the hypothesized causal mechanism—that corporate funders can and do use their actual or promised financial contributions to the IASCF to gain influence over IASB standard setting—would provide strong support for the club-theoretic argument. Such an analysis, however, is beyond the scope of this chapter.

Financing Financial Standards Setting: Some Preliminary Empirical Observations

The empirical analysis of the IASB and its funding faces two major impediments. First, in a curious twist for an accounting standard setter, the IASCF only discloses the names of its contributors in its annual reports, but not the size of individual contributions except for the major accounting firms, nor a breakdown of contributions by national origin.[9] Repeated inquiries over the course of more than a year yielded no more than a differentiation of funding by the category of contributors (see below). These data limitations allow an analysis of the national origins of contributors only by the number of contributors, not the size or economic importance of those contributions—and the average size of contributions reportedly varies substantially across countries, with a large number of Japanese corporations, for instance, making on average much smaller contributions than the corporate contributors from other countries.[10] Second, the IASCF Board of Trustees was established in May 2000; the IASB was established in January 2001 (see Camfferman and Zeff 2007, esp. 408ff, 447ff). Given this short history, an analysis of its operations must be somewhat tentative. Yet, seven years of IASCF annual reports, insights shared by senior executives from contributing firms, a few social scientific studies, and recently intensified reporting on the IASCF and IASB in the financial press allow at least a preliminary assessment of some of the hypotheses developed above.[11]

The annual reports list contributors in five categories: the major accounting firms ("Big Five," now "Big Four"), "underwriters," "supporters" (i.e., corporate contributors that were not underwriters), central banks and government entities, and business associations and organizations. I focus here on the corporations that file and publish regular financial statements, rather than the major international accounting firms that audit those corporations' financial reporting and themselves contribute about 20 percent of the IASB's budget. Companies were designated as underwriters if they pledged in 2001 a contribution of $100,000, $150,000, or $200,000 annually (depending on the firm's size) for the IASB's first five years. Supporters made usually smaller contributions in any given year and had no obligation to contribute for multiple years. In 2006, the distinction between these two groups of private sector contributors was dropped in favor of a single designation: "corporate and other private sector supporters." The IASB/IASCF has had a total of 440 such contributors since 2001. Some of them have given money for only one year, and some for all seven years. The IASB/IASCF started with 136 contributors in 2001 (including underwriters); until 2005, the number of private sector contributors for a given year then fluctuated between 126 and 134; in 2006, it jumped to 236 and then to 381 in 2007.

How important are the contributions from these corporate/private sector supporters to the financial viability of the IASB? Figure 8.2 traces the share of the total contributions from corporate and other private sector supporters from 2001 through 2007. In contrast to figure 8.1, which records the percentages of contributions to the IASCF/IASB overall budget, figure 8.2 reports the corporate/private sector contributions as a percentage of the total voluntary contributions received by the IASCF; it does not consider interest income and income from the sale of IASB publications due to data limitations. As the figure shows, the corporate/private contributions have (as a percentage of the total contributions) gradually but consistently declined.

Note, however, that a slowly increasing number of business associations and organizations have made collective contributions on behalf of private sector contributors, such as the Financial Reporting Council of Australia on behalf of the Australian private sector (since 2003) and Emittenti Titoli on behalf of the Italian business community (since 2006). The contributions from corporate/private supporters may therefore be increasingly underreported in an analysis of contributions by type. If contributions from business associations and organizations are counted as corporate contributions, then the marked decline in the share of business contributions, from about 62 percent (US$11 million) in 2001 to 38 percent (US$8.6 million) in 2007 (figure 8.2), turns into a minor decline in relative terms (from 62 to 56 percent) and a small increase

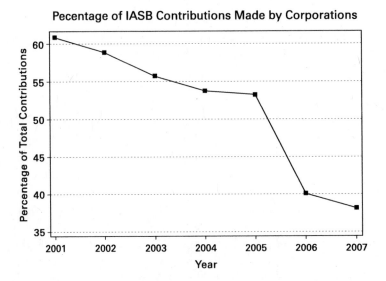

Figure 8.2
Share of voluntary contributions to the IASC foundation from corporate/private sector supporters, 2001–2007

in absolute terms ($11.2 to $12.6 million).[12] Contributions from government entities, international (governmental) organizations, and central banks have been usually much smaller (as shown in figure 8.1, their combined total contribution in 2005 was barely over one-third of the contribution of the Big Four accounting firms), but have been eagerly sought by the IASCF for the legitimizing effect of such public support.[13]

The annual reports (IASCF 2002–2005, 2006b, 2007b, 2008) also confirm the dominant role of the Big Four international accounting firms (all headquartered in the United States, though all multinational in structure and outlook). From 2001 through 2005, they contributed $1 million per year; for 2006, they increased that contribution (at the IASCF's request) to $1.5 million per year and committed to provide the same amount of funding for 2007. For 2008, their contribution was scheduled to increase to $2 million per firm. This finding is consistent with the HST-based account, but does not offer any evidence for these four firms playing the role of the k-group. The accounting firms' business interests may suffice to explain their substantial contributions.

A second issue that might provide insights into the relative explanatory leverage of HST and the club approach for understanding IASB

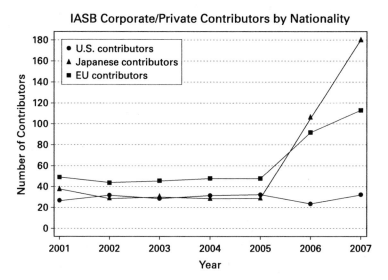

IASB Corporate/Private Contributors by Nationality

Figure 8.3
IASB private/corporate contributors by nationality

funding is the pattern of contributions from private sector firms. Because underwriters undertook a five-year obligation at the outset, they should be considered separately: the thirty-eight underwriters were all either multinationals or internationally oriented firms, which probably indeed require the auditing services of one of the major international accounting firms.[14] But as noted above, the logic of the HST—with the major accounting firms as the collective hegemon—suggests that the cross-national distribution of contributors should approximate the cross-national distribution of those firms' audit business. This observable implication of the HST-based explanation is not borne out—U.S.-based/headquartered corporations are clearly underrepresented among the IASCF underwriters (and supporters) relative to their share in the big accounting firms' audit business.

By contrast, the distribution of private contributors by nationality (tables 8.1 and 8.2, as well as figure 8.3) seems consistent with the expectations derived from the club approach. Firms from the European Union, where the use of IFRSs has been mandatory since 2005 (as planned and announced since 2002), are prominently represented, both among the underwriters (20 out of 38) and supporters (40 of the 131 supporters for 2001–2005). Many of the other contributors over the first seven years of the IASB have also been headquartered (or have subsidiaries) in countries where IFRSs are now required or permitted. A firm's decision to support international standardization financially thus appears to be a function of the stake that it has in the content of those standards—which suggests that funding indeed provides at least some opportunities for influencing the standard setting (the hypothesis that I derived from the club approach).

While there is thus considerable support for the club-theoretic perspective, the contributions from U.S. and especially Japanese firms exceed what might be expected: concrete plans for convergence with or outright adoption of IFRS have surfaced in both countries only quite recently, whereas the number of contributors from both countries has been substantial and relatively stable throughout the first five years. The increasing likelihood of a Japanese move toward IFRSs (which gives Japanese companies an increasing stake in the specific provisions of these international standards) might explain the substantial increase in the number of Japanese contributors from 2005 through 2007, consistent with the club-theoretic logic (see figure 8.3), although the extent of the increase seems disproportionate to the (until recently) rather unspecific pronouncements about IFRS adoption from the Japanese regulator.[15] Moreover, the essentially "flat" number of U.S. contributors seems at odds with what the club approach would lead us to expect, though the Securities and Exchange Comission's commitment to move from U.S. Generally Accepted Accounting Principles to IFRS may have become clear to many U.S. firms only after the Securities and Exchange Commission issued a first concept release about the potential acceptance of IFRS-based accounts in November 2007. The club approach, as applied here, might therefore suggest a significant increase in U.S. contributors only starting in 2008

More generally, changes over time seem to support a club approach explanation more than the HST account: for underwriters, the crucial moment came in 2006, when they had to decide whether to extend their previous five-year pledge with additional annual contributions. As table 8.1 shows, their willingness to continue their financial commitment to the IASB was remarkably high; only four of the thirty-eight underwriters did not continue to contribute (though the fact that those four were all European MNCs is surprising).

Among supporters, the willingness to discontinue financial support for the IASB clearly was higher than among underwriters (see table 8.2), but the general pattern of changes in support corresponds with what we

Table 8.1
Change in contributions 2005–2006 from 2001–2005 underwriters

Country/region	No. of underwriters, 2001–2005	No. of underwriters that discontinued funding in 2006	Discontinued as percentage of underwriters
Brazil	2	0	0%
European Union	20	4	20%
Switzerland	3	0	0%
United States	13	0	0%
Total	*38*	*4*	*10.5%*

would expect based on the club-theoretic account: EU firms with a high, direct stake in the specific provisions of IASB standards have been the least likely to withdraw, especially from 2005 to 2006, when the economic importance of IFRSs must have been clear to them, given the EU requirement to use these standards for consolidated accounts starting in 2005. Also consistent with the expectations derived from the club approach is the increase in South Korean contributors from zero to twenty-one in 2007, after Korea decided to allow the use of IFRSs from 2009 and require it from 2011, and more generally the increase in the number countries from which the IASB/IASCF receives contributions from fifteen in 2001 to twenty-one in 2006–2007.

The analysis so far has relied on drawing inferences from the annual reports, based on a correlational logic. But what direct support, if any, is there for the causal mechanisms stipulated by the two alternative approaches? As discussed earlier, the HST leads us to expect that the major accounting firms, acting as a k-group, bring about corporate contributions by putting (more or less subtle) pressure on their audit clients to make a contribution to finance the IASB with its positive (public good) externalities. Direct evidence of such actions would naturally be hard to come by, even if it existed. To be sure, the major accounting firms play a crucial role at every level, far beyond their financial contributions. Most notably, three of the twenty-one trustees of the IASCF as of December 31, 2006, were current or retired senior partners of the Big Four accounting firms. While the pervasive presence of the representatives from the accounting firms makes it difficult to distinguish cleanly between the firms and the IASCF, I have found no indications that corporate

Table 8.2
Fluctuations in contributions from financial supporters, 2005–2006

| | A | B | Column B as | C | D | Column D as |
	Supporters 1 or more years, 2001–2005	Discontinued funding at some point, 2002–2006[1]	percentage of column A	Supporters in 2005	Discontinued funding from 2005 to 2006	percentage of column C
Country/region						
Australia[2]	1	1	100%	1	1	100%
Brazil	5	3	60%	5	3	60%
Canada	10	9 (1)	90%	6	5	83%
China	5	4	80%	1	0	0%
European Union	40	16 (1)	40%	29	5	17%
Japan	39	17	44%	29	8	28%
Mexico	1	1 (1)	100%	0	—	N/A
South Africa	3	3	100%	2	2	100%
Switzerland	2	2	100%	0	—	N/A
United States	25	19 (1)	76%	20	14	70%
Total	*131*	*75*	*57%*	*93*	*38*	*40%*

Notes:

1. In parentheses: the number of companies that subsequently resumed funding, if any.

2. The figures for Australia underreport the breadth and depth of Australian private sector contributions: in 2003, the Financial Reporting Council of Australia (Australia's domestic [governmental] accounting and auditing standards setter) started to make contributions to the IASB budget "on behalf of private and public sector stakeholders in the Australian accounting standard-setting process" (IASCF 2003).

contributors to the IASCF were approached with a request for such contributions by their auditors rather than the IASCF trustees (acting appropriately in their assigned role of fund-raisers). While such attempts to leverage one's auditing work might have occurred in some instances, they do not seem to have been widespread. I also have found no indications that any of the past or current contributors have sought to broaden the group of contributors to spread the costs of the public good provision, as suggested by the logic of a generalized HST.

By contrast, there is—mostly anecdotal, but cumulatively persuasive—evidence that contributors have indeed used their financial contributions to gain influence. Such leveraging of one's contribution for political influence should of course not happen. The very structure of the organization is supposedly intended to inhibit such threats to the independence of the standard-setting process—with the IASCF Board of Trustee, which is responsible for fund-raising, institutionally separated from the IASB, which develops the international standards. Yet IASB officials and close observers have on several occasions noted, and complained about, threats by some of the funders to discontinue their funding unless the IASB were to reconsider certain provisions in a forthcoming standard or changes to a recently approved one (e.g., Schaub 2006, 14; FT 2006). In fact, the annual report of the IASCF for 2006 indirectly acknowledges this problem when it calls for broad-based, possibly mandatory financing arrangements that would "make free riding very difficult," and would ensure that financing for the IASB is "not contingent on any particular action that would infringe on the independence of the IASC Foundation and the International Accounting Standards Board" (IASCF 2007b, 6).

Conclusion

This chapter has laid out two alternative theoretical perspectives to explain why profit-maximizing corporations might voluntarily finance a private international body, the IASB, which produces public goods. One explanation is based on a variant of HST and the other on club theory. The necessarily preliminary empirical findings presented here suggest that the club approach is useful for understanding the financing (and in that sense the material existence) of the IASB: companies appear to be indeed motivated to provide financial resources for international standard setting with its public goods characteristics because such financial contributions provide them with the club benefit of an enhanced ability to exert influence during the standard-setting process.

A few caveats are in order. While the empirical analysis has offered stronger support for the theoretical argument derived from club theory than for HST, it has also led me to empirical findings that are not well explained by either approach. These anomalous findings suggest that future research might benefit from combining the club-theory-based account of incentives (where the *potential* for influencing the content of international accounting rules creates the incentive for supplying the funds that make the creation of those rules possible) with insights from institutional complementarity theory (Büthe and Mattli 2009, 2010; Mattli and Büthe 2003)—most important, that firms from different countries might have different expectations about their *ability* to influence outcomes at the international level, given the domestic institutions within which they operate.

Moreover, I have focused on nongovernmental institutions that set behavioral standards for economic actors. My analysis draws attention to an aspect of these types of voluntary programs, which is likely critical for firms as they evaluate the attractiveness of such programs, but largely overlooked in the club approach as currently developed by Potoski and Prakash. The well-documented aversion of (especially U.S.) firms and senior managers to government regulation (Bernstein 1953; Vogel 1978, 1996; Büthe 2002; 2006) seems to be grounded in part in an aversion to the loss of autonomy that inevitably results from submitting to rules. But if rules are necessary—maybe to retain consumer confidence in the products of one's industry and sustain demand—then it seems much preferable to be part of, or have a direct influence over, the rule making (i.e., here: standard setting). Firms' willingness to support a particular set of standards might therefore be a function of the extent to which supporting the work of the standard setter yields influence through financial (or other) contributions—and how much promise such a private rule maker holds for keeping government regulation at bay.

Two additional implications of my case study for the club approach should be noted. First, if it is correct that contributing to the IASB budget yields the club benefit of enhanced influence over the specific provisions of IFRSs, then the IASCF might be said to be accommodating differences among firms (differences in the stakes they have in international financial reporting standardization) through an auctionlike scheme, by which the IASCF allows firms to choose the level of their contribution themselves. Each contributing firm thus can choose to contribute at a level consistent not only with the firm's size and financial capacity at any given moment but also based on the importance of IFRSs to the firm (assuming that the club benefits are proportional to the contributions). This feature of the IASB/IASCF as a "club" has interesting implications for the club approach. Insofar as the level of the contribution is the functional equivalent to the stringency of club standards as discussed by Potoski and Prakash (chapter 2), clubs like the IASB/IASCF might through a multitiered structure allow for different levels of stringency under one institutional roof.

Second, I have in this case study focused on the decision (by senior managers on behalf) of corporations and other private sector entities to provide financing for the IASB. The club approach can be useful for explaining this corporate behavior insofar as it leads us to see these financial contributions as simultaneously (1) leading to the creation of public goods in the form of generally highly regarded accounting standards for global financial markets, and (2) generating a club good in the form of increased leverage over the standard setter. From a policy perspective, such dual-effect behavior is unproblematic insofar as corporate influence over the IASB merely affects its selection of one social-welfare-maximizing equilibrium among several. Even if such a choice of equilibria has distributional consequences, with some corporate contributors winning at the expense of others, the benefit for investors or the general public need not be diminished. Under those conditions, the central policy challenge is indeed, as Potoski and Prakash note, "to find ways to curb free riding among firms through a mechanism that creates excludable benefits that can be appropriated only by those firms that bear the costs of producing positive social externalities" (chapter 2, p. 18). However, if those excludable club benefits lead to something like the global private politics equivalent of regulatory capture, then the normative assessment of such voluntary programs would be rather less favorable. The legitimacy of the voluntary financing arrangement of the IASB thus depends on the standard setter's ability to produce technical standards that deliver the positive (social welfare) externalities that global market participants expect from the international harmonization of financial reporting based on IASB standards. The history of voluntarily financed U.S. domestic accounting standard setting (Büthe 2006) does not bode well for the IASB in this respect—which may be why some in the IASB (though not any of the current contributors) are seeking to move to a system of transnationally government-mandated contributions.

9

How Universal Are Club Standards? Emerging Markets and Volunteerism

Daniel W. Drezner and Mimi Lu

Over the past decade or two, the proliferation of voluntary programs, including voluntary standards and corporate codes of conduct, has been impressive (Kolk, Tulder, and Welter 1999). The rise of these voluntary programs has fostered a growing literature, affecting discussions about global civil society (Wapner 1995), world polity approaches (Boli and Thomas 1999), corporate culture (Prakash 2000a; Garcia-Johnson 2000), civil regulation (Vogel 2007), transnational networks (Djelic and Sahlin-Andersson 2006), and corporate management (Beardsley, Burgov, and Enriquez 2005).

The club approach as outlined by Prakash and Potoski in chapter 2 of this volume seeks to create a unifying methodology for analyzing and understanding voluntary programs. For the club approach to be valid it must be applicable across an array of stakeholders and firms. One aim of this chapter will be to test the universality of the club approach by examining the diffusion of voluntary programs in the Pacific Rim region. Understanding the behavior of emerging market firms and which program design works the most effectively in the Pacific Rim is of increasing importance because of both of market trends and heightened civil society attention regarding this region. Each program discussed in this chapter produces a different set of social externalities ranging from democratic regime change to improved environmental stewardship. Each program sets forth a formal rule structure that permits, prohibits, or encourages specific behavior. ISO 14001 promotes sustainable environmental practices through the development of a corporate environmental management system. The UN Global Compact encourages adherence to a universal declaration regarding human rights, environmental protection, and labor standards. The Free Burma campaign discourages companies from trading with and investing in Burma by blacklisting offending firms. ISO

14001 and the Free Burma "Dirty List" campaign represent "weak sword" programs with lax enforcement mechanisms while the UN Global Compact represents a "strong sword" program that more rigidly ensures firm compliance and sanctions shirking. These three voluntary programs together serve as test cases for examining the universality of the club approach by looking at the patterns of program adoption in non-OECD economies.

The work on voluntary programs to date rests on an unspoken premise: the bulk of the multinational corporations (MNCs) adhering to voluntary standards have been headquartered in Western, advanced, industrialized democracies. There has been little examination of whether multinational firms headquartered in either non-Western or less developed countries (LDCs) embrace voluntary programs in the same way. It is possible that the costs and benefits of voluntary program membership are different for firms based in non-Western economies. This gives rise to an obvious but important question: Are voluntary programs a truly global phenomenon, or has the predominance of multinational firms from European and North American countries created a misperception among global political economy scholars?

This question is both intrinsically and theoretically significant. The focus to date on MNCs based in the transatlantic area has been appropriate; as of 2006, 94 percent of the *Financial Times'* five hundred largest firms were headquartered in OECD economies. Yet global firms are increasingly emanating from emerging markets (Matthews 2006; Sinha 2005). The recent pattern of global savings and investment flows suggests that multinational firms headquartered in emerging markets will increasingly establish footholds in established markets. In the past few years, there have been cross-border merger and acquisition disputes involving the acquisition of OECD properties by Mittal Steel, CNOOC, Gazprom, and Dubai Ports World. Disparate adherence to voluntary standards could heighten economic tensions. Protests about myriad aspects of Chinese behavior in the run-up to the Beijing Olympics in 2008 also highlight the growing social divergence between Western civil society and Pacific Rim countries. If emerging multinational firms were to value adherence to voluntary standards differently than established multinational firms, then institutionalized mechanisms to encourage voluntary compliance could break down over time. OECD-based firms would have an incentive to backslide on their own commitments, arguing that they cannot compete with less developed countries–based firms that operate on a different playing field (Vogel 2007).

The diffusion of voluntary programs outside the transatlantic economy also represents a critical test of the explanatory power of several different theoretical paradigms. If non-Western firms reject adherence to voluntary programs, it sharply constrains models designed to predict the spread of business and ethical norms across borders. If non-Western firms embrace adherence to voluntary programs, then this would be strong evidence supporting the generalizability of the literature on private orders (Cutler, Haufler, and Porter 1998; Prakash and Potoski 2006b). If there is variation in the degree of adherence, then scholars have an ideal testing ground to parse out the precise causal mechanisms through which firms decide to adhere to voluntary programs. For example, if adherence is in part a function of home country economic development, then one would expect less compliance by firms based in less developed countries than others. If, on the other hand, regime type is the key factor, then firms headquartered in democratic regimes would be expected to have greater adoption levels.

As noted above, this chapter looks at the power of voluntary programs in emerging markets by examining the participation and compliance of firms headquartered in Pacific Rim developing countries to three different voluntary programs: the UN Global Compact, the Free Burma campaign, and the ISO 14001 regime. The Pacific Rim represents a wide spectrum of economies with different levels of economic and political development, regime type, and varieties of firm-state relations (Baumol, Litan, and Schramm 2007). If firms in this region demonstrate a greater adherence to strong sword programs than weak sword ones, then this would be evidence that Prakash and Potoski's (2006b) club approach model has explanatory power for the future. If adherence is low across the board, however, then a rethinking of the universality of the club approach would be in order. If there is variation in firm adherence, what are the causal mechanisms that can explain this variation? Are these mechanisms different from what drives Western firms to comply?

The chapter concludes that adherence to voluntary programs is not limited to the West. Indeed, the data show that Pacific Rim economies have been more enthusiastic about the International Organization for Standardization (ISO) and the UN Global Compact. The degree of

184 *Daniel W. Drezner and Mimi Lu*

adherence across programs and countries suggests that as Pacific Rim firms seek to build up their brand, they will pay more attention to voluntary programs. At the same time, the data also indicate that firms are more likely to embrace weak sword programs than strong sword ones. Indeed, it is possible that firms view ISO 14001 and the UN Global Compact as substitutes rather than complements—and more often than not, will sign up for clubs with weak swords more than strong swords.

This chapter is divided into six sections. The next section considers arguments for why multinational firms based in the Pacific Rim countries might not adopt voluntary standards at the same rate as firms based in other OECD countries. The third section looks at the counterarguments that suggest Pacific Rim MNCs are simply late adopters. The next section reviews the different countries and standards to be examined, teasing out testable predictions. The fifth section looks at Pacific Rim compliance with the UN Global Compact, the Free Burma campaign, and the ISO 14001 regime. The final section summarizes and concludes.

Why the Pacific Rim Might Be Different

A recent survey of corporate social responsibility practices reveals that compared to U.S. or European corporations, firms based in Asian countries have been relative laggards (Welford 2005). This suggests that the factors driving Western MNCs into accepting voluntary programs appear to be weaker across the Pacific Rim. Is this geographic disparity temporary or permanent? There are valid arguments on both sides of this debate, and we will discuss them in turn.

This discussion rests on a simple premise, articulated in chapter 2: "If private gains from unilaterally taking such actions were sufficient to induce the firm to produce positive social externality, then voluntary clubs (or governmental regulations for that matter) would not be necessary" (pg. 35). In other words, voluntary programs are not *that* voluntary—if they were, every firm would have its own corporate social responsibility program without any outside prodding. In fact, most firms "volunteer" to adhere to standards in response to external pressure by global civil society actors, international governmental organizations, or home governments. In thinking about cross-national adherence to voluntary standards, we need to think about why these external actors might be more or less constrained in their ability to influence MNCs. An important aspect of voluntary clubs is the information asymmetry that they help mitigate. They allow interested stakeholders to attain credible information on firm performance. Therefore any club design should take into consideration the audience of stakeholders, because they ultimately determine the success of the club—by rewarding or sanctioning firms for their behavior. Clubs signal to stakeholders the type and extent of social externalities produced by firms. While some firm may inherently be concerned with doing good, a majority of them will be more concerned with appeasing their stakeholders. A crucial consideration might be that the stakeholders that Eastern MNCs face are inherently different from the ones that Western MNCs face.

There are several contentions supporting the thesis that Pacific Rim MNCs will not embrace voluntary standards at the same rate as Western ones. Despite the globalization of economic activity, there is strong evidence that corporate cultures are embedded within national institutions (Chandler 1990; Pauly and Reich 1997; Doremus, Reich, and Pauly 1998; Hall and Soskice 2001). This affects MNC preferences headquartered in Pacific Rim countries in two ways. First, the "flying geese" pattern of industrial development (Bernard and Ravenhill 1995) renders these firms less sensitive to civil society pressures. Under this pattern of economic and corporate development, Pacific Rim MNCs spend most of their lives operating as original equipment manufacturing(OEM) subcontractors for Western-based firms (Berger 2006). Current figures bear this out; in the 2007 Millward Brown Optimor survey of the top one hundred most powerful brands, only four firms had non-OECD origins (Brandz 2007). For example, the iPod, while sold under the Apple brand, is really assembled by Pacific Rim MNCs (Linden, Kraemer, and Dedrick 2007).

Original equipment manufacturing subcontractors could face a different incentive structure than more brand-conscious firms when deciding to join a voluntary club. The benefits of club membership are decidedly lower. The primary club benefit comes from the goodwill, legitimacy, or other compensation that members receive from external stakeholders in return for affiliating with the club (see chapter 2). Firms less concerned with brand recognition will care less about stakeholder praise or criticism. At the same time, OEM subcontractors compete primarily on price. Any club that imposes even minor costs could place these firms at a competitive disadvantage vis-à-vis their rivals. Indeed, these OEM subcontractors exist primarily in emerging markets because they can exploit the cost advantages of cheaper labor and lax regulatory environments.

The cost-benefit analysis for these flying geese firms would therefore be starker than with brand-conscious firms.

Differences in corporate governance also reduce the civil society pressures on Pacific Rim MNCs. The Asian financial crisis exposed the opacity of corporate governance structures across the region (Iu and Batten 2001; Claessens and Fan 2002). The distribution of shareholder ownership across this region is narrow. In Japan and South Korea, cross-share holdings between firms in the same *keiretsu* or *chaebol* make it difficult to ascertain who owns what. In countries like Malaysia and China, state ownership and the emergence of sovereign wealth funds as investors generates an additional level of opacity in corporate governance (Summers 2007). A study of 1,105 publicly listed Chinese firms found that 84 percent of the companies were either under the direct or indirect control of the state (Yusuf, Nabeshima, and Perkins 2005). While only about 8.5 percent of the listed firms are directly controlled by the government, the nontradable shares of the majority of the listed firms are held by state-owned holding companies and/or state-controlled nonlisted holding companies. These ownership patterns, combined with a general preference for bonds over equity investment, greatly reduce the leverage that stockholders have over the management of Pacific Rim MNCs. In contrast, public shaming campaigns in the United States have been effective even when the campaign targeted a tertiary participant.[1] Opaque corporate governance denies civil society groups a clear causal pathway to influence firm behavior.

Another way in which Pacific Rim countries differ from their Western counterparts is that indigenous civil society groups are both less active and less influential. This is true for several reasons. The first and most obvious reason is that on average, countries in the Pacific Rim are more authoritarian than in Europe or North America. Regime type obviously places greater constraints on civil society groups that want to influence corporate behavior—authoritarian states, and firms headquartered in authoritarian countries, simply possess a wider array of options to thwart civil society pressures. The tighter links between mainstream media outlets, MNCs, and the state imposes a more hostile environment for civil society groups. If NGOs lack the ability to crack this iron triangle of state-firm-media relations, then they lose another technique of mobilizing public pressure for firms to adhere to voluntary standards.

For many Pacific Rim countries, there is a deeper reason for a lack of indigenous civil society placing greater constraints on business activity—

on a per capita basis, these countries are poorer than their Western counterparts. Poorer countries will view even voluntary programs as a luxury good (Drezner 2007, chapter 2). Regulations and corporate codes of conduct impose high opportunity costs, since investments in complying and monitoring such regulations hamper economic growth (Alesina et al. 2003; Scarpetti and Nicoletti 2003). Ceteris paribus, as a country's median level of income decreases, societal preferences for government regulation will shift in favor of less stringent standards. Citizens in emerging markets will therefore not be as interested in ratcheting up standards for corporate behavior.

There is prima facie evidence for this logic. In cross-national polling, citizens living in Pacific Rim economies have evinced less concern about corporate adherence to stringent labor or environmental standards (Program on International Policy Attitudes 2006; Chicago Council on Global Affairs 2007). This lack of concern has only been exacerbated by the fear that developed countries want to use labor and environmental standards as a means to protect uncompetitive home industries (Graham 2000; Drezner 2006). Ronald Inglehart's work on cross-national societal preferences confirms that only when countries enter "middle-income" status is there a marked change in societal priorities. Inglehart (2000, 219) observes that "societies at the early stages of the [development] curve tend to emphasize economic growth at any price. But as they move beyond a given threshold, they begin to emphasize quality of life concerns such as environmental protection and lifestyle issues." Although the Pacific Rim is a region experiencing rapid economic growth, the most populous countries—China, India, and Indonesia—remain quite poor. In these countries, one would expect to see less public enthusiasm for civil society campaigns.

The final argument rests on a cultural logic against adherence to standards that originate in the West. Most countries in the region embrace a Confucianist approach to state-society relations (Huntington 1996). As a philosophy, Confucianism stresses deference to traditional forms of authority and the importance of the group over the individual. As Samuel Huntington (1996, 108) puts it, "For East Asians, East Asian success is particularly the result of the East Asian cultural stress on the collectivity rather than the individual." This kind of deference goes against the type of pressure tactics and political dissent needed to convince firms to adopt standards that they would otherwise choose to ignore. Unless the state has decided that firms should adhere to voluntary clubs, it would go against the civilizational grain for protest groups to pursue a confrontational strategy to affect corporate behavior. Obviously, there are dangers inherent in exaggerating this kind of civilizational effect. On the margins, however, it might help to explain public opinion polls showing that citizens in the Pacific Rim care less about regulating globalization relative to Westerners (Program on International Policy Attitudes 2006; Chicago Council on Global Affairs 2007).

There are many reasons to believe that the club membership benefits for non-Western firms should be lower. At the same time, firms competing on small price margins also face greater costs of membership. Both of these effects should blunt the incentive for voluntary clubs outside the West.

Why the Pacific Rim Is Not Different

There are several counterarguments to the previous section. The most direct one is that the Pacific Rim economies, rather than being fundamentally different economic animals, are simply late adopters. Pac Rim countries are merely at a different stage of economic development; when they reach a comparable level of development as Western states, they will adhere to similar regimes. In other areas in the global political economy—such as free trade agreements—time has revealed that the Pacific Rim economies will behave similarly to the United States or the European Union. It simply takes longer for ideas to diffuse across the Pacific Ocean (Cao 2006). It is possible that late adoption also applies to the case of voluntary programs.

Indeed, over time a variety of the constraints that were discussed in the previous section should be expected to lessen. More and more firms headquartered in the Pacific Rim, for example, are either expanding greenfield investment or acquiring Western brands based in the OECD economies. Increasingly, Pacific Rim MNCs are intent on branding their wares to Western publics. Lenovo, for instance, acquired IBM's personal computer division in 2005, and has started to advertise in Western markets. In summer 2007, a rash of health and safety concerns regarding Chinese imports prompted swift action by Beijing to protect the brand image of "China, Inc."

As these firms market themselves to Western consumers, they also expose themselves to civil society pressures in the host countries. They become more sensitive to brand image and consumer boycotts. Even firms that remain lower in the supply chain are facing new vulnerabilities. As Western NGO activists become more sophisticated, they have targeted the retail sector as an indirect means of pressuring supplier firms (Bartley and Child 2007). While Pacific Rim MNCs might be more resistant to NGO pressure, they will listen if the Gap, Home Depot, or Wal-Mart request compliance with voluntary standards.

Domestic pressure is also building in these countries for private firms to act in a more public manner. Following Inglehart's logic, economic growth in these countries has rendered the citizenry more sympathetic to labor, environmental, and public health concerns than they would have been a decade ago. Even in the People's Republic of China—where close to half of the population lives on less than two dollars a day—the environmental movement has amassed greater political clout (Economy 2004). Civil society pressures in these countries are not absent; they're simply nascent.

Even the civilizational assertion could cut in favor of a greater adherence to voluntary standards. As Miles Kahler (2000) points out, there is a stronger tradition of informal cooperation between private and public actors across the Pacific Rim. Indeed, Chalmers Johnson (1982, 265–272) observes how "administrative guidance" played an important role in Japan's industrial policy for decades. It is possible that these informal state-firm relations can translate to voluntary and civil regulation as well. If firms face a choice between state-imposed mandatory regulation and private standards "suggested" by the state, most Pacific Rim MNCs would take the latter option. The deeper forms of informal consultation thus increase the likelihood that voluntary standards would act as a substitute for mandatory regulation.

Testing Compliance with Voluntary Standards

Three voluntary programs will be examined here, as mentioned earlier. Their attributes are summarized in table 9.1. According to the Potoski and Prakash paradigm, ISO 14001 regime typifies a weak sword program. Monitoring is done via third-party audits, but ISO 14001 does not require public disclosure and does not have mechanisms for punishing shirkers. ISO 14001 is a process-focused regime that does not require specific performance outcomes. The ISO sets out broad guidelines for developing an environmental management system that covers a wide range of environmental and worker safety practices. The scope and

Table 9.1
Program attributes

	Firms attracted	Cost of joining	Desired social externality	Club good	Club standards	Enforcement mechanism
ISO 14001	Firms serving as suppliers to brand-conscious companies, which might already be ISO members or firms that are themselves brand conscious.	Initial cost of implementation and certification can range from $24,000 to $128,000, and the annual cost of maintaining the system can cost between $5,000 to $10,000.	Responsible environmental stewardship through the development of environmental management policies.	Ease of interoperation with other businesses and governments due to compliance with a widely known and respected set of guidelines. For supply-chain firms in developing economies, ISO certification offers possible entry to Western firms facing pressure for greater contractor oversight.	Lenient standards. Specific performance outcomes are not mandated. ISO only requires firms to create an environmental management system; the content and nature of the system are left to the discretion of the firm.	Weak sword program: third-party audits are required, but public disclosures are not. No sanctioning mechanism exists for aggressively punishing shirkers.

UN Global Compact	Internationally minded firms, especially in the export sector, that are brand and image conscious.	Varies depending on sector and level of indigenous government involvement.	Improved environmental, labor, human rights, and anticorruption policies across different sectors.	Prestige, credibility, and positive public image transmitted by authorization to use Global Compact brand. Members have a global network and regional Compact Offices. Membership is not as large as ISO standards, however.	Stringent standards. The ten principles of the Global Compact require compliance in multiple areas: human rights, environment, and labor standards.	Strong sword program: while no third-party audits are required, firms must produce and publicize annual "Communications on Progress." Firms that continue to shirk are dismissed.
Free Burma	Socially conscious firms responsive to civil society appeals.	Costs vary by firm; for certain firms the financial and opportunity cost can be huge, especially in the energy sector. Whereas in the tourism sector, substitutes designation can be easily arranged, and the cost is minimal.	The cutoff of foreign financial capital/support for a notoriously brutal military regime.	The club good provided is that divested companies are publicly identified as "clean." The Free Burma campaign enforcement mechanism and club good are nearly identical, with the only distinction being on which of the two lists the company name appears: "clean" or "dirty."	Stringent standards. Compliance requires complete withdrawal from Burma. Rather than requiring a change in how the firm does business, it require that the firm stop doing business.	Weak sword: firms need only to publicly disclose their withdrawal from Burma; there are no auditing or sanction mechanisms.

depth of each adopting organization's environmental policy and plan is at the organization's discretion. As of January 2006, 103,583 ISO 14001 certifications had been issued worldwide. At the top of the list with the greatest number of certifications was Japan with 19,477, followed by China with 12,683 certifications.[2] These two countries combined account for 31 percent of all ISO 14001 certifications.

Initial plausibility probes suggest variation in the adoption of ISO standards across the Pacific Rim. There are several reasons for this; the main being that the motivation for ISO standard adoption benefits companies with particular aims, especially in the export market. Asian companies adopt ISO standards when a high proportion of output is exported to developed countries or MNCs that value environmental protection, or are themselves adopters of ISO standards. This would explain the high number of certifications attained by Chinese firms, for example. Thus, while companies in Asia are opting for membership in the ISO 14001 "club" at an increasing rate, the impetus for the move is not an indigenous concern for the environment or pressures from civil society groups; rather, the motivation appears to be globalization. It is a premium for doing business with developed countries and corporations that are brand minded. Because the ISO regime is the most widespread, the network effect comes into play, making the club benefits of membership relatively high.

The Free Burma campaign also represents a weak sword program, but it is a weak sword program with stringent standards. It therefore meets the country club definition that Potoski and Prakash discuss in chapter 2 of this volume. While some voluntary clubs require that members do business in a certain way (i.e., requiring that members adopt certain process-oriented standards such as developing management policies, while other clubs require specific performance outcomes such as reduced emissions), the Free Burma campaign requires that members simply stop doing any business with Burma. Numerous human rights and environmental groups have objected to international trade with Burma, arguing that firms doing business with Burma are helping to prop up an odious regime that represses all forms of political dissent. In an effort to persuade companies to voluntarily withdraw from Burma, a coalition of NGOs was formed to coordinate the efforts of an unprecedented number of players. Free Burma Campaign UK is working with other branches of the Free Burma Coalition worldwide to pressure firms and states to divest from Burma. The initial targets of the coalition's campaign were large MNCs including TOTAL Oil (French), Unocal (U.S.), and Daewoo (Korean). More recently, however, Free Burma Campaign UK began publishing a "dirty list" of companies doing business with Burma as part of its campaign of "naming and shaming." Once a company has pulled out of Burma, they are moved from the "dirty list" to the "clean list." The only pressure to comply consists of avoiding the blacklist. This campaign is the most recent of the voluntary programs discussed, and has the fewest number of adherents. From the benefit side of the equation, therefore, the Free Burma campaign should yield the fewest rewards for membership because the network effect is negligible and the brand recognition of the club is limited.

The UN Global Compact represents the strong sword approach; companies are required to produce and publicly disclose an annual Communication on Progress (COP). Companies that fail to comply with reporting measures are dismissed from the compact. The ten universal principles of the UN Global Compact address four main areas of concern: human rights, labor, the environment, and anticorruption. The principles are drawn from the Universal Declaration of Human Rights, the International Labor Organization's Fundamental Principles on Rights at Work, and the Rio Declaration on Environment and Development. A benefit of the compact is that it offers "one-stop shopping" in the three critical areas of greatest external pressure: human rights, the environment, and labor standards; by joining the compact, firms can reduce their transaction cost (Kell and Ruggie 1999). The number of standards, combined with the strong sword enforcement regimen, makes the Global Compact a mandarin program as defined by Potoski and Prakash. As for benefits, the UN imprimatur should yield greater benefits than the Free Burma campaign, but the relative newness of the program makes it less desirable than ISO membership.

As of August 2007, the Global Compact had a total of 3,977 business participants.[3] Of those participants, 436 were noncommunicating (failed to communicate according the Global Compact integrity measures), and 755 were inactive (failed to submit a COP).[4] Examining the inactivated companies reveals that the majority were from the developing world, in particular the Philippines and Brazil. Other researchers suggest that non-OECD firms have been slow to sign up (Blair, Bugg-Levine, and Rippin 2004).

As in the case of ISO 14001, the impetus for small and medium-size enterprises to enter into the compact is related to external market forces.

Table 9.2
Testing compliance with voluntary standards

Theoretical claim	Testable hypothesis across countries	Testable hypothesis across standards
Branding hypothesis: brand-conscious firms more likely to adhere to voluntary standards	Compliance higher in consumer product sectors; small-market countries (Hong Kong, Singapore)	Compliance highest with ISO 14000, lowest with Free Burma
Corporate governance hypothesis: opaque corporate governance limits incentives for adhering to voluntary standards	Compliance higher in countries with less corruption, greater rule of law (Hong Kong, Singapore, Japan)	Compliance highest with UN Global Compact, lowest with Free Burma
Regime hypothesis: civil society strength determines the extent to which corporations feel compelled to adhere to voluntary standards	Compliance higher in countries with lower Freedom House scores (Japan, Korea, India, Indonesia, Philippines)	Compliance highest with Free Burma, lowest with ISO 14000
Development hypothesis: populations in richer economies will support voluntary standards more	Compliance higher in countries with higher per capita GDP (Japan, Korea, Singapore)	No difference in compliance across standards
Cultural hypothesis: Confucian societies will resist Western-imposed standards	Compliance higher in non-Confucian societies (India, Indonesia)	Compliance highest with ISO 14000, lowest for Free Burma

A McKinsey study of the Global Compact noted that many developing country companies are participating in the Global Compact to enhance their chances of entering into supplier relationships with MNCs (Blair, Bugg-Levine, and Rippin 2004).

Table 9.2 outlines how the candidate hypotheses discussed in the previous two sections are projected to map out in terms of variation in compliance across different countries and different standards. The *branding hypothesis* represents the cost-benefit approach discussed in chapter 2 in this volume. It predicts that firms are more likely to comply when they must be conscious of consumer response. This leads to the direct prediction that firms in consumer sectors should be more likely to be voluntary compliers. Indirectly, this hypothesis would predict that firms based in small markets should be more willing to comply. Firms based in these countries must be concerned about access to export markets, and hence must please both foreign consumers and foreign governments. Finally, the branding effect should have its strongest impact on standards that have attracted the widest publicity and legitimacy. Of the three programs listed, ISO 14001 possesses the greatest degree of name recognition; the Free Burma campaign has the lowest profile.[5]

The *corporate governance hypothesis* predicts that firms with opaque or corrupt ownership patterns have fewer incentives to volunteer. Across countries, this hypothesis would predict greater compliance in countries that rank low in terms of corruption and high in terms of the rule of law. Firms based in societies with transparent legal systems and low levels of corruption will have well-defined corporate governance structures. This opens up an additional avenue—shareholder and stakeholder pressure—through which civil society groups can influence firms. Across standards, we posit that strong sword programs with state participation should have the greatest effect on firms with opaque governance structures. Therefore, the Global Compact should have the greatest impact. In contrast, the Free Burma campaign, which is the province of NGOs, should have the lowest level of compliance.

The *regime hypothesis* argues that firms are likelier to comply with voluntary standards if civil society is stronger within their home country. Across nations, this hypothesis would predict greater compliance in countries that score well on the Freedom House index of political and civil rights. Civil society networks should be stronger in open societies like South Korea, India, and the Philippines. Across standards, this hypothesis would predict greater compliance with standards "owned" by civil society groups. This implies that the Free Burma campaign would generate the greatest degree of compliance; the ISO 14001 standard, which has no NGO participation, should generate lower adherence.

The *development hypothesis* contends that as countries become wealthier, firms based in those countries should be more interested in noneconomic concerns related to voluntary standards. The costs of compliance would also be expected to decrease. Across countries, this hypothesis would predict greater compliance in wealthier societies. Using the GDP per capita as our metric for income, compliance should be greatest in OECD member states like South Korea and Japan, and wealthy entrepôt economies like Singapore and Hong Kong. Poorer economies like India should be less compliant. Across standards, this hypothesis would not make any predictions.

Finally, the *culture hypothesis* asserts that Confucian societies would be more reluctant to adhere to voluntary standards—especially if the origins of those standards come from the West. Across countries, this hypothesis would predict greater compliance in non-Confucian societies like India or Indonesia, and low levels of compliance in predominantly Confucian societies like China. Across standards, compliance should be lowest for standards that are perceived as "Western imposed." This clearly implies that the Free Burma campaign would generate the lowest level of compliance.

Adherence to Voluntary Standards in the Pacific Rim Economies

In order to determine whether Pacific Rim countries are adopting voluntary standards at the same rate as Western countries the ideal measure would be to compare the number of participating firms to the total number of businesses that could theoretically join. Unfortunately, such data are not available for non-OECD economies (Kollman and Prakash 2001). Standard with the existing literature, we use the GDP of respective countries as a proxy for the total number of firms. The aggregate size of a country's economy should roughly reflect the number of indigenous enterprises operating within the country.

The UN Global Compact   As mentioned above, all business participants in the Global Compact are required to annually produce and make public a COP. The COP communicates to the stakeholders the progress being made by the firm on implementing the ten principles of the compact and serves as a learning resource for other participants. The annual submission of a COP ensures that participants are continuously working to incorporate and promote the ten principles, and that initial accession to the principle is followed by substantive action, thereby protecting the integrity of the compact. Notable COPs are featured on the Global Compact Web site as best practices. Firms that fail to produce a COP are labeled as "noncommunicating" participants on the compact's Web site. The failure to submit a COP for two years renders a participant "inactive." A continued failure may lead to the dismissal of the firm.[6] The Web site contains a full database of all business signatories of the compact by country and their status.

To better understand the commitment of firms to the Global Compact and its ten principles, we can break down the number of compact participants by country. We then examine the extent of compliance by looking at the percentage of participants that are noncommunicating or inactive members. These figures are available in table 9.3. As an outside reference point, participation figures are also provided for the United States, the United Kingdom, France, and Germany. In terms of both raw numbers and participation as a fraction of the GDP, France would appear to be the most active country.

Looking at the Pacific Rim, in terms of meeting the basic commitment to the Global Compact (e.g., submitting a progress report), Japan and Singapore do best. Japan has a total of 50 business participants, out of which only 2 are noncommunicating and there are no inactive members. Singapore has 30 total participants, of which only 1 is noncommunicating and none are inactive. The Philippines does the worst; out of a total of 111 participants, 97 are inactive and 8 are noncommunicating. There are about seven times the delinquent participants as compared to active ones (97 to 14).

Looking at participation rates, a few surprising facts reveal themselves. Contrary to expectation, firms in most of the Pacific Rim economies have been relatively eager to join the UN Global Compact. As a fraction of the GDP, five Pacific Rim economies—India, Indonesia, the Philippines, Singapore, and South Korea—have greater participation in the compact than Germany or Great Britain. Japan, Malaysia, and Thailand have the lowest participation rates.

ISO 14001 Environmental Standards   Table 9.4 displays the extent to which ISO 14001 standards have penetrated Pacific Rim economies. Clearly, firms have adopted ISO standards in substantially greater numbers than the Global Compact. For example, there are 50 total Japanese business participants in the compact compared to the 19,477 Japanese sites that have ISO 14001 certification. In South Korea, 4,955 sites have ISO 14001 certification as compared to 41 compact participants.

Comparing the Pacific Rim economies, the pattern is intriguing. India, Indonesia, and Hong Kong have the lowest participation rates. The highest participation rates come from a heterogeneous mix of countries: China, Japan, South Korea, Thailand, and Singapore. What is particularly interesting is that most of the Pacific Rim economies have higher participation rates as a fraction of the GDP than the Western economies.

Table 9.3
Compliance rates with UN Global Compact

Country	Total # of participants	Participation rate	2006 GDP (in $ billions)	Nominal participation/ GDP ratio	Real participation/ GDP ratio
China (PRC)	113	68.1%	2630.11	.043	.029
India	125	47.2%	886.9	.141	.067
Indonesia	29	96.6%	364.2	.080	.077
Japan	50	96.0%	4367.5	.011	.011
Malaysia	2	50.0%	150.9	.013	.007
Philippines	111	5.4%	116.93	.949	.051
Singapore	30	96.7%	132.16	.227	.219
South Korea	41	100%	888.27	.046	.046
Thailand	12	0.0%	206.26	.058	.000
France	471	59.23%	2231.7	.211	.125
Germany	92	90.2%	2897.0	.032	.029
United Kingdom	82	84.1%	2373.7	.035	.029
United States	128	67.2%	13244.6	.010	.006

Table 9.4
Compliance rates with ISO 14001

Country	Certified ISO 14001 sites	2006 GDP (in $ millions)	ISO certification as a fraction of GDP
China (PRC)	12683	2630.11	4.82
India	1500	886.9	1.69
Indonesia	369	364.2	1.01
Hong Kong S.A.R.	385	189.5	2.03
Japan	19477	4367.5	4.46
Malaysia	566	150.9	3.75
Philippines	361	116.93	3.09
Singapore	658	132.16	4.98
South Korea	4955	888.27	5.58
Thailand	1153	206.26	5.59
France	2089	2231.7	0.94
Germany	5094	2897.0	1.76
United Kingdom	6223	2373.7	2.62
United States	5100	13244.6	0.39

Source: International Monetary Fund, World Economic Outlook Database, April 2007

Indonesia is the only Pacific Rim economy to have a lower participation rate in the ISO 14001 standard than the average of the Western OECD economies. As with the UN Global Compact, firms headquartered in the Pacific Rim appear to be eager to participate in voluntary standards.

The Free Burma Campaign   Trade and investment interest in Burma from the Pacific Rim region has centered largely on its rich natural resources such as coal, natural gas, petroleum, timber, copper, tin, zinc, precious stones, and teak. The targets of the Free Burma Coalition's campaign are large MNCs including, as noted above, TOTAL Oil, Unocal, and Daewoo. The campaign against TOTAL is the largest international campaign ever mounted against a company working in Burma, and includes 18 different countries and 50 organizations.[7]

Of the 139 companies currently on the dirty list of companies doing business with Burma are 44 Asian companies. Of the 44 so-called dirty Asian companies, 13 are Japanese, 10 are Singaporean, and 7 are Thai. China, Malaysia, and India each have 3 companies on the list; Hong

Kong and Korea both have 2 companies on the list.[8] Once a company has pulled out of Burma, it is moved from the dirty list to the clean list. Since 2001, a number of companies have withdrawn from the country, and many others have vowed not to enter. The reasons cited for terminating business with Burma include difficulties in working with the regime, consumer boycotts, damage to company reputation, and incompatibility with corporate values.

In contrast to both ISO 14001 and the UN Global Compact, the Free Burma campaign has not made any inroads into the Pacific Rim. The campaign has moved 20 companies from the dirty list to the clean list—including Texaco, Adidas, Premier Oil, Triumph International, Levi Strauss, PepsiCo, Erickson, Heineken, Carlsberg, British Home Stores, Burton, River Island, Apple, and Compaq.[9] While some Japanese firms have vowed to not do business with Burma, no Asian firm has been moved from the dirty to the clean list. This fact remains true despite the greater awareness of the Burmese problem following the aborted Saffron Revolution in fall 2007.[10]

Indeed, a closer examination suggests an explicit rejection of the principles underlying the Free Burma campaign. In 1993, the planned development of the Yadana pipeline from Burma into Thailand was met with international outrage. The involvement of the Burmese military in the development of the pipeline led to numerous documented human rights violations. The planned Shwe gas field, twenty miles off Burma's coast to India, is likely to follow a similar pattern. Construction on the pipeline has not begun yet, but feasibility studies are complete and gas extraction may begin as soon as 2009. The construction of the two hundred miles of the Burmese portion of the pipeline will be overseen by Daewoo International, a firm on the Free Burma campaign's dirty list.

The Shwe natural gas development deal between the Burmese government, Daewoo International, India, and China is fertile ground for corruption, and bodes ill for the Burmese villagers along the pipeline route. Rajiv Mathur, who oversees sourcing at the Gas Authority of India (which holds a 10 percent stake in the consortium developing the pipeline), was challenged about possible human rights violations by the Burmese military. His response was, "What they do there is their business." He added, "We hope they proceed by international laws, ethics, and norms."[11]

Daewoo International has also been accused by Earth Rights International of supplying military munitions technology to Burma's ruling military regime. In an open letter issued by NGOs and civil society groups in South Korea, Daewoo is accused of "exporting key munitions technology to Burma, such as lathes and other materials used for fabricating the fuses of bombs."[12] A coalition of NGOs and other civil society members has mobilized against Daewoo, and began focusing media attention in the West. PBS stations across the United States aired "Burma: State of Fear," a *Frontline* documentary about the situation, in October 2006. Unocal and TOTAL have suffered court action and bitter protests due to their involvement with Burma. Despite all of this, Daewoo, the Gas Authority of India, and China are planning to travel the same path as Unocal and TOTAL. It would appear that global civil society has little leverage on these actors. In terms of the strategies that the global civil society can employ to change norms—that is, to bring attention to environmental concerns and human rights abuses, and engage in dramatic actions to highlight the seriousness of the situation—the global civil society seems to have exhausted its options. Overall, there is no evidence that civil society pressure has forced Pacific Rim firms investing in Burma to observe basic human rights standards. The Free Burma campaign serves as a clear counterexample to the regime hypothesis.

Summary of Findings

To sum up the data analysis: there is a clear rank ordering of Pacific Rim adherence to voluntary standards. Firms headquartered in East Asia were the most receptive to ISO 14001, followed by the UN Global Compact. They have, to date, categorically rejected adherence to the Free Burma campaign. In comparison to major Western OECD countries, the Pacific Rim economies do relatively well in participating in both the ISO and UN programs.

Free Burma's divestment campaign differs in two ways from the other voluntary standards programs. First, the Free Burma campaign proffers smaller incentives. The positive appeal of the ISO 14001 and UN Global Compact regimes is their international branding and visibility. The ISO standards are the most influential ones in the world, in particular the ISO 9000 standards. Hence, the ISO 14001 standards have the greatest perceived legitimacy and international recognition. Furthermore, ISO 14001 standards provide private benefits to Asian companies. Having ISO certification helps Asian export companies attract Western MNCs that have already adopted ISO standards or face civil society pressure to ensure that their suppliers are engaging in environmentally substantial practices (Jiang and Bansal 2003). The Global Compact has the prestige and clout of the United Nations behind it. The participants in the Global Compact are allowed to use its name and logo. On the other hand, the Free Burma campaign has neither the name recognition nor clout. In terms of the incentives, other than recognition as a "clean company," Asian firms have little incentive to adhere to the standards. For firms seeking to access the Burmese market, the costs are direct and concentrated.

The second difference is that the Free Burma campaign's origins are exclusively Western. Cries for divestment have mainly come from Western civil society. The threat of consumer boycotts has encouraged brand-conscious firms to bypass or divest from Burma. Such threats do not carry much weight in Asia. One could argue that the ISO 14001 regime and the UN Global Compact also have Western origins. The perception of both the ISO and the United Nations differs from the Free Burma coalition, however. The United Nations is a universal membership international global organization; its legitimacy emanates from the global character of its membership (Drezner 2007, chapter 3). The ISO has a similar universal cast to it. The contrast with the Free Burma Coalition is stark.

Consistent with the arguments developed in chapter 2, the hierarchy of adherence to standards—the ISO followed by the Global Compact, followed by Free Burma—lends strong support to the branding hypothesis. As Pacific Rim firms attempt to brand, they will be more likely to join voluntary standards programs. The country prediction that follows is that the entrepôt economies—relying more on export markets than internal ones—should be the most enthusiastic about adherence. Figure 9.1 shows a scatter plot of penetration ratios for Pacific Rim economies for both the UN Global Compact and the ISO 14001 standard. As can be seen, Singapore is the outlier; it scores well on both dimensions. This lends further support to the branding hypothesis.

Beyond Singapore, there is an apparent *inverse* correlation between ISO 14001 and Global Compact adherence. Thailand has the lowest degree of genuine UN Global Compact participation, but the highest degree of ISO penetration. Conversely, Indonesia has the lowest participation rate in the ISO 14001 program, but is among the regional leaders in UN Global Compact participation. One possible explanation for this puzzle is that Pacific Rim economies view the ISO and UN programs as

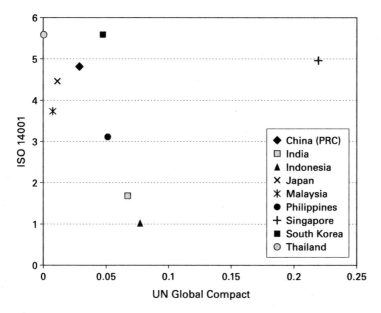

Figure 9.1
Scatter plot of variation in ISO and UN Global Compact penetration

substitutes rather than complements. Countries that already embraced the ISO standards at a high rate were less likely to think of the UN Global Compact as a significant standard.

Another possibility is that it is arguably easier to maintain ISO certification. The UN Global Compact has initiated strict measures to guard the integrity of the Global Compact brand, whereas the ISO has a relatively lax monitoring policy. While the ISO 14001 regime has relatively lenient standards and weak enforcement, it is not necessarily a sham club. The size and scope of ISO regimes bestow on club members sizable network effects, enabling ISO firms to more easily do business with other ISO adopters and countries that value the ISO regimes. Corporations interested in the branding aspects of environmental standards would therefore be more likely to opt for ISO 14001 over the UN Global Compact because it grants firms similar benefits without the requirement of adopting strict standards. This would expand the higher overall adoption rate of ISO standards in the Pacific Rim.

Thus, of the causal theories outlined in this chapter, the branding hypothesis is the most promising. The regime hypothesis has been shown to be false. The corporate governance hypothesis does not appear to carry much water either. It predicts that compliance with voluntary standards would be higher in countries with lower levels of corruption and stronger rule of law systems, although China, a country that does not do well on either front, appears to be an enthusiastic adopter of the ISO regime. The cultural hypothesis does prove to have explanatory power and could be useful in moving forward with different programs designed for the Pacific Rim region. The development hypothesis seems to be sound, yet its validity will need to be tested in the long term as economies in the Pacific Rim continue to grow and mature.

Conclusion

Most voluntary standards have their origins in the United States and Europe; most of the corporate adherents are also headquartered in those countries. As global economic forces foster the rise of Pacific Rim economies, it is worth asking whether theories of voluntary adherence can translate to that region. The theory and categorization posited by Potoski and Prakash highlight the importance of looking at club design to maximize standards adoption and the production of social externalities. The effectiveness of different program designs will become increasingly significant as voluntary clubs strive for a global reach. In terms of the issues that civil society is most concerned with—the environment, human rights, and labor conditions—the Pacific Rim region is fertile ground for improvement.

To test Pacific Rim adherence to voluntary standards, this chapter has examined how the economies of the region have reacted to the ISO 14001 standard, the UN Global Compact, and the Free Burma campaign. The data suggest that Asian firms have not been laggards in either the UN or ISO programs—though they have lagged in divesting from Burma. The variation of adherence by standard and country indicates that as Pacific Rim firms try to build out their brand names, they will be more and more likely to adhere to voluntary standards.

The differing rates of uptake among the three voluntary clubs examined in this chapter likely cannot be explained using the club approach alone, however. There may be cultural influences in play. A close study of the actors involved may also be necessary. Because of the close links between the government and business in Asia, any measure intent on inducing firms to go beyond the letter of the law to create social externalities could require tacit support from the government. Future club design might have to take this structural dynamic into greater consideration.

The value of using the club approach to study the diffusion of these programs in developing countries is that it provides a relatively universal framework within which different types of organizations can be studied and compared. The three voluntary clubs examined in this chapter are similar only in the rough alignment of their ultimate objectives, and yet the club approach admits to a systematic comparison. Table 9.1 outlines where the three voluntary programs explored here fit within the club approaches and what types of firms would be most attracted by each program. The club framework permits a systematic way to analyze discrepancies in participation rates across regions and cultures. For example, enforcement mechanisms based on public naming and shaming may have differing levels of effectiveness in different media environments and different consumer markets. Another important component of the clubs framework is the creation and design of standards structures that would best encourage desired firm behavior. While there is a seemingly high adoption rate of the club standard with the most lenient standards and the weakest sword (of the three discussed in this chapter, that would be the ISO14001 regime), as noted by Potoski and Prakash, this does not necessarily mean good results are not achieved. ISO 14001 might only induce firms to mildly improve their environmental management policies, but the shear volume of firms involved in the regime could produce aggregate benefits that well exceed the level of social externalities produced by regimes with stringent standards and strong swords, but low membership.

Clearly, the results delineated in this chapter are tentative, and further research is necessary. On the one hand, the branding hypothesis appears to travel beyond the transatlantic area. On the other hand, the inverse correlation between ISO 14001 and UN Global Compact acceptance suggests that countries and firms view voluntary standards as substitutes rather than complements. It is possible that consistent with Aaron Chatterji and Siona Listokin (2007), firms in the Pacific Rim will begin to game the voluntary standards system, embracing those standards with the weakest swords.

The narrative of the Free Burma campaign offers a different cautionary tale. The failure of the Free Burma campaign to elicit Asian firms to adopt club standards may be attributed to several different causes: weak indigenous civil society organization, the low visibility of the club brand,

and/or Western, NGO-based origins of the campaign. Ultimately, the Free Burma campaign failed to create the necessary incentives to induce firms to desire membership. The club standard (complete divestment) is extremely stringent, and the payoffs/benefits for firms are preclusively small. A possible remedy for this situation is to change the terms of the payoffs/benefits equation. This means that for voluntary clubs that address issues similar to the Free Burma campaign, incentive structures and standards requirements that may work for Western firms will not work for Pacific Rim ones. The Free Burma campaign, of course, is only a snapshot of the NGOs and civil society activity in the Pacific Rim region. A more wide-ranging survey of success of NGO-lead initiatives and the nature of these initiatives needs to be examined before broad assumptions regarding different explanatory theories can be confirmed or denied.

III

Governmental and NGO Clubs

10

Green Clubs: A New Tool for Government?

Daniel J. Fiorino

As governments around the world have gained experience with environmental protection, they increasingly have diversified their policy strategies. After relying almost entirely on regulation in the 1970s, they incorporated incentive and information-based approaches in the 1980s and 1990s (Gunningham and Grabosky 1998; Kettl 2002; National Research Council 2002). More recently, governments have turned to voluntary programs as yet another strategy for achieving their environmental goals.

Government-business voluntary programs are qualitatively different from strategies based on regulation, incentives, and information (Brouhle, Griffiths, and Wolverton 2005). The most obvious difference is that they are optional for both government and firms. For environmental agencies, voluntary programs often are initiated without specific statutory authority or mandates. They are a way to respond flexibly and collaboratively to problems for which no established legal mechanisms apply. For industry, whether or not to participate is optional. They cannot opt out of regulations or community-right-to-know rules, but they can decide not to enter into voluntary programs, just as government can decide not to create them in the first place.

Of the many forms that these programs may take, one of the more popular ones in recent years has been government-sponsored green clubs. These clubs conform in their purpose and design with the definition of green clubs presented in this volume, but they are distinctive. They are created and managed by government, and are justified as mechanisms that environmental agencies may use to achieve their goals. In some cases, such as in many U.S. states, green clubs are authorized specifically by statute. In others, such as for most voluntary programs that have been adopted by the EPA, they are not specifically authorized but are created under more generic statutory authorities. In either case, government-sponsored clubs are different from others, such as ISO 14001 or Responsible Care, because of the role that government plays.

Government clubs enjoyed something of a free ride politically for years. They were voluntary, consumed few resources, and appeared to deliver environmental results. They drew on the better intentions of industry and allowed agencies to experiment with a newer, more creative approach to doing their jobs. Firms could earn recognition for doing well and achieve social objectives without government coercion. Government-sponsored clubs have been seen as a low-cost and flexible way to align the interests of firms and other organizations with the collective interests of society. They enabled government and other actors to build collaborative relationships in a traditionally adversarial setting, while producing societal benefits in the form of reduced pollution, the more efficient use of resources, and better information about environmental performance.

More recently, though, government clubs have drawn criticism. However few their resources, they have been challenged for using money and staff that should be dedicated to "core" regulatory and enforcement programs. Some critics see government clubs and their emphasis on positive recognition and collaboration as a threat to agency independence; they prefer that agencies maintain a consistently adversarial stance toward regulated firms. Critics also claim there is little evidence that clubs change behavior; instead, they merely recognize what people would have done anyway, for other reasons.

This chapter examines government-sponsored green clubs as they have developed in the United States and evaluates them as policy tools. The next section considers government clubs in the context of club theory. It then gives a brief overview of clubs that the EPA has created, followed by a discussion of green clubs that are being used at the state level to complement regulatory strategies. The premise here is that green clubs will not replace regulation and other strategies, yet may augment them and produce positive externalities, not only in the form of less pollution and the more efficient use of resources, but in better capacities for learning, trust building, information sharing, and innovation.

A particular focus of this chapter is the EPA's National Environmental Performance Track and similar programs that have been adopted at the state level. As prototypical examples of the concept of government-sponsored green clubs, these programs apply in practice many of the ideas that have been proposed in recent years for making regulation in the United States more flexible, collaborative, and performance based (Durant, Fiorino, and O'Leary 2004). By improving government's ability to measure environmental performance, developing means of discriminating among the levels of performance, and applying approaches that have been used in the European context to use networks effectively, these programs are designed to chart a path toward long-term regulatory innovation. Although the results they achieve are important, just as significant are the lessons they offer regarding government's role in environmental sustainability, especially in transforming relationships from largely being adversarial and punitive, to more collaborative and focused on outcomes.

Although this chapter addresses many of the same issues as those considered in chapter 11, the intent and purposes are different. This chapter examines government-sponsored green clubs as the basis for a new and more active role for government in promoting socially desirable environmental behavior. Chapter 11 considers government-sponsored green clubs as well as their strengths and weaknesses at their current stage of development, with less concern over their fit within the larger regulatory system and their long-term potential for changing governmental capacities. This chapter approaches green clubs in the context of the need for developing broader systems of environmental governance.

The Characteristics of Government-Sponsored Green Clubs

Government clubs meet the characteristics for green clubs generally (Prakash and Potoski 2006b, 17–27). They offer excludable benefits in that membership status, which is controlled by government, distinguishes those who are in the club from those who are not. At the same time, the benefits are nonrival, because membership by one firm does not make the benefits unavailable to others. Indeed, an increase in the number and quality of members usually will increase the value of the club's benefits to members, at least to the point at which overcrowding may occur.

What distinguishes government green clubs from others is that government controls membership. Of course, under conventional regulation, government controls another kind of membership: it defines who is and is not subject to regulations. The green club is different, however, in that membership is at the discretion of the firm as well as the agency, and is based on the promise of benefits, not the threat of punishment. This involves a fundamental shift—from finding and punishing socially bad behavior, to recognizing and encouraging good behavior—that does not come easily to regulators.

Government clubs share several characteristics. Government defines the criteria for and controls membership. There is, by definition, a quid pro quo: members agree to provide information and follow specified standards of behavior in return for the benefits that government makes available to them. Members are explicitly defined as being in or out of the club—otherwise the value of differentiation is lost. Clubs typically grant some form of increased interaction with government officials as well as public recognition. In addition, many government green clubs offer other inducements for participation, such as providing information and assistance that would not readily be available otherwise, or treating club members differently within the regulatory system.

Clubs also differ in several ways. Some government clubs have only one kind of membership; others involve two or more levels based on qualifications that have been established or commitments that are made. Some clubs define expected levels of performance or require information, while others expect little accountability. Some provide for limited terms of membership, while others are more open-ended. All clubs supply at a minimum some form of recognition or branding; several also offer regulatory incentives such as reduced transaction costs or flexibility. Clubs differ too in the extent to which they involve external groups in decision making, including the selection of club members and the sanctions that may be applied for the nonperformance of obligations.

Green Clubs at the EPA

Over the last few decades, governments around the world have turned to green clubs as a policy tool (OECD 1997). In the European Union, for example, the Eco-Management and Auditing Scheme (EMAS) was created in 1993 and modified in 2001 (Gouldson 2005). In April 2007, some thirty-six hundred organizations covering nearly fifty-four hundred sites were registered under the Eco-Management and Auditing Scheme. In Mexico, Industria Limpia defines membership criteria based on adopting an environmental management system (EMS) auditing for compliance and preventing pollution. In 2003, China's environmental agency created the Environmentally Friendly Enterprises program for recognizing organizations that go beyond legal compliance, use management systems, and meet acceptable standards.

Three forces were especially influential in promoting green clubs in the United States in the 1990s and early 2000s. One was a problem, the second was an approach, and the third was a strategy. The problem was greenhouse gases, for which few regulatory mechanisms were available in the United States. Most EPA voluntary programs in the 1990s were designed to address these emissions. To advocates, such programs were a way to get federal agencies in the climate business and take advantage of forces outside of government that were pushing many firms to develop climate action strategies. To critics, they were merely excuses for not regulating. The point for now is that voluntary programs, some of which qualify as green clubs, were used to fill a vacuum that the lack of regulatory authority had created (Carmin, Darnall, and Mil-Homens 2003; Darnall and Carmin 2005).

The approach was the Environmental Management Systems (EMS). Indeed, for the clubs considered here, the perceived need by environmental agencies to incorporate EMSs into government policy was a driving force behind their creation (Coglianese and Nash 2001). In the EPA's most comprehensive club, the National Environmental Performance Track, and the state equivalents discussed below, the EMS has been central. For EMS advocates, the carrot of membership in a green club presented a more effective and available mechanism for promoting an EMS than did the traditional stick of regulation.

The strategy was pollution prevention. The focus in the early environmental programs was on pollution control through required technologies. In the late 1970s and 1980s, firms and later government began to see the value of an alternative approach that looked to the causes as well as the symptoms of environmental problems (Geiser 2004). Still, a prevention strategy is difficult to implement through regulation. Many environmental agencies have concluded that voluntary partnerships, including green clubs, are a better way to encourage pollution prevention. Nearly all of the green clubs discussed here incorporate pollution prevention into their program designs.

The earliest and best-known EPA green club was the 33/50 program, created under administrator William Reilly in 1992. Announced as an alternative to regulation, the EPA invited firms to commit publicly to reducing releases of seventeen priority chemicals tracked under the

Toxics Release Inventory (TRI) by 33 percent in 1992 and 50 percent in 1995. In exchange, the EPA publicly recognized the firms for their participation. Although there have been mixed evaluations of the program's effects, it cast a mold for the voluntary partnership programs that have followed (Khanna 2007), including some green clubs.

As of August 2007, the EPA was implementing some fifty-five voluntary programs nationally. Nearly half (43 percent) were located in the air office, followed by 25 percent in the toxics and pollution prevention office, 13 percent in waste, 11 percent in water, 4 percent in the policy office, and 4 percent in research and administration. Not all would meet the definition of a green club used in this book. Of these fifty-five, nine could be defined as a government-sponsored green club. Green clubs at the EPA would likely include Climate Leaders, Energy Star, the Green Power Partnership, the National Environmental Performance Track, the National Partnership for Environmental Priorities, the Pesticide Environmental Stewardship Program, the Smart Way Transportation Partnership, WasteWise, and Water Sense. The degree of rigor in these programs varies (Darnall and Carmin 2005). WasteWise, for example, has been criticized for obtaining annual reports from only about 20 percent of its members (Delmas and Keller 2005). Although more research is needed to evaluate these programs, they likely range across the typology of weak, medium, and strong sword programs. Table 10.1 lists the EPA partnership programs that may be classified as green clubs.

Of the green clubs that the EPA has created, the Performance Track was the most comprehensive and rigorous, and the one most explicitly linked to the existing regulatory system.[1] Launched in June 2000, near the end of administrator Carol Browner's tenure, the Performance Track was the EPA's response to a number of advisory bodies active in the 1990s, including the President's Council for Sustainable Development, the Aspen Institute, and the National Academy of Public Administration (Fiorino 2006, 127–128). Its purpose was to complement a conventional regulatory strategy with a more positive one that encourages facilities to do better than compliance and use more effective management practices. To qualify, applicants commited to measurable improvements in environmental performance that go beyond what is required legally, implemented an EMS, reached out to the community, and demonstrated a record of sustained compliance with environmental regulations at all levels of government. In return, they were recognized in several ways by the EPA, became eligible for regulatory flexibility (such as flexible or

Table 10.1
Green clubs at the EPA

EPA program	Year established	Approximate number of participants*	Office
Climate Leaders	2002	150	air
Energy Star	1992	9,000	air
Green Power Partnership	2001	700	air
Partnership for Environmental Priorities	2002	130	waste
Performance Track	2000	500	policy
Pesticides Environmental Stewardship	1994	190	toxics
SmartWay Transport	2004	600	air
WasteWise	1994	1,900	waste
WaterSense	2006	30	water

*The number of participants is approximate as of August 2007. The numbers change over time and should be seen as a rough indicator of the level of activity in the club.

expedited permits) or reduced reporting, and were provided opportunities for more constructive interactions with the EPA and state environmental agencies. By August 2008, some 550 facilities (mostly private, but also including public and nonprofit facilities) were members of the Performance Track.

A major question regarding green clubs is why people join. The EPA conducted Performance Track member surveys in 2004 and 2006 that shed light on this issue. The most common reason for members' interest in applying for and remaining in the program in 2004 was to build a more collaborative and constructive relationship with regulators. The second most common reason was public recognition from the EPA. In 2006, the most common reason given in the survey was to improve environmental performance. Improved relationships with agencies and public recognition that may be gained through use of the Performance Track brand also ranked high in this second survey (EPA 2007a).

A study by the Kennedy School of Government concluded that Performance Track members "are distinguished by a distinct tendency to value and seek external recognition" (Coglianese and Nash 2006, 5). The study found that participants in the Performance Track tend to have a stronger and more open orientation to the outside world than comparable organizations that do not participate. The program attracts "those who already cultivate an identity of environmental responsibility and environmental leadership, who value recognition and actively seek to engage regulators and communities, and who enjoy managerial support for such efforts" (ibid.). The study cautioned that because of a lack of comparable performance data, it is difficult to state definitively that Performance Track members are better performers than other facilities with strong compliance records and management systems. It is their openness and management styles that may more clearly distinguish them from their peers.

The experience with government green clubs illustrates the difficulties to implementing collaborative efforts within a traditionally adversarial regulatory culture. For example, the EPA's inspector general issued a critique of the Performance Track in 2007 that evaluated members' environmental goals as legally required standards rather than results they would aim to achieve and report on annually (EPA 2007c). As the EPA reported in its response to the critique, most members met or exceeded their goals and measurably improved their performance, as is discussed later in the chapter. In addition, as the EPA noted in its response (attached to the main report), the inspector general critique made assertions about compliance records that were based on faulty and outdated data, or failed to place relatively minor compliance issues in context. Similarly, claims about increases in emissions reported in the Toxic Release Inventory failed to account for changes in the EPA's calculation methodologies that made it appear as if emissions had increased when in most cases they had not—an issue that the EPA addressed in its response as well.

There also has been debate, as is suggested in chapter 11, that members of green clubs are not clearly and demonstrably superior in their environmental performance to other facilities, whether regulated or unregulated. The problem in investigating this issue is that the larger quantity of information available on Performance Track members is not matched by what is available on nonmembers, simply because members report on several environmental indicators for which they have set goals. Comparable data are not available on nonmembers, who have not reported and in most cases probably have not even tracked these indicators. Data from the Toxics Release Inventory (TRI) have been used in a wide range of empirical studies as the dependent variable, but this is a limited indicator of overall performance, and because of changes in measurement methods from year to year and other factors, not a particularly reliable indicator of facility performance. Relying just on the TRI data also omits most of the important indicators of environmental sustainability, such as energy, water, and materials use; a range of air and water pollution indicators; product design and supply chain management, habitat conservation, and protection; many kinds of waste; and greenhouse gas emissions, among others. In fact, many active participants in green clubs, such as Johnson & Johnson, Hewlett-Packard, Intel, Coca-Cola, and Toyota, consistently place high in environmental rankings of major firms. Nonetheless, better information on the environmental performance of members of green clubs relative to other facilities would be valuable in assessing the design of these programs and their criteria for membership.

Green Clubs in the U.S. States

Much of the effort to create government-sponsored clubs in the United States has been occurring at the state level. Although interest has grown steadily over the past ten years, there were false starts. In 2000, Oregon and New Jersey created green clubs (the Green Permits and the Gold and Silver Track programs, respectively) that have largely been discontinued. Since then, several states have created voluntary partnership programs that fit the definition of a green club. As of September 2007, twenty-two states had created programs that meet the definition of a green club as presented here; five others (New Hampshire, New York, Mississippi, Washington, and West Virginia) were developing one.[2]

Although they all meet my definition of a government green club, these state programs vary (EPA 2007b). The main sources of variation are the number of levels, criteria for membership, standards for member accountability, involvement of outsiders in decision making, and member benefits. Some states, such as Arizona and Indiana, have only one level. Others, such as Virginia and Colorado, have three or four. Nearly all require an annual report. South Carolina and North Carolina have created external advisory groups to evaluate applications, but most states have not. Some state clubs have only a few members; others number in the dozens. Several states have linked their application process with the EPA, while others maintain separate application processes.

Table 10.2 lists and compares sixteen of the clubs along several of these dimensions. (The other six states are not included on this list

Table 10.2
State-level green clubs

State	Year created	Number of tiers	Compares to Performance Track	Joint application*	State regulatory benefits*	Specific legal authority*
Arizona Performance Track	2005	1	One-level	X	X	
Colorado Environmental Leadership	1998	4	Gold leader	X	X	
Georgia P2 Partnership	2004	4	Blue	X	X	
Idaho GEMStars	1998	3	One-level	X	X	
Indiana Environmental Stewardship	2006	1	One-level			
Kentucky EXCEL	2005	4	Master			
Maine STEP-UP	2000	3	Leadership		X	X
Missouri Environmental Partnership	2002	4	Advanced partner		X	
New Mexico Green Zia	1998	3	Excellence			X
North Carolina Environmental Stewardship	2002	3	Rising steward			
South Carolina Environmental Excellence	1996	1	One-level		X	
Tennessee P2 Partnership	2000	6	Performer			
Clean Texas	1998	4	Gold	X	X	X
Clean Utah!	2004	3	Leader	X	X	
Virginia Environmental Excellence	2000	3	Extraordinary environmental enterprise		X	X
Wisconsin Green Tier	2004	2	Tier 2		X	X

* Denotes states having joint applications with the EPA's Performance Track, states authorizing additional regulatory benefits to members, and states that have enacted specific legal authority for a green club.

because they are relatively inactive or there is a lack of comparable information about them.) The table lists the number of tiers or levels in each program, the name of the level (if there is more than one) most comparable to the EPA's Performance Track, the number of members in that specific tier, if the EPA and the state have adopted a joint application, whether the state offers any regulatory benefits to members beyond those that were available to members of the national Performance Track, and the programs for which the state legislature has enacted specific statutory authority.

The theory behind government clubs is that their benefits will encourage members to produce positive externalities. These benefits to members fall into two groups. One is intangible or "soft" benefits, such as public recognition, networking, and better relationships with government and communities. The second is tangible or "hard" benefits, which may translate directly into financial advantages and operating efficiency. These include regulatory flexibility (e.g., flexible permitting) and reduced transaction costs (e.g., expedited permitting and reduced reporting). The first allows a member to create social and regulatory capital, and indirectly, to achieve top line and bottom line business advantage from membership. The second provides more immediate financial benefits that firms can assign to the bottom line. The second group is available only from government; they are a nonrival benefit that nongovernmental clubs may not offer.

All sixteen of the state clubs listed in table 10.2 offer recognition. These include public recognition from the agency (such as listing on a Web site or in press releases), the use of a program logo, public events with the governor or environmental agency head, and others. Most of these also either state or imply that membership leads to a different relationship with regulators. In their public materials, eleven of the sixteen state green clubs promise or make available hard benefits related to permitting, reporting, or reduced permit fees. The other five do not offer hard benefits that are specific to members of the state club, although four of these do offer regulatory benefits that have been developed by the EPA that are available only for members of the Performance Track program. Only Idaho makes no mention of benefits other than recognition on its program Web site.

In a federal system, organizations have three choices, at least in states having a green club. They may apply for the state program, the federal program, or both. Again, there has not been comparative research, but state and federal programs are able to offer different inducements. Because state agencies carry out the bulk of the permitting and enforcement within the federal system, they are in the best position to provide members with tangible regulatory benefits, such as expedited or flexible permitting and reduced inspections. For firms competing in national markets, the EPA recognition is valued. For the firm that wants to maximize the benefit of the green club, of course, participation at both levels would be desirable. The characteristics of the firm as well as the level of alignment between a state and federal program would affect the level of interest.

The timing for the creation of federal and state clubs is interesting. The median year for the creation of the sixteen green clubs listed in table 10.2 is 2002. Assuming that the programs in the five pending states were launched as planned in 2008, the median year rises to 2004. The EPA's Performance Track was created in 2000. Of the twenty-two state clubs that the EPA tracks, nineteen were created between 1998 and 2005. There are two explanations for this timing. One is that the EPA and states were responding to the same pressures and sense of opportunity. The second is that there was a "diffusion of innovation" effect in which the adoption of green clubs in one jurisdiction stimulated their adoption in others. Although there is evidence of both, the second may be readily documented. In creating the Performance Track, the EPA drew on experiences from Oregon, Wisconsin, and New Jersey. More important, the EPA's launch of a Performance Track as well as its efforts to coordinate and align state programs with that program stimulated activity in the states (on this diffusion of innovation effect generally, see Rabe 1999). The EPA also has provided financial support for state green clubs as part of its State Innovation Grant program in recent years.

State green clubs offer a fruitful area for empirical research. Their growth has been one of the more interesting trends in environmental policy—one that is consistent with evidence that states have become more innovative and progressive (Rabe 2006). The EPA's program has stimulated interest among states, but many states likely would have moved in this direction even had the EPA not. State legislatures and agencies that create green clubs are responding to the same motivations that drove the EPA to create the Performance Track: they are trying to reconcile citizen demands for environmental protection with concerns about jobs and growth. They are seeking collaborative, flexible, and results-based approaches to problems. State agencies still define themselves as regulators, but they are responding to the limits of the old regulatory model by developing new strategies (Fiorino 1999, 2001, 2006), of which green clubs are a prominent example.

Issues in Implementing Government Green Clubs

Like any others, government clubs face many design and implementation issues. Three are examined here. First, to what extent may overcrowding affect their success, especially given the limited resources that now are dedicated to them? Second, to what degree does shirking threaten their credibility, and how may it be minimized? Third, the justification for government green clubs is that they cause their members to produce positive externalities. How effective are they in producing these externalities?

Overcrowding in Government Clubs

The benefits of government clubs are nonrival, so there is no equivalent of a commons that is being consumed and reducing the benefits available for others. To a point, additional members, especially if they exemplify the attributes sought for the club, will serve to enhance the value of membership. Other clubs that offer impure public goods illustrate the effects of overcrowding on membership. At a fitness club, for example, the number of members may grow to the point that equipment is unavailable, staffing is insufficient, and maintenance declines—all of which reduces membership value.

Similarly, the value of government green clubs could erode if they grow too rapidly or beyond the level of government resources that are available to support them. Voluntary programs usually are funded at the margins, because hard-pressed agencies find it difficult to take resources away from regulatory programs to fund what are seen as discretionary activities. Staffing for state green club programs typically is from one to three positions. Similarly, at the EPA, staffing for the Performance Track remained essentially the same as the number of members grew from three hundred to over five hundred. If the membership exceeds the capacities of the club managers, such basic member services as recognition opportunities, flexible permitting, and others could suffer, and thus the value of membership could decline.

Another consequence of overcrowding for government clubs is that agencies will have difficulty in maintaining the quality of the club and its members. Unlike other voluntary programs, credible clubs involve a system of obligations and expectations from both government and members. For example, in the EPA's Performance Track, members submitted an Annual Performance Report, maintained the quality of their EMS and compliance, conducted audits at regular intervals, and had to be available for site visits from the EPA and states. Each of these involves corresponding obligations from government, which had to evaluate the reports, monitor systems quality and compliance, and conduct the site visits. Membership could grow to the point that an agency could not meet these obligations, and the quality of members and hence the credibility of the program could suffer.

Shirking in Government Clubs

As the theoretical framework for this collection suggests, shirking is a potential problem for green clubs. Members who do not meet their obligations may undermine confidence in the club and tarnish its reputation. To maintain the credibility and thus the club's value to members, agencies should be able to prevent or at least minimize shirking.

Green clubs may avoid shirking through three mechanisms: third-party auditing of member qualifications and performance; public disclosure of conformance with program criteria; and through sanctioning, such as removal from the club. Weak sword clubs include only the first; medium sword clubs require the first two; strong sword clubs involve all three mechanisms (Potoski and Prakash 2005a).

The Performance Track may be classed as a strong sword club because it included all three measures. Members at a minimum must have had an independent assessment of their EMS under defined protocols. They were subject to a site visit from the EPA and the state to evaluate their performance. The EPA had conducted some 260 site visits as of August 2008, and aimed to visit 5 to 10 percent of its members annually. As for public disclosure, all applications, renewals, and Annual Performance Reports were made public on the program Web site, and members took measures to inform the local community. Those failing to maintain their qualifications or report as required were removed. As of August 2008, sixty-six members had been removed or not renewed for failing to maintain their qualifications or meet program obligations, such as the Annual Performance Report. From the beginning, these measures were seen to be necessary to protect the program's credibility, particularly since membership involves recognition and different treatment in the regulatory system.

State programs vary in their efforts to minimize shirking. It is difficult to classify them, because many have the authority to remove members but try to avoid exercising it. Because admission into state green clubs is at the discretion of the agency, nearly all states appear to have formal authority to remove members. Like the Performance Track, however, they preferred to use this authority with a soft touch, by asking members to leave rather than putting them through a formal removal process. Most but not all require some kind of third-party audit, usually of the EMS rather than of the full program requirements. All of the state programs involve some measure of public disclosure, although the specific requirements vary. In sum, it is difficult to determine how rigorous these programs are without a more detailed empirical examination of their operation. Yet at a formal level, most appear to fall into the medium sword category, with some (e.g., Texas, Virginia, and North Carolina) potentially meeting the strong sword criteria.

The Effectiveness of Green Clubs

As creations of government, the green clubs discussed in this chapter are expected to produce benefits for society. Although lightly funded (e.g., the Performance Track uses less than .01 percent of the EPA's total budget), they still consume resources that could be used for more traditional regulatory functions, such as permitting or inspections. Moreover, members incur opportunity costs by participating in the club. Are clubs worth the effort?

Green clubs may produce several kinds of benefits for society. The first and most obvious are environmental results that otherwise may not be achieved. To the extent that members reduce pollution, save energy and water, protect habitat, or redesign products, they are fulfilling a prime purpose of clubs. These are measurable results and may be documented. The EPA has been systematic in documenting results in member Annual Performance Reports that are publicly available, and annual *Progress Reports* that compile and analyze these data. Between 2001 and 2006, the EPA reported, among other results, that Performance Track members reduced greenhouse gases by 310,000 tons of carbon dioxide equivalent, sulfur oxides by 43,000 tons, nitrogen oxides by 12,800 tons, volatile organic compounds by 3,000 tons, nontoxic discharges to water by 33,000 tons and toxics to water by 3,000 tons, and water use by 5.2 billion gallons (EPA 2008b). All of these results extended beyond the existing legal requirements. The benefits to society of these reductions may be substantial. For the three air pollutants (sulfur oxides, nitrogen oxides, and volatile organic compounds) for which the EPA has developed methods for monetizing the health benefits of emission reductions, for example, the benefits fall in a range of $93 to $974 million (ibid.). Even if a small percentage of the results may be attributed to the club, the environmental returns on the government's investment could be significant.

To what extent would these results have been achieved anyway? Critics of government clubs argue that agencies merely are recognizing firms for doing what they would have done without the club. Clearly, many forces are pushing firms to achieve environmental results that government does not require (see, e.g., Reinhardt 2000; Esty and Winston 2006). It would not be valid to attribute all of the reported gains to the effects of the clubs alone. Still, there is evidence that payoffs from club membership do affect behavior. Anecdotally, members of these clubs report that being in a government green club helps to solidify internal support for environmental initiatives, reinforces a long-term commitment to environmental improvement, and encourages firms to set more stringent goals or improve their management systems. In a survey that the EPA conducted in 2007, 53 percent of Performance Track members reported that their participation had led them to seek innovative solutions to environmental problems, 40 percent noted that they had reduced environmental impacts in ways that would not have occurred otherwise, and 30 percent said they had improved their EMS to be able to qualify for the program. Although more research is needed, these results suggest that clubs generate environmental benefits (EPA 2007a).

The literature on government voluntary programs generally (which includes more than green clubs) indicates that they offer modest but measurable benefits. One set of case studies, for instance, concluded that "voluntary programs have a real but limited effect, particularly among energy-related activities" (Morgenstern and Pizer 2007, 182). One of the first government green clubs, the 33/50 program, appeared to have a small but statistically significant effect on emissions by the participants relative to the nonparticipants (Khanna 2007). There is also evidence, this same analysis concluded, that 33/50 paid longer-term dividends by encouraging more integrated environmental management, more sharing of information within and among firms, and more awareness of the avoidable costs of waste generation and disposal. A study of another early EPA green club (Climate Wise, which ran from 1993 to 1999, and was replaced by Climate Leaders) concluded it had a short-term and transient effect on greenhouse gas emissions by the participants, reducing the emissions by about 3 percent over a one- to two-year period. The study noted that later programs, such as Climate Leaders, incorporated more rigorous goal setting and reporting, and that may increase their effect on emissions. A longer-term program with a different design, especially if linked to a threat of regulatory action, could have a more substantial effect.

Based on these and their other case studies, Richard Morgenstern and William Pizer (2007, 183) conclude that voluntary programs may play an important role in environmental protection when legal authority or political support for mandatory action is lacking, but that "it is hard to argue for voluntary programs when there is a clear desire for major changes in behavior." They also recognize that voluntary programs offer soft benefits that are difficult to quantify, such as "changes in attitudes or management practices that are viewed by participants and stakeholders as significant steps in improving long-term stewardship" (182). Similarly, incremental yet measurable improvements in performance, augmented by longer-term social benefits, may define the core strengths of green clubs.

Although the emphasis has been on producing environmental results beyond what is legally required, green clubs also may produce benefits in terms of better compliance. In a study of thirty-seven hundred regulated facilities, Potoski and Prakash (2005a) found that those with ISO certifications demonstrated a better compliance rate with air quality rules than did comparable facilities without certification. They attribute this higher rate of compliance to a sense of obligation to uphold club standards and meet commitments made publicly.

A second kind of benefits to society comes in improved problem-solving capacities gained by having more collaborative, open, and trust-based relationships. For both agencies and members, these are the primary purposes of forming and participating in clubs. Indeed, in the Performance Track members' survey, the opportunity to build a different relationship with regulators was cited as a principal motivation for joining. Much of the literature on regulation suggests that lower transaction costs, more trust, and better information sharing facilitate innovation and problem solving (Kagan 2000; Wallace 1995; May 2004, 2005). These constitute long-term system benefits that are difficult to quantify, but they may constitute some of the most important long-term benefits of government-sponsored green clubs.

Green Clubs as Tools for Government

Using clubs as policy tools within established and often inflexible systems of deterrence-based regulation presents challenges. One is agency and regulatory culture. Environmental protection in the United States relies almost entirely on a regulatory strategy. In this model, legislatures delegate authority to agencies that define standards and procedures to which affected entities must conform (Bardach and Kagan 1982; May 2005). In the United States, regulation has taken on a more legalistic and adversarial style than it has in many other countries (Kagan 2000; Gunningham, Kagan, and Thornton 2003). These contrasts in regulatory style have been a prominent theme in the literature on comparative regulation.

The relationships created by government green clubs clash directly with this style of governance. For advocates of the conventional approach, nearly any collaboration may undermine the enforcement underpinnings of the regulatory system. Such programs have been criticized as a distraction from the "core" regulatory programs. Any attempt to reduce oversight based on performance or management criteria (i.e., being a member of the club) are seen as an opportunity for cheating. These arguments have been made by critics of the EPA's Performance Track, for example, and surely will be applied to state green clubs also. Opposition within agencies—largely from enforcement staff—and from some environmental activists will challenge green clubs at all levels of government.

A second challenge is the statutory framework. So long as the benefits of programs are limited to recognition, agencies generally have been able to carry them out without specific statutory authority. Given that the EPA's and many state green clubs now aim to provide regulatory flexibility or reduce transaction costs for members, however, the lack of explicit statutory authority has become an issue. Agencies now wish to grant exceptions to rules for club members, and that may be difficult to accomplish under existing laws. This issue is not unique to green clubs; a similar lack of legal flexibility impeded such earlier reform initiatives as the EPA's Project XL in the 1990s (Mank 1998).

The concept of treating entities that distinguish themselves from others is not one that has been incorporated into environmental laws. Although the law may authorize or require differential treatment based on size, industry sector, or the age of a facility, it is difficult to find provisions that authorize agencies to treat members of a green club differently from nonmembers based on performance. The first regulatory provision that offered flexibility to Performance Track members (granting extensions for hazardous waste storage) was not justified as a way to recognize their performance, because that was not acknowledged in the statute. Instead, it was justified as a way to collect data on a possibly better approach to regulation. Some of the laws authorizing state green clubs have addressed this issue by granting specific authority for agencies to vary requirements based on membership in the club. Given the litigious nature of the U.S. regulatory culture, the long-term survival of government green clubs depends on their having a clear statutory basis, particularly in authorizing agencies to treat club members differently.

The Future of Green Clubs in Government

Club theory offers a useful framework for studying and evaluating government-sponsored green clubs. It provides an analytic basis for distinguishing clubs from other voluntary programs, and more generally from regulation and other approaches that government has used in the past. As this chapter illustrates, the concepts of excludable and nonrival benefits, member accountability to maintain the club's reputation, the enforcement of club standards, and the positive externalities that clubs offer are valuable for understanding the strengths and challenges of using clubs as a tool for government.

Government clubs are similar conceptually to such nongovernmental clubs as ISO 14000, Responsible Care, and the Forest Stewardship Council. They offer nonrival, excludable benefits to their members in recognition of members' efforts to achieve social goals. Their rapid growth in the last decade makes them an important area for research.

Despite these similarities, government clubs also differ fundamentally from those in which government plays no role. They carry the imprimatur of government. It is a delicate matter for government agencies to confer benefits on one set of firms and not others. An even greater complication is that it is *regulatory* agencies that are conferring these benefits. Legally, culturally, and historically, regulatory agencies are designed to establish rules, control behavior, find fault, and exact penalties when necessary. It is not an easy transition from this well-established, largely punitive role to one in which agencies offer positive incentives, encouragement, information, and networks to influence behavior in the desired directions.

A major issue is what actions are necessary from government to induce both private and public sector organizations to commit to green clubs and produce positive social externalities. This is a crucial area for research and lesson drawing from existing programs. The authors assert in chapter 11, that to expand membership in these clubs, government agencies must offer more program incentives (such as flexible permits or reduced routine compliance reporting) that will in turn draw more scrutiny from environmental activists and other critics of innovative approaches. Chapter 11 offers no empirical support for this assertion regarding expanded participation. It is just as likely that the soft benefits of green clubs—the reputational and relationship value, and the opportunity to engage with government and others in more productive problem solving—will turn out to be the more significant motivators of beyond compliance performance. Moreover, the logic of tailoring regulatory processes and paperwork to the performance characteristics of different organizations may eventually convince critics that the opportunities for more efficient governance and greater trust building are among the most important benefits of green clubs.

Within government, the most likely skeptics of green clubs are enforcement officials who find it difficult to reconcile a carrot-based approach to one that traditionally has relied on sticks. Outside of government, the likely critics are environmental activists who long have relied on adversarial tactics, including litigation and public shaming, to achieve their goals. On the other hand, program managers within agencies often view green clubs as an appealing extension of their influence and a way to get beyond compliance. NGOs that work collaboratively with business may view government clubs as yet another path to effective partnerships. In sum, the political landscape offers both barriers and support for the further adoption of green clubs.

The key to integrating green clubs into existing strategies lies in their credibility and effectiveness. To the extent that shirking is allowed, members fail to realize benefits, or measurable environmental outcomes are not demonstrated, green clubs will be difficult to sustain. Yet when properly designed, government-sponsored green clubs offer a valuable complement to existing strategies and a means of building more flexible, collaborative approaches to achieving environmental results. The evidence suggests that when used in conjunction with regulation (OECD 2002; O'Toole et al. 1997; Morgenstern and Pizer 2007), green clubs and other partnerships may offer an effective tool for achieving environmental results beyond what is accomplished through regulation.

Regulatory agencies still are grappling with the role of green clubs in their overall policy strategies. To this point, green clubs have been seen as a complement rather than a substitute for conventional regulation. To the extent that club membership is used to justify different treatment by regulators, as it was for the Performance Track and most of the state green clubs that were reviewed here, clubs offer a path for systemic change as well as a short-term tool for achieving results and promoting collaboration. In time, the successful implementation of green clubs by government may prove that carrots as well as sticks offer effective tools, not only for environmental protection, but in fulfilling a longer-term vision of environmental sustainability. At this stage in their development, though, the potential of green clubs as a tool for government is yet to be fully tested.

11

Government Clubs: Theory and Evidence from Voluntary Environmental Programs

Cary Coglianese and Jennifer Nash

In the preceding chapter, Daniel J. Fiorino offers a conceptual account of how governments use green clubs to try to achieve environmental results. In this chapter, we analyze the way green clubs run by the U.S. Environmental Protection Agency (EPA) manage a tension inherent in all clubs: attracting members while upholding standards.[1] As Matthew Potoski and Aseem Prakash explain in chapter 1, the positive social externalities that a green club achieves will depend both on the number of club members as well as the requirements for membership. The challenge for institutions that establish green clubs is to encourage large numbers of facilities to join while maintaining rigorous conditions for entry and ongoing membership.

All things being equal, the greater the benefits that can be offered to members, the more readily clubs can achieve both high membership rolls and high standards. Many green clubs, like the nongovernmental ISO 14001 (Prakash and Potoski 2006b), only promise enhanced reputation—that is, the possibility that investors, employees, and environmental regulators will look on members more favorably (Lyon and Maxwell 2004). Green clubs run by government, by contrast, can offer members more than an enhanced reputation; they can also offer relief from regulatory requirements. For example, the EPA's Performance Track program offered its members a low priority for routine regulatory inspections as well as the reduction in burdens associated with reporting and permitting regulations (see previous chapter). Only green clubs run by government can offer such regulatory benefits, so it would seem that government clubs would have a clear advantage when it comes to attracting members that meet high standards, at least compared to clubs run by other institutions.

Surprisingly, though, membership in some *non*governmental clubs significantly dwarfs membership in comparable governmental clubs. ISO 14001 has about ten times as many members in the United States as the Performance Track program, even though both have similar requirements and even though membership in Performance Track offered greater rewards than the ISO. After eight years of operation as the EPA's flagship voluntary program, however, Performance Track had only been able to recruit and retain about 550 individual facilities from across the nation—a fraction of the facilities with ISO-compliant EMSs. Assuming Performance Track's experience is emblematic of government clubs more generally, why has the level of participation in government clubs remained comparatively low?

In this chapter, we investigate why government clubs with the greatest benefits paradoxically have the fewest members. We explain this puzzling outcome by focusing first on the relationship between clubs' entry procedures and the rewards they offer members, and then on the relationship between membership levels and entry procedures. While government agencies in theory have the most to offer facilities that participate in their voluntary programs, in practice these agencies face a political environment that leads them to combine greater rewards with more demanding entry requirements. As Fiorino indicates, conferring benefits on individual regulated entities is a "delicate matter" for government officials, particularly when the benefits take the form of regulatory relief.

Our analysis accepts club theory's premise of a trade-off between attracting members and preventing them from shirking. We show that government clubs can achieve one or the other of these objectives—high growth or high standards—but not both. As a result, unlike Fiorino who optimistically views government clubs as "a path for systemic change," we suggest a substantially more limited role for government clubs. Club theory and our data lead us to predict that the level of participation in government clubs will continue to remain relatively low, especially when they offer substantial membership rewards. These rewards are simply not significant enough for many firms to overcome the additional demands that agencies place on potential members that are to receive those additional rewards. If "clubs with few members can hardly be considered successful" (Prakash and Potoski 2006b, 21), then in contrast with Fiorino, we actually should expect little from government clubs, notwithstanding their ability to offer additional inducements for membership.

Club Design and Participation

As Potoski and Prakash have emphasized, green clubs meet the challenges of attracting members and enforcing club standards through institutional attributes that provide sufficient incentives for businesses to join, while still ensuring adequate monitoring and enforcement of standards. Prakash and Potoski's (2006b) emphasis on institutional design points to an important way of explaining membership levels across green clubs. At least until Prakash and Potoski's work, scholars had paid remarkably little attention to how the design of voluntary environmental programs might affect participation. In a comprehensive review of the literature on voluntary programs, for example, Thomas Lyon and John Maxwell (2002) offered a series of eight factors affecting participation in voluntary programs and these programs' performance—none of which directly related to the issue of program design. The relative lack of attention to the design of voluntary programs is striking because any potential member's assessment of the costs and benefits of participation presumably rests not only on that prospective member's own business model and organizational characteristics but also on what kinds of benefits and costs the voluntary program actually offers and imposes.[2]

One reason institutional design has been so little emphasized may be that existing research has used the individual firm as the unit of analysis, seeking to explain varying firms' decisions while holding the voluntary program—or government club—constant. For example, Madhu Khanna and Lisa Damon (1999) and Seema Arora and Timothy Casson (1995, 1996) analyze differences between participants and nonparticipants in the EPA's 33/50 program, while Prakash and Potoski (2006b) use a single club—ISO 14001—as their main example. Restricting attention to participation in individual voluntary programs has allowed researchers to gain analytic traction on the firm- or facility-level characteristics that correlate with participation. Nevertheless, such an approach does not allow researchers to assess whether or how differences in program design may also influence firms' decisions.

To see how design differences may affect participation, we begin by considering three of the EPA's most prominent voluntary programs: the 33/50 program, Performance Track, and Project XL. For each, we describe the package of benefits that the EPA has offered, and the standards it has set for entry and ongoing participation. We also describe the numbers and characteristics of facilities that have joined each program. These three programs represent a progression in terms of their standards for participation and the rewards they offer. Although the EPA has given high priority to each of these programs, membership in them has varied substantially. The 33/50 program engaged roughly twenty-five times the number of facilities as Project XL, and membership in Performance Track reached a level between the extremes of 33/50 and XL.

The 33/50 Program

The EPA's 33/50 program, launched in early 1991, sought to encourage businesses voluntarily to reduce emissions and transfers of seventeen targeted chemicals required to be reported under the TRI, an environmental disclosure system that Congress mandated in 1986 under the Emergency Planning and Community Right to Know Act. The program received the name 33/50 because it aimed to reduce overall TRI releases of the targeted chemicals by 33 percent by 1992 and 50 percent by 1995.

The EPA developed its list of seventeen targeted chemicals by asking its regulatory offices to name their high-priority chemicals. Any TRI chemical making the list of more than one office came under the rubric of 33/50. The program's interim goal of 33 percent and its ultimate goal of 50 percent were based largely on a suggestion made in an earlier report published by the Office of Technology Assessment that a 50 percent reduction in toxic releases would be feasible (U.S. Congress 1986).

Any company that released any one of the targeted chemicals was eligible to participate. To join, a company needed only to commit to reducing at least one of these chemicals—and to do so by any amount. The 33 and 50 percent reduction goals applied to overall emissions of the targeted chemicals, not necessarily targets for individual businesses.

The EPA faced the decision of what baseline year to use to measure the attainment of its toxics reduction goals. Companies and trade associations that had already undertaken major efforts to reduce toxic releases before 1991 argued against using 1991 or 1990 as a baseline year because it might advantage those companies that waited longer to begin reducing releases. According to EPA staff, industry also wanted to make the voluntary program a success by meeting the EPA's reduction goal— something that would be more assured if the agency selected an earlier baseline year. In the end, the EPA used a 1988 baseline, which in early 1991 was the most recent year for which aggregate data on toxics releases were available.

The EPA actively recruited companies to join the program, targeting at the outset those companies with facilities having the largest volumes of toxic releases (Khanna 2007). The EPA sent an initial batch of invitation letters to the CEOs of the "Top 600" companies, which together accounted for about 66 percent of releases of the seventeen targeted chemicals based on 1988 data (EPA 1999). Of these businesses, 328 (64 percent) chose to join (Khanna 2007). In July 1991, the EPA sent letters to an additional 5,400 companies and followed up with telephone calls. It sent out a third round of invitations in 1992, to an additional 2,512 companies (ibid.). The businesses that the EPA contacted in the second and third rounds were smaller in size, had lower releases than the initial Top 600 group, and were relatively less responsive to the EPA's invitation, with only about 13 percent signing up (Davies and Mazurek 1996). Out of about 10,000 companies eligible for the program because they reported toxic releases, the EPA overall invited about 8,000 to participate, and by the end of the program, about 1,300 facilities had joined (EPA 1999; Khanna 2007).

Perhaps not surprisingly given the EPA's initial outreach to businesses with the largest volumes of toxic releases, 33/50 participants tended overall to be large, profitable businesses with large emissions (Arora and Casson 1995; Gamper-Rabindran 2006). They also tended to market their products directly to consumers, have large advertising and research budgets (Arora and Casson 1996), and be publicly traded (Gamper-Rabindran 2006). Beyond these common features, other characteristics varied according to the participants' sector. In the transport industry, for example, plants surrounded by poorer households were less likely to participate. In the chemical industry, plants were more likely to join if the EPA had recently inspected them (ibid.).

For businesses that joined, the participation costs were minimal. A manager simply had to write the EPA a short letter committing to reduce any amount of one or all of the seventeen targeted chemicals against their 1988 level of releases.[3] On the EPA's receipt of such a letter, the company was "in" the 33/50 club. The EPA then recognized these companies by sending them a certificate of appreciation signed by the administrator. The commitments were in no way legally binding, and the EPA made this clear to the participants. The EPA encouraged businesses to set their own goals and time frames. As noted, individual facilities did not need to commit to reducing their own releases by 33 or 50 percent. Indeed, a notable proportion of companies—up to 40 percent according to a 1995 evaluation commissioned by the EPA—received certificates even though the EPA could not quantify any specific level of reductions stated in their commitment letters (EPA 1995a). Each company received the same certificate of appreciation regardless of the level of its commitment. Furthermore, the EPA made no effort to see whether individual companies followed through on whatever commitments they made.

The overall releases from both participating and nonparticipating companies declined enough to meet the EPA's national 33 and 50 percent goals. By the end of the first year of the program, the total reported releases of the seventeen targeted chemicals were down more than 33 percent compared with 1988 levels. By the end of 1995, the total releases of the targeted chemicals had dropped by 55 percent, or 824 million pounds, since 1988 (Khanna 2007).

The 33/50 program has been the subject of numerous research studies that present a complex picture of the program's impact (Khanna and Damon 1999; Sam and Innes 2005; Gamper-Rabindran 2006). No one seriously thinks that 33/50 led to the entire 55 percent reduction in the release of targeted chemicals from 1988 to 1995. Khanna (2007) observed, based on a review of EPA (1999) data, that 28 percent of the reduction attributed to the program occurred in the period 1988–1990, before 33/50 even began. Obviously, these reductions should be attributed to other factors besides 33/50.[4] Furthermore, other TRI chemicals not included in the 33/50 program also declined, suggesting that factors having nothing to do with 33/50 probably contributed to reductions in the targeted chemicals, including preexisting corporate pollution control programs, the closure of facilities, the elimination of product lines, the incentives provided by the public availability of TRI data, and traditional regulations aimed at the targeted chemicals. The EPA, in fact, issued a proposed or final rule directed at reducing almost every one of the seventeen target chemicals between 1988 and 1991. The 33/50 chemical having the single largest percentage reduction—1,1,1-trichloroethane, an ozone-depleting chemical found in industrial solvents—was subject to a regulatory ban under the Montreal Protocol (EPA 1999). The reductions in this one chemical alone accounted for approximately 20 percent of the total reductions in 33/50 chemicals from 1988 to 1996 (ibid.).

In addition, TRI data themselves raise questions. Since the EPA uses industry's own reporting, if companies devote more attention to estimating their releases they may be able to report reductions on paper that do not necessarily reflect real reductions. Companies also can escape the requirement to report releases if they reduce their use of designated toxic chemicals to below given thresholds, a reporting artifact that may account for as much as 40 percent of the reductions in reported releases (Bennear 2008). Of course, concerns about TRI data are not restricted to 33/50 companies, so it might make sense to compare the progress of participants with that of nonparticipants. According to the EPA, the participants in 33/50 reduced targeted chemicals by 49 percent between 1991 and 1994, while the nonparticipants reduced the same chemicals by only 30 percent during the same time period (Davies and Mazurek 1996, 15). The overall release of targeted chemicals dropped 42 percent during the same period, while other TRI-reported chemicals dropped only 22 percent (ibid.). These findings, however, do not take into account the fact that companies signing up for 33/50 may have been predisposed to reduce their releases and that the same factors that led them to join also prompted them to reduce.

Using regression analysis, Khanna and Damon (1999) examined the effect of the program on releases in the chemical industry, reporting that the 33/50 program was associated with about a 28 percent decline in the target chemicals during the period 1991–1993. Abdoul Sam and Robert Innes (2005) similarly reported that the program corresponded with a reduction in releases and a decline in inspection rates. Shanti Gamper-Rabindran (2006, 408) eliminated from analysis two 33/50 chemicals required to be phased out under the Montreal Protocol and found that for the remaining fifteen chemicals, "the program did not reduce emissions in most industries." Only in the fabricated metals and paper industries did overall emissions decrease, and releases in the chemicals and primary metals industry actually increased. Moreover, reductions in releases in the fabricated metals industry were due to off-site transfers to recyclers, not source reduction, the preferred method under the program (Gamper-Rabindran 2006).

If 33/50's benefit to society came from incremental reduction in toxic releases, the primary benefit that the EPA offered participants was recognition—literally, a certificate of appreciation mailed a few weeks after the EPA received a company's letter of commitment. Companies could display their EPA certificates of appreciation in their headquarters' lobbies. The EPA also included the names of participating companies in its annual Progress Update Reports and other publications. In the later years of the program, the EPA decided to allow companies to submit "success stories" describing their environmental efforts—stories that the

EPA then disseminated. The EPA also much later decided to cooperate with the publisher McGraw-Hill on a more selective awards program, called Environmental Champions, based on corporate-level performance as measured in TRI reports. The 33/50 program was officially "enforcement neutral," which is to say that the EPA did not offer any regulatory relief or enforcement discretion to the participants.[5]

The simplicity of 33/50's joining requirements made it easy for businesses to participate in this club, but those simple requirements also made it more difficult for the EPA to demonstrate the program's credibility. The 33/50 program failed to win the support of the national environmental community, which had actively sought a stronger voluntary program that would have promoted reductions in the use—not just the release—of toxic chemicals instead. Environmental groups were also concerned that companies could reduce releases in the target chemicals by switching to other toxic chemicals or by making "paper reductions" based on different estimation techniques rather than on real environmental gains. Instead of recognizing companies simply for making a commitment, environmentalists urged that the EPA require companies to submit additional documentation on their use-reduction efforts before being recognized under this program. Although they were not opposed to the idea of a voluntary pollution prevention program, they wanted to see that the program could achieve genuine and well-documented environmental results. Overall, environmentalists have not been convinced that 33/50 had a significant impact on the environment, tending to see it as basically a public relations ploy.

National Environmental Performance Track

Five years after 33/50 came to an end, the EPA launched its National Environmental Performance Track program. Like 33/50, Performance Track sought to induce individual facilities to make measurable environmental improvements by recognizing and encouraging facilities that commit to going above and beyond what they are required to do by law. The standards for entry and ongoing participation, however, were significantly higher than 33/50. To qualify for membership in Performance Track, a facility needed to have implemented a formal, independently assessed environmental management system, demonstrated a history of past environmental achievements, maintained a record of sustained compliance with environmental regulations, committed to improving its environmental performance, and engaged in community outreach activities.

To encourage facilities to join this club, the EPA initially contacted the participants in its other voluntary programs, including 33/50. Two hundred twenty-seven facilities joined during the initial application round in 2000. After that, Performance Track staff members focused recruitment efforts in three areas: facilities that met the program's environmental management system requirement, facilities that met the program's compliance requirement, and facilities that expressed interest in the program at conferences that the agency attended or organized. EPA staff members routinely contacted managers of the nearly 5,600 facilities that are certified to ISO 14001, since these facilities already met Performance Track's management system requirement. A much larger number, approximately 65,000 facilities, satisfied Performance Track's compliance requirement by having a generally clean record in the EPA's enforcement database; several years ago, the EPA sent program information to some of those facilities as well. Performance Track staff also regularly attended and spoke at a variety of professional and industry conferences in an effort to promote the program.

The Performance Track program staff reviewed applications for new members twice each year. After 2000, membership in Performance Track grew by about 12 percent annually. As of October 2008, the membership stood at 548 facilities. While members represented a wide range of economic activities, four major manufacturing sectors made up the substantial portion of the program's membership: chemical products, electronic and other electric equipment, pharmaceuticals and medical equipment, and transportation equipment. Yet many nonmanufacturing facilities participated along with a large number of public sector facilities (EPA 2007c). Nearly 15 percent of Performance Track facilities were operated by local, state, or federal governments.

Performance Track facilities tended to be located in relatively densely populated communities, where poverty levels are relatively low and people are relatively highly educated (Booz Allen Hamilton 2005).[6] Performance Track facilities were diverse in terms of size. In 2004, about 12 percent of facilities had fewer than 50 employees, and nearly 20 percent had fewer than 100 (EPA 2006a). The remaining 80 percent were distributed about evenly among the following size categories: 10–499 (29 percent), 500–1,000 (24 percent), and over 1,000 (27 percent) (ibid.).

Slightly less than half of all Performance Track facilities (47 percent) held environmental permits under the Clean Water, Clean Air, or Resource Conservation and Recovery Acts (Booz Allen Hamilton 2005).[7] About 30 percent had been designated large-quantity hazardous waste generators under the Resources Conservation and Recovery Act, 25 percent designated as major sources of air pollution, 9 percent were major sources of water pollution, and 7 percent were Hazardous Waste Treatment, Storage, and Disposal Facilities (Booz Allen Hamilton 2005). About half of all Performance Track plants held no major environmental permits (ibid.).

The costs of participation were considerably higher for Performance Track than they were for the 33/50 program. In order to have joined Performance Track, a facility must have completed a twenty-two-page application that asked questions about its location, size, and business sector, environmental management system, and past environmental accomplishments. The facility needed to describe four areas in which it promised to make future environmental commitments over the coming three years. Applications needed to include three community references and needed to be signed by a senior officer in the applying organization. The EPA reviewed each application and conducted its own screening to ensure each facility was in compliance with federal, state, and local regulations.

Once accepted into Performance Track, a facility's membership was valid for three years, at which point the facility needed to reapply. The EPA's expectation was that members would make progress toward achieving their performance commitments, and thus the program also required that members complete a twelve-page Annual Performance Report. The annual report, which needed also to be signed by the senior manager responsible for the facility, required facilities to "normalize" their current performance vis-à-vis a baseline level. The EPA posted facility Annual Performance Reports on its Web site, and facility managers were expected to make the report generally available to the public. EPA headquarters and regional staff visited about 10 percent of member facilities annually to confirm application information and assess progress toward facilities' commitments.

The EPA has claimed that Performance Track's positive social impacts were significant. During the period 2000–2006, members reported having reduced water consumption by 3.66 billion gallons, energy use by 4.25 million MMBTU, and hazardous waste generated by 52,266 tons

(EPA 2008b). They reported conserving some 16,809 acres of land (ibid.).

The results of the program have not yet been extensively reviewed by outside researchers, and as was true for 33/50, the key question is whether the reductions made by Performance Track facilities would have otherwise occurred in the absence of the program. Presumably even facilities not in Performance Track have reasons to reduce their environmental impacts, especially in terms of their use of materials, energy, and water where improvements to environmental performance can also result in private cost savings.

From the EPA's perspective, Performance Track offered three significant benefits to member facilities: recognition, networking opportunities, and regulatory and administrative incentives. In the first benefits category, the EPA offered several types of recognition. The agency listed members on its Web site, issued press releases announcing new members, and sent letters to relevant elected officials announcing a facility's acceptance to the program. The EPA allowed members to use the Performance Track logo at facility sites and in promotional materials. In addition, the EPA persuaded some social investment advisory firms to treat Performance Track membership as a factor in rating companies. Finally, the agency gave out several special awards only to Performance Track members (EPA 2006b).

The second benefits category included a number of networking opportunities for Performance Track members. The EPA occasionally invited member facilities to information sessions with senior EPA officials to discuss regulatory and administrative incentives. The EPA organized a members' event annually, regional roundtables, and a mentoring program that matched current and potential Performance Track members to share information about the application process and ways to improve environmental performance. In addition, members themselves created a separate Performance Track Participants Association that worked closely with the EPA to support the program.

Finally, the EPA worked with state agencies to offer a variety of regulatory and administrative benefits to participating members. These included reducing some of the routine administrative costs of environmental regulation. For example, the EPA deemed Performance Track facilities to be a low priority for routine inspections. The EPA also gave at least two formal regulatory exemptions to Performance Track members (EPA 2004).

First, members could file reports less frequently under the Maximum Achievable Control Technology (MACT) hazardous air pollutant provisions of the Clean Air Act. Second, Performance Track facilities could accumulate hazardous wastes on-site for up to 180 days, and in some cases 270 days, without a RCRA permit (in comparison to the usual 90 days) (EPA 2004). In announcing these regulatory benefits, the EPA estimated that overall, facilities would stand to gain about $700,000 over the next three years from reduced monitoring costs and increased flexibility, or on average about $1,350 annually per facility (ibid.).

The EPA proposed offering additional modifications in regulatory requirements to Performance Track members. Environmental advocacy organizations sharply criticized such proposals, however, thereby demonstrating the political climate within which government clubs operate. For example, in comments on the EPA's 2005 proposal to expand Performance Track benefits, the Natural Resources Defense Council objected to incentives that would reduce monitoring, record keeping, and reporting for Performance Track members, and would reduce EPA and state oversight (Walke 2005). The Environmental Integrity Project, a nonprofit environmental organization, similarly called on the EPA to step back from "ever more ambitious regulatory breaks" for Performance Track members (Ware 2006). Both the Natural Resources Defense Council and the Environmental Integrity Project raised concerns that the Performance Track entry criteria failed to ensure that members could demonstrate truly "superior" environmental performance that would warrant such benefits. In a letter to then-EPA administrator Stephen Johnson, the Environmental Integrity Project and thirty other environmental organizations called on the agency to delay expanding Performance Track until it could "show that the program's [societal] benefits justify reducing oversight, relaxing legal requirements, or excusing violations of the law" (Schaeffer et al. 2006).

At the time, the EPA disagreed with the environmentalists' criticisms, and it did issue a further exemption in 2006 that allows certain Performance Track plants to reduce the frequency with which they self-inspect their hazardous waste processing (EPA 2006d). Yet even this form of regulatory relief was still markedly more modest than the regulatory benefits originally proposed by the EPA when it created Performance Track.

In addition to criticisms from environmental groups, Performance Track elicited broader concerns. It received negative media coverage and criticisms from members of Congress (Coglianese and Nash 2008).

The agency's own Inspector General (IG) voiced similar apprehensions, finding that some Performance Track members' regulatory compliance and releases of toxic chemicals fell below the average performance level for their sector. The IG argued that these underperforming facilities undermined the integrity of the program (EPA IG 2007).

Although the EPA's Performance Track office disputed the IG's criticisms (EPA 2007b), their very existence demonstrates a core vulnerability facing green clubs run by government. As government attempts to broaden the benefits offered to participants, it can expect pressure from both within and outside government to tighten the membership process to ensure participants are truly worthy of the benefits they receive. Given the political climate within which government clubs operate, it should come as little surprise that a program like Performance Track that offered more benefits than 33/50 also had entry requirements more demanding than 33/50. Even with these more demanding entry requirements, Performance Track had been subjected to substantial criticism, and in March 2009 President Obama's EPA administrator terminated the program.

Project XL

The EPA's design for Project XL was decidedly more ambitious than 33/50's and Performance Track's. In the wake of a Republican sweep of congressional elections in 1994, President Bill Clinton and Vice President Al Gore announced Project XL as part of an initiative to "to develop innovative alternatives to the current regulatory system" (Clinton and Gore 1995). The EPA intended Project XL to encourage "eXcellence and Leadership" in environmental management—hence the name XL. Viewed at the time as the EPA's flagship voluntary program, Project XL sought to promote superior environmental results by offering participants individualized regulatory exemptions. The EPA committed to considering proposals to waive virtually any regulatory requirement if an applicant facility could demonstrate that doing so would enable the facility to achieve superior environmental performance through alternative technologies or processes.[8]

Both Project XL and Performance Track trace their ideological roots to a set of discussions convened by the Aspen Institute in the early 1990s about alternatives to existing environmental regulation. One recommended alternative was to recognize and treat differently organizations if they meet high standards and pledge to attain "superior environmental performance" (Aspen Institute 1994, 4). While the Aspen Institute did not use the language of club theory, in essence it was proposing the establishment of a government club for environmental leaders for whom usual regulatory requirements would not apply. In addition to favorable publicity, government would provide participants with "increased flexibility as to how the environmental goals are achieved" and waivers of some regulatory requirements (ibid.).

In announcing Project XL, the EPA stated its intention "to give regulated sources the flexibility to develop alternative regulatory strategies that will replace or modify specific regulatory requirements on the condition that they produce greater environmental benefits" (EPA 1995b). The agency established a detailed set of criteria for facilities seeking to qualify for benefits under Project XL. To be eligible, facilities were required to demonstrate superior environmental performance improvements, reduce paperwork and cost, involve outside constituencies, prevent pollution in multiple media, establish measurable objectives, and broadly disseminate information. Facilities seeking regulatory flexibility under Project XL would first submit a proposal to the federal Regulatory Reinvention Docket. A team of EPA headquarters, regional, and state agency staff members would review each proposal to determine if it merited further consideration. If so, the facility could then decide whether to adapt its proposal in response to EPA feedback—usually by providing substantial additional information. If the facility chose to develop its proposal further, the EPA would then determine whether the revised proposal met the stated criteria for Project XL. If it cleared this hurdle, a proposal would come before the associate administrator for reinvention, who would consult with other EPA personnel before deciding whether to advance the proposal. At this point, the agency and the proposing facility would start developing a "Final Project Agreement," a negotiation that also included officials from the applicable state and local governments as well as representatives from interested environmental and community groups (ibid.). If the negotiations among these varied players yielded a consensus, the EPA and the facility would draw up a contract describing the project in detail (Caballero 1998).

When Project XL was first announced, many agency officials anticipated attracting an extensive competition among project proposals. President Clinton even declared that the EPA would complete fifty Project XL agreements within the first year. The agency received far fewer applications than expected, though. It was not until December 2000, five years after the program was launched, that the EPA could announce it had reached its fiftieth Project XL agreement. Even two years later, when the EPA announced that it would be permanently closing down Project XL, it had only completed a handful of additional agreements.

Project XL was open to any organization subject to EPA regulation. The early participants in Project XL were mostly large businesses. The first members, announced by President Clinton in fall 1995, included facilities operated by 3M, Hadco, Intel, Lucent, and Merck as well as by two public entities, the South Coast Air Quality Management District, and the Minnesota Pollution Control Agency (Lund 2000). Over time, Project XL's membership shifted to include still larger numbers of public sector organizations including cities, post offices, and sewer authorities. By October 2000, about half of all Project XL members were public facilities (Marcus, Geffen, and Sexton 2005).[9] In Project XL's later years, businesses seem "to have shied away from becoming involved in XL" (ibid., 300) due to the high costs and controversy surrounding the program.

Project XL was plagued with "process barriers" (Marcus, Geffen, and Sexton 2002). An EPA (1998, 41) review found that "most stakeholders commented the process was too long or much longer than they expected or felt was warranted." The negotiation of final agreements often required thousands of hours of time over many months (Marcus, Geffen, and Sexton 2002). The average duration needed to complete final agreements was twenty-six months (Delmas and Marcus 2004). The EPA emphasized from the start the importance of obtaining support from community and environmental advocacy groups before it would approve an XL application, even though involvement of these groups proved cumbersome. In addition, after the applicant secured agreement from the EPA, state regulators, community groups, and environmentalists, the EPA then proceeded to develop a site-specific rule making to implement the regulatory waiver sought by the applicant—a rule-making process conducted in Washington through the normal notice-and-comment procedures including publication in the *Federal Register* (Caballero 1998; Hirsch 1998).

According to an independent study of eleven of the earliest XL projects, the process of developing proposals and securing agreement imposed significant costs on businesses, averaging about $350,000 per proposal and rising to more than $500,000 in some cases (Blackman and Mazurek 1999). The most costly parts of the process were interacting with the EPA at both the regional and federal levels. Together, these interactions were responsible for half the costs to companies of advancing an XL proposal (ibid.). The costs to the EPA were also substantial. Not counting the costs to the EPA headquarters to run the program overall, the EPA regional offices spent on average about $111,000 to negotiate and approve each proposal, and in some cases the costs reached about $200,000 per proposal (ibid.). The costs were greatest for complex and innovative projects—"precisely the type of proposals that Project XL was designed to foster in order to improve the efficiency of the regulatory system" (ibid., 1). Companies were discouraged by the high transaction costs of participation, time-consuming review process, and complex negotiations required with a seemingly vast array of interest groups (Davies and Mazurek 1996).

In an effort to gauge the cumulative environmental benefits from Project XL, the EPA has attempted to aggregate the environmental benefits listed in the approved project proposals. Assuming these proposals accurately predicted actual environmental impacts, the cumulative benefits of nineteen such projects over the period 1997–2001 included the elimination of as much as 28,319 tons of criteria pollutants, 2,467 tons of volatile organic compound emissions, and 467 tons of hazardous air pollutants as well as the recycling of 20,540 tons of solid waste (EPA 2001). The EPA also claimed that the program was associated with a number of community benefits. Since people living near a Project XL facility were invited to participate in decision making about environmental management, they presumably enjoyed increased access to information about facility environmental impacts and operations (ibid.).

The benefits to the organizations that completed XL agreements with the EPA varied. Of course, as the program's name implies, the EPA gave recognition to participants for their "excellence and leadership," something that the EPA has claimed was "very helpful in improving relations with regulatory agencies and communities and in meeting the expectations of environmentally conscious consumers and shareholders" (ibid., 5). The waivers that the EPA promised Project XL participants were more substantial than the regulatory incentives provided through Performance Track. Intel's Project XL agreement, for example, allowed it to reduce the time to secure environmental permits for one of its semiconductor manufacturing facilities in Arizona. By eliminating the need for a permit every time the plant changed manufacturing processes to bring new products to market, the company was able to eliminate some thirty to fifty reviews annually (Lund 2000). Intel's cost savings were substantial, estimated to be in the millions of dollars, because permit delays were a key concern for a firm producing products in the fast-paced computer technology marketplace (ibid.).

Despite the fact that Project XL involved only a modest number of participating facilities, it generated widespread controversy similar to that sparked by Performance Track and, to a lesser extent, the 33/50 program (Susskind and Secunda 1998). For instance, frequent complaints arose over the vague and contested nature of the project's mission to achieve "superior environmental performance" (Marcus, Geffen, and Sexton 2002). Participants debated whether "superior" was to be understood relative to the level imposed by law on a facility or to its actual level of performance, which could already be cleaner than legally required. If a company were already performing better than the standards allowed, did it need to go further beyond compliance to secure an XL agreement? Or was it sufficient to continue to achieve any level of performance better than the regulatory standards, even if worse than before the agreement? Businesses preferred the latter, while environmentalists wanted the former. The agency frequently found itself in the middle.

In addition, critics both inside and outside the EPA charged that the program violated the law, since it was far from clear how the EPA had the authority to waive statutory requirements. It became commonplace to quip, "If it isn't illegal, it isn't XL" (Caballero 1998). Many at the EPA saw Project XL "as a threat" to the environmental regulatory system that they were charged with upholding (Susskind and Secunda 1998, 96). Aware that even one major environmental problem arising from an XL project had the potential to discredit the EPA and all XL facilities, agency officials painstakingly scrutinized XL proposals. Environmental advocacy groups viewed Project XL with suspicion, with some apparently claiming that XL stood for "EXtra Leniency" (Steinzor 1998, 125). Among other things, they feared that "business would subvert XL by offering EPA multimedia emissions trade-offs that could pose new and more serious hazards to workers and the environment" (Susskind and Secunda 1998).

Program Design and Participation

Although 33/50, Performance Track, and Project XL were all examples of green clubs, they exhibited striking differences in their overall design. The requirements for entry into these programs varied considerably, ranging in increasing stringency from a minimal letter of general commitment for 33/50, to completion of an extensive application and documentation of multiple beyond-compliance commitments for Performance Track, to an application process followed by an intensive multistakeholder negotiation followed by a site-specific rule making for Project XL. As the entry stringency increased across these three programs, the participation levels declined, from over 1,300 in 33/50 to about 550 in Performance Track to about 50 in Project XL.

What explains these varied levels of stringency? The insights of principal-agent theory should lead us to expect that the stringency of entry requirements for government clubs will be affected by the level of recognition and rewards to the participants of these programs. The standard principal-agent problem arises when individuals or organizations delegate authority to third parties (agents) to act on their behalf, since principals do not fully control their agents and agents' interests are not always fully aligned with those of their principals (Zeckhauser and Pratt 1985). While government regulators certainly do not make the participants in clubs their agents per se, they do give participating businesses something valuable—namely, the regulators' imprimatur. And like agents more generally, the businesses that participate do not have interests fully aligned with the government's goals. A principal whose agent shirks (i.e., exploits its discretion to pursue its own interests rather than those of the principal) will harm the principal. Similarly, businesses that participate in a green club, and thereby receive government recognition if not even exemption from normal regulations, can harm the reputation of the government agency sponsoring the club if they later are found to have created serious environmental problems or have violated normal environmental regulations.

An agency assumes a risk to its own reputation, and more important, a risk to its standing with its political overseers and the source of its budgetary appropriations, when it recognizes a facility or firm for some action of environmental leadership. When the agency gives businesses still greater recognition and rewards, it assumes as well a still greater exposure to risk of repercussions against the agency. We have seen that each of the three EPA programs failed to receive enthusiastic support from environmental organizations. Significantly, environmentalist criticisms grew stronger as the EPA gave, or proposed giving, members greater regulatory incentives. Since bureaucracies tend to be risk averse, we can expect they will be sensitive to criticisms that their programs are recognizing and rewarding the wrong companies, or that their claims of environmental gains from the programs lack credibility. In addition, for any given business an agency recognizes or rewards, there is at least a small potential that the business will later create a significant environmental problem, or have an accident or fatality on-site. Any regulatory agency that creates a club for "leaders" inherently risks public and political embarrassment should such an incident occur—not to mention the resulting legislative hearings along with the potential for legislative termination of voluntary programs or their appropriations.

The underlying general problem for principals in controlling their agents is an informational one. The principal usually does not know nearly as much as the agent does, nor can the principal fully know everything about the agent's actions. This informational asymmetry gives rise to various solutions that seek either to overcome this asymmetry or help encourage the agent to see it in its interests to serve the principal's interests. These solutions include: contracting, monitoring, power sharing, and reversibility (Coglianese and Nicolaidis 2001). Through contracting, principals either create incentive structures that realign agents' incentives with the principals' interests, or that delineate the authority granted to the agent so that it is defined in a way that restricts departures from the principals' interests. Monitoring refers to reporting and other mechanisms designed to overcome the information asymmetry that afflicts principals. Under power-sharing arrangements, agents must get authorization from or otherwise involve their principals in final decisions. And reversibility mechanisms allow principals the opportunity to override agents' decisions and even terminate the agency relationship.

When government agencies recognize and reward industry, their underlying informational problem is the same as that of any principal. How does the EPA know if a business it decides to recognize for reducing pollution will actually do what it commits to do? How will it know the business will not later turn out to be (or create) an environmental disaster that embarrasses the agency and subjects it to accusations of having cozied up to industry? The solutions for the regulator's problem are similar to the kinds of contracting, monitoring, power sharing, and reversibility used in addressing principal-agent problems more generally. The entry requirements that government imposes on prospective club members as well as the overall terms and conditions for participation reflect these kinds of solutions. Under Performance Track, for example, the EPA monitored facility environmental performance by requiring managers to complete a relatively lengthy application, visiting the participating facility, and reviewing annual progress reports. It also reserved the right to end the membership of any facility that did not live up to the program requirements, and it exercised this discretion on numerous occasions. Under Project XL, the EPA added a power-sharing mechanism, not only requiring a buy-in by community groups and environmentalists but also retaining the authority to reject the terms of a final project agreement.

For the same kinds of reasons that underlie principal-agent theory, then, we can expect that the greater the reward an agency gives to businesses that participate in government clubs, the greater will be the stringency of the club's entry requirements. That appears to be exactly what we observe with 33/50, Performance Track, and Project XL. The stringency of the entry requirements for these three clubs corresponds to the level of reward and recognition that each program provided to its participants. Under the 33/50 program, the EPA simply supplied participants with a certificate of membership, and so the entry requirements were minimal. Under Performance Track, the EPA offered participants higher-profile recognition by listing them on the agency's Web site—as well as inviting them to annual meetings with high-level EPA officials and providing modest exemptions from certain regulatory requirements. Performance Track's entry requirements were correspondingly more stringent than 33/50's. Under Project XL, the EPA promised participants a still more substantial benefit—namely, actual waivers from substantive environmental standards—and its entry requirements were the most stringent and intensive of all. Furthermore, as we have seen, as entry stringency increased across each of these three clubs, business participation declined, notwithstanding the changes in the level of rewards.

Design and Participation across All EPA Partnership Programs

Do the relationships between government rewards, entry stringency, and business participation generalize beyond the cases of 33/50, Performance Track, and Project XL? We believe they do. To assess the general validity of the conclusions drawn from these three cases, we collected and analyzed data on all similar EPA clubs that were in existence in 2004.

We began our study by identifying and reviewing all of the national voluntary programs administered by the EPA.[10] As one might imagine, what the EPA designates as a voluntary program can mean several things. The EPA appears to consider as a voluntary program any agency effort that is designed to induce firms or facilities to undertake voluntary action—that is, action that goes beyond current regulations or is not addressed by current regulations. This category includes educational programs, grants, competitive awards, product certifications, and partnership programs. Of the several types of voluntary programs, we considered only partnership programs as constituting government clubs.[11]

In a partnership program, the EPA establishes criteria for designating some firms or facilities as "members." Membership requires organizations to make some kind of commitment or other demonstration, and in return the EPA offers members some benefit or package of benefits.[12] Of all the EPA voluntary programs we examined, twenty-nine could be classified as voluntary partnership programs—that is, clubs. A complete list of these clubs is provided in box 11.1. Notwithstanding the actual names that the EPA had given these programs, each had an element of exchange or agreement between the applicant and the government. Even the two programs the EPA labeled as awards programs were in fact partnership programs in the sense we mean, since the awards were not limited or competitive but instead were available to any qualifying applicant.[13]

For each of the programs in box 11.1, we reviewed official program material describing the application process and the qualifications for membership. Three researchers (the two authors and a graduate student) participated in coding the stringency of each program's entry requirements, with differences in coding reconciled through agreement and further investigation. In cases where there was uncertainty in the written materials, we contacted the EPA staff responsible for administering the programs.

We coded programs on a three-point scale for their entry stringency. Programs rated at "1" (lowest stringency) only called for the participants to send in a short note or complete a brief application making a commitment to undertaking a voluntary action—much like 33/50. For example, to join the SunWise School Program, a school needed only to provide the EPA with contact information, a promise to increase awareness of the dangers of sun exposure by trying at least one of five suggested activities, and a brief description of how it intends to use information that the EPA provides about avoiding sun exposure.

Programs rated "2" required both commitment and action, such as a description of a project or other undertaking that demonstrated the participant's commitment. For instance, the Best Workplaces for Commuters Program recognized companies that encouraged employees to

Box 11.1
National EPA voluntary partnership programs (2004)

- Best Workplaces for Commuters
- Climate Leaders
- Coal Combustion Products Partnership
- Combined Heat and Power Partnership
- Energy Star Business Improvement
- Green Power Partnership
- GreenScapes
- High Production Volume Challenge
- Indoor Air Quality Tools for Schools—Great Start Awards Program
- Indoor Air Quality Tools for Schools—Leadership Awards Program
- Labs 21
- Landfill Methane Outreach Program
- Methane to Markets Partnership
- Mobile Air Conditioning Climate Protection Partnership
- National Environmental Performance Track
- National Partnership for Environmental Priorities
- Natural Gas Star Program
- Partnership for Safe Water
- Pesticide Environmental Stewardship Program
- PFC Emission Reduction Partnerships
- Plug-In to eCycling
- SF-6 Emission Reduction Partnership for Electric Power Systems
- SF-6 Emission Reduction Partnership for Magnesium Industry
- SmartWay Transport Partnership
- Sunwise School Program
- Sustainable Futures
- Voluntary Aluminum Industrial Partnership
- Voluntary Children's Chemical Evaluation Program
- WasteWise

get to work in ways other than by drive-alone commuting. It required prospective members to complete a three-page checklist that included information about the employer's actions to promote carpooling and public transportation. Each year, an employer would need to complete an eight-page update form describing the benefits it offered to commuters. To join SmartWay Transport Partners, another EPA partnership program rated a 2, businesses needed to complete a two-page application committing to use the EPA's performance model to measure their vehicle fleets' environmental performance, set specific and measurable performance goals, develop action plans for implementing the goals, submit the goals and action plans to the EPA, and report progress. Most programs were like these examples, in that they required both a commitment and some demonstration or declaration of action, however minor.

Programs rated "3" also required both a commitment and some demonstration of action, but in addition they involved training or screening by the EPA or a third party to verify the applicant met all the qualifications. The Performance Track, described in the previous section, illustrates this highest level of stringency. Facilities wishing to join Performance Track needed to clear a compliance screening by the agency, meet eligibility requirements, commit to improve performance in four areas, and complete a twenty-two-page application and a twelve-page annual report. The Sustainable Futures program also imposed substantial procedural and substantive requirements on prospective participants. To be eligible for relief from certain Toxic Substances Control Act testing requirements offered to the members of Sustainable Futures, facilities needed to enroll in a $2\frac{1}{2}$-day training program to learn about the EPA's Pollution Prevention Framework. Facilities then needed to use the EPA's framework to assess the risks associated with new chemicals that they plan to develop and show they use the framework in making product development decisions. They must submit to the EPA between five and ten assessments that include their views about how well the EPA's framework helped in comparing alternatives and selecting more benign chemicals.

In addition to entry stringency, we also coded programs based on the benefits they offered members. For most of the programs, the benefits were basically the same: public recognition (including listing on the EPA's Web site), a plaque, logo, or certificate, a point of contact with the EPA, and access to technical assistance or educational materials. Only one program offered less than these benefits, the SunWise program,

		Benefits		
		Low	Med	High
	Low	0	5	0
Entry Stringency	**Med**	0	18	1
	High	0	0	3

Figure 11.1
Matching entry stringency to benefits

which did not even list participating schools on the EPA's Web site. We rated it a 1 for its level of benefits. A handful of programs provided benefits exceeding the basic package, in particular some form of regulatory relief; we rated these programs a 3 for their level of benefits.

Finally, we collected data on the number of members of each partnership program. For most programs, members were listed on the EPA's Web site, so we used the number of members contained on those lists as of the end of October 2005 for our analysis. Where no lists were posted we contacted the EPA to obtain current data. For those programs that distinguished members based on their sector or organization type, we aggregated members from across all categories and used the total membership numbers.

The basic contours of our data are consistent with the theoretical expectations growing out of our examination of 33/50, Performance Track, and Project XL. Programs with low entry stringency did not offer high benefits, and programs with high entry stringency tended to have high benefits. Of course, as figure 11.1 shows, the variation between entry stringency and program benefits is not significant because more than half of the programs provided the standard package of program benefits and possessed the typical level of entry stringency, requiring both a commitment and some action on the part of their members. A few programs with low entry stringency offered medium benefits, but none supplied a high level of benefits. Similarly, most of the programs with high stringency also provided high levels of benefits.

As expected, the degree of entry stringency was inversely related to the number of members (figure 11.2). That is, the average membership in programs with low stringency was higher than the average membership in those with high stringency. Even taking into account the fact that

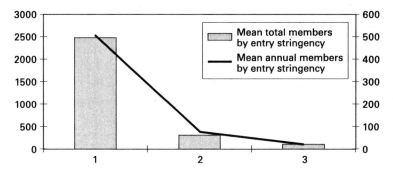

Figure 11.2
Average membership by membership entry stringency

some programs were older than others, the average number of members per year was higher for those programs with lower entry stringency.

Admittedly, even though we examined all of the EPA's existing voluntary partnership programs, the overall numbers in our sample were low. The average membership level for programs with low stringency was no doubt dramatically affected by a single program—SunWise—which boasted about thirteen thousand members. That program, though, seems instructive: it offered no benefits to members beyond some educational materials, and despite a stipulation requiring members to participate in a student and teacher evaluation, it really demanded nothing other than completing an online form with contact information.[14]

At the other extreme from SunWise lay the Sustainable Futures program. As noted, Sustainable Futures required that prospective members send representatives to a multiday training course, conduct extensive risk assessments, and go through the EPA screening, but in exchange it offered expedited regulatory relief from the Toxic Substances Control Act testing protocols. Although it was nearly three years old at the time of our data collection, the program had attracted only three businesses that qualified for regulatory relief.

In between these extremes, the bulk of the programs appeared to be "middle of the road"—both in terms of entry stringency and benefits. The membership levels correspondingly appeared quite modest. The average number of members per year for all these programs was 157, with a standard deviation of 495. Dropping the programs with the highest and lowest number of members, the average number of members per year was 72, with a standard deviation of 96.

Given the sample size, we did not control for other factors that would seem likely to affect variation in membership levels across partnership programs, including the number of firms or facilities that could be potential members, the underlying costs and benefits of the kind of environmental controls encouraged by the program, the existence of regulatory or other liability pressures that might additionally encourage businesses to undertake the actions called for by members, the degree of aggressiveness with which the EPA promotes the program, and the probability of the EPA taking regulatory action on issues related to the program and the costliness that any likely regulatory action would have for affected entities. We certainly do not pretend to have developed a full model explaining variation in membership levels across businesses, nor can we say how much of this variation can be explained by entry stringency.

There is one interesting comparison among the EPA's programs that appears to be a natural experiment. The EPA's Indoor Air Quality Tools for Schools program had two membership levels: the Great Start Awards (with low stringency and moderate benefits) and the Leadership Awards (with moderate stringency and moderate benefits). Neither program had attracted many members, but they did target the same kinds of organizations (school districts), address the same set of environmental issues, and operate within the same regulatory climate. Consistent with expectations, the lower stringency Great Start Awards level had attracted about 25 percent more members than had the Leadership Awards level (54 versus 44, respectively).

Conclusion

In the introduction to this volume, Potoski and Prakash explain that effective clubs develop strategies to attract new members and ensure that they meet club standards. If industry and NGOs are able to create clubs that meet these two challenges, then government should presumably be able to do so as well. In practice, though, government faces distinctive constraints that make it difficult, if not impossible, to use green clubs to induce both high levels of participation and high levels of environmental improvement. The EPA has tended to design its programs so that entry stringency increases with rewards. As a result, the *addition* of rewards corresponds with a *reduction* in participation.

This counterintuitive result appears to be a function of how government tries to manage the risks of publicly recognizing and rewarding businesses that it is otherwise charged with regulating. Moreover, it appears that the EPA and business managers place different value on the rewards and information demands associated with participation in government clubs. The regulatory incentives that the EPA worked to provide as part of Performance Track, for example, have been significant enough to generate criticism of the EPA by environmentalists, members of Congress, and the EPA's own inspector general. Yet for many businesses, the program's regulatory relief was trivial, if not entirely inconsequential. Some environmental managers even told us that having hazardous waste stored on-site longer, as Performance Track allowed, was actually a way to increase their risks of a spill or accident—as well as their concomitant tort liability risks.

Although much work remains to explain the variation in participation across different green clubs run by government, the case studies and data we present in this chapter show that fewer firms will assume the increased costs associated with gaining entry to clubs with higher stringency, even when these clubs promise greater rewards. Even if the transaction costs associated with joining a program like Performance Track seemed modest and reasonable to an outside observer, many of those in business found completing the EPA's twenty-two-page application and twelve-page annual progress report to be a significant enough burden to lead them to pass on applying to Performance Track. In principle, government agencies like the EPA could presumably increase their rewards so dramatically that businesses would flock to join, even if the entry requirements were as stringent as those of Performance Track, Project XL, or Sustainable Futures. But the present political and legal reality is such that either government agencies simply cannot offer rewards that are so substantial or they can only do so by increasing entry stringency still further.

Our analysis leads to the prediction that the level of participation in green clubs run by government will remain quite modest. If government moves to increase rewards, it will also be compelled to increase entry stringency. The net result will be to decrease or at least constrain program membership. Although in theory government has substantial rewards to offer businesses that participate in its green clubs, in practice it only offers strong rewards to those willing to submit to exceedingly strong swords. Few businesses are eager to accept that bargain.

12

Self-regulation and Voluntary Programs among Nonprofit Organizations

Mary Kay Gugerty

This chapter examines the rise of voluntary regulation programs among nonprofit organizations (NPOs). The vast majority of the literature on voluntary regulation examines such efforts among private, commercial firms. But the number of voluntary regulation initiatives among nonprofits has increased dramatically in recent years. The demand for nonprofit voluntary regulation comes from a number of sources, both national and transnational. Over the last two decades the rapid growth in NPOs around the globe created what some have characterized as a fundamental "powershift" in which nonprofits play a major part in reshaping world politics by constraining the actions of states and intergovernmental institutions (Matthews 1997). In most countries, NPOs fill increasingly important roles in the delivery of basic public goods and services (Smith and Lipsky 1993; Edwards and Hulme 1997).

This growing influence has raised concerns over the lack of accountability and oversight of NPOs. As the power of nonprofits rose, the capacity of many states for regulation and oversight of the sector was in decline, with the result that many governments, particularly in developing and transition economies, began to consider how to restructure the regulatory framework governing nonprofits. Proposed changes to regulations constituted both a threat and an opportunity for nonprofits. As a result of these factors, nonprofits around the world began to debate the meaning of nonprofit accountability, and develop mechanisms by which more institutionalized forms of accountability might be constructed among nonprofits themselves.

The result has been a tremendous increase in efforts at collective, nonstate, nonprofit voluntary regulation. Robert Lloyd (2005) documents twenty-four different self-regulation and accountability initiatives globally; I document twelve country-level efforts in sub-Saharan Africa

(Gugerty 2007), and Mark Sidel (2003) finds seventeen in Asia. The majority of these programs are voluntary codes of conduct developed and maintained by national or industry associations. The Web site for the U.S.-based nonprofit association the Independent Sector, for example, lists over fifty collective codes of conduct in the United States alone.

In spite of the increased interest in nonprofit accountability, there have been few efforts to systematically characterize the emerging voluntary regimes and understand how nonprofits seek to collectively correct their own accountability shortfalls. This chapter addresses this gap by analyzing the emergence and structure of voluntary regulation across thirteen nonprofit voluntary clubs. A key question of this chapter is whether and how nonprofit voluntary programs differ from their commercial counterparts, and the extent to which the voluntary clubs framework is useful to understanding similar collective action efforts among nonprofits.

Benefits and Costs in Nonprofit Clubs

The social benefits created by nonprofit clubs differ somewhat from many commercial clubs. A key feature of many environmentally focused clubs is the mitigation of public "bads," such as pollution. The policy rationale for most nonprofit clubs might be conceptualized instead as the maximization of public goods produced by nonprofits. Nonprofits typically receive subsidies from governments in the form of tax-exempt status; they also raise funds through donations from individual and institutional donors and governments. Such implicit and explicit subsidies are given largely on the basis of nonprofit commitment to social welfare, often in the belief that nonprofits are more trustworthy than for-profit firms because they are prohibited from distributing profits to shareholders (Hansmann 1980).

Additional rationales for public support of nonprofit activity include the creation of important social externalities such as building social capital (Putnam, Leonardi, and Nanetti 1993), providing citizens with civic experience (Almond and Verba 1965; Verba, Brady, and Scholzmann 1995), and providing goods and services that are underprovided by markets and government (Weisbrod 1988). To the extent that such benefits flow largely from legitimate, high-performing organizations and such organizations are hard to identify, one policy rationale for nonprofit clubs is to create social capital and civic capacity through a higher volume of high-quality nonprofit activity. Since nonprofits often receive public subsidies, governments also have an interest in regulating the non-profit sector to ensure the proper use of public funds. Private individuals and organizations that provide donations to nonprofits have an interest in verifying that their funds were used to further the nonprofit's stated mission.

While the beyond-compliance behavior mandated by voluntary club standards produces social benefits, such behavior has private costs to organizations. The extent of private costs depends on the costs organizations must incur that go beyond baseline standards organizations are required to meet. Given that legal nonprofit reporting requirements in many countries are quite minimal, we might expect that donor reporting requirements will play a crucial role in determining what constitutes beyond-compliance behavior for NPOs.

The costs of participating in a voluntary club need to be offset by club benefits in order to provide a motivation for participation. Voluntary regulation among nonprofits can generate both collective or club benefits, and may also offer private benefits to individual organizations.

Club theory proposes that club benefits are a function of the stringency of club standards as well as the credibility and strength of its monitoring and enforcement mechanisms. If clubs have stringent standards along with robust monitoring and enforcement, than the reputational signal created by the club is more credible and creates larger potential benefits for participation. For nonprofits, there are several potential benefits tied to this reputational signal. To the extent that nonprofit donors, whether individual or institutional, have difficulty distinguishing among high- and low-quality organizations, nonprofits have incentives to create credible signals about nonprofit quality. Such a signal is a collective benefit, since all club participants enjoy the benefits. In addition, in countries where government attitudes toward nonprofits and NPOs are hostile, such a signal may also help protect an organization from unwanted government interference or scapegoating. Thus for nonprofit clubs, the collective benefits generated for members are likely to be as important a rationale for club formation as the social benefits it may produce.

Nonprofit clubs may create private benefits too. Organizations may benefit from organizational learning in the certification process, or may be able to find ways to streamline or reduce the costs of other reporting requirements. Compliance procedures may encourage the more efficient or effective use of donor or government funds; to the extent this increased effectiveness can be documented, this may in turn lead to both increased funding and higher social benefit. Most nonprofit certification programs promote organizational learning as a key benefit of participation.

In addition to the collective benefits created by reputational signaling, a number of nonprofit clubs provide quite concrete material benefits to participants. In some countries, certification is a prerequisite for tax-exempt status. In other countries, credentialing is a prerequisite for receiving government grants or contracts. Other clubs supply tangible immediate benefits in the form of club-mediated access as well as connection to individual and institutional donors. Where clubs are sponsored by industry associations, participation may include association benefits.

If signaling to donors and governments offers the most important rationale for participation in nonprofit voluntary clubs, voluntary clubs may be more prominent among service delivery nonprofits than among membership and advocacy organizations. Service delivery nonprofits face high hurdles in communicating quality to donors, governments, and beneficiaries, creating potentially large benefits to mechanisms that can give credible signals about nonprofit quality. This signal will be especially significant for nonprofits that are mediating between donors and distant or hard to reach beneficiaries where the information asymmetries between donors and nonprofits and between nonprofits and their beneficiaries will be particularly large. Given the highly operational and managerially intensive nature of service delivery organizations, it is also possible that they can more easily find common management standards than can advocacy organizations (Johnson and Prakash 2007).

Collective Action and Club Structure among Nonprofits

Just as in commercial clubs, nonprofit clubs face potential problems of collective action among members. Club sponsors must design institutions that attract participants willing to meet standards beyond those required by law or standard practice, and must find ways to credibly commit these participants to adhering to standards once they are admitted. These two attributes, club standards and club enforcement, are the key institutional attributes of voluntary programs. This section first presents the specific standard-setting and enforcement problems faced by nonprofit clubs, and then illustrates how clubs are designed in practice through an examination of thirteen nonprofit clubs.

Club Standards and Stringency

Club standards consist of the rules governing entry and the actual content of the regulatory regime. Standards serve two functions: first, they establish the amount of beyond-compliance behavior required by the program, which should in turn be related to the level of social benefits created by the program. Standards also serve the second function of creating strong signals about participant quality. The stringency of club standards depends on the baseline reporting requirements faced by the average organization. The actual cost of compliance to an individual organization, however, can be expected to vary; organizations that are already closer to the voluntary standards will incur lower additional costs to join. Thus, the expectation is that high-quality organizations will be more likely to join voluntary programs, potentially increasing the strength of the reputational signal provided by the club.

In nonprofit clubs, the determination of club costs requires determining the extant compliance requirements across a range of legal and donor regimes. Legal requirements for nonprofit reporting in many countries are relatively minimal and typically include only aggregate financial data. Unlike commercial firms, nonprofits have no clear owners (principals), and are not embedded in an institutional environment (such as a stock market) that requires extensive information provision and provides incentives for managers (agents) to act responsibly (Johnson and Prakash 2007; Lynn and Smith 2007). Given that the signaling benefit offered by nonprofit regulation is often aimed at institutional and individual donors, the determination of beyond-compliance standards must incorporate donor as well as legal requirements. To complicate matters, the average service delivery nonprofit may receive funds from a number of different donors or sources, all of which have different reporting requirements. Typically, most donors require some annual project-level reporting on expenditures and the associated outputs produced. Donors and nonprofits may vary in the extent to which they require reporting on the actual outcomes or results of programming. Nonprofits that receive government funds or operate with government contracts also face an additional set of reporting requirements. Government contracts are frequently awarded on a fee-for-service basis, meaning the nonprofit is reimbursed for services provided, although performance-based contracting is on the rise.

In general, it therefore seems reasonable to assume that levels of standard stringency will not always be comparable between commercial and nonprofit clubs, and that the typical "high-cost" nonprofit club will have standards that are lower than the typical high-cost commercial club. We would expect to find that nonprofit clubs focus on process-oriented management and financial standards, and that few clubs will develop standards related to performance.

Monitoring and Enforcement

The second determinant of club strength is the strength of enforcement, meaning the extent to which the club can credibly prevent shirking among members. Mitigating shirking is an essential component of club credibility and therefore of club benefits. Enforcement includes at least three features: the specification of monitoring and other forms of performance measurement, the rules governing the disclosure of monitoring information, and the specification of sanctions in cases of noncompliance. Verification of compliance can range from little or no formal reporting or other verification, to self-reported compliance reports, with the most stringent systems requiring third- or fourth-party monitoring in which experts outside the organization certify compliance. Regimes also vary in the amount of public disclosure that accompanies the information provided. Such information can be kept completely private, shared among the participants, or made publicly available. Finally, self-regulatory regimes may specify sanctions or actions to be taken in cases of noncompliance. These may be graduated with the most severe sanctions being expulsion from the regime. Intermediate actions may include disclosure within the regime, fines, or public disclosure.

Empirical Data on Nonprofit Clubs

This section describes and evaluates the club characteristics of thirteen nonprofit voluntary regulation programs. Candidate programs were identified through a comprehensive literature review, Web searches, and by interviews with nonprofit managers and industry analysts. Programs were considered without regard for industry, location, sponsorship, or geographic scope, although educational and health care accreditation programs are excluded from this initial study. The thirteen programs that form the final sample are distinguished from the numerous existing nonprofit codes of conduct by having met the minimum club criteria of requiring organizations to pledge commitment to the code through a written document, and by having at a minimum an established

Table 12.1
Characteristics of nonprofit voluntary clubs

	Characteristic	Number of organizations (13 total)
Membership characteristics		
Geographic scope	National	12
	Transnational	1
Industry scope	Industry specific	7
	Sectorwide	6
Sponsorship	Industry association	10
	Independent agency	3
Club size	More than half of potential members participate	3
	Less than half participate	10
Club structure		
Type of standards	Broad principle-based standards	1
	Management/financial processes	10
	Outcome/performance	2
Monitoring and certification	Third-party	3
	Second-party	5
	First-party	3
	None	2
Disclosure/ sanctions	Public complaints process	9
	Public disclosure of compliance status	8
	Public disclosure of compliance info	3

complaints and review mechanism as a monitoring device. Data on the structure, requirements, and current membership for each program were gathered from a detailed review of agency documents. While this data set likely does not include all the qualifying programs, it is a reasonable enumeration of the best developed and strongest initiatives globally.

A full list of the programs and their characteristics is provided in appendix 12.1. Table 12.1 above summarizes their key characteristics. A few features deserve comment. All the programs except for one are national, rather than transnational, in scope. The only transnational nonprofit voluntary program meeting the club definition is the Humanitarian Accountability Partnership (HAP). HAP is an outgrowth of a series of collective processes among international humanitarian and relief agencies to develop more formalized accountability structures. Although at least six of these initiatives have been undertaken to date, HAP is the only program that requires any form of reporting on compliance. The prevalence of national systems is likely the result of several factors. Nonprofits have particular accountability requirements to their host government (such as the 990 form required by the U.S. Internal Revenue Service) that may facilitate common reporting standards. National governments may also more easily grant privileges or rights to program participants than transnational or intergovernmental institutions.

In addition to being largely nationally based, half the programs identified in the sample are based in developing countries—a potentially surprising feature. The regulatory capacity of governments in these countries tends to be lower, and the regulations governing nonprofits relatively underdeveloped. In many developing countries, the rapid growth in NPO activity has led governments to reexamine the laws and statutes governing nonprofit activity, often in ways that nonprofits find threatening or intrusive. All of these factors may motivate the development of private regulation in these contexts.

The programs are almost evenly divided between those that are specific to a particular nonprofit "industry" (such as humanitarian relief) and those that span the sector. Most are sponsored by industry or sector membership associations, rather than by independent agencies. None are directly sponsored by governments, although four programs have substantial government involvement, either through the provision of benefits or by the delegation of quasi-judicial regulatory authority.

The club size in most cases is quite small relative to the potential, suggesting that there may be substantial costs to participation even in weaker clubs. In two of the three high-membership cases, participation in the club is essentially a compulsory condition for nonprofit operation. Since the potential membership size varies widely across each country and industry, it is somewhat difficult to interpret the membership figures, but only two programs number more than five hundred members and most have fewer than two hundred. Preliminary analysis suggests that only three of the programs cover more than 50 percent of the potential membership. Most national-level programs probably cover less than 10 percent of the potential organizations.

Most programs are focused on process-oriented management standards, rather than on performance or outcome metrics. Only two programs make any attempt to incorporate performance measures. This indicates both the difficulty of specifying common performance measurements across diverse organizations, and a tendency for voluntary programs to focus on the concerns of donors and governments for financial accountability. The majority of clubs appear to be comprised primarily of operational service delivery nonprofits that are highly donor reliant, soliciting funds to operate social service and humanitarian relief and development programs on behalf of beneficiaries and clients.

Evaluating Nonprofit Club Attributes

To assess the extent to which nonprofit voluntary programs fit the voluntary clubs model, the two key attributes of clubs, standards and enforcement, are evaluated by assigning a numeric ranking to each club attribute. The criteria used to evaluate programs are given below. The analysis suggests that even the strongest nonprofit programs would be considered no more than country clubs according to the typology of chapter 1; most would be categorized as shams. Yet to dismiss these programs as shams may not fully appreciate the ways in which good-faith attempts by nonprofits to increase their accountability and transparency can affect organizational behavior, nor appreciate the extent to which these clubs can improve the performance of members. The typology of clubs may require an extension that can better incorporate nonprofit clubs.

The club standards are evaluated according to two sets of criteria. First, the level of specificity and detail in the standards was evaluated through a review of club documentation. Clubs specifying only broad, principle-based behaviors were awarded one point, while those detailing more specific, process-oriented standards were given two or three points, depending on the level of details, specificity, and number of standards. Those clubs that also attempt to measure the performance of participants were awarded four points. The second set of standards evaluates the level of detail specified in terms of how organizations will meet the standards, the level of documentation required for entry, and whether or not compliance with each standard must be documented. Each of those components was awarded one point. The maximum possible score for club standards is thus seven.

The strength of enforcement is evaluated across three components: monitoring, disclosure, and sanctions. The monitoring strength was assessed by characterizing the nature of the verification mechanism for each program. These ranged from no formal reporting requirements (zero points) to various forms of certification. First-party certification in nonprofit clubs is characterized by self-certification of compliance by the managers of the organization. Second-party certification in these clubs denotes peer review or review by teams appointed by the club sponsor. Third-party certification is conducted by independent bodies approved by the club sponsor. Points were awarded for each form of verification with third-party certification receiving the most points for strength (four points). Clubs received an additional point if the standards are written and publicly available, if compliance is formally monitored on a periodic basis, and if the documentation of compliance is required. The total possible standards score is seven.

The disclosure policies are assessed by examining the program rules on the public disclosure of application status, compliance information, and complaint status (one point each). One additional point is given if the club maintains a permanently staffed complaints board and/or has a clear, written publicized complaints procedure. Finally, the use of sanctions is evaluated by assessing whether the club has a credible option for sanctioning or removing noncompliant organizations, whether such action had ever been undertaken, and whether sanctions are made public. The maximum enforcement score is fourteen.

Together, the evaluation of clubs standards and club enforcement allows us to characterize the thirteen programs according to their strength. The results are presented in table 12.2; the rows represent the strength of club standards, while the columns indicate the strength of monitoring and enforcement. The strength of the two club attributes appears to be fairly well correlated. There are no programs with strong monitoring, but weak standards, nor any with stringent standards and weak enforcement. This suggests that nonprofit voluntary regimes can be categorized by four types, represented by the four shaded blocks. The first and weakest program type is a "minimal club," characterized by minimal reporting requirements and broad standards. Both programs in this category are run by nonprofit industry associations, and participation is mandatory for membership in the association. The second set of programs are "self-help" clubs. These regimes require self-certification of compliance, and the club standards are reasonably detailed and specific. These programs are also all run by industry associations, and participation is a requirement of association membership.

The third set of programs are "peer-review clubs" in which nonprofits provide detailed data through an application process that is reviewed and

Table 12.2
Institutional structure of nonprofit voluntary regulation clubs

Club standards	Enforcement and monitoring rules			
	Minimal club Minimal monitoring, complaints mechanism (1–3 points)	Self-help club Self-certification, some disclosure or complaints (4–6 points)	Peer review club Peer certification, modest disclosure, and complaints (7–9 points)	Standard-bearer club Third-party verification, or second-party with on-site review and strong disclosure (10–14 points)
Lenient standards (1 point)	Ethiopia Code Kenya Code			
Medium standards (2–3 points)		Canadian Council for International Cooperation Australian Council for International Development	Uganda Quality Assurance Mechanism	
Strong standards (5–6 points)		Interaction Self-Certification Plus	Land Trust Alliance Standards for Excellence	Interaction Child Sponsorship Evangelical Council for Financial Accountability Humanitarian Accountability Partnership Philippines Council on Nonprofit Certification
Stringent standards (7 points)				Pakistan Council on Philanthropy Certification

certified by an independent commission or committee of peers appointed by the club sponsor. All three of these programs are sponsored by industry associations, but the association has established a quasi-independent unit for certification that includes independent, nonassociation staff. These programs also include detailed management and financial processes that must be met through certification.

The final set of programs are the nonprofit "standard-bearers" since they are currently the strongest nonprofit voluntary regulation regimes globally (although they correspond most closely to the weakest type of commercial club, the country club). These clubs have third-party certification systems in place with strong or stringent standards that require certification of detailed management practices and in some cases organizational performance. This category also includes programs that use second-party certification, but combine this weaker monitoring with strong public disclosure requirements, sanctions, or an on-site (as opposed to desk) review.

Club theory suggests that the club strength will be related to the level of benefits provided by participation because the strength of the club is directly related to the reputational benefits it produces. Strong clubs with stringent standards and strong enforcement are more credible. Because they are high cost, it is expected that high-performing organizations will be more likely to join. If the club provides visible benefits over time, then other firms may find it in their interest to undertake the costs required to join. But club sponsors must also persuade organizations to join, and the reputational benefits may not be apparent a priori. Clubs may therefore need to provide tangible benefits in addition to potential reputational benefits in order to attract participants. Stronger clubs may require stronger inducements. Many clubs try to create stronger signals by developing a license or seal that club members can display or publicize to document their quality. In clubs run by industry associations, the benefits of association membership can offer an additional inducement to join the association and participate in the program. Some clubs provide quite tangible benefits to participants, such as access to government funds or tax-exempt status.

Club benefits for the thirteen programs are evaluated using five categories: public recognition via a Web site or public list of club participants, certification or seals of approval, benefits from access to an industry association, tax exemption or access to government funds, and finally, preferential access to donor agencies or individuals. Table 12.3 relates

Table 12.3
Club strength and club benefits

	Club benefits		
Club type	Low	Med	High
Minimal	Ethiopia Kenya		
Self-help	Interaction Self-Certification Canadian Council		Australian Council
Peer review		Land Trust Alliance Standards for Excellence Uganda	Interaction Child Sponsorship
Standard bearer		Humanitarian Accountability Partnership Evangelical Council	Pakistan Philippines

the club type to the strength of the club benefits. In general, stronger clubs supply larger benefits, with a few exceptions. The Australian program has high benefits in relation to its strength because the participants become eligible to receive funds from the Australian government development agency. The HAP-I and Evangelical Council programs are evaluated as having somewhat lower levels of benefits relative to their strength; this is largely because they do not have such tangible benefits associated with participation. HAP-I is a relatively new club, so it is difficult to evaluate the benefits that will ultimately be associated with participation. Further empirical investigation might also indicate that Evangelical Council participation has important benefits in terms of fundraising and financing that are not apparent from this somewhat approximate evaluation.

Before turning to the implications of this analysis, we provide short case studies of each club type to illustrate the typical requirements and benefits of each.

The Standard-Bearer: Pakistan Council for Philanthropy (PCP) Certification

In 2001, the PCP was formed as a nonprofit with the mission of promoting the volume and effectiveness of philanthropic giving in Pakistan. In 2003, the PCP began its certification program—an idea that had emerged from extensive stakeholder consultations. The government of Pakistan backed this initiative by authorizing the PCP as an official non-profit certification agency, meaning that certified organizations qualify for tax-exempt status. In addition to this benefit, the PCP connects certified organizations with potential donors.

The PCP certification process is the most comprehensive of any non-profit regime in the sample. Applicants complete an extensive (thirty-page) application form that lists the detailed supporting documentation required. This application is desk reviewed by a three-person team (including an independent evaluator) at the PCP. If the materials are complete and the organization is a good candidate for certification, a field evaluation is organized in which the team visits the headquarters office and selected field offices to verify the application, and give the organization numeric ratings on eighty-three different standards and practices. The evaluation team then prepares a final report that includes a numeric rating that quantifies the extent of compliance (the criteria vary slightly with the size of the organization). The final report is then presented to an evaluation panel with a recommendation of certification, deferral, or rejection. The independent panel consists of three PCP nominees and two government representatives. The panel has the final word on certification, which if issued is valid for three years. To date, the PCP has received 182 applications from nonprofits, of which 121 have received certification. This represents but a small portion of the 10,000 to 16,000 NGOs estimated to be operating in Pakistan.

A Peer-review Club: Standards for Excellence (SFX) Institute Nonprofit Certification Program

The SFX Institute is an operating division of the Maryland Association of Nonprofit Organizations that maintains an ethics and accountability code along with a nonprofit certification program. The institute is an outgrowth of the successful certification program originally developed by the association. State associations can now apply to become replication partners that are officially designated to offer certification training programs and license certification consultants. The certification process involves a twelve-page application that verifies roughly fifty management practices and requires the applicant to furnish supporting documentation for each standard. The applications are reviewed by a team of licensed peer reviewers, which makes a recommendation on certification to the SFX Ethics Standards Committee, which makes the final decisions. On-site meetings may be requested, and a formal appeals process exists as well as a formal process by which complaints can be brought and heard against certified organizations. Certification and the right to use the SFX logo is granted for a three-year period. By 2008 the SFX program had certified 150 organizations. Twenty of these organizations are large non-profits or local affiliates of large national federations such as the YMCA or United Way. The rest appear to be medium-size local NPOs. The program is still scaling up, but data from the initial Maryland site (63 organizations certified from 2001-08) suggest that the program may never reach a large scale.

A Self-help Club: Interaction Self-certification Plus (SCP)

Interaction is a membership association of 160 U.S.-based international development NPOs. Interaction first developed member standards in 1992, and until 2004, compliance consisted of only a short letter to the association stating that the organization was in compliance. Beginning in 2006, all member organizations must participate in SCP. SCP requires organizations to complete an annual self-assessment, supported by a thirty-five-page resource guide that lists the required supporting documentation. On completion of the self-assessment, organizations complete a three-page compliance form that certifies compliance with forty-five standards and lists the documents used internally by the organization to verify compliance. Where organizations are not in compliance, they must certify that they have developed an action plan to come into compliance, although the action plan does not need to be submitted to the association. Self-certification is a requirement for Interaction membership, and organizations that do not comply can potentially face suspension, although Interaction's policy is to offer assistance before sanctions. Interaction plans to pilot a peer-review process for certification as well. Interaction's membership base includes almost all of the mid- to large-size U.S.-based international NPOs, but does not include many smaller international organizations; club members likely account for the majority of international development funds raised in the United States, but the club includes a minority of the existing organizations.

A Minimal Club: Christian Relief and Development Association (CRDA) of Ethiopia Code of Conduct

Among the weakest clubs in this sample is the code of conduct maintained by the CRDA of Ethiopia. The CRDA is the oldest NPO in

Ethiopia and is the only broad-based NPO association in the country; roughly 60 percent of the officially registered NPOs are members. The CRDA spearheaded the development of the code of conduct in 1998. The original intent was to establish a general assembly of code signatories that would elect a code observance committee, but creating and maintaining such a body appeared to be a strong barrier to implementation, and so the committee was housed at the CRDA. The code itself is a mix of aspirational values along with a number of verifiable financial and management practices, including the provision of publicly available annual reports and audited financial statements. CRDA members are required to sign on to the code on joining the association. Because the CRDA vets its members prior to entry and there is currently a waiting list for entry, membership provides a clear reputational signal about member quality to donors and the government. Once organizations are admitted to the CRDA, however, there is not a strong ongoing reporting or monitoring system to ensure that that members are abiding by the standards, nor does the complaints system appear to function well, except in cases of egregious violations.

Conclusions and Areas for Future Research

This chapter provides some of the first systematic data on nonprofit voluntary programs, and examines the emergence and structure of nonprofit voluntary clubs across a range of domains. The analysis indicates that nonprofit clubs are generally weaker than their commercial counterparts, particularly in terms of their monitoring and disclosure. I argue that in spite of the apparent weakness of nonprofit clubs, they should nonetheless be viewed as serious attempts to create credible, private forms of regulation among NPOs. The chapter suggests three additional club types to supplement the introductory typology—the member club, the self-help club, and the peer-review club—and notes that the relatively weak country club in the commercial firms is actually the standard-bearer club for nonprofits. Yet each of these clubs represents a potentially important advance over current efforts at nonprofit voluntary regulation, which consist largely of passive codes of conduct.

Agency documents and interviews with key stakeholders confirm that the sponsors and participants in voluntary programs have invested significant amounts of time and effort to develop credible programs. Moreover, nonprofits, most of which are heavily donor reliant, have strong incentives to develop credible signals to the donor community. Most nonprofit voluntary regulation schemes appear to be more than mere "whitewashes," and most programs have been steadily increasing their standards and stringency over time. As noted earlier, nonprofits are subject to less stringent reporting requirements than are for-profit firms, so nonprofit programs are starting from a lower initial base in terms of organizational capacity for reporting.

The low participation rates in nonprofit clubs illustrate the difficulty of creating and scaling up nonprofit voluntary programs, similar to the limits faced by the government-sponsored programs discussed in chapters 10 and 11 in this volume. Many obstacles to club formation are not different from those in the for-profit sector. NPOs and representative industry associations are reluctant to police their peers, and are also reluctant to share information when they are in competition for the same donors. As in the private sector, the formation of credible clubs involves a delicate balance between the stringency of standards and the willingness of organizations to join. Nonprofits may face some additional hurdles. As discussed in this chapter, many nonprofits have a relatively low capacity for monitoring and reporting, and few donors are willing to fund these activities. Many nonprofits lack the capacity and personnel to comply with stringent program requirements, even if they only require self-certification. The lack of funding for reporting activity also makes it more difficult for nonprofits to pay accreditation agencies fees that would help them cover the costs of their services. Quite often club sponsors must seek external funding for the development of voluntary programs, since high participation fees would crowd out most nonprofits.

This chapter has focused largely on describing the institutional structure of nonprofit voluntary programs. To fully understand their rationale and effectiveness, we need better information on who joins these clubs (and who does not) as well as more nuanced ways of evaluating both the benefits of club membership and the impact of participation on nonprofit behavior and performance. In many cases, participation may be motivated by the threat of government regulation or the pressure resulting from a high-profile nonprofit scandal. More concrete measures of the costs of participation also would help in understanding both participation decisions and the level of benefits provided by clubs. In addition, future work should consider the clubs studied here in comparison with voluntary accreditation programs comprised largely of nonprofits, such as educational accreditation programs, and with voluntary programs

Appendix 12.1
List of nonprofit clubs included in sample

Program	Scope	Sectorwide or industry based	Sponsor	Year initiated	Number of participants
Interaction Self-Certification Plus	National	Industry	Industry association	2001	160
Interaction Child Sponsorship Certification	National	Industry	Industry association	2004	5
Australian Council for International Development	National	Industry	Industry association	1997	110
Evangelical Council for Financial Accountability	National	Industry	Independent agency	1979	2,092
Land Trust Alliance Accreditation Program	National	Industry	Industry association	2006	44
Canadian Council for International Cooperation Code of Ethics	National	Industry	Industry association	1997	90
Humanitarian Accountability Partnership— International	Trans- national	Industry	Industry association	2006	2
National Standards for Excellence Institute	National	Sectorwide	Industry association	1998, national in 2001	150
Philippine Council for NGO Certification	National	Sectorwide	Independent agency	1999	424
Pakistan Council on Philanthropy Certification Program	National	Sectorwide	Independent agency	2003	121
Uganda Quality Assurance Mechanism	National	Sectorwide	Two industry associations	2007	brand new
Kenya National NGO Council Code of Conduct	National	Sectorwide	Quasi-governmental agency	1993	3,000+
Christian Relief and Development Agency, Code of Conduct	National	Sectorwide	Industry association	1999	262

that include both commercial firms and NPOs. Finally, the political roots of these clubs deserve attention—a point also made in chapter 6 in this volume. Why have governments actively supported the development of nonprofit clubs in some contexts, but resisted them in others?

The strength of club theory in the analysis of nonprofit voluntary regulation is that it can provide a coherent institutional explanation of the structure of such regimes. This chapter indicates that club theory has a significant role to play in expanding our understanding of nonprofit voluntary accountability programs. This incentive-based approach to understanding voluntary programs, however, could be supplemented by a norm-based approach that may be particularly important in understanding mission-based nonprofit behavior. For example, the literature on nonprofit advocacy and accountability politics suggests that verbal commitments made by international actors can be used to pressure them to change their behavior (Keck and Sikkink 1998; Fox and Brown 1998). The same tactics could be used to pressure NPOs, and there are an increasing number of watchdog groups doing so. Moreover, as nonprofit voluntary programs proliferate, they diffuse new norms and standards for judging nonprofit behavior and performance. The full impact of nonprofit clubs may therefore include the ways in which clubs raise the bar for generally accepted monitoring and reporting behavior among nonprofit organizations.

IV

Conclusion

13

Voluntary Clubs: Future Prospects

Aseem Prakash and Matthew Potoski

This volume shows how the club approach sheds light on voluntary governance research using case studies and rigorous formal models. The chapters apply the club approach to study voluntary programs across industries (diamonds, shipping, apparel, and accounting), issue areas (labor rights, human rights, and the environment), sponsorship types (government, industry, and NGOs), actor types (firms, governments, and nonprofits), economic (developed and developing countries), and policy contexts (weak and strong governmental institutions). The club approach provides important theoretical and empirical insights by directing focus on two central challenges that voluntary programs face: recruitment to the program, and the efficacy of the program. The recruitment challenge is crucial given the "voluntary" nature of clubs. The efficacy challenge is significant because the programs' uneven monitoring and enforcement mechanisms have lead to skepticism about their usefulness as policy tools. Finally, the chapters also highlight some of the club approach's limitations, as we discuss later in this conclusion.

We first take up the issue of the club approach's contributions to the broader voluntary regulation literature and its frameworks, such as the CERNA framework, which focuses on the involvement of public authorities as the sponsoring actor (Börkey, Glachant, and Lévêque 1998).[1] Our aim is to show that the club approach does much more than simply substitute the phrase club for voluntary program. In doing so, we demonstrate how much of the voluntary program literature employs club theory concepts, such as free-riding and shirking problems (Arora and Casson 1996; Nunan 1999; King and Lenox 2000; Rivera and deLeon 2004; Delmas and Keller 2005), program membership as a signaling mechanism (Darnall and Carmin 2005; Terlaak and King 2006), the collective nature of reputations (Hoffman 1997; Cashore,

Auld, and Newsom 2004; Barnett and King 2006), and the importance of monitoring and enforcement to prevent shirking (Börkey, Glachant, and Lévêque 1998; Kolk and Tulder 2002).

As a tool for systematic institutional analysis, the club approach offers several contributions to these voluntary program literatures. First, it provides an analytic framework (as opposed to descriptive typology) that identifies key variables as well as posits their causal relationships in voluntary program design and functioning. The club approach also offers a deductive framework that link insights generated from prior research's program-by-program studies. Second, the club approach creates a unifying framework and a common vocabulary that pulls insights from prior research's program-by-program studies. The club approach focuses attention on program design as an exogenous driver of program recruitment and efficacy. Previous research has examined the role of firm characteristics (Khanna and Damon 1999), industry characteristics (Gunningham and Rees 1997; Rivera and deLeon 2004; Press 2007), management's environmental preferences (Prakash 2000a; Gunningham, Kagan, and Thornton 2003), trade association sponsorship (Cashore, Auld, and Newsom 2004; King and Lenox 2000), the political and regulatory context (Delmas 2002; Potoski and Prakash 2004), consumer pressure (Arora and Casson 1996), supply chain pressure (Kolk and Tulder 2002; Prakash and Potoski 2007b), NGO pressure (Sasser et al. 2006), and sponsors' characteristics (Darnall and Carmin 2005) as drivers of recruitment. The research has not synthesized these studies into a systematic focus on the nonrival but excludable nature of membership benefits and how program design contributes to their production.

A third benefit of the club approach is that it offers powerful insights for the more general study of the production, provision, and distribution of collective goods through mandatory (i.e., governments) as well as voluntary clubs. Club theory evolved in public finance and local public economy literatures in the 1950s and over the last four decades, it has been employed to study collective goods problems at the subnational, national, and international levels (Cornes and Sandler [1986] 1996). The recruitment and enforcement challenges that are salient for voluntary programs also tend to be relevant for public regulation. One way to think about these issues is to view public regulation as a mandatory club since any actor living in its jurisdiction is obliged to become its member. Notwithstanding compulsory membership, shirking with public law is pervasive. With imperfect monitoring and enforcement, individuals can have considerable autonomy in responding to governmental law (Scholz and Lubell 1998). At a broader level, one could even question compulsory membership because jurisdictional boundaries are porous: capital and labor mobility has been a persistent theme from Charles Tiebout (1956) to the globalization literature (Berger and Dore 1996). "Reputational issues" are increasingly recognized as salient in countries' efforts to recruit capital and skilled labor—as the "credible commitment" literature indicates. It is not an exaggeration to say that the voluntary and mandatory regulation face similar institutional design, recruitment, and rule enforcement challenges. Thus, the club approach can identify key characteristics of different types of governance systems and facilitate their comparative study. This book contributes to this objective.

Key Lessons

Looking across this volume's empirical chapters, we can see some broad themes that the club approach raises. First, while voluntary programs offer opportunities for firms to appropriate reputational gains (as in ISO 14001 and the Global Compact), the programs are often industry creations to respond to collective reputational issues. The Kimberley Process looks to safeguard the reputation of the diamond industry by purging the stain of blood diamonds (chapter 5). While it is early to comment definitively about the program's efficacy—we do not know how much it has curbed the flow of illicit diamonds—the program has established a brand image and created effective monitoring systems. Assaults on the shipping industry's reputation come from several fronts: labor conflicts, environmental mishaps, insurance hazards, and so on; several voluntary programs look to parry the assaults (chapter 7). Programs in the apparel industry sought to repair the industry's tarnished image in the wake of bad publicity, with varying success (chapter 6). As chapter 12 discusses, even nonprofits have collective reputation problems and have sought to employ clubs to respond to them. Later in this chapter, we offer detailed comments on the analytic properties of collective reputations to lay out a stronger theoretical foundation of how these reputations are maintained and the nature of the threats that may damage them.

A second broad theme that emerges from this volume's chapters is that firms use voluntary program membership to signal firms' intentions to generate positive social externalities. Membership in a voluntary program can reduce external stakeholder's search costs for identifying socially responsible firms and their transaction costs to monitor firms' policies and performance. Recalling the theoretical discussion in chapter 2, effective voluntary programs provide signals about their members' attributes and behaviors that would otherwise be difficult for external stakeholders to verify. The empirical chapters lend support to this claim.

The signaling function has been noted by other scholars of voluntary programs (Börkey, Glachant, and Lévêque 1998; Terlaak and King 2006). Club reputations are multifaceted signals, with different meanings across audiences, depending on program design, characteristics of the participating firms and their stakeholders, and the political, economic, and policy context. What is important is that whether in the apparel, diamond, or shipping cases, the signals conveyed by voluntary clubs have generally struggled to reach final consumers. Instead, a common theme in this volume's chapters is that voluntary clubs appear to be most effective in signaling to other organizations in supply chains (such as in accounting, diamond, and shipping industries) or activists organizations (such as labor rights advocates and labor unions). Firms can influence other firms through market exchanges, and as Baron's formal model of voluntary programs (chapter 3) suggests, NGOs can engage in private politics by targeting firms for boycotts (although in some circumstances, membership in a voluntary program makes firms more attractive boycott targets). Consumers may not have either the sophistication to interpret the voluntary program signal or sufficient means (or willingness) to reward firms for the action they take through program membership. Thus, a focus on both business-NGO dynamics as well as supply-chain dynamics seems to offer promise for future work in this area.

A third learning emerging from this volume pertains to the importance of monitoring and enforcement, or in short the programs' swords. Voluntary clubs with strong enforcement mechanisms and sound club standards more clearly signal their members' intentions. Ineffective programs, such as the apparel industry's early voluntary programs (chapter 6), are marked by ineffective monitoring and enforcement mechanisms. A promising trend is that some programs without their own effective enforcement programs have been able to harness public sector institutions to improve enforcement, such as in the accounting industry (chapter 8). The Kimberley Process (chapter 5), however, offers a cautionary note on voluntary programs' outsourcing enforcement to the public sector: effective enforcement is often most needed where government institutions are feeble.

Shortcomings of the Club Approach

The chapters in this volume also highlight the shortcomings of the club approach. An initial observation is that the club perspective appears to be a better fit for some types of voluntary programs than others. Clubs help participating firms signal their intentions to various stakeholders regarding the production of social externalities. Signaling is a critical aspect of the club story. It follows, therefore, that the club approach may be more useful in three situations. First, the club approach is more useful in information-scarce environments where external stakeholders know little about the firms' internal operations and firms do not have credible mechanisms to convey this information. Second, the club approach is more applicable where firms pursue reputational value. Thus, the club approach can be usefully employed to explain recruitment to industry-level clubs in industries that are either vulnerable to bad publicity (as in the chemical and diamond industries) or where there is a high salience of branded products (as in the apparel and footwear industries).

The club approach has analytic value where "brand signals" enable the participating firms to appropriate the excludable reputational benefits. The club approach has marginal payoffs for studying agreements negotiated directly between public authorities and individual firms, where the agreements have clear reporting, monitoring, and enforcement mechanisms (as in the Performance Track; see chapters 10 and 11). In these cases, the participating firms' activities are clear and the regulators can differentiate the participants from the nonparticipants at low costs. In such cases, the theoretical arguments outlined by the club approach regarding how voluntary programs solve the collective action dilemmas related to recruitment and shirking are less germane. The broad lesson is that to understand the usefulness and limitations of the club approach, it is important to study the informational demands the context makes on the participants and their stakeholders, and the reputational payoffs for the club participants of joining the club.[2]

The club approach is also likely to be less useful for voluntary programs that are concerned primarily with the provision of technical information to participating firms. Indeed, Tom Lyon and John Maxwell

(2007) suggest that some voluntary programs sponsored by public authorities focus on disseminating information about best industrial practices. Reputational considerations are likely to play a minor role in recruiting firms to these programs. Instead, the carrot is the ability to access the valuable information at low costs.

A third limitation pertains to the assumption that club design is an exogenous driver of club recruitment and club efficacy—an echo of criticisms levied against the broader institutionalist research program. While most agree that institutions matter, it is less clear how institutions are established in the first place. Two issues are important here. First, factors that drive the emergence of the institution might also influence their efficacy. Second, as several chapters indicate, the club theory as outlined in this book does not adequately address how clubs are established, how this influences their institutional design, and how the dynamics of their emergence shape how they function. These are valid criticisms. An institution's rule configuration, credibility with stakeholders, and ultimately its performance are structured considerably by the processes and the context in which it emerged. In the social science lexicon, we can say voluntary program features are endogenous to the process of club formation. The significance of program formation and governance is raised explicitly in the analysis of the apparel industry's voluntary programs in chapter 6, and appears elsewhere throughout this volume. Indeed, chapter 4 suggests that government and nongovernmental voluntary club sponsors have quite different incentives for the types of programs they create. Furthermore, stakeholders have varying preferences regarding which clubs firms should join (or not join) a club and varying abilities to induce firms to pay membership costs. Stakeholders may send conflicting signals about a club to the firm. The sponsoring actor also can influence the brand reputation directly through its own reputation as well as indirectly though its choice of club design. We need to bring sponsors' attributes as well as the contextual factors in which the clubs emerge explicitly into the discussion on club design, and therefore the reputational benefits a voluntary program can produce.

The fourth limitation is that the club perspective underspecifies mechanisms by which club design shapes club reputation and, consequently, the incentives for firms to join the club and produce social externalities. Given the multifaceted nature of brand reputations, future research needs to document how various stakeholders interpret and prioritize what they learn of firms from their club memberships. While information disclosures might be important for one stakeholder, commitment to quantitative targets might be salient for others (Morgenstern and Pfizer 2007). Future research should explore in more detail how club brands are established and communicated, and how brands influence firms' incentives to join clubs.

While exploring the processes by which reputations are established and communicated, scholars need to pay close attention to how individual firms appropriate and exploit the reputation of the clubs they have joined. After all, firms are likely to benefit asymmetrically from the club reputation. This appropriation question is quite significant because there might be a tendency to incorrectly interpret the analytic features of club reputation. Because club reputations are nonrival and excludable, scholars should not confuse them with common-pool resources that are rival and nonexcludable—a tendency that is evident in some discussions on industry-level clubs.

This volume does not address how the incentives faced by early and late joiners might differ (Delmas and Montes 2007; Lyon and Maxwell 2007), and how the program design might have different implications for them. While the club approach draws on the concept of network effects in explaining the increasing returns to club size, it does not explicitly theorize as to which firms are likely to join early and why. This is because the club perspective does not adequately explore the issue of the multifaceted nature of club reputations, or how club reputations are developed and communicated, and how different firms might find different facets of the reputation to be most attractive. Is the firm accused of violating labor rights more likely to join a given club or a firm that treats its labor well? Why? Are the reputational benefits each seeking the same? Assume that the former is looking for "insurance benefits" to protect from the backlash while the latter is looking for ways to differentiate itself from others. How would club standards and the club swords signal which types of benefits the club might offer, and therefore predict which type of firm is likely to become an early joiner? Hence, the spartan nature of the club framework with its focus on two attributes of club design is less useful to respond to some types of questions.

In the remainder of this chapter, we address two crucial issues that this book has raised. We begin with a call for sharpening the theoretical analytics for studying club reputations, and then discussing some important theoretical concerns for a political theory of voluntary program establishment and governance. We then provide a few concluding thoughts on the role of voluntary programs in public policy.

Club Reputation Analytics

Reputations are an important, multifaceted asset for firms.[3] Firms have their own reputations. Their products have reputations, which to some extent are independent of the firm's reputation. The industry in which firms operate has its own reputation as well. The overall perceptions about the Honda Accord are influenced by the reputation of the car, Honda's corporate reputation, and the Japanese automobile industry's reputation. Voluntary programs can be designed to focus their reputational effects on firms, specific products, or the industry. How these reputations interact in specific contexts is a question worthy of further research. Below, we examine one key analytic challenge in sorting through this issue.

Voluntary clubs are sometimes tailored for the needs of a single industry. Examples of industry-level clubs examined in this volume pertain to the apparel, shipping, accounting, and diamond industries. It is clear that an industry can acquire a reputation of its own, and this reputation reflects on individual firms. This is because stakeholders often make inferences about a firm based on the reputation of the industry in which it operates. It is therefore fair to say that firms operating in a given industry share a common reputation, or to put it differently, the industry reputation is held in common by firms.

What are the analytic features of such reputations held in common? What kind of collective action dilemmas are posed (or not posed) when a firm seeks to appropriate or augment this reputation? Some scholars characterize industry reputations and industry clubs as "reputational commons," and relate their production and appropriation to the broader literature on common-pool resources (Barnett and King 2006). While efforts to link reputational issues with voluntary programs are worthwhile, it is important to differentiate a *reputation held in common* by firms operating together in an industry (or as part of the same cross-industry voluntary program) from a *reputational commons* in a common-pool resource sense (Ostrom 1990; Dolsak and Ostrom 2003). The distinction between the two is not just semantics because the collective action dilemmas, and the institutional means to mitigate them, are quite different in each case.

The reputational commons concept can indeed be confusing, so we begin with some conceptual clarifications. The word commons has a specific connotation in political economy and public policy. Where a club good is nonrival and excludable, a common-pool resource (often simply called a commons) is rival and nonexcludable. To illustrate the difference between a good held in common and a common-pool resource, it is useful to return to Garrett Hardin's (1968) pasture, a celebrated example of a common-pool resource. For Hardin, the tragedy of the commons arises because one herder cannot exclude others from increasing the flock size, dictated by the nonexcludability dimension in the Elinor Ostrom (1990) framework. Because the pasture can support only up to a certain number of sheep (rivalry dimension), adding additional sheep decreases the availability of the good for other herders, leaving each herder with the incentives to increase the size of their own herd because they expect others to do so in short order. The herder wants to be the first mover—the first to put more sheep on the common—lest they lose out on gains from the commons. The herder realizes that by adding a sheep to their herd, he enjoys the benefit of raising an extra sheep, but bears only a small portion of the incremental cost associated with degrading the pasture. Thus, it is rational for the herder to add sheep to his herd without limit. As all herders seek to appropriate the resource before the others do, the common is degraded. Note that the rivalry dimension is accentuated by the nonexcludability dimension because the first-mover advantage associated with overconsumption compels the participants to move quickly.

Hardin's pastures are open-access resources: anybody can appropriate them by becoming a herder and to any extent they want by choosing for themselves the size of their herd. To avert the commons tragedy, the access to the resource needs to be limited only to a given group of herders. That is, rules are required to create excludability. Addressing the rivalry dimension by limiting the herd size also reduces the commons tragedy. If rules limit herd size, then every herder will be prohibited from increasing the herd size indefinitely and will also have the assurance that others face the same constraint. With the diminished possibility of facing a "sucker's payoff," the herder is less likely to overconsume the pasture. In sum, the solution to the commons problem is to establish property rights that limit the number of herds on the commons (excludability) *and* the size of each of the allowed herds (rivalry).

Applying the herding analogy to industry reputations suggests focusing on whether a given industry's reputation is rivalrous (as in common-pool resources) or not rivalrous (as in clubs goods). We suggest that an industry's (or voluntary club's) reputation is a nonrivalrous good held in common by firms of the industry (or club). A firm "consumes" a positive (or negative) industry reputation by enjoying goodwill (or suffering ill will) from stakeholders that see the industry—and consequently the firm—in a positive (or negative) light. While a firm has consumed the reputation in this way, this reputation is still available for other firms to consume: they too can receive goodwill (or ill will) from stakeholders as a result of the industry's reputation. If the reputation were rivalrous, once the first firm had consumed the reputation, it would no longer be available for the second firm to consume, and firms would consequently race to lower their own environmental standards to exploit the limited and dwindling stock of industry reputation—a dynamic similar to Hardin's herders racing to add sheep to their herd before the pasture is completely overgrazed by sheep of other herders. Since the industry reputation is nonrivalrous, it is not a common-pool resource.

Actions of one firm in an industry have positive or negative consequences for the other industry firms, which is what we mean when we say that the industry reputation is held in common by firms. A good held in common can be damaged, to the detriment of all who would consume the good. Environmental mishaps by one firm impose negative reputational externalities on other firms in the industry, thereby diminishing the industry's reputation. Firms in an industry realize they all sink or swim together: one firm cannot externalize the costs of the diminished industry reputation on to others and emerge unscathed. While Hardin's herder bears only 1/nth of the incremental cost of their commons consumption, firms all bear the full (or substantial) brunt of the declining industry reputation simply because all firms get tarred by the same negative brush. Of course, firms show varying vulnerabilities to such tarring. Indeed, the bigger and more reputable firms may suffer the most. The point we are trying to make is that unlike Harding's herder who bears a small proportion of the cost (and therefore has the incentives to overconsume the common-pool resource), the firm whose actions are tarring the industry's reputation is getting substantially tarred itself.

The upshot of this discussion is that industry reputations are a shared, nonrivalrous resource. Actions that enhance an industry's reputation, such as creating an industry-level club, create nonrivalrous benefits for all, and actions that diminish an industry's reputations impose nonrivalrous costs for all. The implication for institutional design is that club rules should focus on the excludability dimension so that the reputational gains of taking beyond-compliance environmental actions are appropriated only by members of the club. Because free-rider incentives are strong—firms in an industry cannot be excluded from enjoying the benefits of a positive industry reputation—industry clubs need to ensure that all firms in the industry join the club. This explains why industry associations such as the American Chemistry Council and the American Forest and Paper Association *require* their members to join their own voluntary clubs.

In contrast, solving the commons problems requires not only an exclusion mechanism but also a partitioning mechanism for solving the rivalry problem. A partitioning mechanism divides reputation among industry members. In Hardin's herd example, an exclusion mechanism would limit the number of herders allowed to use the pasture while a partitioning mechanism would limit the number of sheep any herder can place into the common pasture. The partitioning mechanism would counter herders' incentives to move first and quickly consume the commons before other herders did the same. We do not think any industry-level club has mechanisms to partition its shared reputation among its members, most likely because the industry reputation is a nonrivalrous good that is quite difficult to partition. Indeed, since reputations are nonrivalrous, there is no need to solve the rivalry dimension: no rationing is necessary among firms consuming an industry reputation. In fact, absent crowding or other externality affects, such rationing would be a welfare loss because it would needlessly prevent the consumption of the good.

Voluntary Club Formation and Governance

The club perspective we presented in the introductory chapter does not yet take into account the fact that club features may be endogenous to the sponsors' efforts to recruit members. Most scholars studying voluntary programs begin their inquiry in the context of an established club, and then explore how club features influence recruitment efforts and recruitment success (see, for example, Arora and Casson 1996; for a recent review, see Koehler 2007). In the voluntary club research program, there is an interesting prior question as well—how the club was established in the first place, and how the dynamics surrounding club's formation might influence the recruitment efforts. An important next step, then, is to explore how the stringency of club standards as well as the strength of monitoring and enforcement swords might be shaped by (or endogenous to) the club's founding. Club sponsors decide on stringency levels not only in anticipation of desired membership levels and what types of firms they want to join the club but also in response to the events that lead them to establish the club in the first place. A club established in the wake of an NGO criticism about labor practices of the overseas suppliers (chapter 6) is likely to have different stringency levels in relation to a club established in the same industry in more "normal" circumstances (chapter 7 on shipping clubs).

Clubs established in the same industry by different actors may have different rule configurations and stringency levels because of different political and economic dynamics. In the forestry industry, NGOs established the FSC and began lobbying forestry firms to join this voluntary club. Forestry firms, especially the U.S. ones, were not comfortable with this club because they did not want an adversarial actor (the founding NGOs) to decide the configuration and stringency of club standards (Sasser et al. 2006). In response, important firms in the industry established their own industry-sponsored club, the SFI. The idea was that this club would shield forestry firms from pressure to join an NGO-sponsored forestry club because firms could always claim that they are already members of a different club. Not surprisingly, the NGOs have not welcomed the industry initiative and have actively discouraged firms from joining the SFI (ibid.). The SFI has adopted more stringent standards in response to the criticisms by activist groups. At the same time, the FSC has also rationalized its standards to make the club more appealing to forestry firms. Thus, voluntary club sponsors design and modify their program both in anticipation of and response to a variety of stakeholders. Future research should explore these issues of club emergence and evolution, and their influence on club design.

On the one hand, it is a welcome development to observe that club sponsors are willing to respond to stakeholder criticism and change club structure. After all, rigid governance structures are bound to become dated and obsolete in a fast-changing world. But this is a mixed blessing simply because the ability to change program rules raises the specter of credible commitment problems. Any governance system must provide a sense of stability and continuity to its members if it wants them to operate with a long shadow of the future. Clubs need to credibly commit to their stakeholders as well as potential members about the nature and stringency of club rules.

The credible commitment problem facing firms' stakeholders is that the voluntary club may ease its standards over time, without publicly announcing or discussing the changes. After gaining a reputation for strong environmental standards, program sponsors may then secretly dilute the standards—capitalizing on reputations' sticky nature (Weigel and Camerer 1988; Schultz, Mouritsen, and Gabrielsen 2001). Stakeholders may withhold benefits from members until they are confident that sponsors are committed to maintaining their club's standards. Voluntary clubs established by industry associations may be especially vulnerable to such credible commitment problems because of the obvious incentives to decrease the "regulatory" burden on their members.

The credible commitment problem toward potential participants is that the voluntary club may tighten its standards after firms have become members, opportunistically exploiting the fact that exiting the program might be costly for firms. Club membership might require investments in infrastructure, technology, or competency assets that are specific to the program, and are difficult to apply to alternative uses (Williamson 1985). Firms may be reluctant to join a program that requires asset-specific investments that would leave them vulnerable to opportunistic exploitation by sponsors. Retribution costs may also impede firms' ability to leave a program, as stakeholders are likely to punish firms that leave a voluntary club. Because the exit option is costly, voluntary clubs, particularly those sponsored by NGOs, need to signal to potential members that they will not opportunistically tighten the program standards.

We can suggest three institutional features that voluntary clubs can adopt to address credible commitment problems. First, voluntary clubs can stipulate "rules for making rules" or "collective choice rules," as Ostrom (1990) terms them, in ways that assure stakeholders that club requirements will not changed surreptitiously. One approach is for voluntary clubs to grant external stakeholders—including participating firms and NGOs—political authority in deciding future changes to its rules. The notice and comment provisions of the United States under the Administrative Procedures Act are examples of this approach on a broader scale. The industry-sponsored SFI is an interesting instance of a voluntary club that has designed collective choice rules to mitigate its credible commitment problem. The club sponsors have sought to tie their own hands by creating the External Review Board comprising eighteen environmental, professional, and academic experts (http://www.sfiprogram.org).

The second credible commitment mechanism is stipulating supermajority voting rules for changing club standards. Consider the case of the ISO, which requires that any new standards that it develops as well as changes in existing standards need to be approved by two-thirds of the members that have participated in the standards development process, and by three-fourths of all voting members of the club (http://www.iso.org). Supermajority voting rules mean the standards cannot be changed easily. The process of standard development is reasonably transparent, and outside observers, even when not represented on technical committees, have a fair amount of information about the deliberations.

A third institutional feature for addressing the credible commitment problem is to submit the voluntary club to an external certification standard for how the program is managed. Indeed, we can see the beginnings of an interesting example of a supravoluntary club for certifying the quality of other voluntary clubs. The International Social and Environmental Accreditation and Labeling Alliance is an international NGO made up of international standards-setting organizations (http://www.isealalliance.org). The alliance's Code of Good Practice for Social and Environmental Standard Setting, launched in 2004, is a set of program standards to guide the development, implementation, and oversight of voluntary social and environmental clubs. The code's standards specify processes for developing a program's standards, such as extensive stakeholder participation, and procedures for handling disputes. The code's monitoring and enforcement mechanisms are being refined: there is currently a peer-review procedure in place, and the alliance is in the process of developing tools and processes to assess compliance. The goal is to help sponsors develop their clubs by providing best practices benchmarks, and provide governments, NGOs, citizens, and other stakeholders a way to evaluate the quality of different voluntary clubs.

In sum, the attributes of the club sponsor can lead to different types of credible commitment challenges. When a club is sponsored by an organization favorably disposed toward businesses, it needs to signal to its stakeholders that it will not opportunistically loosen the rules. When a club is sponsored by an organization adversarial toward businesses, it needs to make a credible commitment to potential members that it will not opportunistically tighten the rules after firms have joined. Club design is not entirely exogenous to the context in which the club is established and functions. Future research must seek to systematically link club formation with club recruitment and club efficacy.

Concluding Remarks

Voluntary clubs are instruments for inducing firms (and nonprofits as well) to generate positive externalities beyond the requirements of the law. Dinah Koehler (2007) correctly points out that voluntary clubs can be employed to address issues outside the purview of the existing regulatory framework. For example, while the U.S. government has yet to enact regulations to mitigate global warming, the EPA has established eighteen voluntary programs to respond to climate change challenges.

Some scholars suggest that a proliferation of voluntary clubs might lead to a retreat of the state, as voluntary clubs substitute for public law. If nongovernmental institutions such as voluntary clubs are "less democratic" or "less accountable" than public law (Gunnigham and Rees 1997), this could be worrisome—an issue we first raised in the introductory chapter of this book.

It is clear from the chapters presented in this volume that voluntary clubs operate under the shadow of public law, and frequently in coordinating with public law, end up reinforcing public law. In fact, as chapters 10 and 11 point out, public regulators may themselves establish voluntary clubs as instruments of public policy and vehicles to strengthen compliance with public law. Furthermore, as chapters 7 and 8 suggest, voluntary programs can fill in the gap in underregulated areas. Thus, the evolution, diffusion, working, and efficacy of voluntary clubs should be understood only in the context of public law and the institutions in which they are situated. We firmly believe that public law should be the fundamental governance foundation for any society; voluntary clubs should be viewed as supplements.

Having said this, we recognize that under some conditions, actors may establish voluntary programs to preempt public law (Segerson and Miceli 1998; Lyon and Maxwell 2004; Heritier and Eckert 2008). The shipping case examined in chapter 7 as well as the apparel case examined in chapter 6 provide useful commentaries on this subject. As these chapters show, voluntary clubs can potentially "crowd out" public law or blunt its stringency. This of course assumes that public law would have been supplied had voluntary clubs not been established—an assertion that is difficult to verify. Nevertheless, we recognize that actors have varying motivations to establish a club or join them. Researchers need to carefully assess such motivations and how they may bear on public policy.

Voluntary clubs are potential responses to specific market and government failures. Yet voluntary clubs themselves are amenable to failure. They are not perfect institutions. Clubs may address some types of institutional failures, but they themselves create or become vulnerable to other types of failures. While recognizing that we live and function in an imperfectly governed world, the challenge is to think of the portfolio of policy instruments for specific categories of social challenges, and how might voluntary clubs contribute to this portfolio. We believe future research should look more closely at the portfolio approach to governance.

In sum, while much has been written about voluntary clubs, this volume's contribution is to examine a variety of voluntary programs via a deductive framework that links program efficacy to specific collective action challenges and their mitigation strategies. We hope that future research will draw on this volume and the club framework to study how the interplay among varying sponsors' attributes, stakeholder and institutional contexts, and firm characteristics influence programs' efficacy. The second-generation research, we hope, will consider not only specific programs but also systematically compare various programs, and hopefully compare voluntary clubs with other policy instruments.

Notes

Chapter 2

1. Olson (1965) employed the phrase selective benefits, which pertains to excludable benefits emanating from membership in a group. Olson's selective benefits could take the form of rival and excludable benefits as well as nonrival and excludable benefits. We do not employ the phrase selective benefits because we want to focus on the nonrival but excludable benefits that voluntary programs provide. Consistent with our framework, we term them as branding benefits.

2. Our framework focuses on two program attributes—club standards and monitoring/enforcement rules—because they bear on the two collective action dilemmas we believe to be most important in the study of program efficacy. Other scholars have sought to privilege other program characteristics. For example, Morgenstern and Pizer (2007, 10) concentrate on different program contexts as well as program characteristics as drivers of outcomes. For the latter, they identify one salient characteristic: quantitative versus qualitative targets. Given that our analytic strategy differs in terms of squarely looking at collective action issues, we focus on club standards and monitoring/enforcement as key program attributes.

3. The CERNA group studies the first three only. Madhu Khanna (2001), Thomas Lyon and John Maxwell (2003), Dinah Koehler (2007), and Morgenstern and Pizer (2007) also adopt the same threefold typology.

Chapter 3

1. I would like to thank Bard Harstad, Matthew Kotchen, and Erica Plambeck for their comments on an earlier draft of this chapter, and Alexander V. Hirsch for his research assistance.

2. I (Baron 2001, 2003) introduced the concept of private politics.

3. Such organizations have also been formed in other timber-producing countries. Virtually the entire U.S. timber industry participates in the SFI, in part because its formation was facilitated by the American Forest and Paper Association,

which required participation in the SFI for membership in the association. See Cashore, Auld, and Newsom (2004); see also Sasser et al. (2006).

4. For example, the NGOs want "no-go zones" for certain ecosystems.

5. Andrew King and Michael Lenox (2000) found no evidence that the firms participating in Responsible Care had improved their safety and environmental performance relative to those firms that did not participate. Moreover, the firms that participated in Responsible Care were dirtier on average than the industry as a whole. Responsible Care had no inspection or compliance mechanisms at the time. In the model considered here, all firms are assumed to comply with the standard.

6. Credible assurance is referred to as branding in chapter 2, and in contrast to the typical notion of branding, the firms that do not participate in the club can benefit from the branding of the club firms. This results because the nonclub firms can benefit from the higher price charged by the club firms.

7. A bargaining model could also be used, and the qualitative results would be unchanged.

8. Andrew Whitford (2003) studied coalitions of NGOs that participated as amicus curiae in environmental litigation against firms.

9. This formulation is equivalent to one in which the activist expends an amount. A directed at all the club firms plus an amount a directed at each club firm, where the probability of a successful campaign depends on $A + ma$ rather than A in equation (3.3).

10. This follows because the lowest-cost firms join the club so $K_i(s_A) < K_j(s_A)$, $\forall i \in C, j \in \mathcal{N}$.

11. See http://www.globescan.com/news_archives/WEF_trust2005.html.

12. Jamie Hendry (2006) evaluated propositions relating to target selection based on case studies of five NGOs. In my work with Daniel Diermeier, I provide an analysis of target selection by an activist, and identify conditions under which a soft target is selected (Baron and Diermeier 2007).

13. There are six other equilibriums.

Chapter 4

1. For a comprehensive review of the economics literature on club theory, see Cornes and Sandler ([1986] 1996).

2. For the original formulations of warm glow preferences in the context of privately provided public goods, see Andreoni (1989, 1990). Note that chapter 3 in this volume considers warm glow preferences as well.

3. Our initial setup of consumer preferences and producer costs is similar to that in Besley and Ghatak's (2007) model of corporate social responsibility.

4. With perfect competition among firms, the price would be driven down to equal firm costs c, and consumers would enjoy all the surplus. In contrast, with

imperfect competition, the price may be set as high as the consumer benefit *b*, in which case firms would enjoy all the surplus as profit.

5. This specification of preferences implies that the club-certified good is an impure public good, with the joint production of private and public characteristics. For applications of the impure public good model to green markets, see Kotchen (2005, 2006a).

Chapter 5

1. The research for this chapter was supported in part by a grant from the U.S. Institute of Peace. The opinions, findings, and conclusions or recommendations expressed here are those of the author, and do not necessarily reflect the views of the U.S. Institute of Peace.

Chapter 6

1. This section and the next draw on Bartley (2007).

2. In a previous article (Bartley 2003), I reported that government funding accounted for "most" of the SAI's funding, when the portion was actually substantial but less than 50 percent. I thank SAI officials for pointing out this error.

3. For more information on the sample, see Bartley and Child (2007).

4. Those nine were Nike, Reebok, Levi Strauss, the Gap, Liz Claiborne, Phillips-Van Heusen, Nordstrom, Polo Ralph Lauren, and Eddie Bauer (Spiegel).

5. I use the natural log of the total assets as the measure of a firm size. Among these firms, this measure is highly correlated with other possible measures of size, such as the total sales (r = .93).

6. Since the dependent variable in the stage one model is a count of the number of years that a company was targeted, I use negative binomial regression.

Chapter 7

1. Despite these incentives, however, what is odd is that P&I clubs rarely remove ships from their organization once the ship has been admitted.

Chapter 8

1. This research was made possible, in part, by a research fellowship from the Robert Wood Johnson Foundation at the University of California at Berkeley. I am grateful to Ana Barton, Ashley Kustu, and Tammy Hwang for research assistance, the IASB/IASCF and Yasuhiro Uozumi for sharing data, and Steve Hanson, Aseem Prakash, and Matthew Potoski for comments.

2. All references below to IFRSs should be read as references to IFRSs or revised International Accounting Standards.

3. For a recent, in-depth analysis of the IASB's predecessor organization, though, compare Camfferman and Zeff (2007); see also Büthe (2008).

4. The seventy-four countries are: Armenia, Australia, Austria, Bahamas, Bahrain, Barbados, Belgium, Bulgaria, Costa Rica, Croatia, Cyprus, the Czech Republic, Denmark, the Dominican Republic, Ecuador, Egypt, Estonia, Finland, France, Germany, Georgia, Ghana, Greece, Guatemala, Guyana, Haiti, Honduras, Hong Kong, Hungary, Iceland, Ireland, Italy, Jamaica, Jordan, Kenya, Kuwait, Kyrgyzstan, Latvia, Lebanon, Liechtenstein, Lithuania, Luxembourg, Macedonia, Malawi, Malta, Mauritius, Namibia, the Netherlands, Nepal, New Zealand, Nicaragua, Norway, Oman, Panama, Papua New Guinea, Peru, the Philippines, Poland, Portugal, Romania, Singapore, Slovenia, the Slovak Republic, South Africa, Spain, Sweden, Tajikistan, Tanzania, Trinidad and Tobago, Turkey, Ukraine, the United Kingdom, Venezuela, and Yugoslavia (see Deloitte 2007, 12–16).

5. The institutional structure surrounding the IASB is discussed in greater detail in Mattli and Büthe (2005b).

6. The process of IASB standard setting therefore is in some respects akin to forms of business self-regulation seen in numerous other issue areas (see, e.g., Braithwaite and Drahos 2000; Haufler 2001; Kollman and Prakash 2001; Bartley 2003; Cashore, Auld, and Newsom 2004).

7. Concentrated interests might be more important than size. As Duncan Snidal (1985, 589) has pointed out, the argument about "size" is also about having the *capability* to provide the public good.

8. In this respect, the club good "produced" by IASB financing is not strictly nonrival.

9. In the annual report for 2007 (IASCF 2008), the IASCF for the first time differentiates three broad categories of contributors (from "less than £25,000" to "£50,000+") and discloses total amounts per country. The categories, however, are still very broad, and no such information is available for past years, making it impossible to trace the monetary level of contributions by country over time.

10. A small number of corporations from a given country therefore in some cases makes a larger contribution (and might carry more weight with the IASB) than a large number of corporations from another country (not-for-attribution interview with IASB official, March 2008; see also IASCF 2008, 54ff).

11. Particularly notable here among the social scientific studies is the one by Yasuhiro Uozumi (2007), on which I have built for some of the analyses below. Uozumi assumed equal average contributions by firms in each category in order to estimate the national distribution of contributions, given the lack of information from the IASCF about the exact amounts of individual contributions. I have not followed that approach in light of the IASB's statement that average contributions have varied greatly across countries.

12. The IASB budget is in British pounds, but contributions have been pledged and made in U.S. dollars, even by British and Eurozone contributors.

13. Not-for-attribution interview with an IASCF official.

14. Many supporters were also MNCs, though on average slightly smaller.

15. For the EU figures, I assume here and below that the four Italian companies that contributed in 2005 continued to do so via Emittenti in 2006 (IASCF 2007b, 39n7), and that a total of thirty Italian companies contributed via Emittenti in 2007 (as reported in IASCF 2008, 56). The time series are *not* adjusted for the switch to a levy-based for all publicly traded companies in the United Kingdom, which became effective late in 2007 and might have depressed the recorded number of UK contributors.

Chapter 9

1. An example of stockholder targeting by civil society groups is the campaign against Fidelity for its holding of shares in two Chinese firms that do business in Sudan. In this case, activists were targeting a Western company that invested in a Chinese company that did business in Sudan. Despite this somewhat attenuated relationship, the public shaming campaign seems to have yielded results— Fidelity did submit to criticism, selling 90 percent of its U.S. shares in the firms in question.

2. ISO 14001 statistics were compiled by Reinhard Peglau of the Federal Environmental Agency in Germany, and the Corporate Risk Management Company in Japan. A complete listing of countries and certificates figures is available at http://www.ecology.or.jp/isoworld/english/analy14k.htm (accessed June 5, 2007).

3. UN Global Compact, available at http://www.unglobalcompact.org/ParticipantsAndStakeholders/index.html (accessed August 2007).

4. UN Global Compact, available at http://www.unglobalcompact.org/CommunicatingProgress/index.html (accessed August 2007).

5. A Google search of "Free Burma," "UN Global Compact," and "ISO 14000" revealed 118,000 hits, 378,000 hits, and 1.5 million hits, respectively. A Lexis/Nexis news search of those same terms in headlines or lead paragraphs over the past two years yielded 7, 14, and 77 stories, respectively.

6. Communication on Progress, UN Global Compact. Available at http://www.unglobalcompact.org/COP/index.html (accessed June 10, 2007).

7. More details about the campaign can be found on the Web site for Free Burma Campaign UK, available at http://www.burmacampaign.org.uk/total.php.

8. As for the remainder of the list, Taiwan and Hong Kong each have a single company on the dirty list.

9. "The Dirty List," Free Burma Campaign UK, available at http://www
.burmacampaign.org.uk/dirty_list/dirty_list_briefing.html (accessed December
12, 2006).

10. Ibid. (accessed April 25, 2008).

11. Daniel Pepper, "Myanmar: In Harm's Way," November 20, 2006, available at http://money.cnn.com/magazines/fortune/fortune_archive/2006/11/27/
8394466/index.htm.

12. "The Prosecution Must Crack Down on Daewoo International's Suspicious
Illegal Exports of Defense Industry Materials to Burma, and Daewoo Should Expose the Truth," open letter issued by Earths Rights International, signed by
twenty-six South Korean NGOs, available at http://www.earthrights.org/
burmafeature/money_guns_and_gas__south_koreas_relationship_with_burmas
_military.html.

Chapter 10

1. As the book goes to print, the EPA Administrator has decided to terminate the Performance Track program. This chapter, however, focuses on design
and implementation issues, which remain relevant to the broader subject of
government-sponsored green clubs. The Performance Track remains an important case study, because it defined the most comprehensive and rigorous of EPA's
efforts to implement the concept of a green club and reflected a bipartisan approach based on the recommendations of several organizations, such as the President's Council for Sustainable Development and the Aspen Institute.

2. The twenty-two states that the EPA tracks as having green clubs are Arizona,
Colorado, Delaware, Georgia, Idaho, Indiana, Kentucky, Louisiana, Maine,
Michigan, Missouri, New Mexico, North Carolina, Oklahoma, Oregon, South
Carolina, Texas, Utah, Vermont, Virginia, and Wisconsin. Oregon has elimi-
nated funding for its program, which has largely been terminated. Implementa-
tion of the New Hampshire, New York, Mississippi, Washington, and West
Virginia programs is expected to begin in late 2007 or 2008.

Chapter 11

1. Gopal Raman provided invaluable research assistance in many facets of this
project, most especially with coding and collecting data. We are also grateful for
helpful comments we received from Natasha Besch-Turner, Dan Fiorino, Deb
Gallagher, Peter May, John Mendeloff, Dinah Koehler, Matt Potoski, Aseem Prakash, Evan Ringquist, Thane Thompson, Michael Toffel, and Terry Yosie. We
presented an earlier version of this chapter at the 2005 meeting of the Association of Public Policy and Management, and appreciate the comments of those
participants. Our research was supported by the EPA, Office of Policy, Economics, and Innovation (grant no. R-83056701), and an award from the Corporate
Social Responsibility Initiative at Harvard University's John F. Kennedy School

of Government. We alone—and neither our funders nor colleagues—are responsible for the views and conclusions expressed herein.

2. The rewards offered to members, and the behavior expected of them to join and remain in the club, are key aspects of what we mean by a club's institutional design. To be sure, several previous studies have noted that positive inducements offered by clubs can motivate participation (Segerson and Li 1999; Davies and Mazurek 1996; Khanna 2001). Others recognize that government can provide different types of membership benefits than NGOs. In addition to supplying technical information about ways to reduce waste and other forms of pollution (Khanna 2001; Delmas and Keller 2005), government can offer regulatory or procedural flexibility to participating firms (Delmas and Terlaak 2001; EPA 1998). Other government programs seek to encourage firms to undertake action that can benefit their bottom line, such as through energy efficiency or other actions that firms presumably have an incentive to take even in the absence of the program (Morgenstern and Pizer 2007).

3. The EPA even prepared a sample letter, just one paragraph long, for firms to use to make their commitments.

4. The General Accounting Office (1994) has criticized the EPA for adopting the 1988 baseline, arguing that only reductions from the period 1991 to 1994 should be attributed to the program.

5. Sam and Innes's (2005) finding that the participants were subject to less frequent inspections suggests that in practice, 33/50 members may have reaped some decreased regulatory scrutiny.

6. The information about the demographic characteristics of Performance Track plants is taken from Booz Allen Hamilton (2005), which includes data from Performance Track facility applications through Round 7 (February 2004).

7. The information about environmental permitting is taken from Booz Allen Hamilton (2005), which includes data from Performance Track facility applications through Round 7 (February 2004).

8. Some scholars might well characterize Project XL as a negotiated agreement as opposed to a green club (Delmas and Marcus 2004; Carraro and Lévêque 1999). Project XL did involve negotiations with individual facilities, but the program also bears an affinity with other EPA voluntary programs in that it sought to encourage individual facilities with records of strong regulatory compliance to cooperate with the EPA, states, and environmental or community organizations, and experiment with new ways to achieve superior environmental performance. We therefore follow Prakash and Potoski (2006b, 63–65) in treating Project XL as an example of a green club.

9. For a list of Project XL agreements, see http://www.epa.gov/ProjectXL/projects.htm.

10. We examined all the programs listed on the EPA's Web site as voluntary programs, available at http://www.epa.gov/partners/. In addition, we reviewed those listed on internal documents that we obtained from the EPA staff. All the

programs were national ones; we excluded exclusively regional voluntary programs. We did not include any past EPA programs—such as 33/50 or Project XL—that the agency no longer considered active. In total, we examined sixty-two programs. Data collection took place in October 2005.

11. Confusingly, the EPA sometimes refers to all of its voluntary programs as "partnerships." We use the term *partnership program* in a more restricted sense, as a standardized program that enables an exchange between the EPA and a regulated entity. The EPA offers a package of benefits (usually recognition) in exchange for certain types of beyond-compliance activities on the part of the facility. To be clear, we distinguish partnership programs from the following four alternative types of voluntary programs. *Educational programs* offer educational resources to firms, local governments, NGOs, and citizens. Resources take the form of publications or Web sites that inform parties of environmentally benign ways of operating. The "It All Adds Up to Clean Air" program is an example. *Grants* provide financial support for projects that demonstrate beyond-compliance practices, and we considered technical assistance programs as a grant-in-kind to businesses. The EPA's AgSTAR Program is an example. *Competitive awards* recognize firms that distinguish themselves beyond their peers. These are competitive, one-time awards, not a sustained partnership. The EPA's Clean Water Act Recognition Program is an example. *Product certifications* seek to promote a market in "green" products by developing standards for the environmental characteristics of these products and a process for certifying that specific products meet these standards. The part of the Energy Star program that establishes standards for energy-efficient appliances is an example.

12. Unlike with product certification, in voluntary partnership programs the membership decision is made based on the qualities of the organization, not the product.

13. Our list includes the nine programs that Fiorino describes in chapter 10 with the exception of WaterSense, which the EPA began in 2006, after we collected our data. We include twenty additional programs that fit our definition of partnership programs. Through these programs, the EPA designated some firms as members that are required to commit to specific practices that the EPA rewards with defined benefits. While in his chapter Fiorino includes the entire Energy Star program (which includes a product certification program), our analysis includes only the Energy Star Business Improvement program, a component of Energy Star for business operations.

14. Finally, were it not for the fact that the EPA clearly treats SunWise as a partnership program, replete with membership requirements that make the program a club, we probably would have characterized SunWise as an educational program.

Chapter 13

1. There are several other characterizations of voluntary programs such as governance without government (Rosenau and Czempiel 1992), private authority

regimes (Cutler, Haufler, and T. Porter 1999), nonstate market-driven systems (Cashore, Auld, and Newsom 2003), civil regulations (Vogel 2007), reflexive regulation (Teubner 1983), and public-private partnerships (Risse 2004). While these characterizations are useful and illuminating, they tend not to explicitly outline analytic frameworks that identify exogenous drivers of recruitment into and the efficacy of voluntary governance programs.

2. Ans Kolk and Rob van Tulder (2002) point out that in addition to club design, a critical factor for the success of codes of conduct on child labor is the availability of alternative employment opportunities for children who would lose employment if such codes were put in practice. Thus, the external political and social environment might have crucial bearing on the efficacy of the voluntary code.

3. This section draws on Prakash and Potoski (2007a).

References

Abend, J. 1996. CFA in the Corner of California Manufacturers. *Bobbin*, February, 26–29.

Abrams, A. 1994. Tanker Association Seeks to Require Pollution Insurance. *Journal of Commerce* (May 12): 7B.

Akerlof, G. A. 1970. The Market for "Lemons." *Quarterly Journal of Economics* 84 (3): 488–500.

Alesina, A., S. Ardagna, G. Nicoletti, and F. Schiantarelli. 2003. Regulation and Investment. NBER working paper no. 9560, Cambridge, MA, March.

Almond, G., and S. Verba. 1965. *The Civic Culture*. Boston: Little and Brown.

Andreoni, J. 1989. Giving with Impure Altruism: Applications to Charity and Ricardian Equivalence. *Journal of Political Economy* 97:1447–1458.

Andreoni, J. 1990. Impure Altruism and Donations to Public Goods: A Theory of Warm-Glow Giving. *Economic Journal* 100:464–477.

Argenti, P. 2004. Collaborating with Activists: How Starbucks Works with NGOs. *California Management Review* 47:91–114.

Armbruster-Sandoval, R. 2005. *Globalization and Cross-Border Labor Solidarity in the Americas*. New York: Routledge.

Arnold and Porter, LLP. 1996. *Monitoring Precedents*. Prepared for Apparel Industry Partnership. Archives of FLA organizer.

Arora, S. and T. Casson. 1995. An Experiment in Voluntary Environmental Regulation: Participation in EPA's 33/50 Program. *Journal of Environmental Economics and Management* 28 (3): 271–286.

Arora, S., and T. Cason. 1996. Why Do Firms Volunteer to Exceed Environmental Regulations? Understanding Participation in EPA's 33/50 Program. *Land Economics* 72:413–432.

Aspen Institute. 1994. *The Alternative Path: A Cleaner, Cheaper Way to Protect and Enhance the Environment*. Washington, DC: Aspen Institute.

Banner, S. 1998. *Anglo-American Securities Regulation*. New York: Cambridge University Press.

Bardach, E., and R. Kagan. 1982. *Going by the Book: The Problem of Regulatory Unreasonableness.* Philadelphia: Temple University Press.

Barnett, M., and A. King. 2006. Good Fences Make Good Neighbors. Paper presented at the Academy of Management Best Paper Proceedings, Atlanta, GA.

Baron, D. 2001. Private Politics, Corporate Social Responsibility, and Integrated Strategy. *Journal of Economics and Management Strategy* 10:7–45.

Baron, D. 2003. Private Politics. *Journal of Economics and Management Strategy* 21:31–66.

Baron, D. 2007. Corporate Social Responsibility and Social Entrepreneurship. *Journal of Economics and Management Strategy* 16:683–717.

Baron, D. 2008. Managerial Contracting and Corporate Social Responsibility. *Journal of Public Economics* 92:268–288.

Baron, D. 2009. A Positive Theory of Moral Management, Social Pressure, and Corporate Social Performance. *Journal of Economics and Management Strategy*, 18: 7–43.

Baron, D. 2009b. Credence Attributes, Voluntary Organizations, and Social Pressure. Working paper. Stanford University.

Baron, D., and D. Diermeier. 2007. Strategic Activism and Nonmarket Strategy. *Journal of Economics and Management Strategy* 16:599–634.

Barrett, J. 1994. Senate Hears of Brutal Child Labor Conditions. *Women's Wear Daily*, September 22, 9–10.

Bartley, T. 2005. Corporate Accountability and the Privatization of Labor Standards. *Research in Political Sociology* 12:211–244.

Bartley, T. 2007. Institutional Emergence in an Era of Globalization: The Rise of Transnational Private Regulation of Labor and Environmental Conditions. *American Journal of Sociology* 113(2):297–351.

Bartley, T. 2003. Certifying Forests and Factories. *Politics and Society* 31 (3): 433–464.

Bartley, T., and C. Child. 2007. Shaming the Corporation. Working paper. Department of Sociology, Indiana University.

Baumol, W., R. Litan, and C. Schramm. 2007. *Good Capitalism, Bad Capitalism, and the Economics of Growth and Prosperity.* New Haven, CT: Yale University Press.

Beardsley, S., D. Burgov, and L. Enriquez. 2005. The Role of Regulation in Strategy. *McKinsey Quarterly* 4:92–102.

Bennear, L. 2008. What Do We Really Know? The Effect of Reporting Thresholds on Inferences Using Environmental Right-to-Know Data. *Regulation and Governance* 2 (3): 293–315.

Benner, T., W. Reinicke, and J. Witte. 2004. Multisectoral Networks in Global Governance. *Government and Opposition* 39 (2): 191–210.

Bennett, P. 2001. Mutual Risk: P&I Insurance Clubs and Maritime Safety and Environmental Performance. *Marine Policy* 25:13–21.

Benston, G. 1975. Accounting Standards in the United States and the United Kingdom. *Vanderbilt Law Review* 28 (1): 235–267.

Berger S, 2006. *How We Compete*. New York: Doubleday.

Berger, S., and R. Dore, eds. 1996. *National Diversity and Global Capitalism*. Ithaca, NY: Cornell University Press.

Bernard, M., and J. Ravenhill. 1995. Beyond Product Cycles and Flying Geese. *World Politics* (January): 173–209.

Bernstein, M. 1953. Political Ideas of Selected American Business Journals. *Public Opinion Quarterly* 17 (Summer): 258–267.

Bernstein, S., and B. Cashore. 2004. Non-State Global Governance: Is Forest Certification a Legitimate Alternative to a Global Forest Convention? In *Hard Choices, Soft Law*, ed. J. Kirton and M. Trebilcock, 33–63. Aldershot, UK: Ashgate.

Besley, T., and M. Ghatak. 2007. Retailing Public Goods: The Economics of Corporate Social Responsibility. *Journal of Public Economics* 91:1645–1663.

Bessen S., and G. Saloner. 1988. *Compatibility Standards and the Market for Telecommunication Services*. Santa Monica, CA: Rand.

Bhagwati, J. 2004. *In Defense of Globalization*. New York: Oxford University Press.

Binder, S., and E. Neumayer. 2005. Environmental Pressure Group Strength and Air Pollution: An Empirical Analysis. *Ecological Economic* 55:527–538.

Black, S. 1995. Bad Apples Need Not Apply. *Bobbin*, October, 2.

Black, S. 1997. Can We Live With Big Brother? *Bobbin*, June, 1.

Black, S. 1998. AAMA's Compliance Plan-A Mammoth Undertaking. Bobbin, November, 1.

Blackman, A., and J. Mazurek. 1999. *The Cost of Developing Site-Specific Environmental Regulations: Evidence from EPA's Project XL*. Resources for the Future discussion paper, 99-35-REV. Washington, DC: Resources for the Future.

Blair, M., A. Bugg-Levine, and T. Rippin. 2004. The UN's Role in Corporate Social Responsibility. *McKinsey Quarterly* 4:21–24.

Bobbin. 1997. CAIC Works Toward Non-Profit Compliance. *Bobbin*, February, 44.

Boli, J., and G. Thomas, eds. 1999. *Constructing World Culture*. Palo Alto, CA: Stanford University Press.

Bonacich, E., and R. Appelbaum. 2000. *Behind the Label*. Berkeley: University of California Press.

Booz Allen Hamilton. 2005. *Performance Track Database Report*. Joint Project of Booz Allen Hamilton and the Center for Business and Government, John F. Kennedy School of Government, Harvard University. On file with the authors.

Börkey, P., M. Glachant, and F. Lévêque. 1998. *Voluntary Approaches for Environmental Policy in OEDC Countries: An Assessment.* Available at http://www.cerna.ensmp.fr/Documents/PBMGFL-OECDVAs.pdf (accessed February 2, 2008).

Braithwaite, J., and P. Drahos. 2000. *Global Business Regulation.* Cambridge: Cambridge University Press.

Braudel, F. 1981. *Civilization and Capitalism.* New York: Harper and Row.

Bray, J. 1997. Intercargo Poised to Set Up Safety Scheme. *Lloyd's List* (June 11): 1.

Brouhle, K., C. Griffiths, and A. Wolverton. 2005. The Use of Voluntary Approaches for Environmental Policymaking in the U.S. In *The Handbook of Voluntary Environmental Agreements*, ed. Edoardo Croce, 107–134. New York: Springer-Verlag.

Buchanan, J. M. 1965. An Economic Theory of Clubs. *Economica* 32:1–14.

Büthe, T. 1998. The State as Facilitator of Collective Action. Manuscript. Columbia University.

Büthe, T. 2002. The Political Sources of Business Confidence. PhD diss., Columbia University.

Büthe, T. 2004. Governance through Private Authority? Non-State Actors in World Politics. *Journal of International Affairs* 58 (1): 281–290.

Büthe, T. 2006. *The Dynamics of Principals and Agents.* Manuscript. Duke University.

Büthe, T. 2008. Politics and Institutions in the Regulation of Global Capital: A Review Article. *Review of International Organizations* 3 (2): 207–220.

Büthe, T., and W. Mattli. 2010. *Assessing the IASB: Results of a Business Survey about International Financial Reporting Standards and IASB's Operations, Accountability, and Responsiveness to Stakeholders.* Durham, NC/Oxford, England Duke and Oxford Universities

Büthe, T., and W. Mattli. 2009. Standards for Global Markets: Domestic and International Institutions for Setting International Product Standards. In *Handbook on Multi-Level Governance*, ed. H. Enderlein, S. Wälti, and M. Zürn. Cheltenham, UK: Edward Elgar.

Büthe, T., and J. Witte. 2004. *Product Standards in Transatlantic Trade and Investment.* Washington, DC: American Institute for Contemporary German Studies.

Caballero, T. 1998. Project XL: Making It Legal, Making It Work. *Stanford Environmental Law Journal* 17:399.

Calveras, A., J. Ganuza, and G. Llobet. 2007. Regulation, Corporate Social Responsibility, and Activism. *Journal of Economics and Management Strategy* 16:719–740.

Camfferman, K., and S. Zeff. 2007. *Financial Reporting and Global Capital Markets.* Oxford: Oxford University Press.

Campaign for Labor Rights. 1997. Newsletter no. 9. Washington, DC: Campaign for Labor Rights.

Cao, X. 2006. Convergence, Divergence, and Networks in the Age of Globalization. Paper presented at the International Political Economy Society Conference, Princeton University, Princeton, NJ, November.

Carmin, J., N. Darnall, and J. Mil-Homens. 2003. Stakeholder Involvement in the Design of U.S. Voluntary Programs: Does Sponsorship Matter? *Policy Studies Journal* 31:527–543.

Carmona, S. 2002. History Matters. *European Accounting Review* 11 (1): 9–32.

Carpenter, D. P. 2001. *The Forging of Bureaucratic Autonomy*. Princeton, NJ: Princeton University Press.

Carraro, C., and F. Lévêque. 1999. Introduction: The Rationale and Potential of Voluntary Approaches. In *Voluntary Approaches in Environmental Policy*, ed. C. Carraro and F. Lévêque, 1–16. Boston: Kluwer Academic Publishers.

Casella, A. 2001. Product Standards and International Trade. *Kyklos* 54 (2–3): 243–264.

Cashore, B., G. Auld, and D. Newsom. 2004. *Governing through Markets: Forest Certification and the Emergence of Non-State Authority*. New Haven, CT: Yale University Press.

Cashore, B., F. Gale, E. Meidinger, and D. Newsom. 2006. Forest Certification in Developing and Transitioning Countries. *Environment* 48:6–25.

Cavanagh, J. 1997. The Global Resistance to Sweatshops. In *No Sweat: Fashion, Free Trade, and the Rights of Garment Workers*, ed. A. Ross, 39–50. New York: Verso.

CDI. 2007. "Main" and "Participants." Available at http://www.cdi.org.uk/main.html.

Chandler, A. 1990. *Scale and Scope: The Dynamics of Industrial Capitalism*. Cambridge, MA: Belknap Press.

Chatterji, A., and S. Listokin. 2007. Corporate Social Irresponsibility. *Democracy: A Journal of Ideas* 3 (Winter): 52–63.

Chicago Council on Global Affairs. 2007. World Public Favors Globalization and Trade but Wants to Protect Environment and Jobs. Available at http://www.worldpublicopinion.org/pipa/pdf/apr07/CCGA+_GlobTrade_article.pdf.

Claessens, S., and J. Fan. 2002. Corporate Governance in Asia: A Survey. *International Review of Finance* 3 (June): 71–103.

Clinton, W., and A. Gore. 1995. Reinventing Environmental Regulation. Washington, DC: EPA Office of Policy Analysis and Review.

Coase, R. 1960. The Problem of Social Cost. *Journal of Law and Economics* 3:1–44.

Coglianese, C., and J. Nash, eds. 2001. *Regulating from the Inside: Can Environmental Management Systems Achieve Policy Goals?* Washington, DC: Resources for the Future.

Coglianese, C., and J. Nash. 2006. Beyond Compliance: Business Decision Making and the US EPA's Performance Track Program. Regulatory Policy Program, Kennedy School of Government, Harvard University.

Coglianese, C., and J. Nash. 2008. EPA's National Environmental Performance Track: What Is Iit Tracking? What Is It Performing? Unpublished manuscript.

Coglianese, C., and K. Nicolaidis. 2001. Securing Subsidiarity. In *The Federal Vision*, ed. K. Nicolaidis and R. Howse. Oxford: Oxford University Press.

Collingsworth, T., W. Goold, and P. Harvey. 1994. Time for a Global New Deal. *Foreign Affairs* 48:8–13.

Cornes, R., and Sandler, T. [1986] 1996. *The Theory of Externalities, Public Goods, and Club Goods.* 2nd ed. Cambridge: Cambridge University Press.

Council on Economic Priorities. 1994. *How to Develop Guidelines for Corporate Action on Child Labor.* New York: Council on Economic Priorities.

Cutler, C., V. Haufler, and T. Porter, eds. 1998. *Private Authority and International Affairs.* Albany: State University of New York Press.

Darnall, N., and J. Carmin. 2005. Greener and Cleaner? The Signaling Accuracy of U.S. Voluntary Environmental Programs. *Policy Sciences* 38 (1): 71–90.

Dasgupta, S., H. Hettige, and D. Wheeler. 2000. What Improves Environmental Compliance? Evidence from Mexican Industry. *Journal of Environmental Economics and Management* 39:39–66.

Davies, T., and J. Mazurek. 1996. *Industry Incentives for Environmental Improvement: Evaluation of U.S. Federal Initiatives.* Global Environmental Management Initiative, September.

Delmas, M. 2001. Stakeholders and Competitive Advantage: The Case of ISO 14001. *Production and Operation Management* 10 (3): 343–358.

Delmas, M. 2002. The Diffusion of Environmental Management Standards in Europe and in the United States. *Policy Sciences* 35 (1): 1–119.

Delmas, M. 2006. Collective Corporate Political Activity: Are Late Joiners the Free Riders? Working paper. University of California at Santa Barbara.

Delmas, M., and A. Keller. 2005. Strategic Free Riding in Voluntary Programs: The Case of the US EPA Wastewise Program. *Policy Sciences* 38:91–106.

Delmas, M., and A. Marcus. 2004. Firms' Choice of Regulatory Instruments to Reduce Pollution: A Transaction Cost Approach. *Business and Politics* 6 (3): article 3.

Delmas, M., and M. Montes. 2007. Voluntary Agreements to Improve Environmental Quality: Are Late Joiners the Free Riders? Institute for Social, Behavioral, and Economic Research. ISBER Publications. Paper 07.

Delmas, M., and A. Terlaak. 2001. A Framework for Analyzing Environmental Voluntary Agreements. *California Management Review* 43 (3): 44–63.

Deloitte. 2007. *IFRSs in Your Pocket 2007: An IAS Plus Guide.* London: Deloitte Touche Tohmatsu.

Deloitte. 2008. Use of IFRS by Jurisdiction. Available at http://www.iasplus
.com/country/useias.htm (accessed August 15, 2008).

Dempsey, P., and L. Helling. 1980. Oil Pollution by Ocean Vessels. *Journal of
International Law and Policy* 10:37–87.

DeSombre, E. 2000. *Domestic Sources of International Environmental Policy.*
Cambridge, MA: MIT Press.

DeSombre, E.. 2005a. Fishing under Flags of Convenience. *Global Environmental Politics 5*, no. 4 (November): 73–94.

DeSombre, E. 2005b. Globalization and Environmental Protection on the High
Seas. In *International Handbook of Environmental Politics*, ed. Peter Dauvergne.
Cheltenham, UK: Edward Elgar.

DeSombre, E. 2006. *Flagging Standards.* Cambridge, MA: MIT Press.

de Swaan, A. 1988. *In Care of the State.* New York: Oxford University Press.

Djelic, M., and K. Sahlin-Andersson, eds. 2006. *Transnational Governance:
Institutional Dynamics of Regulation.* New York: Cambridge University Press.

Djelic, M., and K. Sahlin-Andersson. 2006. Introduction: A World of Governance. In *Transnational Governance*, ed. M. Djelic and K. Sahlin-Andersson,
1–28. New York: Cambridge University Press.

Dolsak, N., and E. Ostrom, eds. 2003. *The Commons in the New Millennium.*
Cambridge, MA: MIT Press.

Doremus, P., S. Reich, and L. Pauly. 1998. *The Myth of the Global Corporation.*
Princeton, NJ: Princeton University Press.

Drezner, D. 2006. *U.S. Trade Strategy.* New York: Council on Foreign Relations
Press.

Drezner, D. 2007. *All Politics Is Global.* Princeton, NJ: Princeton University
Press.

Durant, R., D. Fiorino, and R. O'Leary, eds. 2004. *Environmental Governance
Reconsidered.* Cambridge, MA: MIT Press.

Ebrahim, A. 2003. Accountability in Practice: Mechanisms for NGOs. *World
Development* 31 (5): 813–829.

Economist Intelligence Unit Democracy Index 2006. 2007. *Economist.* Available at http://www.economist.com/media/pdf/DEMOCRACY_TABLE_2007_v3
.pdf (accessed August 8, 2007).

Economy, E. 2004. *The River Runs Black: The Environmental Challenge to
China's Future.* Ithaca, NY: Cornell University Press.

Edwards, L. 2005. Starting with a Name Only. *Advertising Age*, March 28, 7.

Edwards, M., and D. Hulme, eds. 1996. *Beyond the Magic Bullet.* West Hart-
ford, CT: Kumarian Press.

Eesley, C., and M. Lenox. 2006. Firm Responses to Secondary Stakeholder
Action. *Strategic Management Journal* 27:765–781.

Esbenshade, J. 2004. *Monitoring Sweatshops*. Philadelphia: Temple University Press.

Egels-Zanden, N. 2007. Suppliers' Compliance with MNCs' Codes of Conduct. *Journal of Business Ethics*, 74.

Elliott, K., and R. Freeman. 2003. Can Labor Standards Improve under Globalization? *Environmental Law Journal* 17:399–471.

Esty, D., and A. Winston. 2006. *Green to Gold*. New Haven, CT: Yale University Press.

Ethical Trading Initiative. 2006. *Getting Smarter at Auditing*. London: Ethical Trading Initiative. Available at www.eti2.org.uk/Z/lib/2006/11/smart-audit/eti-smarter-auditing-2006.pdf.

Fair Labor Association. 2007. *FLA 3.0: Toward Sustainable Compliance*. Available at http://www.fairlabor.org/about/fla_30_-_toward_sustainable_compliance.

Falkner R. 2003. Private Environmental Governance and International Relations. *Global Environmental Politics* 3 (2): 72–87.

Finnemore, M. 2003. *The Purpose of Intervention*. Ithaca, NY: Cornell University Press.

Finnemore, M., and K. Sikkink. 1998. International Norm Dynamics and Political Change. *International Organization* 52 (4): 887–917.

Fiorino, D. 1999. Rethinking Environmental Regulation. *Harvard Environmental Law Review* 23:441–469.

Fiorino, D. 2001. Environmental Policy as Learning. *Public Administration Review* 61:322–334.

Fiorino, D. 2006. *The New Environmental Regulation*. Cambridge, MA: MIT Press.

Fombrun, C. 1996. *Reputation: Realizing Value from the Corporate Image*. Boston: Harvard Business School Press.

Fombrun, C., and M. Shanley.1990. What's in a Name? Reputation Building and Corporate Strategy. *Academy of Management Journal* 33:233–258.

Foster, L., and A. Harney. 2005. Doctored Records on Working Hours and Pay Are Causing Problems for Consumer Multinationals as They Source More of Their Goods in Asia. *Financial Times*, April 22.

Fowler, R. 2000. *Report of the Panel of Experts on Violations of Security Council Sanctions against Unita*, 1–184. New York: UN Security Council.

Fox, J., and D. Brown. 1998. *The Struggle for Accountability*. Cambridge, MA: MIT Press.

Frenkel, S. 2001. Globalization, Athletic Footwear Commodity Chains, and Employment Relations in China. *Organization Studies* 22:531–562.

Gamper-Rabindran, S. 2006. Did the EPA's Voluntary Industrial Toxics Program Reduce Emissions? *Journal of Environmental Economics and Management* 52 (1): 391–410.

Garcia-Johnson, R. 2000. *Exporting Environmentalism*. Cambridge, MA: MIT Press.

Garcia-Johnson, R. 2001. Beyond Corporate Culture. Unpublished paper, Duke University.

Geiser, K. 2004. Pollution Prevention. In *Environmental Governance Reconsidered*, ed. R. Durant, D. Fiorino, and R. O'Leary, 427–454. Cambridge, MA: MIT Press.

Gilpin, R. 1981. *War and Change in World Politics*. New York: Cambridge University Press.

Global Witness. 1999. *A Crude Awakening: The Role of Oil and Banking Industries in Angolan Civil War and the Plunder of State Assets*. London: Global Witness.

Global Witness. 1998. *Rough Trade: The Role of Companies and Governments in the Angolan Conflict*. London: Global Witness.

Global Witness and P. Wexler. 2006. *An Independent Commissioned Review Evaluating the Effectiveness of the Kimberley Process*, 1–25. London: Global Witness.

Gouldson, A. 2005. Voluntary Regulation and Capacities for Environmental Improvement. In *Industrial Transformation: Environmental Policy Innovations in the United States and Europe*, ed. T. Bruijn and V. Norberg-Bohm, 229–252. Cambridge, MA: MIT Press.

Graham, E. 2000. *Fighting the Wrong Enemy*. Washington, DC: Institute for International Economics.

Grant, R., and R. Keohane. 2005. Accountability and Abuses of Power in World Politics. *American Political Science Review* 99 (1): 29–43.

Gugerty, Mary Kay, 2007. "The Emergence of NGO Self-Regulation in Africa." Paper presented at the Symposium on Nonprofit Self-Regulation in Comparative Perspective, University of Washington, March 2007.

Gunningham, N., and P. Grabosky. 1998. *Smart Regulation*. Oxford: Oxford University Press.

Gunningham, N., R. Kagan, and D. Thornton. 2003. *Shades of Green*. Palo Alto, CA: Stanford University Press.

Gunningham, N., and J. Rees. 1997. Industry Self-Regulation. *Law and Policy* 19 (4): 363–414.

Gunningham, N., and D. Sinclair. 2002. *Leaders and Laggards*. Sheffield, UK: Greenleaf Publishing.

Hall, P., and D. Soskice, eds. 2001. *Varieties of Capitalism*. New York: Oxford University Press.

Hansmann, H. 1980. The Role of Nonprofit Enterprise. *Yale Law Review* 89:835–898.

Harbaugh, R., J. W. Maxwell, and B. Roussillon. 2006. The Groucho Effect of Uncertain Standards. Working paper, Indiana University, Kelley School of Business, Department of Business Economics and Public Policy.

Hardin, G. 1968. The Tragedy of the Commons. *Science* 162:1243–1248.

Hardin, R. 1982. *Collective Action*. Baltimore: Johns Hopkins University Press.

Harrison, A., and J. Scorse. 2006. Improving the Conditions of Workers? Minimum Wage Legislation and Anti-Sweatshop Activism. *California Management Review* 48:144–160.

Haufler, V. 2001. *A Public Role for the Private Sector*. Washington, DC: Carnegie Endowment for International Peace.

Hendry, J. 2006. Taking Aim at Business: What Factors Lead Environmental Non-Governmental Organizations to Target Particular Firms? *Business and Society* 45:47–86.

Heritier, A., and S. Eckert. 2008. New Modes of Governance in the Shadow of Hierarchy. *Journal of Public Policy* 28 (1): 113–138.

Hirsch, D. 1998. Bill & Al's XL-ent Adventur. *University of Illinois Law Review* 1:129–172.

Hoffman, A. 1997. *From Heresy to Dogma*. San Francisco; New Lexington Press.

Hopwood, A. 2002. Creating a New Community. *European Accounting Review* 11 (May): 33–41.

Huntington, S. 1996. *The Clash of Civilizations and the Remaking of World Order*. New York: Simon and Schuster.

IASCF (International Accounting Standards Committee Foundation). 2002. *Annual Report 2001*. London: IASCF Publications Department.

IASCF. 2003. *Annual Report 2002*. London: IASCF Publications Department.

IASCF. 2004. *Annual Report 2003*. London: IASCF Publications Department.

IASCF. 2005. *Annual Report 2004*. London: IASCF Publications Department.

IASCF. 2006a. Future Funding. Available at ⟨http://www.iasb.org/About+Us/About+the+Foundation/Future+Funding.htm⟩ (accessed March 23, 2007).

IASCF. 2006b. *Annual Report 2005*. London: IASCF Publications Department.

IASCF. 2007a. *Preliminary Budget: 2008 Calendar Year*. London: IASB.

IASCF. 2007b. *Annual Report 2006*. London: IASCF Publications Department.

IASCF. 2008. *Annual Report 2007*. London: IASCF Publications Department.

Inglehart, R. 1990. *Culture Shift in Advanced Industrial Society*. Princeton, NJ: Princeton University Press.

Innes, R. 2006. A Theory of Consumer Boycotts under Symmetric Information and Imperfect Competition. *Economic Journal* 116:355–381.

Institute of Shipping Economics and Logistics. 2004. *ISL Shipping Statistics Yearbook 2004*. Bremen: ISL

ITF (International Transport Workers Federation). 2001. ITF Standard Collective Agreement for Crews on Flag of Convenience Ships, 1 January 2006. Flags of convenience campaign, "Agreements." Available at http://www.itfglobal.org/files/seealsodocs/1467/ITF%20Standard%20CBA%202006.pdf (accessed July 15, 2007).

Iu, J., and J. Batten. 2001. The Implementation of OECD Corporate Governance Principles in Post-Crisis Asia. *Journal of Corporate Citizenship* 4 (Winter): 47–62.

Jiang, R. J., and P. Bansal. 2003. Seeing the Need for ISO 14001. *Journal of Management Studies* 40 (June): 1047–1067.

Johnson, C. 1982. *MITI and the Japanese Miracle*. Palo Alto, CA: Stanford University Press.

Johnson, E., and A. Prakash. 2007. NGO Research Program: A Collective Action Perspective. *Policy Sciences* 40 (3).

Jupille, J., W. Mattli, and D. Snidal. 2008. International Institutional Choice for Global Commerce. Manuscript. University of Colorado at Boulder.

Kagan, R. 2000. Introduction: Comparing National Styles of Regulation in Japan and the United States. *Law and Policy* 22:225–244.

Kahler, M. 2000. Legalization as Strategy. *International Organization* 54 (June): 549–571.

Keck, M., and K. Sikkink. 1998. *Activists beyond Borders*. Ithaca, NY: Cornell University Press.

Kell, G., and J. Ruggie. 1999. Global Markets and Social Legitimacy: The Case of the "Global Compact." Paper presented at Governing the Public Domain beyond the Era of the Washington Consensus? Redrawing the Line between the State and the Market, York University, Toronto, November 4–6.

Keohane, R. 1980. The Theory of Hegemonic Stability and Changes in International Economic Regimes. In *Change in the International System*, ed. O. Holsti, R. Siverson, and A. George. Boulder, CO: Westview Press.

Keohane, R. 1984. *After Hegemony*. Princeton, NJ: Princeton University Press.

Kettl, D. 2002. *Environmental Governance*. Washington, DC: Brookings Institution.

Khanna, M. 2001. Non-Mandatory Approaches to Environmental Protection. *Journal of Economic Surveys* 15 (3): 291–324.

Khanna, M. 2007. The U.S. 33/50 Program: Its Design and Effectiveness. In *Reality Check*, ed. R. Morgenstern and W. Pizer, 15–42. Washington, DC: Resources for the Future.

Khanna, M., and L. Damon. 1999. EPA's Voluntary 33/50 Program. *Journal of Environmental Economics and Management* 37 (1): 1–25.

Kindleberger, C. 1983. Standards as Public, Collective, and Private Goods. *Kyklos* 36 (3): 377–396.

Kindleberger, C. 1986. *The World In Depression*. Berkeley: University of California Press.

King, A., and Lenox, M. 2000. Industry Self-Regulation without Sanctions: The Chemical Industry's Responsible Care Program. *Academy of Management Journal* 43 (August): 698–716.

King, A., and M. Lenox. 2002. Exploring the Locus of Profitable Pollution Reduction. *Management Science* 48:289–299.

King, A., M. Lenox, and M. Barnett. 2002. Strategic Responses to the Reputation Commons Problem. In *Organizations, Policy, and the Natural Environment*, ed. A. Hoffman and M. Ventresca, 393–406. Palo Alto, CA: Stanford University Press.

Klein, N. 1999. *No Logo*. New York: Picador.

Koehler, D. 2007. The Effectiveness of Voluntary Environmental Programs. *Policy Studies Journal* 35 (4): 689–722.

Kolk, A., and R. Tulder. 2002. The Effectiveness of Self-regulation. *European Management Journal* 20 (3): 260–271.

Kolk, A., R. Tulder, and C. Welter. 1999. International Codes of Conduct and Corporate Social Responsibility. *Transnational Corporations* 8 (April): 143–180.

Kollman, K., and A. Prakash. 2001. Green by Choice? *World Politics* 53 (April): 399–430.

Kollman, K., and A. Prakash. 2002. EMS-Based Environmental Regimes as Club Goods. *Policy Sciences* 35 (1): 43–67.

Kotchen, M. 2005. Impure Public Goods and the Comparative Statics of Environmentally Friendly Consumption. *Journal of Environmental Economics and Management* 49:281–300.

Kotchen, M. 2006a. Green Markets and Private Provision of Public Goods. *Journal of Political Economy* 114:816–834.

Kotchen, M. 2006b. Voluntary Provision of Public Goods for Bads. Working paper. University of California at Santa Barbara.

Krasner, S. 1976. State Power and the Structure of International Trade. *World Politics* 28 (April): 317–347.

Krasner, S. 1999. *Sovereignty: Organized Hypocrisy?* Princeton, NJ: Princeton University Press.

Krupat, K. 1997. From War Zone to Free Trade Zone. In *No Sweat: Fashion, Free Trade, and the Rights of Garment Workers*, ed. A. Ross, 51–77. New York: Verso.

Labor Rights in China. 1999. *No Illusions: Against the Global Cosmetic SA8000*. Hong Kong: Labor Rights in China.

Lake, D. 1983. International Economic Structures and American Foreign Economic Policy, 1887–1934. *World Politics* 36:517–543.

Lake, D. 1993. Leadership, Hegemony, and the International Economy. *International Studies Quarterly* 37 (4): 459–489.

Le Billon, P. 2006. Fatal Transactions: Conflict Diamonds and the (Anti)Terrorist Consumer. *Antipode* 38 (4): 778–801.

Leblond, P. 2006. Making the EU Count: Institutional Leadership and the Global Convergence of Accounting Standards. Manuscript. HEC Montreal, February.

Lenox, M., and C. Eesley. 2009. Private Environmental Activism and the Selection and Response of Firm Targets. *Journal of Economics and Management Strategy* 18:45–73.

Lenox, M., and J. Nash. 2003. Industry Self-Regulation and Adverse Selection: A Comparison across Four Trade Association Programs. *Business Strategy and the Environment* 12:343–356.

Levy, S. 1998. Testimony, U.S. House of Representatives Committee on Education and the Workforce, American Worker at a Crossroads Project. Available at http://commdocs.house.gov/committees/edu/hedo&i5-105.000/hedo&i5-105.htm.

Linden, G., K. Kraemer, and J. Dedrick. 2007. Who Captures Value in a Global Innovation System? Personal Computing Industry Center, Irvine, CA, June. Available at http://pcic.merage.uci.edu/papers/2007/AppleiPod.pdf (accessed July 2007).

Lloyd, R. 2005. *The Role of NGO Self-Regulation in Promoting Stakeholder Accountability*. London: One World Trust.

Locke, R., F. Qin, and A. Brause. 2007. Does Monitoring Improve Labor Standards? Lessons from Nike. *Industrial and Labor Relations Review* 61:3–31.

Louie, M. 2001. *Sweatshop Warriors*. Boston: South End Press.

Lund, L. 2000. Project XL: Good for the Environment, Good for Business, Good for Communities. *ELR News and Analysis* 2-2000:10140–10152.

Lynn, L., and S. R. Smith. 2007. The Performance Challenge in Nonprofit Organizations. Unpublished manuscript.

Lyon, T. P., and J. W. Maxwell. 2002. Voluntary Approaches to Environmental Regulation. In *Economic Institutions and Environmental Policy*, ed. M. Franzini and A. Nicita, 75–120. Chippenham, UK: Ashgate.

Lyon, T. P., and J. W. Maxwell. 2003. Self-regulation, Taxation, and Public Voluntary Environmental Agreement. *Journal of Public Economics* 75:1453–1486.

Lyon, T. P., and J. W. Maxwell. 2004. *Corporate Environmentalism and Public Policy*. Cambridge, UK: Cambridge University Press.

Lyon, T. P., and J. W. Maxwell. 2007. Environmental Public Voluntary Programs Reconsidered. *Policy Studies Journal* 35 (4): 723–750.

Manheim, J. 2001. *The Death of a Thousand Cuts*. Mahwah, NJ: Lawrence Erlbaum Associates.

Mank, B. 1998. The Environmental Protection Agency's Project XL and Other Regulatory Reform Initiatives. *Ecology Law Quarterly* 1:25.

March, J., and J. Olsen. 1998. The Institutional Dynamics of International Political Orders. *International Organization* 52 (Fall): 943–969.

Marcus, A., D. Geffen, and K. Sexton. 2002. *Reinventing Environmental Regulation: Lessons from Project XL*. Washington, DC: Resources for the Future/Johns Hopkins University Press.

Marcus, A., D. Geffen, and K. Sexton. 2005. Cooperative Environmental Regulation: Examining Project XL. In *Industrial Transformation*, ed. T. Bruijn and V. Norberg-Bohm. Cambridge, MA: MIT Press.

Marlow, M. 1995. L.A. Contractors: A New Set of Rules. *Women's Wear Daily*, June 22, 9–10.

Matthews, J. 1997. Powershift. *Foreign Affairs*, January–February: 50–66.

Matthews, J. 2006. Dragon Multinationals. *Asia Pacific Journal of Management* 23 (March): 5–27.

Mattli, W. 1999. *The Logic of Regional Integration*. Cambridge: Cambridge University Press.

Mattli, W. 2001. The Politics and Economics of International Institutionalized Standards Setting. *Journal of European Public Policy* 8 (3): 328–345.

Mattli, W., and T. Büthe. 2003. Setting International Standards: Technological Rationality or Primacy of Power? *World Politics* 56 (1): 1–42.

Mattli, W., and T. Büthe. 2005a. Accountability in Accounting? *Governance* 18 (3): 399–429.

Mattli, W., and T. Büthe. 2005b. Global Private Governance. *Law and Contemporary Problems* 68 (3–4): 225–262.

Maxwell, J., T. Lyon, and S. Hackett. 2000. Self-Regulation and Social Welfare: The Political Economy of Corporate Environmentalism. *Journal of Law and Economics* 43:583–618.

May, P. 2004. Compliance Motivations: Affirmative and Negative Biases. *Law and Society Review* 38:41–68.

May, P. 2005. Compliance Motivations: Perspectives of Farmers, Homebuilders, and Marine Facilities. *Law and Policy* 27:317–347.

McGuire, M. 1972. Private Good Clubs and Public Goods Club. *Swedish Journal of Economics* 74:84–99.

Meidinger, E. 2006. The Administrative Law of Global Public-Private Regulation. *European Journal of International Law* 17 (1): 47–87.

Meidinger, E., C. Elliott, and G. Oesten, eds. 2003. *Social and Political Dimensions of Forest Certification*. Available at http://www.Forstbuch.de.

Milgrom, P., D. North, and B. Weingast. 1990. The Role of Institutions in the Revival of Trade. *Economics and Politics* 2:1–23.

Moloney, S. 1997. Societies Force Ship Fault Move. *Lloyd's List*, February 7, 3.

Moonitz, M. 1970. Three Contributions to the Development of Accounting Principles Prior to 1930. *Journal of Accounting Research* (Spring): 145–155.

Morgenstern, R., and W. Pizer, eds. 2007. *Reality Check: The Nature and Performance of Voluntary Environmental Programs in the United States, Europe, and Japan*. Washington, DC: RFF Press.

National Research Council. 2002. *New Tools for Environmental Protection.* Washington, DC: National Academy Press.

Nett, A. 1997. California Makers Squeezed, Come Out Fighting. *Bobbin*, December, 34–38.

Nobes, C., and R. Parker, eds. 2008. *Comparative International Accounting.* Harlow, UK: Prentice Hall.

Nölke, A. 2005. Introduction to the Special Issue: The Globalization of Accounting Standards. *Business and Politics* 7 (3).

North, D. 1990. *Institutions, Institutional Change, and Economic Performance.* New York: Cambridge University Press.

North, D., and B. Weingast. 1989. Constitutions and Commitment. *Journal of Economic History* 49:803–832.

Northrup, H., and R. Rowan. 1983. The International Transport Workers Federation and Flag of Convenience Shipping. Philadelphia: Industrial Relations Research Unit, Wharton School.

Northrup, H., and P. Scrase. 1996. The International Transport Workers' Federation Flag of Convenience Shipping Campaign, 1983–1995. *Transportation Law Journal* 23 (3): 369–423.

Nunan, F. 1999. Barriers to the Use of Voluntary Agreements. *European Environment* 9 (6): 238–248.

Oatley, T., and R. Nabors. 1998. Redistributive Cooperation. *International Organization* 52 (Winter): 35–54.

OECD (Organization for Economic Cooperation and Development). 1997. *Voluntary Approaches for Environmental Policy: An Assessment.* Paris: OECD.

OECD. 2002. *Voluntary Approaches in Environmental Policy.* Paris: OECD.

OCIMF (Oil Companies International Marine For). 2007. Organization. Available at http://www.ocimf.com/custom.cfm?action=members (accessed June 19, 2007).

Olson, M. 1965. *The Logic of Collective Action.* Cambridge, MA: Harvard University Press.

O'Rourke, D. 1997. Smoke from a Hired Gun: A Critique of Nike's Labor and Environmental Auditing in Vietnam as Performed by Ernst & Young. Transnational Resource and Action Center. Available at http://nature.berkeley.edu/orourke/PDF/smoke.pdf.

O'Rourke, D. 2002. Monitoring the Monitors: A critique of corporate third-party labor monitoring. In *Corporate Responsibility and Labour Rights*, ed. R. Jenkins, R. Pearson, and G. Seyfang, 196–208. London: Earthscan.

O'Rourke, D. 2003. Outsourcing Regulation: Analyzing Nongovernmental Systems of Labor Standards and Monitoring. *Policy Studies Journal* 31 (1): 1–29.

Ostrom, E. 1990. *Governing the Commons.* Cambridge: Cambridge University Press.

O'Toole, L. J., C. Yu, J. Cooley, G. M. Cowie, S. Crow, T. Demeo, and S. Herbert. 1997. Reducing Toxic Chemical Releases: Explaining Outcomes for a Voluntary Program. *Policy Studies Journal* 25:11–26.

Pauly, L., and S. Reich. 1997. National Structures and Multinational Corporate Behavior. *International Organization* 51 (Winter): 1–30.

Pfaff, A., and C. Sanchirico. 2000. Environmental Self-Auditing. *Journal of Law, Economics, and Organization* 16 (1): 189–208.

Pigou, A. [1920] 1960. *The Economics of Welfare.* 4th ed. London: Macmillan.

Piore, M. 1997. The Economics of the Sweatshop. In *No Sweat: Fashion, Free Trade, and the Rights of Garment Workers,* ed. A. Ross, 135–142. New York: Verso.

Podolny, J. 2005. *Status Signals.* Princeton, NJ: Princeton University Press.

Porter, J. 1994. INTERTANKO to Discuss Stricter Guidelines. *Journal of Commerce* (May 5): 8B.

Porter, J. 1995a. Bulker Group to Tighten Membership Conditions. *Journal of Commerce* (June 22): 13B.

Porter, J. 1995b. INTERTANKO Expels Greek Tanker Owner. *Journal of Commerce* (May 24): 8B.

Porter, M., and C. van der Linde. 1995. Toward a New Conception of the Environment-Competitiveness Relationship. *Journal of Economic Perspectives* 9:97–118.

Porter, T. 2001. The Democratic Deficit in the Institutional Arrangements for Regulating Global Finance. *Global Governance* 7 (November): 427–439.

Porter, T. 2005. Private Authority, Technical Authority, and the Globalization of Accounting Standards. *Business and Politics* 7 (3).

Posner, E. 2007. Institutional Origins of Bargaining Power: The New Transatlantic Regulatory Relations in Financial Services (or: The End of Regulator Hegemony in Financial Services). Manuscript. Case Western Reserve University, May.

Potoski, M., and A. Prakash. 2004. Regulatory Convergence in Non-Governmental Regimes. *Journal of Politics* 66 (3): 885–905.

Potoski, M., and A. Prakash. 2005a. Covenants with Weak Swords. *Journal of Policy Analysis and Management* 24 (4): 745–769.

Potoski, M., and A. Prakash. 2005b. Green Clubs and Voluntary Governance: ISO 14001 and Firms' Regulatory Compliance. *American Journal of Political Science* 49 (2): 235–248.Prakash, A. 2000a. *Greening the Firm.* Cambridge: Cambridge University Press.

Prakash, A. 2000b. Responsible Care: An Assessment. *Business and Society* 39 (2): 183–209.

Prakash, A., and M. Potoski. 2006a. Racing to the Bottom? Trade, Environmental Governance, and ISO 14001. *American Journal of Political Science* 50 (2): 350–364.

Prakash, A., and M. Potoski. 2006b. *The Voluntary Environmentalists: Green Clubs, ISO 14001, and Voluntary Environmental Regulations.* Cambridge: Cambridge University Press.

Prakash, A., and M. Potoski. 2007a. Collective Action through Voluntary Environmental Programs: A Club Theory Perspective. *Policy Studies Journal* 35 (4): 773–792.

Prakash, A., and M. Potoski. 2007b. Investing Up: FDI and the Cross-National Diffusion of ISO 14001. *International Studies Quarterly* 51 (3): 723–744.

Press, D. 2007. Industry, Environmental Policy, and Environmental Outcomes. *Annual Review of Environment and Resources* 32:317–344.

Program on International Policy Attitudes. 2006. 20 Nation Poll Finds Strong Global Consensus: Support for Free Market System, but Also More Regulation of Large Companies, 11 January. Available at http://65.109.167.118/pipa/pdf/jan06/FreeMarkets_Jan06_quaire.pdf.

PRS Must Shake Off Taint Left by IACS Explusion. 2005. Lloyd's List (7 January): 12.

Putnam, R., R. Leonardi, and R. Nanetti. 1993. *Making Democracy Work.* Princeton, NJ: Princeton University Press.

Rabe, B. 1999. Federalism and Entrepreneurship: Explaining American and Canadian Innovation in Pollution Prevention and Regulatory Innovation. *Policy Studies Journal* 27:288–306.

Rabe, B. 2006. Power to the States: The Promise and Pitfalls of Decentralization. In *Environmental Policy: New Directions for the 21st Century*, ed. N. Vig and M. Kraft, 34–56. 6th ed. Washington, DC: CQ Press.

Ramey, J. 1997. Textile, Apparel Importers Set Up PAC. *Women's Wear Daily*, November 25, 13–14.

Ramey, J., and J. Barrett. 1996. Apparel's Ethics Dilemma. *WWD*, March 18, 1996, 10–13.

Ramus, C., and I. Montiel. 2005. When Are Corporate Environmental Policies a Form of Greenwashing? *Business and Society* 44 (4): 377–314.

Rapaport Tradewire. 2000. World Diamond Council Calls for International Government Action on Conflict Diamonds. Rapaport TradeWire, September 8.

Reich Says Kathie Lee Joining His Campaign against Sweatshops. 1996. *Women's Wear Daily*, May 24, 1–2.

Reinhardt, F. 2000. *Down to Earth.* Cambridge, MA: Harvard University Press.

Risse, T. 2004. Global Governance and Communicative Action. *Government and Opposition* 39 (2): 288–313.

Rivera, J., and deLeon, P. 2004. Is Greener Whiter? *Policy Studies Journal* 32 (3): 417–437.

Roberts, C., P. Weetman, and P. Gordon. 2008. *International Corporate Reporting: A Comparative Approach.* 4th ed. Harlow, UK: Prentice Hall.

Rodríguez-Garavito, C. 2005. Global Governance and Labor Rights. *Politics and Society* 33:203–233.

Rolnick, A. 1997. Muzzling the Offshore Watchdogs. *Bobbin*, February, 72–73.

Rosenau, J., and E. Czempiel, eds. 1992. *Governance without Government*. Cambridge: Cambridge University Press.

Ross, A. 1997. *No Sweat: Fashion, Free Trade, and the Rights of Garment Workers*. New York: Verso.

Ruggie, J. 2004. Reconstituting the Global Public Domain. *European Journal of International Relations* 10 (4): 499–531.

Salter, L. 1999. The Standards Regime for Communication and Information Technologies. In *Private Authority and International Affairs*, ed. C. Cutler, V. Haufler, and T. Porter, 97–127. Albany: State University of New York Press.

Sam, A., and R. Innes. 2005. Voluntary Pollution Reductions and the Enforcement of Environmental Law. Manuscript. Department of Agricultural and Resource Economics, University of Arizona at Tucson.

Samuelson, P. 1954. A Pure Theory of Public Expenditure. *Review of Economic and Statistics* 36:387–389.

Sandler, T., and J. Tschirhart. 1997. Club Theory: Thirty Years Later. *Public Choice* 93:335–355.

Sasser, E., A. Prakash, B. Cashore, and G. Auld. 2006. Direct Targeting as NGO Political Strategy: Examining Private Authority Regimes in the Forestry Sector. *Business and Politics* 8 (3): 1–32.

Scarpetti, S., and G. Nicoletti. 2003. Regulation, Productivity, and Growth. World Bank Policy Research working paper no. 2944, Washington, DC, January.

Schaeffer, E., et al. 2006. Letter to the Honorable Stephen Johnson, Administrator, U.S. Environmental Protection Agency, January 25.

Schaub, A. 2006. Opening Remarks. In *The Future of IASB Funding: Conference at the Deutsches Aktieninstitut, 30/31 March 2006*. Frankfurt: Deutsches Aktieninstitut.

Schelling, T. 1978. *Micromotives and Macrobehavior*. New York: W. W. Norton and Co.

Scholz, J., and M. Lubell. 1998. Trust and Taxpaying. *American Journal of Political Science* 42:398–417.

Schrage, E. 2004. *Promoting International Worker Rights through Private Voluntary Initiatives*. University of Iowa, Center for Human Rights.

Schultz, M., J. Mouritsen, and G. Gabrielsen. 2001. Sticky Reputation. *Corporate Reputation Review* 4 (1): 24–41.

SEC (Securities and Exchange Commission). 2008. SEC Proposes Roadmap toward Global Accounting Standards to Help Investors Compare Financial Information More Easily. Press release, August 27. Washington, DC: Securities and Exchange Commission. Available at http://www.sec.gov/news/press/2008/2008-184.htm (accessed October 22, 2008).

Secrets, Lies, and Sweatshops. 2006. *Business Week*, November 27.

Segerson, K., and N. Li. 1999. Voluntary Approaches to Environmental Protection. In *International Yearbook of Environmental and Resource Economics, 1999/2000*, ed. H. Folmer and T. Tietenberg, 273–306. Cheltenham, UK: Edward Elgar.

Segerson, K., and T. Miceli. 1998. Voluntary Environmental Agreements. *Journal of Environmental Economics and Management* 6 (2): 109–130.

Seidman, G. 2007. *Beyond the Boycott*. New York: Russell Sage Foundation/ ASA Rose Series.

Shapiro, S. 1987. The Social Control of Impersonal Trust. *American Journal of Sociology* 93:623–658.

Shaw, R. 1999. *Reclaiming America*. Berkeley: University of California Press.

Sidel, M. 2003. Trends in Nonprofit Self-Regulation in the Asia Pacific Region. Mimeo. University of Iowa Law School.

Silverstein, K. 2001. Diamonds of Death. *The Nation* 272,16: 19–22.

Singer, D. 2007. *Regulating Capital*. Ithaca, NY: Cornell University Press.

Sinha, J. 2005. Global Champions from Emerging Markets. *McKinsey Quarterly* 2:26–36.

Smillie, I., L. Gberie, and R. Hazleton. 2000. *The Heart of the Matter*. Ottawa: Partnership Africa Canada.

Smith, S., and M. Lipsky, 1993. *Nonprofits for Hire*. Cambridge, MA: Harvard University Press.

Snidal, D. 1985. The Limits of Hegemonic Stability Theory. *International Organization* 39 (Fall): 579–614.

Snyder, J. 1991. *Myths of Empire*. Ithaca, NY: Cornell University Press.

Solomons, D. 1983. The Political Implications of Accounting and Accounting Standards Setting. *Accounting and Business Research* 13 (50): 107–118.

Spar, D.1994. The Cooperative Edge. Ithaca, NY: Cornell University Press.

Spar, D. 1998. The Spotlight and the Bottom Line. *Foreign Affairs* 77:7–12.

Spar, D., and D. Yoffie. 2000. A Race to the Bottom or Governance from the Top? In *Coping with Globalization*, ed. A. Prakash and J. Hart, 31–51. New York: Routledge.

Spielberg, E. 1997. The Myth of Nimble Fingers. In *No Sweat: Fashion, Free Trade, and the Rights of Garment Workers*, ed. A. Ross, 113–122. New York: Verso.

Spiro, P. 2002. Accounting for NGOs. *Chicago Journal of International Law* 3 (1): 161–169.

Steinberg, M., D. Arner, and C. Olive. 2002. Internationalisation of Accounting Standards. In *International Financial Sector Reform*, ed. S. Goo, D. Arner, and Z. Zhou, 87–117. London: Kluwer Law.

Steinzor, R. 1998. Reinventing Environmental Regulation. *Harvard Environmental Law Review* 22 (1): 103–202.

Stevens, M. 1981. *The Big Eight*. New York: Macmillan.

Stevens, M. 1985. *The Accounting Wars*. New York: Macmillan.

Stevens, M., with C. Stevens. 1991. *The Big Six*. New York: Simon and Schuster.

Stigler, G. 1971. The Theory of Economic Regulation. *Bell Journal of Economic and Management Science* 2 (1): 321.

Strange, S. 1996. *The Retreat of the State*. Cambridge: Cambridge University Press.

Su, J. 1997. El Monte Thai Garment Workers. In *No Sweat: Fashion, Free Trade, and the Rights of Garment Workers*, ed. A. Ross, 143–149. New York: Verso.

Summers, L. 2007. Funds That Shake Capitalist Logic. *Financial Times*, July 29. Available at http://www.ft.com/cms/s/2/bb8f50b8-3dcc-11dc-8f6a-0000779fd2ac.html.

Susskind, L., and J. Secunda. 1998. The Risks and the Advantages of Agency Discretion: Evidence from EPA's Project XL. *UCLA Journal of Environmental Law and Policy* 17 (1): 67–116.

Terlaak, A., and A. King. 2006. The Effect of Certification with the ISO 9000 Quality Management Standard. *Journal of Economic Behavior and Organization* 60 (4): 579–602.

Teubner, G. 1983. Substantive and Reflexive Elements in Modern Law. *Law and Society Review* 17:239–285.

The Economist. 2007. "Changing Facets." 382: 75–76.

Tiebout, C. 1956. A Pure Theory of Public Expenditure. *Journal of Political Economy* 64:416–424.

Tsogas, G. 2001. *Labor Regulation in a Global Economy*. Armonk, NY: M. E. Sharpe.

Tweedie, D. 2007. Ken Spencer Memorial Lecture. Slide presentation. March. Available at http://www.iasplus.com/au/0703tweedie.pdf (accessed September 13, 2007).

United Press International. 2000. DeBeers Wants Improved Us Relations. UPI Wire Service, January 31.

Uozumi, Y. 2007. *Japanese Business and International Convergence of Accounting Standards*. Program on U.S.-Japan Relations Occasional Paper Series no. 13/ 2007, 1–52.

U.S. Congress, Office of Technology Assessment. 1986. Serious Reduction of Hazardous Waste: For Pollution Prevention and Industrial Efficiency. OTA-ITE-317. Washington, DC: U.S. Government Printing Office.

U.S. EPA. 1995a. 33/50 Program Progress Update: TRI Reporting Profiles for 33/50 Program Chemicals. Washington, DC: U.S. EPA.

U.S. EPA. 1995b. Regulatory Reinvention (XL) Pilot Projects. *Federal Register* 60:27282–27290.

U.S. EPA. 1998. Evaluation of Project XL Stakeholder Processes: Final Report. Washington, DC: U.S. EPA.

U.S. EPA. 1999. 33/50 Program: The Final Record. EPA-745-R-99-004. Washington, DC: U.S. EPA.

U.S. EPA. 2001. Project XL: Directory of Project Experiments and Results. EPA 100-R-01-003. Washington, DC: U.S. EPA.

U.S. EPA. 2004. National Environmental Performance Track Program. *Federal Register* 69:21737–21754.

U.S. EPA. 2006a. Leading Change: Performance Track Fourth Annual Progress Report. Office of Policy, Economics, and Innovation (MC 1808T), EPA-100-R-06-001. Washington, DC: U.S. EPA.

U.S. EPA. 2006b. Performance Track Hall of Fame. Washington, DC: U.S. EPA. Available at http://www.epa.gov/performancetrack/benefits/halloffame.htm#out (accessed September 22, 2006).

U.S. EPA. 2006d. Resource Conservation and Recovery Act Burden Reduction Initiative. *Federal Register* 71:16862–16915.

U.S. EPA. 2007a. Results of the 2006 Performance Track Members Survey, June. Available at http://www.epa.gov/performancetrack/members.

U.S. EPA. 2007b. State Performance-Based Program Directory. Office of Policy, Planning, and Innovation, May. Available at http://www.epa.gov/performancetrack/states.

U.S. EPA. 2007c. Today's Commitments. Tomorrow's World. Five Years of Environmental Leadership. EPA 100-R-07-004. Washington, DC: U.S. EPA. Available at http://www.epa.gov/performancetrack/downloads/PTPRreport_05final.pdf.

U.S. EPA. 2008a. Performance Track Results: Detailed Results. Available at http://www.epa.gov/performancetrack/results/detailed-results.htm.

U.S. EPA. 2008b. Performance Track Sixth Annual Progress Report. Washington, DC: U.S. EPA. Available at http://www.epa.gov/ performancetrack/downloads/PT_ProgRprt_2008.pdf.

U.S. EPA IG, Office of the Inspector General. 2007. Performance Track Could Improve Program Design and Management to Ensure Value. Report no. 2007-P-00013. Washington, DC: U.S. EPA. Available at http://www.epa.gov/oig/reports/2007/20070329-2007-P-00013.pdf.

U.S. General Accounting Office. 1994. Toxic Substances: Status of EPA's Efforts to Reduce Toxic Releases. GAO/RCED-94-207. Washington, DC: U.S. General Accounting Office.

U.S. Department of Labor. 1996. *The Apparel Industry and Codes of Conduct.* Washington, DC: U.S. Department of Labor, Bureau of International Affairs.

US/LEAP. 2003. Guatemala Surprise. *US/LEAP newsletter*, July.

Varley, P., ed. 1998. *The Sweatshop Quandary.* Washington, DC: Investor Responsibility Research Center.

Verba, Sidney, Kay L. Schlozman, and Howard E. Brady, 1995. Voice and Equality: Civic Voluntarism in American Politics. Cambridge, MA: Harvard University Press.

Véron, N. 2007. *The Global Accounting Experiment.* Brussels: Bruegel.

Véron, N., M. Autret, and A. Galichon. 2006. *Smoke & Mirrors, Inc.* Ithaca, NY: Cornell University Press.

Viscusi, W. 1978. A Note on "Lemons" Markets with Quality Certification. *Bell Journal of Economics and Management Science* 9:277–279.

Vogel, D. 1978. Why Businessmen Distrust Their State. *British Journal of Political Science* 8 (January): 45–78.

Vogel, D. 1995. *Trading Up: Consumer and Environmental Regulation in a Global Economy.* Cambridge, MA: Harvard University Press.

Vogel, D. 1996. *Kindred Strangers: The Uneasy Relationship between Politics and Business in America.* Princeton, NJ: Princeton University Press.

Vogel, D. 2005. *Market for Virtue.* Washington, DC: Brookings Press.

Vogel, D. 2007. The Private Regulation of Global Corporate Conduct. Paper prepared for the Global Economic Governance Programme, Oxford University, Summer.

Vogel, D. 2008. Private Global Business Regulation. *Annual Review of Political Science* 11:261–282.

Walke, J. 2005. Letter to Administrator Johnson on Behalf of the Natural Resources Defense Council. Docket ID OA-2005-0003, November 3.

Wallace, D. 1995. *Environmental Policy and Industrial Innovation.* London: Earthscan.

Wapner, P. 1995. Politics beyond the State. *World Politics* 47 (April): 311–340.

Ward, H. 1996. Common but Differentiated Debates: Environment, Labour, and the World Trade Organization. *International and Comparative Law Quarterly* 45:592–632.

Ware, P. 2006. Benefits of "Performance Track" Program in Question, Environmental Groups Says. *Environment Reporter* 37, no. 6 (February 10): 309–310.

Webb, K., ed. 2004. *Voluntary Codes.* Ottawa: Carleton Research Unit for Innovation, Carleton University.

Weisbrod, B. 1988. *The Nonprofit Economy.* Cambridge, MA: Harvard University Press.

Welford, R. 2005. Corporate Social Responsibility in Europe, North America, and Asia. *Journal of Corporate Citizenship* 17 (Spring): 33–52.

Whitford, A. 2003. The Structures of Interest Coalitions: Evidence from Environmental Litigation. *Business and Politics* 5:article 3.

Williamson, O. 1985. *Economic Institutions of Capitalism*. New York: Free Press.

Wilson, G. 2002. Regulatory Reform on the World Stage. In *Environmental Governance*, ed. Donald Kettl, 118–145. Washington, DC: Brookings Institution Press.

Wiseman, J. 1957. The Theory of Public Utility: An Empty Box. *Oxford Economic Papers* 9:56–74

Wolf, C. 1979. Theory of Nonmarket Failure. *Journal of Law and Economics* 22 (April): 107–139.

WTO (World Trade Organization). 2005. *World Trade Report 2005*. Geneva: World Trade Organization.

Yusuf, S., K. Nabeshima, and D. Perkins. 2005. *Under New Ownership*. Palo Alto, CA: Stanford University Press.

Zarsky, L. 2002. Stuck in the Mid? Nation States, Globalization, and the Environment. In *The Earthscan Reader of International Trade and Sustainable Development*, ed. K. Gallagher and J. Werksman, 9–44 London: Earthscan Publications.

Zeckhauser, R., and J. Pratt. 1985. Principals and Agents: An Overview. In *Principals and Agents*, ed. J. Pratt and R. Zeckhauser, 1–35. Boston: Harvard Business School Press.

Zeff, S. 1972. *Forging Accounting Principles in Five Countries*. Champaign, IL: Stipes Publishing Co.

Contributors

David P. Baron is the David S. and Ann M. Barlow Professor (Emeritus) of Political Economy and Strategy at the Graduate School of Business, Stanford University. He has authored over one hundred articles and three books, including *The Export-Import Bank: An Economic Analysis* (1983) and *Business and Its Environment*, the sixth edition of which was published in 2009.

Tim Bartley is an assistant professor of sociology at Indiana University at Bloomington. He has published articles on transnational private regulation, corporate social responsibility, and institutional change in the *American Journal of Sociology*, *Social Problems*, *Politics and Society*, and other journals.

Tim Büthe is an assistant professor of political science at Duke University and co-principal investigator of the International Standards Project. His research on global private politics seeks to advance our understanding of how and why outcomes differ when decision-making authority is delegated to nongovernmental (private) organizations. His work has been published in the *American Political Science Review*, the *American Journal of Political Science*, *World Politics*, *Governance*, and other journals.

Cary Coglianese is the Edward B. Shils Professor of Law and a professor of political science at the University of Pennsylvania Law School. He is also the director of the Penn Program on Regulation and is a senior research fellow at Harvard University's John F. Kennedy School of Government. Coglianese is the coauthor (with Robert Kagan) of *Regulation and Regulatory Processes* (2007), and the coeditor (with Jennifer Nash) of *Leveraging the Private Sector: Management-Based Strategies for Improving Environmental Performance* (2006) and *Regulating from the Inside: Can Environmental Management Systems Achieve Policy Goals?* (2001). He is the coeditor of the new peer-reviewed journal *Regulation and Governance*.

Elizabeth R. DeSombre is the Frost Professor of Environmental Studies and a professor of political science at Wellesley College. DeSombre's recent books include *Flagging Standards: Globalization and Environmental, Safety, and Labor Standards at Sea* (2006) and *Global Environmental Institutions* (2006). Her first book, *Domestic Sources of International Environmental Policy: Industry*,

Environmentalists, and U.S. Power (2000), won the 2001 Chadwick F. Alger Prize for the best book published in 2000 in the area of international organization and the 2001 Lynton Caldwell Award for the best book published on environmental policy. A second edition of her textbook *The Global Environment and World Politics* was published in 2007.

Daniel W. Drezner is a professor of international politics at the Fletcher School of Law and Diplomacy at Tufts University. He is the author of *All Politics Is Global: Explaining International Regulatory Regimes* (2007), *U. S. Trade Strategy* (2006), and *The Sanctions Paradox* (1999).

Daniel J. Fiorino is the director of the National Environmental Performance Track program at the U.S. Environmental Protection Agency in Washington, DC. He has authored or coauthored four books on environmental policy and regulation. His publications have been recognized with seven national awards. Fiorino's most recent book is *The New Environmental Regulation* (2006).

Mary Kay Gugerty is an assistant professor of public affairs at the Daniel J. Evans School of Public Affairs at the University of Washington.

Virginia Haufler is an associate professor of government and politics at the University of Maryland at College Park. She is the author of *A Public Role for the Private Sector: Industry Self-Regulation in a Global Economy* (2001) and *Dangerous Commerce: Insurance and the Management of International Risk* (1997), the coeditor (with A. Claire Cutler and Tony Porter) of *Private Authority and International Affairs* (1999), and the coeditor (with Karol Soltan and Eric Uslaner) of *Institutions and Social Order* (1998).

Matthew J. Kotchen is an assistant professor in the Bren School of Environmental Science and Management and the Department of Economics at the University of California at Santa Barbara.

Mimi Lu is a candidate for a masters of arts in law and diplomacy at the Fletcher School of Law and Diplomacy, specializing in international political economy and East Asia.

Jennifer Nash is the director of policy and programs at the Product Stewardship Institute and a Regulation Fellow at the John F. Kennedy School of Government at Harvard University. She is coeditor, with Cary Coglianese, of two books on environmental policy innovation: *Leveraging the Private Sector: Management-Based Strategies for Improving Environmental Performance* (2006) and *Regulating from the Inside: Can Environmental Management Systems Achieve Policy Goals?* (2001).

Matthew Potoski is an associate professor at Iowa State University, where he teaches courses on politics, administration, and policy. Potoski is the coauthor of *The Voluntary Environmentalists* (2006). He is the coeditor of the *International Public Management Journal*.

Aseem Prakash is a professor of political science at University of Washington at Seattle. Prakash is the author of *Greening the Firm* (2000), the coauthor of

The Voluntary Environmentalists (2006), and the coeditor of *Globalization and Governance* (1999), *Coping with Globalization* (2000), and *Responding to Globalization* (2000). He serves as the general editor of the Public Policy and Business series at Cambridge University Press.

Klaas van 't Veld is an assistant professor in the Department of Economics and Finance at the University of Wyoming.

Author Index

Subject Index